# Christian Social Witness and Teaching

## Volume II

# Christian Social Witness
# and
# Teaching

## The Catholic Tradition from
## Genesis to *Centesimus Annus*

## Volume II

The Modern Social Teaching:
Contexts : Summaries : Analysis

*Rodger Charles SJ*

Gracewing.

First published in 1998


Gracewing
Fowler Wright Books
2 Southern Avenue, Leominster
Herefordshire HR6 0QF

Vol I paperback ISBN 0 85244 460 5
Vol II paperback ISBN 0 85244 461 3


Typesetting by Action Typesetting Ltd,
Gloucester, GL1 1SP


Printed by Cromwell Press,
Trowbridge, Wiltshire BA14 0XB

# Contents

# Analytical Contents

## Chapter 16
## Leo XIII (1878–1903)

## Chapter 17
## Pius X (1903–14) and
## Benedict XV (1914–22)

# Chapter 18
## Pius XI (1922–39)

# Chapter 19
## Pius XII (1939–58)

## Chapter 20
## John XXIII (1958–63)

## Chapter 21
## The background to the Church's social teaching 1962–78

## Chapter 22
## The Second Vatican Council (1962–65)

## Chapter 23
## Paul VI (1962–78) and the Second Meeting of the
## Council of Latin American Bishops (CELAM II)
## Medellín, Colombia 1968

## Chapter 24
## John Paul II and CELAM III at Puebla, Mexico 1979

## Chapter 25
## John Paul II's Social Encyclicals 1979–81

## Chapter 26
## Liberation Theology
## Congregation for the Doctrine of the Faith 1984–86
## John Paul II 1986

## Chapter 27
## John Paul II's social encyclicals 1987–91

# Chapter 28
# John Paul II and CELAM IV at San Domingo, the Dominican Republic 1992

# Chapter 29
# A summary analysis of the social teaching of the Church

# Foreword

When this work was first projected it was intended that it would be just one volume which would contain both the study of the tradition down to the nineteenth century, and the modern teaching, because the two are a continuum and to understand the latter properly it is necessary to understand its foundations in the experience of the Church throughout her history and in the development of her theological and philosophical tradition. For example, the modern teaching is insistent that the Church is not to be identified with any particular political, social or economic system – yet for several hundreds of years in the middle ages there was one Christian society and the Church was very much identified with it. Unless the reasons why this should be so are examined, the enquiring mind will be left with many questions unanswered. The human condition is such that patterns of problems, and responses to them, tend to some extent to repeat themselves; the past has lessons for us, unless we understand what experience has taught the Church on the nature of its relationship with society in the various eras of its existence we will not be able to appreciate the successes it has had in that relationship nor understand the reasons for its failures.

As the scope and size of the enquiry became apparent however it was clear that one volume would be unmanageable and that from many points of view it was better to divide it – its organization into a historical section and the modern teaching favoured it anyway. But we must keep the historical perspective in mind. One reason is that already mentioned, the question of the Church's role in political society. Another is that the main impetus for development of the modern social teaching came from the impact on society of the industrial revolution which took place when liberal capitalism reigned free and unfettered. It is necessary to understand the full evils of that system, and the philosophy behind it if the strictures of

*Rerum Novarum* and the violence of the Marxist reaction against those evils are to be appreciated. There are a host of other questions arising out of the historical experience of the Church which presenting the modern social teaching has taught me need to be explored – for example, its attitude to intellectual and political freedom, to slavery and many other issues. Hence, while I am glad that by publishing in two volumes we will be able to make the modern teaching more readily available to potential readers, and students especially, it is important to remember that for a balanced and complete understanding of it, acquaintance with the main elements of the historical and other data the first volume contains is desirable, indeed essential.

In this volume we examine some thirty four of the major social documents of the Church since 1878. They are mainly social encyclicals and other Papal statements of equal authority, together with the relevant documents from the Second Vatican Council, from the Council of the Latin American Bishops [CELAM] and the Congregation for the Doctrine of the Faith [CDF]; they range in length from the two or three pages of John Paul II's *Letter* on Liberation theology of the two hundred or so pages of the Report of CELAM III at Puebla. The method of presenting them is to consider first their contexts, the circumstances in response to which they were issued, then they are summarized paragraph by paragraph or page by page, mostly in full, but where this is not necessary, selectively. Each document or related group of them is then analyzed in summary and the final Chapter of the Book gives a summary analysis of the whole teaching in some forty six pages.

As explained in the Foreword to Volume One, the greatest problem with presenting the teaching of the Church is to prevent oneself doing so in a way biased in favour of one's own particular social, political and economic opinions. In a free society it is necessary to have such opinions in order to discharge one's duties as a citizen, but it is important when putting the social teaching of the Church across, that that teaching should be left to speak for itself, rather than be presented in the context of one's own opinions which results in using predigested versions of some parts of some documents as illustrations of points. This latter approach too easily excludes from consideration or treats ungenerously aspects of the teaching with which the presenter does not agree, in whole or in part. This of course presents a distorted view of the teaching.

The documents, as explained in pages twelve and following below, are primarily for the guidance of believing Catholics on the ethical issues raised by social living. These do not demand that all have the same social, political and economic opinions, though all must choose options which give them freedom to commit themselves to social justice in a manner compatible with the divine eternal, the divine revealed and the natural law. This is not the same as saying that those options must respect all of those laws as the Christian understands them. All political, social and economic systems have to cater for every member of society, believers and non believers, and those of other religious affiliations which are neither Christian nor Catholic, and will therefore involve some tolerance of things which do not square in detail or substance with Catholic belief. Within them we have to choose the option which we think best offers us the chance of working for charity and justice in society as Christians. Excluded from our range of choice then would be any party which specifically denies a matter of charity or justice of such importance that it poisons the whole of that choice. An essentially racist creed, or one based on hatred or contempt for those of other social economic or political groups, or having as its central committment to any other absolute moral evil, these are excluded. The political parties in modern democracies may then be committed to policies in particular areas which do not sit easily to the law of God but until the teaching Church decides that one or other is to be totally rejected on moral grounds we should respect the options taken by our fellow Christians and others whether we agree with them or not and we must present the Church's social teaching accordingly. The historical experience of her identifying with one social, political or economic groups has not been a happy one, inevitably it ends with it being expected to support policies with which it cannot identify.

Each document has been summarized, with paragraph or page references being given and with quotations that seem to highlight essentials; in this way the reader can see each as a whole, and its thought developing accordingly. There is no substitute for acquaintance with the documents in full but, failing that, where the summary or analysis is such that it sparks interest, the reader will know the exact place to which to refer. The summary analysis of each document or related group highlights the main points of ethical theory or recommendation of practice, and the final summary analysis presents both as a whole in outline. In this way I hope I will be able to help the reader to understand more fully the insights of the tradition.

Rodger Charles SJ
Campion Hall,
14th February 1998

# Abbreviations

| | |
|---|---|
| AB | *Ad Beatissimi* |
| AMS | *Au Milieu des Solicitudes* |
| AN | *Acerba Nimis* |
| CC | *Casti Connubii* |
| CCC | *Catechism of the Catholic Church* |
| CELAM | Consejo Episcopal LatinoAmericano |
| CA | *Centesimus Annus* |
| CEB's | Comunidades eclesiales de base |
| CDF | Congregation for the Doctrine of the Faith |
| DI | *Diuturmum Illud* |
| DIM | *Divini Illius Magistri* |
| DR | *Divini Redemptoris* |
| ESA | *E Supremi Apostolatus* |
| EN | *Evangelii Nuntiandi* |
| EP | *Evangelii Praecones* |
| EV | *Evangelium Vitae* |
| FDP | *Fin Dalla Prima* |
| FC | *Familiaris Consortio* |
| FUCI | Federazione degli Universitari Cattolici Italiani |
| FD | *Fidei Donum* |
| GDC | *Graves de Communi* |
| GS | *Gaudium et Spes* |
| HV | *Humanae Vitae* |
| IFP | *Il Fermo Proposito* |
| ID | *Immortale Dei* |
| IDC | *Inscrutabile Dei Consilio* |
| LE | *Laborem Exercens* |
| LC | *Libertatis Conscientia* |
| LN | *Libertatis Nuntius* |
| MM | *Mater et Magistra* |
| MBS | *Mit Brennender Sorge* |

| MC | *Mystici Corporis* |
| NAB | *Non Abbiamo Bisogno* |
| NDCST | New Dictionary of Catholic Social Thought |
| NKVD | Narodny Kommisariat Vnutrennikh Del |
| NEP | New Economic Plan |
| OA | *Octogesima Adveniens* |
| ODC | Opera Dei Congressi |
| PDM | *Pacem Dei Munus* |
| PT | *Pacem in Terris* |
| PP | *Populorum Progressio* |
| PPI | Partito Popolare Italiano |
| QA | *Quadragesimo Anno* |
| QAM | *Quod Apostolici Muneris* |
| RH | *Redemptor Hominis* |
| RN | *Rerum Novarum* |
| SC | *Sapientiae Christianae* |
| SODEPAX | Society for Development and Peace |
| SQ | *Singulari Quadam* |
| SRS | *Sollicitudo Rei Socialis* |
| SP | *Summi Pontificatus* |
| UAD | *Ubi Arcano Dei* |
| USSR | Union of Soviet Socialist Republics |
| VS | *Veritatis Splendor* |

Part 4

# The Modern Social Teaching: Contexts : Summaries : Analysis

# 16

# Leo XIII (1878–1903)

## 1 Leo and the nineteenth-century Church

The Papacy, which by the end of the eighteenth century seemed to be on the point of final disappearance, in fact emerged reinvigorated in the nineteenth: the Church which Leo XIII was elected to lead in 1878 was one which was strong and vibrant in the essentials of its spirit and life.[1] The first part of the century had been a time of prodigious expansion of foreign missions and of the emergence of new teaching orders who rechristianized the education of a large part of Europe, especially through their work among its young women. The Dominican friars and the Benedictine monks were reformed, and the Society of Jesus was restored; outstanding priests like St Jean-Baptiste Vianney and St John Bosco gave new examples of holiness among the clergy. The definition of the Church's belief in the Immaculate Conception in 1854 and the Lourdes apparitions of 1858 were signs of a new spiritual and doctrinal growth. The First Vatican Council's declaration of the universal primacy of the Pope, and its implications, gave promise of a reduction of the dangerous level of the disputes which had disfigured the Church and weakened her mission since the fourteenth century. The respect and affection that Pius IX had won from his people because of his courage and cheerfulness in the difficulties that beset him helped the Papacy as an institution to secure its rightful place at the centre of the mission of the international Church. At the same time there were tensions within the Church between those who saw the influence of Rome as excessive,[2] and those who saw in it the restoration of the Christ-intended order long needed; certainly the overall importance of the Papacy in the continuing revival of the Church's vitality became clearer as

* The notes and references for Chapter 16 are to be found on p. 437ff

the years went by. That Leo XIII was able to respond so effectively to the need for leadership in face of the conflicts over the social problem and responses to it was one striking example of this.

For there was still much to be done; foundations had been strengthened and new vitality had been imparted to most of the main structures of the Church's life, but the modern industrializing world was changing with alarming rapidity. There was no precedent for the situation. The social question was of vast complexity and immediate urgency. It affected all aspects of social, political and economic life in the industrializing nations of the old world. At the same time, because their trade and their need for raw materials was transforming the world's economy, the rise and fall of its fortunes had an international impact and affected the well-being of the nations which had not yet started on the road to industrialization themselves. Moral judgements involved were on sociological, political, economic, industrial and organizational matters which had never been considered adequately by the Church's theologians before, let alone in the explosive mix that was now presented to them. The world was in turmoil because of this economic revolution. We take it for granted now that the Church, through the Papacy, would speak, and speak exactly to the point, on this matter; but in the last quarter of the nineteenth century it seemed highly unlikely that a lead would come from her. The achievements of the Papacy since 1815 in rebuilding after the previous decades of disaster were not of much interest to the world at large, especially the Western world, bedazzled by the achievements of the new industrial and liberal capitalist age. A Frenchman who was present at the coronation of Leo XIII saw it as the last act of an era and institution which had had its day.[3] Even those who supported the 68-year-old Leo XIII's candidacy did not think that, given his quiet scholarly nature and unspectacular though solid career, he would make waves if elected.

Vincenzo Gioacchino Pecci[4] was born in 1811 in Carpineto near Siena in central Italy, of a bourgeois family which had served the Papacy for centuries. A brilliant student at the Gregorianum in Rome, he was educated for the papal diplomatic service, only deciding on the priesthood in 1837. After ordination he served as civil governor of Benevento, Brescia and Perugia successively, and there gained experience of administration and a reputation as a fair, enlightened and competent ruler, establishing schools and hospitals, reducing taxes and encouraging economic progress. Then, in 1843 when he was 32 years old, he was appointed archbishop and nuncio in Brussels. The new nuncio had previously no experience of any world but that of the Papal States, which had changed little in three hundred years; Belgium was then by contrast undergoing its Industrial Revolution by means of liberal capitalism, and the new nuncio became familiar for the first time with railways, modern factories, and the proletariat. He was able to be present incognito at working-class political gatherings and he also crossed the Channel to London to see more of this new Europe. Belgium's King Leopold, however, was at odds with the liberals, and found Pecci unwilling to pressure the bishops to abandon the Catholic alliance with them: he was then regarded as weak and indecisive;[5] he was recalled to Rome in 1845 and appointed Bishop of Perugia. He did not see eye to eye with Cardinal Antonelli, Pius IX's Secretary of State, especially on the matter of Sardinia/Piedmont,[6] and this meant there was no further promotion for him in the papal diplomatic service. He remained at Perugia for thirty-one years until 1877.

This also meant he was free of involvement in Roman politics at this time, and though he was made cardinal in 1853 he restricted his interests to his see, while maintaining contact with the wider world through careful perusal of the international press. His pastoral letters often dealt with the social question; in one of them he argued that labour was the source of prosperity, of public and private wealth and that the Church backed all who laboured, both the manual and non-manual workers.[7] Yet his concern was pastoral and he was almost unknown in the world outside Church circles when Pius IX died in 1877. The need of the time seemed to require a man who could reduce the tensions between the Holy See and the Italian State. Cardinal Manning backed the candidacy of Pecci, but there would not seem to have been any expectation that the new Pontiff would take any decisive lead in regard to the social question.

## 2  Leo XIII's social encyclicals before *Rerum Novarum*

His short first encyclical *Inscrutabili Dei Consilio*[8] (28 April 1878) was on 'The evils affecting modern society' and those evils were seen to stem from the rejection by the modern world of Rome, the Church and her civilizing mission [3]. Rome and its bishop must be given the respect which is their due and [7] and in particular papal political sovereignty over its territories must be restored [12]. From a strictly juridical point of view this plea was justified, but it was not a message calculated to convince the outsider that

the Papacy had much to say to the modern world which the latter
might think relevant. However, the new Pope showed that he could
be flexible in other directions; within two days of his election he
took the initiative in approaching Wilhelm I on the situation of the
Church in Germany where for seven years the *Kulturkampf* had
been in progress. Bismarck was not at first forthcoming but eventually found it suited his policies in other directions to settle the
matter amicably, although it was 1887 before all the problems were
successfully overcome.

*Quod Apostolici Muneris* (QAM)[9] published on 28 December 1878
was on socialism. He spoke of that

> sect of men who ... are called socialists, communists or nihilists
> ... spread all over the world [and] bound ... in a wicked confed-
> eracy ... no longer seek the shelter of secret meetings but
> openly and boldly ... strive ... to overthrow all civil government
> whatsoever[1],

seeming to have in mind the Marxist International and the
Anarchists. The answer to these dangers is the apostolic precept
that all power comes from God and that he who resists the power
resists God [6]. Rulers for their part must remember that they must
rule justly and that God will judge them very strictly on this.
Tyranny however cannot be countered by insurrection on private
authority, for fear of greater evil.[10] When faced with evil governments, Christian patience is recommended when there is no other
hope of safety, unless anything against divine or natural law is
commanded [7]. Socialism claims that goods should be held in
common and that the rich may in consequence be despoiled, but
this disregards the natural inequalities between men and encourages what is simply theft. The Church for her part does not neglect
the needs of the poor but has always cared for them, and she is
constantly reminding the rich of their duty to be generous to them
[9]. Her bishops must strive to ensure that this teaching, on the
order God has placed in society, is known to all. Since workers are
susceptible to the allurements of the socialists, it is well to encourage societies for them which will help to keep them contented with
their lot[11].

There was here little appreciation of the growing anger and frustration of the workers. Rulers were told that they must rule justly,
but there was no recognition that rigidly controlled governments
encouraged men to think of violent remedies because they could
see no way to getting redress by peaceful means; nor was the appeal
to the charitable feelings of the rich a sufficient response to the

situation. But in *Diuturnum Illud* Leo addressed this problem more positively and directly.

*Diuturnum Illud* (DI),[11] 'On the origin of Civil power', was published on 29 June 1881[12], in the wake of the assassination by nihilists of Alexander II of Russia on 13 March 1881. It comments on the contempt for authority that it sees as a characteristic of the times [1–2] and it asserts the right of the Church to give guidance on ways of ensuring the stability and order of States [3]. In so doing it moves a little nearer to understanding the imperatives of the time, particularly the desire for democracy. The origin of the power of the State is the first matter dealt with. This is not, as has been argued, for the people[13] to delegate to those who are to use it or to revoke it when they wish. The power of the State on the contrary comes from God, and the right to rule accordingly is from him [4–5]. However, those in authority 'may be chosen by the will and decision of the multitude'[6] 'provided [their rule] is just and it tends to the common advantage'. Hence

> so long as justice be respected, the people are not hindered from choosing for themselves that sort of government which best suits their own disposition, or the institutions and customs of their ancestors[7].

But God is the source of the power that the rulers wield [8], because if the authority of the State is to be equal to its task it must be able to bind its subjects to obedience in conscience and no man and no merely human power can command them so [11] but God only, through the ruler.[14] Such a power commands greater respect and obedience than one based purely on human consent [13] and the only limit on such authority is the natural or divine law, giving to Caesar only the things which are truly his, and obeying God rather than man if we are facing a choice between them [15]. It also has to be remembered that justice demands use of State power for the common good, not for private advantage; rulers will one day be judged by God according to this standard [16]. If power is used as it was intended to be used, the cause of seditions is removed and the good of all in society is secure [17]. The Church throughout her history has sought to ensure that a system of government compatible with God's law should exist in those societies on which she has had influence [18–23], while later theories have produced great evils, resulting in communism and nihilism. The Church

> cannot be an object of suspicion to rulers, nor of hatred to the people; for it urges rulers to follow justice, and in nothing to

decline from their duty; while in many ways it supports their authority ... never opposed to honest liberty, the Church has always detested a tyrant's rule[26].

Her bishops should strive 'to make men understand and show forth in their lives what the Catholic Church teaches on government and the duty of obedience' so that the people 'are frequently urged to ... abhor all conspiracy and have nothing to do with sedition'[27].

Since the encyclical repeats the traditional teaching that the people can decide who may rule over them, the strong recommendation of obedience and the specific exclusion of conspiracy and sedition do not rule out peaceful movements in favour of democracy and greater political involvement. Conspiracy and sedition are evils, since they involve the use of force to overthrow government; peaceful desire for political change to democracy is, however, of its nature legitimate. The possibility of the State being tyrannous is mentioned in regard to the Roman Empire's persecution of the early Christians and their consequent peaceful refusal to obey [20], but the moral right, in principle, to rebel against a tyrant in the last resort, which is found in the tradition and in St Thomas in particular, is not, though *Quod Apostolici Muneris* [7] excludes only insurrection on private authority. There is always a question of prudence involved in the use of this teaching and in the circumstances it was clearly thought that the teaching should not be stressed. The tenor of *Diuturnum Illud* overall is in favour of monarchy but avoids the implication that this is the only form of government Christians can happily live under. It is much more positive about democracy and much more realistic about the possible defects of the State than *Quod Apostolici Muneris*, stressing that the Church has always said justice was the purpose of the State, and condemned tyrants.

In *Immortale Dei* (ID) (1 November 1885),[15] 'On the Christian constitution of States', Leo XIII sought to clarify the situation in France and help steer the Church there into more positive channels. It summarizes the Catholic teaching about the relationship between Church and State, both of which have their authority from God [3]. The type of State and the form of government are variable but all must be there to serve the common and not a private good, under God's law; if they do this they can expect obedience from their people [5]. It is therefore to the State's advantage to favour religion and the Catholic Church and it is its duty to do so [6–9]. That God has given to both their powers means that each should render to each what is its own – to Caesar what is his, and to God what is his [13–14]. Christian Europe subdued barbarous nations, was their leader and teacher and founded institutions for the relief of suffering [21]. After the Reformation there emerged the idea of the sovereignty of the people without any reference to God [31] together with an understanding of liberty as a right unconditioned by virtue or truth [32].

As to political forms, it is wrong to say that the Church supports one rather than another; in so far as they are capable of ensuring the welfare of the State all are compatible with her teaching. Participation of the people in government may be of obligation and rulers are not condemned when, for the sake of securing some great good or hindering some great evil, they patiently allow custom or usage to be a kind of sanction for each kind of religion having its place in the State '... no one shall be forced to embrace the Catholic faith against his will'[36]. She will however never approve of liberty which is in fact license, which destroys liberty [37].

The Church then is not hostile to modern political regimes.

> Our eyes are not closed to the spirit of the times. We repudiate not the assured and useful improvements of our age but ... wish the affairs of state ... to rest on a more firm foundation without injury to the true freedom of the people, for the best guardian of liberty is the truth; 'the truth will make you free' (John 8:2) [40].

Save where special circumstances dictate, it is in general fitting and salutary that Catholics should ... give their attention to national politics [44], to seek the 'genuine and true public good'. The example of the early Christians reveals how well they served the world; they were

> of yesterday, yet we swarm in all your institutions, we crowd your cities, islands, villages, towns, assemblies, the army itself, your wards and corporations, palace, senate ... law courts[45].[16]

In matters of practical politics such as 'the best form of government, and this or that form of administration' [48] differences are to be expected.

Unfortunately the Royalist Catholics in France ignored this teaching and Leo issued another encyclical *Sapientiae Christianae* (SC),[17] on 'Christians as citizens', on 10 January 1890. It sets out in full the duties of the members of the Church, and the Church as a whole, towards the secular, political order. In particular it states that the Church refuses,

prompted alike by right and by duty ... to subject herself to the
fleeting exigencies of politics ... it is not her province to decide
which is the best among many diverse forms of government[28].
[Therefore] to attempt to involve the Church in party strife, and
seek to bring her support to bear against those who take oppo-
site views, is only worthy of partisans [29].

This did not have the impact required either, so the Pope arranged
with Cardinal Lavigerie to stage a spectacular demonstration for
the French people. The latter entertained the officers of the
French Fleet at a banquet on 12 November 1890, during which he
pledged a toast to the Republic and then had a band, all of whom
were priests of the White Fathers, strike up the Marseillaise.[18] The
event caused a great outcry, but it had the desired effect of beginning to concentrate minds. Then in 1892 came *Au Milieu des
Sollicitudes*,[19] (AMS) 'On the Church and the State in France',
which spelt out the obligation of the French Catholics to rally to
the Republic; the *Ralliement* as it came to be called was partly
successful in that the bishops accepted the directive and many of
the younger clergy followed suit. The diehards remained to identify with the anti-Semites in the Dreyfus case and bring further
disrepute on the Church.

### 3 Leo XIII and the social problem

In the background meanwhile throughout the 1880s was the social
problem, and given the uncertain economic conditions of the time
it was of increasing urgency. Despite the long-term overall
improvement that economic development was producing for more
and more of the population, there was still too much that was
wrong with the handling of the human problems which rapid
change involved. The business boom of the early seventies broke
between 1873 and 1875 and the prolonged price fall over the next
two decades depressed industry and trade, with labour agitated by
unemployment and uncertainty. It was no longer ready to accept
these things as acts of God, but saw them as due to a failure of
human intelligence and will, which could be overcome if society
and its leaders set their minds to it: their response therefore was of
increasing protest. These were the years of the great strikes in
Belgium, France, Germany, England, and the USA; May Day 1890
saw trade unions leading extensive stoppages of work in most
major European cities, to draw attention to the social question and
secure minimum standards such as the eight-hour day,[20] and in

1891 the Labour Day marches in Spain, France and Italy led to violence and clashes with police. It was also, as we have seen, the time of anarchism and its assassinations of heads of State, of syndicalism and revolutionary trade unionism, of the Communist International and its apparent threat of organized assault on the existing order.

Everywhere labour was on the march and showing its strength and its greater potential. Even the moderate labour movements like the British had their Marxist as well as their uncompromising if non-revolutionary left wings. It was almost impossible at the time for outsiders to separate the one element from the other. The social ferment puzzled and angered those who felt themselves threatened by it, and it was the subject of discussion by all responsible social commentators. People were looking for guidance and answers. We have seen how the Catholic social movement reflected a concern and sense of urgency and how, by the 1880s, it was at something of an impasse; different individuals and groups were proposing solutions which could not easily be reconciled theoretically, and some were seen as totally impracticable, whatever their apparent theoretical advantages. The role of the State in solving the social question was one problem: should it be more interventionist, or should it be as limited as possible, and if interventionist, how interventionist? Providing justice for the worker in industry was another: does it mean in organizational terms the total replacement of the existing liberal capitalist order, or are trade unions, collective bargaining and conciliation, plus adequate legislation for protection of basic standards, enough?

Private property was also an issue, not only because Marxist socialist theory saw its disappearance as inevitable, necessary and good, but because in the USA Henry George and his disciple Fr McGlynn were attacking it with their theories; some bishops and the Roman authorities considered they were threatening the peace and integrity of the Church in that country.[21]

Given this background and the points of contention, the Union of Fribourg said in a memorandum to the Holy Father in 1888 that everyone was looking to the Vatican for a word on the dignity of work and the rights of the worker.[22] Fribourg and the other meetings of social Catholics at Liège and Angers helped clarify the points of controversy on which guidance was needed. The pilgrimages to Rome led by the industrialist Léon Harmel were evidence that among Catholic employers and workers there was a great desire to make the Pope aware of the problems. The long wrangle over the Knights of Labour had concentrated many minds.

Cardinal Manning's crowning of a life's work with the poor of London by his part in bringing about a peaceful end to the dock strike in 1890 with a settlement that was regarded as fair, testified to the Church's growing significance in the lives of the new working classes who were then becoming an increasing force in society. There were also conservative factions in the Church who saw any independence achieved by the workers, for example in free trade unions, as contrary to the mind of the Church. The Vatican archives give further insight into how these disputes were disturbing consciences: the Pope was being asked in letters from all over Europe especially, but also from other parts of the world, to address the issues, to say something on the worker question.[23]

The decision to give moral guidance by means of an encyclical did not at the time seem a very significant or energetic response to problems that had taxed the minds of politicians and statesman, of economists, of academics and practical men of business, of labour leaders and of leaders of opinion and publicists, for decades. But its reception not only within the Catholic world, for which it was primarily intended, but also outside it, was more than satisfactory. Other encyclicals have followed at intervals so that 'papal' teaching in this field and 'Catholic' social teaching, are taken as synonymous.

## 4  Understanding social encyclicals

The account of how and why the social teaching of the Church became particularly identified with the Papacy is useful in introducing us to a correct understanding of the encyclicals. The word 'encyclical' is a Greek derivative, meaning a letter that goes the rounds, an encyclical letter. From the early days of the Church many bishops referred to their peace and communion letters in this way; these letters, given by their bishops to Christians travelling abroad, stated that they were 'in communion' with, i.e. received communion in, their local church, and were therefore recommended to other local churches. Since the late sixteenth century, the title has been used to refer to papal letters concerned with doctrinal or moral matters, exhortations, warnings or recommendations.[24]

The decision to write an encyclical is the personal one of each pope, and its contents are for him to decide in the light of the tradition and of the current situation as he understands it. If he is expert in the matters in question there is less need for consultation on questions of substance; where he is not such an expert, he will be very reliant on his advisers, though, as in civil government, he takes responsibility for what is issued in his name after such consultation; it is his teaching. Leo XIII was very much so reliant over *Rerum Novarum*, but he kept a very close watch on it and the eventual document bore his authority. There will therefore, always be detectable, within the corpus of such encyclicals, differences of approach and emphasis. They are not prophetic announcements based on a certain knowledge of the future. How a pope and his advisers read the signs of the times, what issues he and they think are most central, how exactly to respond, and what are the best arguments in favour of such advice as is given to the faithful, are therefore all variables and the documents reflect this. Neither *Rerum Novarum* nor any other encyclical presents a once-for-all complete teaching which does not allow of additions, variations, changes of emphasis or direction, in short, of all that is implied in idea of the 'development of doctrine', which is the way the living magisterium adapts to new situations, maintaining the same principles but looking at the needs of those situations in which they have to be applied.

Some have seen *Rerum Novarum* as the equivalent to the Decalogue in terms of social teaching, definitive in all its detail, making any difference of emphasis, style or nuance in later documents a matter of great moment.[25] But this is to ignore the personal nature of encyclicals: it also ignores the provisional element that responsive documents always contain; situations may or may not be adequately analyzed in technical terms from the point of view of this school of thought or that. What is not provisional is the moral guidance they give on human rights which stem from the dignity of men and women made in the image and likeness of God; every school of thought and every policy and practice can be assessed in the light of that teaching. Finally, the social encyclicals are published primarily for the guidance of members of the Church who have faith in her teaching. They are not comparable with political documents which deal with issues in the same field, still less with learned academic tracts which do the same, though there will be an overlap in both cases. They are therefore less polemical and simplistic than the former, and less laboriously teased out than the latter. They are moral tracts or exhortations, faithful to the Scriptures and the tradition, presenting a reasoned case for their moral judgements and for their analysis of the issues involved, seeking to convince a Catholic Christian of good will that what they say should be taken seriously and obeyed. Their moral judgements are those of the ordinary teaching of the Church, which means they are binding in conscience.[26]

The genesis of this first social encyclical should also teach us other things. Leo XIII set out in a few pages his moral guidance to the Church on problems which had produced libraries of books, new political parties, whole new ways of looking at work, economics, industry and society. Clearly he was not challenging the competence or endeavour of the responsible individuals and organizations in these fields; he was carrying out his responsibilities as a spiritual and moral leader, and informing consciences on the moral choices that faced them. He was not seeking to instruct society on what economic, social, political theories and policies it should adopt, but was looking at those it had adopted, or was being exhorted to adopt, in terms of their effect on human dignity and rights. He was concerned to ensure that, in both theory and practice, society in all aspects of its functioning fostered the true good of men and women; he was concerned with the effect on the moral and spiritual values it is the Church's duty to protect. In so doing he showed his agreement with various schools of social reformers while also approving of much of the existing social order. It is to the debate between such reformers and conservatives that society looks for the right theories and policies on which to operate the economic and political system, not to the Church. The latter is there to guide them on the moral problems involved and to indicate what elements in current theories and policies are compatible with the good of man in the light of his eternal destiny, and what other possible theories and policies experts are putting forth that are worth considering in such terms.

What the encyclicals are about and how they should be interpreted in general terms is then clear enough. They give guidance on practical moral or ethical issues which strike a particular pope and his advisers as most important in application at the time, reading the signs of the times, on social, political or economic ethics – in other words, justice and charity. Because they are guided by the Church's teaching based on the Scriptures and the apostolic tradition, the principles of that teaching are known, but they are subject to adaptation and development to meet new situations. They throw light on the obligations of a Christian in the field of social morality, and the binding force of moral judgements on these matters is that of the ordinary teaching or magisterium of the Church.[27] Because circumstances demanded it, Leo XIII undertook the task of elaborating this social teaching; initially there was no other Church agency capable of doing this, and since then the unique international authority and responsibilities of the Papacy have required that it maintain its initiative in this area of the Church's moral theology.

The authority of the encyclicals extends to matters of moral principle and their implications only; in them it is binding on the
conscience of members of the Church. The practical and other
judgements the documents contain, touching on matters on which
good men may rightly disagree concerning society, politics,
economics, and historical judgements, are to be judged on the
knowledge and arguments presented; the Church's authority, by
definition, does not extend to such matters. Examples of the teaching binding in conscience are, for example, that socially responsible
ownership of private property is a moral good, as is the right of association of Christians and other men and women of goodwill, in
trade unions and other private associations, and the right of
peoples to choose their rulers and forms of government is a moral
good also. But the degree to which, in the light of the common
good, private property has to be controlled or not controlled in
practice, or the right of association likewise, or what choice the
people should make on forms of government, these are matters on
which good men may disagree, saving the principle. The moral
guidance given is on points of principle, but that does not mean
they are static; moral principles sincerely held are of their nature
dynamic. They move to action, guiding judgements of right and
wrong in particular circumstances. Theory and practice are linked
in moral judgements, and adherence to sound theory is the only
guarantee of sound action.

## 5  The Social Encyclical *Rerum Novarum* (RN)[28] 1891

### (i) *Introduction*

The manner in which this the first of the modern social encyclicals
evolved in its stages of drafting illustrates for us the way in which
the individuals involved and the circumstances in which they
worked help to give each a personal character. By July 1890 Leo
XIII had decided that he must issue some statement on the social
question and since he had published many encyclicals on ethical
issues in the political field already, this form was to be used again.
Since Leo had no expert knowledge on the social question, he
needed assistance on how to approach it. There were few at hand
in Rome who had much to offer him, but one of the few was the
Jesuit Fr Matteo Liberatore, a social philosopher and former editor
of *La Civiltà Cattolica,* who had dedicated himself to the restoration

of Thomism; he had also published works on ethics and natural law and on political economy, and he had been one of a Roman group which had been meeting, with Leo XIII's approval, to discuss the social question and responses to it. It was Liberatore who produced the first draft of the encyclical, some 6000 words, and gave it the simple title 'The Worker Question'.[29] The draft was added to and emended, in some respects quite significantly, by Cardinal Zigliara OP, also a Thomist, to whom it was passed for revision: it was changed in important detail during the translation from the original Italian into Latin, but at every stage Leo XIII watched carefully over it so that when it was finished it expressed his mind, the original Liberatore text providing the main structure and content of the final document. The drafting process was exhaustive: there were seven, perhaps eight versions in Italian and Latin altogether before, on 15 May 1891, it was ready.

### (ii) Summary of the text of Rerum Novarum

There are three main sections to it: the first is an Introduction in which the problems is outlined [1–3]; the second examines the socialist remedy and rejects it [4–15]; in the third the true remedy is set out [16–64].

### Introduction

'The spirit of revolutionary change [rerum novarum] which has long been disturbing the nations of the world' was produced by the impact of industrialization and has led to anxiety and widespread concern [1], so 'we have thought it expedient now to speak on the condition of the working classes ... the responsibility of the apostolic office urges us to treat of the question' so that 'no misapprehension may exist as to the principles which truth and justice dictate for its settlement' [2]. In particular,

> some opportune remedy must be found for the misery and wretchedness pressing so unjustly on the working class ... a small number of rich men has been able to lay upon the teeming masses of the poor, a yoke little better than slavery itself [3].

### I. The rejection of the socialist remedy

The remedy according to the socialists lies in the abolition of private property [4]. But a man works so that he can use what he earns to dispose of it as he wishes, and he may want to dispose of it by investing savings in property [5]. 'What is of greater moment is that the remedy is manifestly unjust. For every man has by nature the right to possess property as his own.' He differs from the animals in that he cannot only use but hold goods permanently [6]. His nature demands the right because he sees that the land will provide for his future needs and he requires permanent possession of part of it for this purpose. 'There is no need to bring in the State. Man precedes the State and possesses, prior to the formation of the State, the right of providing for the substance of his body' [7]. An objection to private ownership cannot be based on the fact that God has given the earth to the whole human race. He did so

> in general, not in the sense that all without distinction can deal with it as they like, but rather that no part was assigned to anyone in particular, and that the limits of private possession have been left to be fixed by man's own industry and by the laws of individual races [8].

The earth is only truly fruitful when cultivated by man, and when he expends his energy and effort on the task

> he makes his own that portion of nature's field which he culti-vates, that portion on which he leaves as it were, the impress of his personality; it cannot but be just for him to possess that portion[9].[30]

Those who say man is only entitled to the fruits of the land, not the land itself [10] contradict the common opinion of mankind, the natural law and the divine law, all of which defend private ownership [11]. The individual's right to private property is much better understood if it is seen in the light of a man's family responsibilities [12]. A man must provide for his dependants, and productive property 'which he can transmit to his children by inheritance' is needed for this purpose[13]. The State cannot take away this right. It must come to the family's aid when it is in distress but must go no further [14].[31] More than injustice would be done by the abolition of private property. 'The sources of wealth themselves would run dry, for no one would have any interest in exerting his talents or his industry.' All who set out to improve the condition of the worker must start from the fundamental principle of 'the inviolability of private property' [15].

## II. The true remedy

*The action of the Church*
The interest of the Church is to bring the Gospel message to bear
in resolving or lessening social conflict. She 'uses her efforts, not
only to enlighten the mind, but to direct by her precepts the life
and conduct of each and all' [16]. Inequalities and suffering are
part of life and it is to delude people to pretend otherwise [17–18].
Yet the classes are not natural enemies; 'each needs the other;
capital cannot do without labour, nor labour without capital'.
Mutual agreement produces order, perpetual conflict results in
savage barbarity. By stressing the duties of each to the other, the
Church can help society produce such agreement[19].

The workers should 'fully and faithfully ... perform the work
which has freely and equitably been agreed upon' and beyond that
in no way harm the employer or his interests or disturb the peace.
For their part the employers

> must not treat their work people as bondsmen but respect in
> every man his dignity as a person according to Christian teach-
> ing. To work for gain is creditable ... it enables [a man] to earn
> an honourable livelihood, but to misuse men as though they
> were things in the pursuit of gain, or value them solely for their
> physical powers – that is truly shameful.

The spiritual needs and moral needs must be properly cared for.
The employer's principal duty 'is to give each and every man what
is just'. It is true that many things must be considered in deciding
a just wage but masters are reminded that 'to defraud a man of the
wages which are his due is a sin crying to heaven for vengeance'
[20]. The knowledge that there is a life to come should give a true
perspective on the good things of this earth; possessions are good
if we use them well; the following of Christ will teach us the right
attitude to life's pains and sorrows [21]. The wealthy are warned
that riches do not help to attain eternal happiness but are rather a
hindrance to it; they should tremble at the warnings of Jesus
Christ.[32] A most strict account must be given to the supreme judge
for all we possess.

It is one thing to have a right to the possession of things: it is
another to use them as we wish. The right to own is natural and
inviolable[33] but 'man should not consider his possessions as his
own but as common, so as to share them when others are in need'.
He is not compelled to give away what he requires for the reasonable maintenance of his own standard of life[34] but when this is

done, charity demands that he give to the needy what is left. Charity's demands cannot be enforced by law, but the laws of Christ come before those of men; we will be judged by God according to this law of love for others. In summary: those generously endowed by God with material or spiritual gifts must use them for their own perfection and 'as a steward of divine providence to the benefit of others'.

> He who has a talent, said St Gregory the Great ... [should not] hide it ... he who enjoys abundance should watch less he fail in generosity to the poor ... he who possesses the skills of management should be careful to share them and their benefits with his neighbour' [22].[35]

Those who have to work for a living have an example in Christ, the Son of God who spent most of his life working as a carpenter [23]. The poor and unfortunate were his special concern, a consideration to check the pride of the well-to-do and encourage them to be generous, while moderating the desires of the poor [24].

> All men are children of the same common father, who is God ... all are redeemed and made sons of God by Jesus Christ ... the gifts of grace belong to the whole human race.

This should be the basis, not only of friendship between the classes, but of brotherly love [25].[36] The Church seeks to help mankind to follow the commandments of God and uses the agencies given her by Jesus Christ to reach the hearts of men [26]. Human society was once renewed by Christianity and can be again [27]. The Church is not so preoccupied with spiritual matters that she neglects the earthly interests of her people. In particular 'her desire is that the poor should rise above poverty and better their condition of life' and her moral teaching helps to this end by restraining greed and extravagance [28]. From the beginning she cared especially for the poor; Tertullian describes her members, feeding the needy, burying the dead, looking after orphans, the aged, the shipwrecked [29].[37] Her work of charity continues and is still needed, despite efforts to belittle it [30]. Yet the work needs the co-operation of all agencies, the State's especially [31].

*The action of the State*
The purpose of the State is to realize public well-being and private prosperity,

> through moral rule, well-regulated family life, respect for religion and justice, the moderation and fair imposing of public

taxes, the progress of the arts and trade, the abundant yield of the land

so benefiting all classes. And the more that is done for the benefit of the working classes by the general laws of the country, the less need will there be to seek for special means to relieve them' [32]. The State must see that the interests of the working class are protected as are those of the rich, providing for their welfare and comfort, otherwise 'that law of justice will be violated which ordains that each should have his due'. What belongs to the whole in a sense belongs to the part.[38] The ruler's 'first and chief [duty] is to act with strict justice ... distributive justice, towards each and every class alike' [33].[39]

> It is the business of all well-constituted States to see to the provision of those material and external helps 'the use of which is necessary to virtuous action'[40] and for the provision of such commodities the labour of the working class is essential: It may be truly said that it is only by the labour of working men that states grow rich ... it cannot but be good for the commonwealth to shield from misery those on whom it so largely depends for things that it needs [34].

The State should not absorb individual or family but allow them full freedom 'consistent with the common good and the needs of others'[41] but it should safeguard the community and its members; the safety of the commonwealth is the government's reason for existence; it is to rule for the benefit of the people, not of the ruler [35]. If a strike of workers threatens the public peace, if excessive working hours lead to neglect of religious duties or danger to health, or if unhealthy, immoral or degrading working conditions, or excessive burdens, are imposed on labour 'there can be no question but that within certain limits ... it would be right to invoke the aid and authority of the law' to the extent that is necessary to remedy the evil [36]. The law must be even-handed; nevertheless when there is a question of defending the rights of individuals the poor have a special claim to consideration. 'The richer class have many ways of shielding themselves ... whereas the mass of the poor ... must chiefly depend on the assistance of the state'[37].

Private property must be safeguarded. Those who stir up disorder and embrace the principles of revolution must not be allowed to use the honest search for justice of the majority of workers as an excuse for their activities [38]. The grave inconvenience of strikes

> should be obviated by public remedial measures ... laws should forestall and prevent such troubles arising ... lend their influ-

ence and authority to the removal in good time of the cause which led to conflicts between employers and employed [39].

The spiritual interests of the worker must be respected. Life on earth is not the final purpose for which man was created, and it is the soul which is made after the image and likeness of God.

> No man may with impunity outrage that human dignity which God himself treats with great reverence ... more, no man has in this matter power over himself. To consent to any treatment which is calculated to defeat the end and purpose of his being is beyond his right; he cannot give up his soul to servitude; for it is not man's rights which are here in question, but God's [40].

Hence Sunday and certain holy days must be respected, for the purposes of worship and rest [41].

It is necessary 'to save unfortunate working people from the cruelty of men ... who use human beings as mere instruments for moneymaking'. Hours of work should not be excessive, according to the nature of the work and its circumstances. Special provision covering women and children should be made. Further, 'in all contracts between masters and workpeople ... there should be provision for proper rest of soul and body' [42]. In a wage bargain it is not enough that there should be personal consent only [43]. Work is not only personal, it is necessary for livelihood and this must be taken into consideration in the contract; only through what they earn can the poor support themselves [44].

> Let the working man and the employer make free agreements, and in particular let them freely agree as to wages, nevertheless there underlies a dictate of natural justice more imperious and ancient than any bargain ... that wages ought to be sufficient to support a frugal and well-behaved wage earner.

If fear or necessity compel a man to make an agreement which does not do this then he is 'the victim of force and injustice'. Since circumstances differ so widely, societies or boards or some other means of safeguarding workers should be set up to determine the just wage, 'the State being appealed to, should circumstances require,[42] for its sanction and protection' [45]. If wages 'are sufficient to enable him comfortably to support himself, his wife and his children', he will be able to save and secure a modest income from property. The law should favour this and encourage as many as possible to become property owners [46].

The result of 'civil change and revolution has been to divide cities into two classes separated by a wide chasm'. On one side there is the part which 'holds power because it holds wealth, which has in its grasp the whole of labour and trade; which manipulates it for its own benefit and its own purposes all the sources of supply', and whose influence affects government policy. The needy multitude resents this, 'is sick and sore in spirit and ever ready for disturbance'. If such people can obtain a share in the land by their efforts they and their country would benefit. The State however should not tax the property owner unfairly although it has a right to control the use of property in the interests of the public good, but not to absorb it altogether [47].

*The action of the employers and the employed*
Employers' and workers' associations exist and many provide for the welfare of needy members and their families [48]. 'The most important of all are the working men's unions; for these include virtually all the rest.' The artificers' guilds of former times produced excellent results. Some still exist, both of workers only and of workers and employers [49]. It is a natural instinct that draws men together, conscious of their weakness as individuals, into civil society as into other lesser associations which are not independent societies but true societies none the less [50]. The State exists for the common good; it is concerned with the interests of all, a public society. Men establish relations with one another in the setting up of a commonwealth.[43] Private societies are formed with the good of their members in mind: 'to enter into a "society" of this kind is the natural right of man' [51]. Where their purposes are evidently evil the State may intervene, but

> every precaution must be taken not to violate the rights of individuals and impose unreasonable regulations under the pretence of public benefit, for laws only bind when they are in accordance with right reason and hence the eternal law of God [52].

So those who have taken away the rights of the Church's organizations have acted unjustly [53].

'Associations of every kind, and especially those of working men, are now far more common than heretofore.' Some of them are in the hands of men acting against Christian standards and the public good. Christians then have no choice but to form unions of their own [54]. Those in the Catholic community who have helped to better the conditions of the workers by rightful means, including through formation of such associations, are commended [55]. Good administration of them is essential, the details of it depend on the different conditions prevailing [56], but their purpose lies in 'helping each individual member to better his condition to the utmost in body, soul and property'. Religion and morality should have pride of place because Christ told us to seek the kingdom of God first and all else would follow [57]. Proper regard for sound principles of organization is necessary: appointment of good officials with clearly designated responsibilities, and honesty in administration. Committees should be established to settle disputes between masters and men, help ensure the supply of work and create funds to help those injured at work, or suffering from sickness, old age or distress [58]. Christian workers can play their full part in the solution of the condition of the worker question if they build on what is just and right. Their associations will be particularly helpful to Catholics who have fallen away from the practice of their religion as a result of the cruel industrial conditions which surround them [59–61]. The Church will co-operate fully with all who seek to solve the social problem, appealing to all classes and seeking only the common good, knowing that, in Christian charity and the Gospel, law is the answer [62].

## 6  His social teaching after 1891

*Graves de Communi* (GDC) (1901)[44] faced the problems which had been raised by the concept of Christian democracy.[45] The term could mean several things: the Catholic social movement, any kind of Christian social reform, Christian socialism, or a specific form of political party combining Christian religious belief and advocacy of democratic forms. It had been around since the 1830s but came into its own after the publication of *Rerum Novarum* in 1891 when it began to be used more and more in the last sense – political parties with programmes inspired by Catholic social teaching, and its acceptance of trade unionism and of reform aimed at overcoming the social evils of liberal capitalist industrialization.

Belgium was a case in point. The Belgian Democratic League had been founded just before the encyclical was issued and its direction was basically middle class, but from the first it supported free trade unions and social reform[46] and it was to receive the solid support of Cardinal Mercier. But Leo XIII was not sure that the close allegiance of the Church and political action implied by the phrase was a good thing, especially in Italy where the *non expedit* still ran and it was with the situation in Italy that *Graves de Communi* was mainly concerned. The whole question of facing the social problem through some kind of political grouping which was Catholic-orientated, grew up then against the background of older Church and State issues which had their roots in the conflicts of the sixteenth to eighteenth centuries, and where political action was by definition confessional or sectarian.

*Graves de Communi* points out that some find the term 'Christian democracy' objectionable because it suggests that popular government is to be preferred to all other forms [4], but properly understood it can only mean 'beneficent Christian action on behalf of the people' without any overtones of party or partisanship. It therefore favours the working class but not 'with the purpose of introducing one government in place of another' [7]. Nor should it be used in a way which overlooks the contribution made by the upper classes of society [8], or to encourage disobedience to lawful rulers [9]. The social question is not just an economic one but it has moral and religious aspects [11] and 'the two-fold charity of spiritual and corporal works' is still needed in its solution [15]. Charity does not replace justice but complements it. Charity

> neither connotes pride in the giver nor inflicts shame on the one who receives ... justice and charity are linked with each other ... to form an admirable cohesive power in human socity ... a sort of providence in looking after their own and seeking the common good as well [16].

In helping towards the solution of the social problem

> that action of Catholics, of whatever description it may be, will work with greater effect if all of the various associations, while preserving their individual rights, move together under one ... directive force

and 'in Italy we wish this should emanate from the Institute of Catholic Congresses' [23]. That Institute in turn was under the control of the bishops. 'So let it be in other nations' [24].

Leo XIII was providing a general ruling on Christian democracy to prevent confusion of the political preference of Catholics of a particular political cast of mind, wth the Church's official policy on political issues which touch on human rights and the good of souls. The former is necessarily partisan. The latter must never be primarily and *ex professo* partisan, but must deal with moral issues irrespective of their partisan implications. Yet groups of Catholics in various countries were finding it useful, and would find it useful, to make their religious convictions, and the social teaching of the Church, the basis for political commitment, and once it could be made plain that they did so unofficially, and in the broad sense embraced all social classes, the use of the term could be accepted.

Leo XIII, with the Italian situation primarily in mind, was not quite ready for this and not enough experience had been gained for him and his immediate successor to be able to see a way through the difficulties. But Leo did in practice accept a Catholic party, the German Centre Party, whose genesis in many ways anticipated the rise of the Christian Democratic parties elsewhere later. The Centre, as its name suggests, spanned the right and left wings of German politics and was by no means the official party of the Catholic Church in Germany; as we have seen, it had grown up as a result of the initiative of a group of laymen, seeking among other things to give political protection to the Church, but deciding its policy without being subject to the authority of the bishops. Leo also insisted that the Church work with democratically-elected governments as in France, and urged Catholics to accept this form as valid for their country. At the same time, the recent experience of the Church had left him wary of democracy as it had developed since the French Revolution; acceptable in theory, it had too frequently been identified with bloodshed and violence, inspired by less than worthy motives, to be trusted. His reservations about the long-term fruits of the French Revolution were borne out. It was inadequate forms of democracy which made it possible for Lenin, Mussolini and Hitler to cheat, lie and bully their ways to power within the first half of the next century with deplorable results for their countries and for the world. If democracy is to work it must do so within a framework of the divine revealed and natural laws, and be supported by a truly civil society, that is, with protection for personal rights and liberties which exist independent of and antecedent to political society and provide the only sound basis for the latter. This civil society is one founded on respect for person and family, a morally responsible citizenry knowing its rights and fulfilling its duties, built up through a network of voluntary organizations, social, political and economic, and based on respect for morally responsible freedom.

# 7  Summary analysis of his social teaching 1878–1903

## (i) Ethics and civil society

The French and the Industrial Revolutions had posed fundamental challenges to the self-understanding of Western society, civil, political and economic, and Leo XIII had the task of outlining the Church's response to the situation. It is out of the needs of civil society that the political and economic structures develop, it is in that society that its fundamental values are formed and nurtured and it was those values which had been questioned most radically.

His first encyclical was on the evils affecting modern society and he addressed these issues – though not in a way which would endear him to the world at large – appealing directly to the civilizing mission of Rome and asking that it be given the respect to which in consequence it was entitled [IDC 3–7]. The revolutionary forces which had been let loose on the world challenged the whole of the social order and civil government itself; the answer to their false and dangerous claims must lie in the knowledge that all power comes from God [QAM 6]. The origin of civil power therefore is not the people but its divine author. Though the people can choose their own rulers, the power they wield once chosen is based in God, and this knowledge must bind the rulers to use that power according to justice for the common good, not their own private good, in accord with the divine and natural law. Only on the sound basis of these laws can a just society be built. Just rule removes the causes of seditions [DI 3–17]. Since this is her teaching, supporting authority and insisting that it rule justly, she cannot be seen as the enemy of honest liberty [DI 26–7]. The Church is not opposed to the good that there is in modern developments: she insists only that freedom be founded on truth; she will never approve of a liberty which is licence, which destroys liberty [ID 32–40].

Civil society gives man rights which the State cannot take from him [RN 7]. One of them is the right to private property which enables man to support himself by his own efforts. There is also a right of association which exists before the State and which it cannot take from him; man sets up private societies for private purposes, and provided these are not anti-social he cannot be denied that right. In particular the workers can organize peacefully and under the law in trade unions for their own well-being [RN 50–51]. Fundamental to society is the family, which the State has a duty to help should it need it, but otherwise it must be left to develop freely [RN 14]. Moral rule, well-regulated family life, and justice for all are the foundations of civil order [RN 32, 34, 35].

The unity of society has been undermined by civil changes and revolution which have divided it into two conflicting classes: on the one hand are the powerful who control wealth and manipulate all things to their own benefit; on the other hand the injustices done to them make the masses inclined to rebellion [RN 47]. A small number of rich men have been able to lay upon the people a yoke little better than slavery itself [RN 3]. But class is not naturally opposed to class. All are children of God the Father, the creator, and redeemed by his Son Jesus Christ, and this is the basis of their human dignity [RN 24, 27]. Far from capital and labour being of their nature antagonistic to each other, they need each other [RN 19]. Where there are injustices these are to be remedied by the action of the state and of the parties themselves, and the rest of the encyclical is concerned with considering, in some detail, the way in which the Church, State and industry should work for this.

The Church wants the poor to be given the opportunity to better their condition [RN 28] and become property owners [RN 46–7]. Though inequalities are a fact of life which will always be there [RN 17–18] and it is wrong to pretend otherwise, inequality should not mean that anyone is without the means to secure for himself a decent livelihood, and it is for the State to watch over the situation to see that justice is done in this matter [RN 32–5].

## (ii) Ethics and political society

The power of the State therefore comes from God; the people may chose the form of State and their rulers [DI 4–6], but all government must be for the common good. The recent memory of the Church made Leo wary of the democratic totalitarianism of the French Revolution and the irreligion of Italian nationalism. It is the fear of these forms of democracy which lay behind his caution. it is because the revolutionaries claimed that it was *from* the people, not *through* them that political authority came, that the excesses of democratic totalitarianism became possible. If the people are the ultimate source of authority then there is no redress against any evil the State does in their name.

The Church is not identified with any particular form of state or regime, and she may not be exploited in a partisan way to support one form or any interest within it [ID 36, SC 28–9]. She is not opposed to the spirit of the times [ID 40] except in so far as it supports a false liberty [ID 41–2]. That the law of God has to be respected does not mean that the State may not be pluralist; it can tolerate different customs or usages for the greater good. The Church rejects coercion in religious matters; no one can or should be forced to be a Christian [ID 36]. The assured and useful improvements of the modern age are welcomed, not rejected [ID 40] and Catholics, save in special circumstances where it is not possible, are encouraged to be active in national politics, seeking the genuine public good. True liberty is freedom under the law of God [ID 2, 6, 17–18, 21, 32]. The question of Christian democracy showed that Leo XIII was still somewhat uncertain as to how, in some circumstances, all this could be done, and he erred on the side of caution [GDC 23–4], but his successors were gradually able to see their way through the difficulties and accept that, in some circumstances, it could be a valid term in a secular context if it did not tie Catholics to it, nor it to Catholic supporters only.

The purpose of the State is to realize public well-being and prosperity through a sound morality, support of family life, respect for religion and spiritual values, and an economic life to provide for the needs of all, for justice, fair taxes, and promotion of culture. The more that it does for the benefit of the working classes by its legislation, the less need will there be of special means of relief [RN 32]. Although it is its duty to act with strict justice towards every class [RN 33], yet because the rich have many ways of defending their interests, while the poor must depend on the State, the latter have a special claim to its protection [RN 37]. Ensuring that the material and external helps necessary for virtuous action are available to all is the State's concern; since it is by the labour of the workers that the State grows rich, they should not lack for the means to a decent livelihood [RN 34]. It must also act to see that the workers are protected against those who use them as mere instruments for making money. Free contracts must be, and be seen to be, fair contracts [RN 42–3]. The State, however, should not absorb individual or family, but should allow them the full freedom which is consistent with the common good [RN 35].

*(iii) Ethics and economic society*

The end and purpose of the economy is to supply society with its material needs, and only if it is based on private property in productive goods will it be able to do this adequately. If private property is abolished 'the sources of wealth would run dry, for no

one would have any interest in exerting his talents or his industry'
[RN 15]. Only if this system exists will the wealth that will enable
nations to solve the economic aspects of the social problem be
solved. The attempt to establish equality by destroying private
property would result only in want and human degradation. These
observations amount to a recommendation, in principle, of the
market economy. Those who own productive goods do so in order
to make a profit, to create wealth through the mechanism of the
market, buying and selling in the manner appropriate to the sector
of the economy in which they operate. The right to produce goods,
and to prosper by trading them, is one that has always been
respected in principle by the Church, though she reminds us [RN
21] that the possession of wealth in any form can be a threat to
one's spiritual well-being. However, that does not amount to a
condemnation of wealth-making in itself. The wealth of the world
was given to us for our use, but we are to use it in accordance with
charity and justice to our neighbours. On this the encyclical gives
guidance.

Private property in productive goods is morally good, provided it
accepts its moral responsibilities, particularly to the workers. The
wage contract is not unjust, but free contracts must be fair
contracts [RN 45]. Wages must be sufficient to support the wage
earner and his family, and also allow him to save so that he may
own some property [RN 46]. Workers are to have the right of association in free trade unions [RN 49] which have their aim as
'helping each individual to better his condition ... in body, soul
and property' [RN 57], negotiating with their employers on wages
and conditions; conciliation boards are one way of reconciling the
claims of the parties, the State being called on if necessary in the
last resort [RN 45]. Strikes should be forestalled by removing their
causes and the law should lend its authority to this end [RN 39].
Hours of work and conditions should be just, and suited to the age
and sex of the workers; they should be settled by agreement of the
parties but the State can intervene if all else fails [RN 37 and 50].
Private property is to be safeguarded, and those who exploit the
majority of workers in order that they may foster revolution are to
be restrained by the State [RN 38]. The property owner must not
be taxed unfairly [RN 47]. The workers are to work faithfully to
fulfill fair contracts, while for employers to defraud workers of what
is rightfully theirs is a sin crying to heaven for vengeance [RN 20].

It is one thing to own property, it is another to use it as one
wishes. The right to own is inviolable, but what is owned has to be
shared with others in need. What is necessary for maintaining

one's standard of life may be retained, the poor must be helped from the rest; the laws of Christ, which are superior to the laws of man, demand that this be done [RN 21–2]. But private charity is not enough. The state has the right to 'regulate the use of property in keeping with the requirements of the common good' [RN 47].

The encyclical would have been strengthened if St Thomas's teaching on this matter had been given more fully but this is simply a weakness in its framing; in practice at every point it insists on the social responsibilities of private ownership being met to the full. The encyclical saw the wage earners being oppressed by a small number of rich men, and its main thrust is an almost prophetic denunciation of the manner in which they were used as instruments of production. It insisted on humane working conditions, just wages, enough for the support of the wage earner and his family and allowing a surplus for savings; it stresses the duty of State and the wealthy to the poor, that is the workers, by whose labour both grow rich. The social responsibilities of private ownership of productive goods were never more clearly set out than in the encyclical as a whole, nor was the duty of the State to see that they met those commitments.

# 17

# Pius X (1903–14) and Benedict XV (1914–22)

## 1 Introduction

During Leo XIII's pontificate the responsibilities of his office demanded that he concern himself with secular events which deeply affected the life of the Church; in France, the inability of many Catholics to come to terms with the reality of a Republican government which was there to stay severely affected the life of the Church there, and he had to do what he could to ease the situation for the good of both Church and State; likewise, the growing political violence that was encouraged by socialist, nihilist and anarchist influences, and was evidenced in the assassination of Czar Alexander II in 1881, demanded a response from him because of his office. Even more pressing was the social question, which the Church had been able to ignore earlier in the century because it had not become crucial in countries with a large Catholic population, and because there were more immediate and pressing matters concerning her internal life that had to be addressed. By the time Leo was elected this too was a question which could no longer be ignored by the head of the Church on earth.

Hence the great series of encyclical letters that he issued: *Diuturnum Illud* (1881), *Immortale Dei* (1885), *Sapientiae Christianae* (1890) and *Rerum Novarum* (1891). They were of a piece. They gave evidence of the remarkable vitality of the Papacy, an institution which the nineteenth century saw as irrelevant or as at best an interesting and no doubt valuable relic, but a relic none the less. What it represented no longer reckoned for anything in the modern world. One hundred years later, it is clear how wrong that judgement was. Leo XIII had in fact provided the Church with a programme that enabled her to deal more than adequately with

* The notes and references for Chapter 17 are to be found on p. 441ff.

the problems of a tumultuous century and, at the end of it, to have survived with a vigour worthy of her history and tradition in the service of Christ.

The decision to issue encylicals is, as we have noted, very much a personal one of each Pope as he develops the policies of his pontificate, responds to the general responsibilities of his office, and establish his priorities, reading the signs of the times in the light of his own sense of the Church, his intellectual and spiritual talents and his life experience. Because the issues that Leo had to face were those which touched on the relationship of the Church with the secular order, he has come to be regarded as a political Pope. In a sense he was, but not because of his political ambitions, of which he had none. His duty, and that alone, turned him in that direction.

The pontificates of Leo's immediate successors, Pius X and Benedict XV, were beset by an entirely different set of problems. That of Pius X was overshadowed by the conflict over what has come to be called modernism, a series of theological ideas and attitudes which he regarded as dangerous to the faith and to the Church which it was his duty to defend. His predecessor, and the Church of his day, had not been so threatened. Moreover, Pius X's last years were spent in the tense and hectic atmosphere of a Europe girding itself for a fratricidal war, a terrible overture to the enormities and sufferings of the twentieth century. To watch the drama unfolding and to be able, in human terms, to do so little to change the course of events, was the fate of Pius X and of all who yearned for peace.

He died on 20 August 1914, just three weeks after the outbreak of war, and it was Benedict XV who had to try to guide the Church through it. It was a war which had its origins in the conflicts of nations which still regarded themselves as Christian, and on both sides of the political and military divide there were men and women who looked to the Pope as their spiritual leader. Both by inclination and circumstances, mitigating the sufferings of the civilian populations and the wounded and bereaved, and encouraging and supporting those who wanted peace. In the aftermath of war he had the duty of trying to secure a just and lasting peace for the nations who had suffered so much, of supporting their efforts at reconstruction, and assisting them in staving off the revolution that threatened them in the turmoil of demobilization and of social unrest at the disappointment of wartime hopes of a better world. These were in a way political tasks, but they were much more immediately an extension of the corporal works of mercy and

of the role of peacemaker in a fully spiritual sense. Like his immediate predecessor, he was not a political Pope.

## 2  Pius X and his pontificate

The conclave which elected Giuseppe Sarto[1] sensed that the internal
demands of the Church were now more pressing, needing a different emphasis in the style of Papacy, which would be more strictly
pastoral; sacramental and doctrinal matters now required consideration and they chose accordingly. The new Pope was born in Upper
Venetia in 1835, his father being a village postman and his mother a
seamstress. His humble origins marked him out from his predecessors since the French Revolution, all of whom had been from
aristocratic, privileged middle class or professional backgrounds.
Sarto's family was hardworking and poor; not destitute or poverty-
stricken in any absolute sense, but always living simply and frugally,
at times having to struggle to make ends meet. There were no family
funds for his education. He needed the help of his parish priest, the
generosity of friends and the scholarship awarded him by the
Patriarch of Venice, in order to be able to study for the priesthood.

Ordained in 1858, his deeply spiritual nature and his other ster-
ling virtues soon marked him out for promotion in the pastoral
work he loved so much, but he was also seen to have intellectual
gifts, as well as being a good administrator; he was curate, pastor,
chancellor, and then spiritual director at the Seminary of Treviso
before becoming Bishop of Mantua in 1884 and then Cardinal
Patriarch of Venice in 1893. He enjoyed a reputation for sanctity
during his lifetime, one confirmed by canonization in 1954, and
was acutely aware of the dangers of doctrinal deviation.

The manner of his handling this latter question has since caused
controversy among theologians, though it was, and has been, less
of a problem in the Church at large, which appreciated his holiness and his work as a great reforming Pope. In improving the
education of the clergy, modernizing and revising sacramental
practice and Canon Law – all matters of crucial importance to the
vitality of the Church's inner life and external practices – he was an
outstanding reformer, and the fact that he is the only Pope of the
last three centuries to have been canonized testifies to his great
spiritual gifts[2]. As to the doctrinal issues, 'it is unquestionable that
there were troublesome aspects of various reform movements ...
which forced the Pope ... to call to mind certain principles and to
warn of blunders.'[3]

Equally certainly mistakes were made in handling the situation, and they led to innocent men being accused and needless fear being caused to those who only wished to help healthy theological developments in the Church. Great issues were at stake, and in all organizations which face such a situation, strong characters and high ideals are found in conflict and a due sense of proportion and calmness of mind is not always present. So it has always been in the Church at crucial times and so it was during the modernist controversy.

As the son of humble parents himself, and as a priest and bishop known as a friend of the poor, Pius X was very much aware of the social problem and in sympathy with those it affected, though he was more cautious than some in raising hopes of a quick or easy improvement in their lot. He accepted fully the *Rerum Novarum* agenda but he was less sanguine concerning its immediate realization; the programme it had set in motion was continued quietly, but now there were other priorities. They did not prevent him from adopting a more positive approach to the Church's social apostolate on some matters, nor from acting emphatically when right or left sought to dominate the Church's direction in this field, but they were not the uppermost problems he faced.

In what he did in revitalizing the Church spiritually and morally he laid the best foundation for further developments in the rest of the Church's life. His policy for his pontificate was 'to restore all things in Christ'. He made no concessions on what he thought were the Church's rights in dealing with secular rulers and he soon clashed with the French Government; in consequence the Church there lost all her property, and a considerable income, rather than compromise with a viciously anti-clerical regime. Immense sacrifices were asked of her people; they made them, and the Church's life flourished.

## 3 His social teaching[4]

In the encyclical *E Supremi Apostolatus* (ESA)[5] of 4 October 1903, he showed the relevance of his motto – restoring all things in Christ – to the programme proposed for his pontificate. It emphasized the Church's role as the way to Christ, and its teaching on social issues, in the broadest sense, was part of that way. The restoration would embrace

the sanctity of marriage, the education and discipline of youth, the possession and use of property, the duties that men owe to those who rule the State, and lastly ... the equilibrium between the different classes of society [9].

The Church is not only concerned with spiritual welfare but also 'contribute[s] largely to temporal welfare and the advantage of society'. Through fidelity to her teaching the wealthy will be charitable and just and the poor maintain their patience [14]. But there is no mention of how the poor are to work politically for justice. The *motu proprio* on Christian social action, *Fin Dalla Prima* (FDP)[6] reaffirmed the teaching of Leo XIII but was very cautious on Christian democracy.

It was published in the wake of the *Opera Dei Congressi* (ODC) meeting in Bologna, during which there were differences which threatened to split that movement. It set out to reaffirm Leo XIII's teaching, which it did, but in a manner which underlined the static nature of society, and so of its politics. Men are equal before God but they are not equal in society; the order God has established is one in which there are rich and poor, nobles and subjects, masters and men who are to be united by the bond of charity and help one another to material and moral well-being on earth, and so to attain heaven [I–III]. There is a right to private property [IV, V]. Justice and charity are to be distinguished, and the rights and responsibilities of labour and capital as given in Leo's encyclical are repeated [VII–VIII]. The dignity of the poor and the right of workers to free trade unions is mentioned [X–XI] but Christian democracy in Italy must not be politically partisan [XIII, XV] and any stirring up of class hatred is to be avoided [XIX].

In the encyclical *Il Fermo Proposito* (IFP)[7] of 11 June 1905 'On Catholic Social Action', a more positive attitude emerges. It recalls the Church's work as the guardian of civilization in earlier ages [4] which she wishes to continue in this. Catholic social action should be, as *Rerum Novarum* indicated, dedicated to 'the practical solution of the social question according to Catholic principles' [13]. Work for the well-being of persons and society is urged as an essential part of the Christian way of life,

> taking to heart the interests of the people, especially those in the working and agricultural classes ... to improve their economic condition, to endeavour to make public laws conformable to justice' [7].

This action should preserve a spirit of peace and harmony, the Popular Union and the Catholic Congresses in Italy providing suitable examples [14–15].

The findings of social and economic studies, experience gained elsewhere, and full information on the conditions of society and State are to be utilized in this enterprise.

> The present constitution of states offers to all ... the right to influence public opinion, and Catholics ... can prove themselves as capable as others by co-operating in the material and civil welfare of the people [17].

In Italy however, Leo XIII's ruling forbidding Catholics to participate in national politics must in general stand, but in particular cases bishops can authorize such participation if the good of souls and the needs of the Church require it [18].

Catholic action demands a united effort, but this does not mean that 'works, rising out of the zeal of particular persons' should be discouraged: rather, they should be harnessed to the general cause [20]. Such works 'should be directed with a reasonable degree of freedom, since responsible action is theirs in temporal and economic affairs as well as in matters of public administration and life' [22]. It is regrettable therefore that some have undertaken initiatives in this sphere in the name of Christ without reference to those to whom he committed the authority to teach in his name. Such movements are particularly dangerous to the clergy who must remain 'above all human interests, all conflicts, all classes of society' [25]. This does not mean that they cannot

> labour on behalf of the people according to the principles of justice and charity by favouring and promoting those institutions which propose to protect the masses from the invasion of socialism [26].

Like Leo XIII, Pius X was looking at the issue from an Italian perspective where it was not clear how Catholics could relate to a State which had done the Church such injustices. He did not deny that the Church was concerned with social, political and economic affairs of its spiritual and moral mandate. In his first consistorial address he had said

> We are forced to deal with politics: the Pontifex Maximus, invested by God with this highest of offices, does not have the right to divorce politics from the realm of faith and morals.[8]

But partisan politics, the declaration for one section of the political spectrum against another where people may legitimately differ, – that was another matter. The Church was not to be tied to a particular partisan political cause.

The forces within the Church supporting Christian democracy were for their part seeking a way of committing themselves to democracy as Christians, either in reaction against the identification that some thought was natural between 'throne and altar', or because they saw such a commitment as a positive good in itself. The difficulty was that, in some circumstances, the use of the title was bound to lead to the belief that they were an 'official' Catholic party, and the strong though informal links they would continue to have with the Church would not make the charge easier to refute. Some made things worse by refusing to accept any guidance from the bishops even in strictly doctrinal matters.[9]

On particular political issues Pius X was prepared to be pragmatic, mitigating the *non expedit* from the beginning by allowing Catholics to vote in general elections in support of candidates favouring the Church's position against radicals and socialists. In the 1904 elections he effectively lifted the decree and several Catholic deputies were elected; it was a gesture which eventually led to its suspension[10]. In Italy the struggle of the younger Christian Democrats to get control of the *Opera Dei Congressi* had nearly succeeded in 1903[11] and only its second section, that which was concerned with social and economic issues, was retained. Pius X admired the German Catholic Social movement and wanted to model the Italian on it; it was he who had insisted on its second section of the ODC continuing under a new title, and it took responsibility for the credit unions and the labour organizations.[12] But the German Church had developed its social movement in tandem with the Centre Party, which secured them a political voice that was independent of the bishops, but which on relevant issues generally identified with the Church's position; this it could do without risking the charge of manipulation by the latter because it was known the party was independent. The Italian Church on the other hand, was saddled with the problems of the Roman question and its implications, which bedevilled all attempts to work out a positive role for the Catholic laity to commit themselves positively to service of the State or to political leadership; the Italian political system was weak and at the same time showed little respect for the Church's problems in its regard.

The question of Christian democracy was also raised in a crucial form in France with *Le Sillon* (The Furrow) movement. This was founded by a group of young people, prominent among whom was Marc Sangnier, who wished to reconcile post-1789 France and Catholic opinion. Sangnier's energy made it very active; it organized social study meetings where workers and intellectuals came together as equals, institutes which competed with socialist people's universities, and public debates on contemporary issues, until it began to resemble a crusade for the Christianizing of democracy and the winning back of the people to God and the Church. In 1906 it embraced a political programme and also became less of a Catholic, confessional, apostolic body, inviting those of other faiths and none to join it.

Predictably this caused the hierarchy to think twice about support, and they thought even harder when they found some eager and enthusiastic younger clergy, and seminarians, ready to listen to Sangnier rather than to their legitimate superiors. Since the modernist crisis was also causing concern at this time, there was an inevitable linkage between the two movements. The bishops were reacting unfavourably to the situation by 1907 and Pius X, while praising the idealism of the young people involved, grew increasingly concerned, and not without specific cause. The movement was increasingly intolerant of any view other than that democracy was a demand of Christian morality, not merely a political option open to Christians, and Sangnier himself was notably harsh in his handling of dissenters. The right-wing enemies of the movement were on hand to add further criticism, justified or not.

The Pope eventually condemned the movement on three grounds; firstly, that statements contrary to Catholic doctrine and reminiscent of the eighteenth-century philosophers of revolution and liberalism were to be found among those who wrote in its favour; secondly, it sought independence of the hierarchy on moral matters, and in general it was eclectic in its theological views; thirdly, it embraced modernist deviations on christology and ecclesiology. By contrast he initially showed favour to the agnostic and right-wing André Maurras' *Action Française*, though he later agreed that this writer's works be banned because of their theological and other errors; the decision on the matter was not however published before the Pope's death in 1914 because he refused to give comfort to the modernists and anticlericals in this way.[13]

What was essentially the Christian democrat controversy also affected Germany, though the context here was different as we have already seen. Within the German Catholic social movement a split had developed between the so called 'integralists' who were opposed to any attempt at the watering down of Catholic doctrine as they understood it, and the attempt by the Centre Party and the Catholic social movement to continue policies on social and political organization which experience had shown to offer the best chance of the Church serving her people and the society of which she was a part. The immediate issue was one of trade union membership. Should Catholics be allowed to join in such non-Catholic organizations or not? The integralists, who said No, were referred to as the Berlin faction, the others who said Yes were the Cologne faction.

The Berlin faction's objection to the policy of the *Volksverein*, namely interdenominational trade unions – and the acceptance, in the last resort, of the right to strike – was that they were undermining the faith of the workers. This faction had considerable influence in Rome, but Pius X's encyclical *Singulari Quadam*[14] of September 1912 judged that in this exceptional case, interdenominational unions were acceptable and the right to strike was not questioned.[15] Still the integralists kept up their pressure on the increasingly suspicious and rather isolated Pope. Articles were published in the semi-official *La civiltà cattolica* in February 1914, which argued that the moral legitimacy of trade unions was questionable because they limited the liberty of the worker and the property rights of the employer while also encouraging State intervention in industrial affairs, to the further detriment of private property rights.

There seemed to be a danger that the Pope might be persuaded to agree, but the discreet intervention and advocacy of laymen like Toniolo and Harmel, of ecclesiastics such as Cardinals Maffi of Pisa and Mercier of Mechlin, and the General of the Jesuits Fr Franz-Xavier Wernz, headed off any likelihood of this. Since accepting the role of free trade unions was an essential part of the policy of the Christian Democrats, they had made their point.[16] It was possible for Catholics to identify with specific sectional interests provided they did not involve the Church in identifying with those interests also.

## 4  Summary analysis of his social teaching

### (i) Ethics and civil society

There was emphasis on the importance to society of marriage and the family and the education of children, on property and duties towards the State [ESA 9] as the basis of a sound social order. On these foundations justice and charity will flourish and the poor will be assisted in bearing the difficulties of life [ESA 14]. There was no mention of what the poor could do for themselves to improve conditions. Pius X was slightly less static in his understanding of society and its institutions: he urged that the social classes which

God had established should help one another in material well-being, recognizing the dignity of the poor [FDP, I, II, III], and the rights of trade unions [FDP XI].

He continued a more cautious openess as occasion demanded. Practical solutions to social problems were to be sought, based on Catholic principles according to *Rerum Novarum* [IFP 13] so that just laws will be made [IFP 7]. Catholics must co-operate in answering the material and civil welfare needs of the people, supporting those institutions which protected the masses [IFP 17 and 26].

## (ii) Ethics and political society

The main concern was the problems as he saw them of Christian democracy, especially in Italy. These groups of socially aware Catholics, inspired by *Rerum Novarum*, wished to act together politically where national traditions made it difficult for them to identify with other politically active groups. The German Church had overcome this problem with the Centre Party, but its circumstances were unique. In Belgium, France and Italy problems remained. It seemed to Pius X that to identify with a confessionally explicit political party ran the risk of politicizing the Church, whereas her duty was to cater for those of all political opinions. Christian democracy was therefore not to be politically partisan [FDP, XI, XII, XIII] and any suggestion of class hatred was repugnant [FDP XIX]. Political action on a national level by Catholics was ruled out [IFP 18], although the *non expedit* was relaxed in 1904 so that Catholics could help counter radicals and socialists. The principle conceded, so too were partisan politics for laymen, though priests were specifically warned against them. The attempt of the Christian Democrats to get control of the *Opera Dei Congressi,* however, was rebuffed, the organization was overhauled and the whole brought more under the control of the bishops: it was active in encouraging Catholics to help credit unions and labour organizations, but in a manner which did not involve them in political life.

His admiration of the German Catholic social movement made Pius X wish to see something like it appear in Italy, but he seems to have been unaware to the difficulties of doing this. He also seems to have been unaware that his policies in these matters could appear partisan in practice. His handling of the *Le Sillon* affair in France laid him open to the charge that he was stricter on Catholic options for the political left than on those for the right. In fact he did warn the right-wing Catholics of the extreme right in France of their theological and other failings, as he rebuffed right-wing efforts in Germany to prevent the Church supporting labour orga-nizations which encouraged independent trade unions, with the right in principle to strike.

Overall therefore he implicitly accepted Catholic involvement in modern democracy, authorizing the participation in the Italian national elections and showing appreciation of the German Catholics' achievement, which included a political party that accepted the reform programme of *Rerum Novarum*. Though a son of the people himself, he was personally inclined to support the conservative wing in politics, but as Pope he defended the right of the Christian democrats to do what was necessary to ensure that the *Rerum Novarum* agenda was put into practice when that right was challenged by conservatives within the Church.

### (iii) Ethics and economic society

On economic and industrial questions therefore he maintained and applied the teaching of *Rerum Novarum*, which had said all that was necessary on them and simply needed to be put into practice. *Singulari Quadam* defended the right of association for the purposes set out by Leo XIII. To encourage improvement in economic conditions [IFP 17] that section of the ODC concerned with social and economics issues was retained; he approved of the German Catholic social movement's work in these fields.

## 5 Benedict XV and his pontificate

Pius X died on 20 August 1914 and on 3 September Giacomo Della Chiesa was elected Pope, taking the name of Benedict XV. Born in Genoa in 1854 of a patrician family, trained in the law, he had entered the papal diplomatic service after ordination in 1878 and served in various capacities in Spain and in Rome itself until appointed Archbishop of Bologna in 1907 and Cardinal in May 1914. His diplomatic experience had much to do with his being the surprise choice as Pope four months later.[17]

On 1 August Germany had declared war on Russia and three days later her allies, France and England, had come to her support in what has come to be known as the First World War. It is hard for us to imagine what a great impact this conflict had on the people of the time, an impact which reverberated throughout the 1920s and 1930s and loosed on the world terrors which have haunted us down to today. In the century preceding 1914 there had been no major war in Europe, and those which had affected European nations were mainly imperial conflicts and against weaker overseas powers. That which now broke out was a world war, in which all the European nations, save Spain, the Netherlands and Scandinavia, were involved. Australians and Americans fought in Europe – and men from Britain's Indian and from France's African Empire did also. The conflict also embraced the Middle-Eastern region through Turkey's alliance with Germany, and in the Far East Japan declared war on Germany; international waters were the scene of prolonged naval conflicts, most notably in submarine warfare. It was a war whose destructive capacity was unparallelled in history, created and sustained as it was by the vast resources and the new technologies at man's service through industrialization in all its aspects.

The Western Front, from the Channel coast of Flanders to the Swiss frontiers, transfixed Europe as it became probably the greatest killing ground in history, and the brutality of it left Western society and culture deeply wounded.[18] Verdun was a battle of two million men of whom half were casualties. Twenty per cent of Frenchmen of military age laid down their lives between 1914 and 1918. The Somme offensive cost the British 420,000 casualties – 57,000, of which 19,000 were fatal – on the first day alone. Britain lost a generation – 500,000 men under the age of 30 – in the course of the war. The Germans suffered more absolutely, but, with their much larger military age groups, less proportionately than the French – just over 13 per cent. The Russians and the Italians suffered cruelly at the hands of the more efficient German war machine.

Europe was shattered, with ten million dead and incalculable suffering in mind and body inflicted on the millions who yet survived. Russia was crippled militarily, economically and politically by defeat and was under Red domination from 1917. The massive war casualties weakened societies, and the returning troops found society turned upside down by the conflict, politically and economically disorganized, ripe for the attention of agitators of right and left. France was not only crippled by her casualties but also by the sheer physical destruction of the battlefields within her borders, and the drain on her economy. The deep divisions in society were initially obscured by the needs of national unity during the war, but the maltreatment of the ordinary French soldier through incompetent leadership and contempt for human life destroyed that unity and added to post-war tensions. Britain was more fortunate, but only marginally so; there had been no battles within her borders, but the drain on the best of her manpower and on her economic and social resources had been crippling and were to contribute to her economic and political weaknesses in the inter-war years. Tiny Belgium was invaded, occupied and plundered. Both Europe, and the world at large which had been so affected by this First World War, found that their economy was warped and undermined by the short and long-term effects so that recovery from it was more difficult. Indeed it could be said that there was no complete recovery from it before the next world war broke out in 1939. Benedict XV therefore had to guide a Church sundered by war in the first four years of his pontificate and then, in the last four, a Church faced by the mass of problems that the war had left in its immediate wake in Europe and throughout the world.

In Italy the Church had particularly acute problems of economic and political instability and the social unrest they fostered. The country had entered the war in 1915 in the hope, among other things, of gaining territories, Trentino in particular, but she was least prepared of all the states for modern war; there was always a large anti-war minority which resented her involvement, and her ill-equipped army was accordingly not bolstered by solid political support. By 1917 there were serious strikes at home and fraternization at the front, while the defeat at Caporetto in October of that year cost her 600,000 casualties. The end of the war brought no relief; she was disappointed in the negligible gains the war had brought her, social upheavals during it had seriously disturbed the already fragile structures of Italian society, while post-war dislocation and readjustment, combined with rising inflation, meant fewer jobs for the returning soldiers. In the winter of 1919–20 there were strikes and 'sit-ins' by workers and peasants, and for two years the fears of Bolshevism and revolution were real enough, increased by weak governments making concessions to the strikers. By the end of 1920 there was a large gap between the political leaders of the country and many of the landowners, businessmen and increasing number of the middle classes generally who saw chaos mounting around them. Meanwhile universal male suffrage had been introduced in 1919, and the Socialists won 156 of the 508 seats in the elections for the legislature in that year. The Italian Popular Party (PPI), mainly Catholic, were next with 100, but enmity between them and the Socialists made coalition impossible and a series of unstable ministries resulted. It was in this context in 1920–1 that Mussolini's Fascism began to take root and flourish through its paramilitary organizations, which by 1921–2 were in places burgeoning out of his control. When Benedict XIV died on 22 January 1922, the advent of an Italian Fascist state was nigh.[19]


## 6 His social teaching[20]

This was in the first instance concerned with the attempt at peace-making. On 8 September 1914 he renewed the pleas made by Pius X for a negotiated solution of the differences between the Powers, and on 1 November in the encyclical *Ad Beatissimi* (AB)[21] he repeated the same message. 'Surely there are other ways and means whereby violated rights can be rectified. Let them be tried honestly and with goodwill, and let arms meanwhile be laid aside' [4]. He also looked at the other sources of conflict in society which are no less distressful than the armed struggle betwen nations. The causes as he saw them are four – absence of mutual love or solidarity, contempt for authority, injustice between social classes and the making of material prosperity the end and purpose of human life [5]. All men are brethren in Christ [6] but although there was never more talk about the brotherhood of man, much of it ignored Christian teaching; in practice there was little such brotherliness [7].

The rejection of Christian teaching has led to injustices in the relations between classes in society because of the excessive materialism of the times [8]. The lack of respect for authority in general leads to attacks on life and property [9]. But he who resists legitimate authority resists God, as St Paul reminded us [10]. The rulers of nations should then remember that it is because they have ignored the Gospel and the Church that their authority is being questioned. They cannot control by force the unrest it causes [11]. When the cohesion of the social body which comes from the union of all in charity has been destroyed then class is set against class; the frequent strikes ending in bloodshed underline this enmity [12]. The errors of socialism have been exposed by Leo XIII and there is no need to comment further on them here; only a spirit of true charity inspiring rulers to treat the people with justice will counter this class bitterness [13].

The love of wealth undermines all; it is as St Paul tells us (1 Tim 6:10) the root of evil [14]. Surrounded by an ethos in which men are taught that eternal life is a mirage and that only a prosperous life on earth is worth striving for, inevitably each tries to obtain this by any means necessary, while those who have already achieved this wealth seek to hold on to it and increase it. Great inequalities exist and any effort the State makes to prevent injustices breeds hatred for it [15]. The Christian philosophy by contrast is that of the beatitudes [16]. It tells us that if man is to be happy he must put his hope in imperishable goods and not in perishable [17]. If this were the perspective accepted by society then the charity of Christ would remove the causes of strife and unrest [18]. In ecclesiastical matters, the pontificate of Pius X did much to revive the religious spirit of mankind [19-20] and the defence he made of the Christian truth against modernism needs to be continued and will be so [21-30], while the freedom of the Church will also be a main concern [31-3].

With the war in progress, there was charitable work to do, helping those suffering from the effects of the conflict. It took many forms. Where hostilities were conducted with some respect for the existing standards established by international law, the Church could build her work on them. The Pope arranged a general exchange of prisoners of war which was accepted by all the warring parties; he also arranged for the freeing of many civilian prisoners, women, children and the sick, the internment in neutral countries of disabled prisoners of war, exchanges of the seriously wounded, getting news of families and prisoners of war, helping refugees and offering facilities in the search for the missing. The German bishops alone investigated 800,000 applications which the State could not handle. Money was collected and distributed to help finance all these activities and the Vatican itself contributed some 82 million gold lire.[22]

In the Near East, there were atrocities of war which attracted little attention but which the Holy See sought to mitigate. Deportations among the Armenians for example cost about one million lives and tens of thousands of Assyrio-Chaldeans were driven into what is now modern Iraq and left to starve to death. By means of personal letters to the Sultan Mehemed V, Benedict was able partially to halt massacres, to save prisoners from execution and to help rescue those children left orphaned. There was no public recognition of Benedict's and the Church's work in these fields in any Western nation during or after the War. But the Sultan erected a memorial in his capital, dedicated 'To the great Pontiff of the world tragedy, benefactor of peoples without distinction of race or creed'.[23]

The new Pope inherited from his predecessor efforts at ending the conflict; he also sought to prevent the Italians getting involved in it. The period between September 1914 and the opening of hostilities with the Austrians and Hungarians in May 1915 was one in which gradually the majority of the Italian people, who were opposed to it but not active in the cause, was swamped and cajoled by an active minority into accepting the declaration of war. For many reasons Benedict was concerned by these internal conflicts. How the universal Church could be governed with Italy at war was one problem. Another was that the Italian Catholics would be expecting some guidance on the matter. On the one hand, the possibility of Italian defeat at the hands of the Austro-Hungarians raised the spectre in Benedict's mind of revolution from the left in the peninsula. On the other hand, should Austro-Hungary be defeated it meant the end of the last strong Catholic monarchy in Europe. From both points of view then Italian neutrality was preferable, quite apart from the bloodshed that would be avoided. At the same time he did not dispute the right of Italian Catholics who were inclined to support the move to war, to do so. He meanwhile tried to use diplomatic influence on both the Italian government and the Austro-Hungarians to prevent the spread of the conflict to Italy, but in both cases he failed. On 24 May both the German and the Austro-Hungarian diplomatic representatives to the Holy See were withdrawn and on the 25th Italy declared war.[24]

The efforts to achieve a negotiated peace between the combatants already involved continued throughout 1915 and 1916; the Pope made it plain that he was not neutral but impartial in his efforts to establish a stable and equitable settlement by negotiation, with respect for the rights and just aspirations of peoples, not one which was effectively a surrender, an imposition by victors on vanquished. A Vatican committee was established in September 1915, its purpose being to follow up the programme set out in *Ad Beatissimi*, and efforts to do this began at once with an offer to France and its allies of proposals which the Germans were believed to be ready to accept or at least discuss. They included freeing Belgium and Northern France, and the restitution of Alsace-Lorraine in return for colonial concessions. These were soon outdated by the much more ambitious expectations of the German General Staff from any such negotiations, but these expectations were in their turn overtaken by the succession of the Emperor Karl who replaced Franz Josef. Mgr Eugenio Pacelli in Munich sought without success to keep the initiative alive.

Early in 1917, however, it appeared that, with stalemate on the Western front, the time was ripe for a formal suggestion of negotiations, and approaches were made to the Powers to consider this. If negotiations were to be credible, they had to proceed with the reasonable expectation that the Powers which had gained most territory up to that time should show willingness to surrender. The peace proposals of 1 August 1917 therefore included provision that all occupied territories should be evacuated, that freedom of the seas be re-established and that, except in certain cases, all claims for war damage compensation were to be abandoned. Foundations for a lasting peace were to be established on the basis of the legal obligation to settle international disputes by arbitration, a general and proportional reduction of armaments and international sanctions against Powers guilty of aggression.

None of the Powers rejected the Pope's initiative in making the appeal, but the Germans blew hot and cold and their allies followed suit. Russia, France and Italy pointedly ignored it; the USA considered the Germans incapable of talking peace; the English were more hopeful that something could come of it but were cautious in response.[25] It has been suggested that from the German side the Pope's initiative might have succeeded; 'it could have served as the basis for peace', since the Reichstag's recent Peace Resolution echoed much of it,[26] but Ludendorff and his allies undermined the effort that was made by German politicians to this end. Russia's collapse in the autumn seemed to offer the Central Powers the chance of outright victory, while the accession of the USA to the Allied cause gave them hope also and the moment passed. The war was fought on to the bitter end.

Ironically the war improved the acceptance of the Catholic community in various countries: so in Italy and France its wholehearted support of their country's war effort, made its members more favourably regarded afterwards. Some 25,000 French priests, for example, served in the military, 12,000 of them as combatants, and nearly 5000 gave their lives. The Papacy however was not thanked for its efforts at securing a negotiated peace, being blamed by both sides for being too favourable to their enemies. It was excluded from the 1919 Peace Conference, and the treaty making and the vindictiveness of the settlements drew its disapproval. Benedict XV's proposal of 1917 for an international authority to oversee disarmament, and to handle arbitration of international disputes, reflected the scheme set out in detail by the Catholic Union of International Studies which met throughout the war in Switzerland, and the scheme had much in common with Wilson's Fourteen Points, though this was not acknowledged at the time; however, in 1923 the Swiss President, addressing the League

of Nations, did so. 'If mankind one day manages to get rid of war
... it will owe that priceless achievement to the principle of arbitration as proposed by Benedict XV.'[27]

The Vatican was not invited to participate in the League of
Nations, which some Catholics took as an affront at the time, but
was in fact a blessing, given the course of events which followed; in
any case the Vatican would not have been prepared to take part
simply as a sovereign State; some recognition of her spiritual role
in Europe and the world would have had to have been forthcoming and there was no likelihood of that. Benedict XV showed no
sign of being put out by the refusal to recognize the role of the
Holy See; he welcomed the League when it was established, while
recognizing its limitations, and instructed the Catholic
International Studies group to liaise with it.

The post-war situation described above offered new challenges
and opportunities to the Church and the Papacy to which they
responded positively. In 1918 the Pope approved Don Sturzo's
plan for what was a Christian Democratic Party, the *Partito Popolare
Italiano,* and in so doing revealed that a new set of circumstances,
and a new Pope, meant that Christian democracy was now
welcomed. The party was set up by Catholics, but it was non-
confessional in the sense that it was not in any way incorporated
into the well-organized diocesan pattern of Catholic social action.
It was then a lay initiative, not prompted by the hierarchical
Church. In practice, both as inspired by Christian principles and as
initially lacking grass-roots organization, it was organized at parish
level, and attracted its widest support among the faithful. Because
of its largely rural membership, it was interested in the agrarian
question; but it was also on good terms with those in the trade
unions who did not encourage indiscriminate and political strikes,
and with the Socialists it fought for the eight-hour day.

The encyclical *Pacem Dei Munus* (PDM)[28] of 23 May 1920 ('Peace
the gift of God') welcomed and celebrated the gift once more after
the terrible years of war. It appealed to the faithful

> in the mercy and charity of Christ ... not only to abandon hatred
> and to pardon offences ... but to promote all those works of
> Christian benevolence which bring aid to ... all who have
> suffered from the war [13].

It appealed especially to those who had been delivered from the
burdens of war that, 'without prejudice to the rights of justice' [14]
they might resume friendly relations among themselves.

We fervently exhort all the nations, under the inspiration of Christian benevolence, to establish a true peace ... and join together in an alliance which is just and lasting' [19].

The labour question was brought to the Pope's attention by the considerable labour unrest that swept over Italy in the post-war years.[29] On 10 May 1919, recalling *Rerum Novarum*, Benedict emphasized that both justice and charity were needed if the social classes were to work together. In the next year, in a letter to the Bishop of Bergamo, he wrote of the need to ameliorate the lot of the masses, and for the clergy to encourage interest in social and political action because of its importance to the Church and to the general welfare.[30] However, he was clearly not convinced that workers' expectations were realistic enough: they were hoping for more than could be reasonably achieved; but he did what he could to encourage trade unions, co-operatives, friendly societies and political action,[31] and he expanded the Church's social programme.[32] Though the political situation of the Church in post-war Italy remained delicate, given the failure to solve the question of the Vatican States, these measures helped the laity to make a Christian affirmation in political, economic and social life.

From the first, Benedict showed himself accommodating towards the Italian State. If he maintained the Papacy's claims he did so in the least offensive way; when peace came he agreed to receive Catholic heads of State on official visits to Rome, and the search for a solution to the Roman question began again in earnest; the fall of the government in 1920 dashed the hopes raised by the first negotiations but they were high again in 1921. He also finally laid to rest any fears that remained about Catholics participating in Italian politics.

## 7 Summary of his social teaching

### (i) Ethics and society

*Ad Beatissimi*, in reviewing the causes of conflict in society, saw them as stemming from a lack of solidarity, from contempt for authority, from injustice and from the making of material prosperity the end of life [5]. There had never been more talk of brotherhood among men, but it lacked foundation in Christ and so was seldom evident in practice [6–7]. It is the lack of the cohesion which can be given to it by Christian belief which is the cause of class conflict [12]. The love of wealth undermines all; it makes ruthless those seeking it, and relentless those who have it and intend to hold on to it at all costs [13–14]. If men would put their first hope in imperishable goods, not perishable, then they would have true happiness [17].

Benedict's direction of the Church's charitable work during the war and his search for means of bringing hostilities to an end by negotiation showed that his message of solidarity of all in Christ was a sincere and practical one. He also accepted new forms of organization pioneered by social Catholics and expanded the social programmes of the Church. Initially he spoke of the need for justice in society but did not give any indication of how the ordinary people could work for it by their own efforts. In the post-war years he showed himself favourable to the development of new political forms which would give Christians a way of making a positive contribution to the search for a just social order through political commitment.

## (ii) Ethics and political society

Benedict was accommodating to the needs of the Italian State and started the reconciliation process which was to enable a lasting agreement to be made with it. The war experience gave him more insight into the needs of practical politics, and he opened the way to the active participation of the Italian Catholics in the political life of their country when he approved Don Sturzo's plan for an Italian Popular Party, the *Partito Popolare Italiano,* in 1918. In international politics Benedict made a major contribution as a peacemaker during the 1914–18 war, and as a conciliator after it. *Ad Beatissimi* appealed for a better way of settling international disputes, other than by force [4], made proposals for a negotiated settlement of the conflict in 1917, and also put forward a plan for arbitration in international disputes, for overseeing disarmament and for other matters which had much in common with President Wilson's fourteen points. In *Pacem Dei Munus* he appealed for the abandonment of hatred and a just post-war settlement [PDM 9–14].

## (iii) Ethics and economic society

Benedict emphasized the central errors and evils of liberal capitalism, its worship of wealth and material prosperity as the true end of life and the ruthless and amoral individualism it fostered in society [AB 5–7], the answer to it being the programme of reform set out in *Rerum Novarum*. The widespread labour unrest that followed the ending of the war forced the labour question to his notice and he was positive in his approach to it. Both justice and charity were needed to solve it. He also wrote on the need to ameliorate the lot of the masses and for the clergy to concern themselves with the matter because of its importance for the Church's and the general social welfare. At the same time he clearly thought that the workers' expectations were unrealistic in the circumstances of the time, but he did not challenge their right to pursue them peacefully.

# 18

# Pius XI (1922–39)

## 1 Pius XI and his pontificate

Benedict XV died unexpectedly on 22 January 1922, and the conclave which met on 2 February was divided between those who wished to return to the policies of Pius X and those who sought a continuation of those of Benedict. The compromise candidate was Achille Ratti, elected on 6 February. His choice of name placed him in the tradition of Pius IX and X who were noted for their dedication to and success in strengthening the Church internally, rather than giving her a more emphatic role as international leader, but from the first, events compelled the new Pope to pay increasing attention to the state of Europe and the world, since those events profoundly affected the Church and her people and indeed the whole of mankind.[1]

The accession to power of the Fascists under Mussolini inaugurated a period of political totalitarianism[2] which faced the Church with new Problems in dealing with States, and the Papacy was increasingly entangled with them, as the leader of the Italian Church in the first instance and then as bearing ultimate responsibility for the churches through the world as the evil spread. Secondly, the weakness of the international economic and monetary system in the aftermath of the 1914 war threatened international economic stability throughout his reign. There was a period of prosperity (1923–9), but it did not last; the world economy went into recession after 1929, leaving no continent untouched, and recovery was slow throughout the 1930s.

The Church then found herself with problems of social and economic injustice which were at least as pressing as those Leo had had to deal with in the wake of the nineteenth-century industrial

* The notes and references for Chapter 18 are to be found on p. 442ff

revolution. No pope, whatever his personal inclinations, could fail to respond to them as their importance demanded. By the 1930s, totalitarianism was assuming more sinister forms and challenging Christian and civilized values in a manner which few had imagined could be so fundamental. First, the Fascism of Hitler's Nazis in Germany was flourishing, and was a much more malignant growth than Mussolini's version, while Hitler was setting the course for a second and more terrible war. Second, Stalinism in Russia was demonstrating the full force of its evil, an evil which its ambitions were seeking to spread world wide as the clash with Fascist forces in Spain, and the popularity of the People's Front, and other fellow-travellers' organizations in the Western democracies, demonstrated. The result was that Pius XI was willy-nilly more embroiled in the moral problems of international politics than any pope since the restoration of 1815.

Achille Ratti was the son of a Milanese textile factory manager, educated at the Gregorian University in Rome and ordained in 1979, when 22 years old. Academically very able, a paleographer and a linguist, he had served for a spell as a village curate before teaching in the seminary at Milan, moving from there to the Ambrosian Library and subsequently to the Vatican Library, both of which he headed as Director and Prefect respectively; he was then Apostolic Vistor to Poland in 1918–20, staying at his post when the Red armies were at the gates of Warsaw, and was then briefly Archbishop of Milan 1920–2. Cultured and active minded, he was by temperament, background and training, cautious and conservative but he showed himself ready to respond to the challenges of his office firmly and radically when needed.

Initially the circumstances facing the Church were in places favourable. The participation of the clergy in the war effort in France did much to reduce anti-clericalism and made her work less controversial than previously. In Germany the Church gained from the growth of democracy; the Catholic Centre Party was one of the strongest supporters of the new Weimar Government, many of whose ministers were drawn from it. In Italy also, the work of military chaplains and the charitable work of the Church in succouring the victims of the war increased her standing in society generally, while Benedict had encouraged participation in politics after the end of hostilities, and the initial success of the PPI helped demonstrate the positive contribution Catholic influence could make to the Italian political scene. However, the accession of the Fascists[3] to power in 1922 meant that once again the Church was faced with difficult questions concerning political authority.

## 2 Italian Fascism and the Church[4]

Since the movement was based on ideas incompatible with
Christian belief and contained in its ranks a large number of
violent and anti-clerical elements, there was tension between it and
the Church from the beginning. Yet Italian Fascism 'could
compromise with other institutions such as the monarchy and the
Catholic Church',[5] it was not as totalitarian as Hitler's National
Socialism. Its founder, Benito Mussolini, the son of a blacksmith,
after completing his schooling was variously teacher, mason, revolutionary, soldier, socialist journalist and finally newspaper owner
who became an enthusiastic advocate of Italian participation in the
1914–18 war. His Fascist Party, founded in 1919, was not an immediate success. Despite the post-war inflation, disillusionment with
the results of the war effort and the unrest of the unemployed ex-
soldiers, the party had little appeal.[6] Not one candidate was
returned in the elections of 1919; it was the Socialists, with 156
deputies, and Don Sturzo's PPI with 100, who attracted the
support. Many feared that the country was going Communist; in
the summer of 1920 more than half a million strikers in Northern
Italy occupied their factories and announced that they, the
workers, intended to run them. They failed, but the strikes and the
violence and street fighting between the Fascists and the Socialists
gave the middle class pause for thought.

Mussolini's party returned 35 candidates in the May election of
1921. Since the number of deputies was 535 in all, of whom 123
were Socialists and 107 PPI, this was not in absolute terms a great
achievement, but Mussolini proved to be a good politician and, by
presenting himself as conciliatory and statesmanlike, soon began
to exercise a wide influence. He bided his time and the final
collapse of the Italian government in the autumn of 1922 enabled
him to make his move. On 28 October ten thousand Fascists
marched on Rome to claim political power. The king could have
thwarted them by ordering the army to intervene[7] but, though the
Prime Minister asked him to do so, he would not sign the necessary
order, and in this he probably had the support of public opinion;
Mussolini seemed to offer hope. The government resigned,
Mussolini formed a coalition and by 1925 his Fascist revolution was
complete; the parliamentary system was suspended, all political
parties apart from the Fascists were outlawed, and the country was
under a Fascist dictatorship. Economic self-sufficiency for Italy and
the search for a colonial empire became priorities. Administration
was notably improved, grandiose public works were undertaken,

industry was, in theory, reorganized in corporatist form;[8] Italy began to make its mark on the world. In the years to the end of the 1920s most Italians, while they might have reservations about some things, were generally not dissatisfied with the regime, while there were many enthusiasts for it. Mussolini's perceived achievements in reducing chaos, giving purpose to national life and possibly staving off socialist revolution, gave him international as well as national credibility. There were very few who mourned the loss of liberal democracy, Italian style, at home or abroad.

Towards the Church, the Dictator was cynically opportunistic. Though his mother had been a devout Catholic, his father was a bitterly anti-clerical socialist, and the son was utterly without any religious understanding or belief. He realized, however, that it was necessary for him to get the Church's acceptance and in 1923 the crucifix reappeared in schools, army chaplains were appointed, charitable laws were reformed in a manner which favoured the Church and clerical stipends were improved.[9] The attacks against Catholic Action went on but they were reduced and little publicized; international acceptance above all depended to a considerable extent on being seen to maintain friendly relations with the Church.[10]

Pius XI was not displeased with the advent of Fascism. While under no illusions about the potential dangers of a movement, and of a man, with such antecedents, it seemed to him at the time that his kind of firm government, capable of preventing a communist takeover and restoring some sort of order to Italian affairs, was the lesser of several evils in a very disturbed time. For this reason he was distinctly cool towards the PPI after his election; the situation was volatile and he thought that it threatened to split the forces of the Church in facing the dangers before her.[11] As it happened, his attitude made little difference; it was soon clear that Mussolini was not going to tolerate other parties in his new order and the PPI was dissolved with the rest. Nonetheless, Pius XI has attracted some criticism for his coolness to it while it existed, and it reinforces the belief that there was in him a certain sympathy with authoritarian governments.[12] If there was, that sympathy did not extend to positive approval of the Fascist authority; he recognized that modern dictatorship was the most formidable danger to Christianity. At the same time, open challenge to any regime, except on matters explicitly concerned with the law of God and the essential rights of the Church, was not in its brief. For the Pope to have involved himself in conflict with the State on the matter would have been in every sense counterproductive, and as events proved it would have been futile since there was soon only one party, the Fascist.

A solution of the Roman question was, however, in the offing. Contacts made with the Italian authorities before Mussolini took power continued, and resulted in 1929 in the Lateran agreements.[13] The Vatican became a sovereign State and financial compensation for the loss of its territories was paid; the Concordat declared Catholicism the official State religion, ensured Church control over the appointment of bishops, freedom for Catholic Action and full legality for religious marriages.[14]

All this gained Mussolini and his party the gratitude of the Church and enabled them to appear before the world as statesmanlike and conciliatory. But Italian Fascism was and remained totalitarian in tendency, if not so absolutely as its German counterpart was to prove; it claimed the whole of man and his life for the State. Everything in the State, nothing apart from the State and nothing against the State had been its leader's claim in 1925 and he continued to assert it, Lateran Agreements or no. Countering the attempt of Fascism to monopolize education of the young was one reason for the Pope issuing on 31 December 1929 an encyclical *Divini Illius Magistri* on the Christian education of the young. During the winter of 1930–1 the regime and its lackeys stepped up their attacks on Catholic Action, accusing it of being a front for the PPI,[15] and it was in response to this situation that *Non Abbiamo Bisogno* was published in 1931.

## (i) Summary of Ubi Arcano Dei (UAD)(1922)[16]

This, the first encyclical of the Pontificate, issued on 23 December 1922, like all such first encyclicals sets out the programme for the new Pope's reign. He outlines the situation that faces the Church at the time. It is one in which the peoples of the world had found no lasting peace since the end of the Great War [7–9]. New problems and old rivalries have caused more suffering and introduced new tensions [10]. Nations and peoples live in fear because the threat of war still remains [11]. Society itself is threatened as class war is accentuated and political parties ignore the common good, seeking only power to exploit. Democracy, a system good in itself, is particularly vulnerable to these evils [12]. The revolutionary spirit divides not only the State but families, and social restlessness affects all [13–14]. Unemployment is rife and moral standards are threatened [15]. Religious and spiritual ideals are being attacked [16–17]. On the positive side, the patriotism of Christians during the war has done something to reconcile Church and society [18].

Peace treaties have not changed hearts and minds [20]. Men do not see one another as brothers; instead they try to exploit one another [21]. Greed for material possessions and gain causes discord [22]; the inequitable distribution of goods among individuals and nations threatens violence [23]. Class warfare and social egotism prevail, selfishness parades as reasons of State, leading to the neglect of the common good, while patriotism is a disguise for extreme nationalism [24–5]. Hope, however, must not be abandoned [32]. Brotherhood in Christ, justice in peace and love are the answer [33–4]. Justice leads to peace which is the fruit of love (ST IIa IIae Q. 29, art. 3 ad 3). It profits a man nothing to gain the whole world and lose his soul. If we seek first the kingdom of God, earthly goods follow. These are the perspectives which assure peace and justice [35–8].

The denial that legitimate authority comes from God is the origin of the confusion we see in daily life [39–40]. The Church, given authority by Christ to interpret that teaching, can lead man in brotherly love [41–2]. If all obey God's law, all know their mutual responsibilities, and under this law peace could be secured. Each would have faith in the word of others, and disagreements could be ended peacefully. Despite its failings, Christianity once provided a true league of nations because there was an ideal by which nations could be judged [45] and the Church could serve society this way today [46]. 'The peace of Christ in the Kingdom of Christ'[17] is to be the programme for the pontificate [49]. Education, charitable work, the individual and social apostolates are to be encouraged [50–8] and Catholic teaching on social authority, private property and the rights of capital and labour are to be the guide [59–60]. Without involving itself in civil affairs needlessly, the Church must speak out against offences against the laws of God [65]. She will also seek the rightful independence of the Holy See [66–70].

### (ii) Summary of Non Abbiamo Bisogno (NAB)(1931)[18]

This was the encyclical, dated 29 June, which was published in response to Fascist attacks on Catholic Action, in particular the university students' organization the Federazione degli Universitari Cattolici Italiani (FUCI) affiliated to it. These attacks had increased in the spring of 1931 when it was claimed that such organizations were about to challenge their Fascist counterparts. On 21 May

FUCI premises had been attacked in several cities and on 29 May, all Catholic youth movements, FUCI among them, were dissolved.

In noting the campaign by the authorities against Catholic organizations and the Church generally, carried on particularly in the controlled press, the encyclical rejects the charges that both are showing black ingratitude to a party which protests that it 'has been the guarantee of religious liberty'. The truth is that the Church has never failed to acknowledge what has been done for the benefit of religion, but it now looks as though all that was done was actuated not by respect for religion but 'due to pure calculation' with the goal of domination in mind. It is not the Church which is ungrateful but those who gained greatly in the opinion of the whole world for establishing relations with the Holy See, which many thought conceded too much in the process[17].

The attack on the alleged political activities of Catholic Action and the latter's disguised hostility to the regime was part of a plan to 'monopolize the young from their tenderest years ... for the exclusive advantage of a regime and a party based on a real pagan worship of the State ... statolatry' [44]. But 'a conception of the State which makes the young generation belong entirely to it, without any exception ... cannot be reconciled with Catholic doctrine ... nor the natural rights of the family' [52]. The position could not be stated more plainly; the Church could not concede to a State which is effectively pagan in its self-worship, the sole right to educate the young; the Church's duty was to see they were educated in the true way of Christ.

### (iii)  Church and State after 1931

Mussolini was outraged by the encyclical but realized he would have to do something to settle a dispute which had not cast him in a good light. The campaign against Catholic Action ceased, and he entered into negotiations aimed at getting some agreement that would end the dispute.[19] The Pope succeeded in saving Catholic Action as a result, but at some cost; the organization became more restricted in its scope and on occasion was pressured into supporting aspects of Facist policy. Concessions on both sides therefore ushered in a period of comparative peace in the relations between the Holy See and the regime, but these became disturbed again in 1938 when Hitler persuaded Mussolini to pass racial laws which parallelled those of Germany.[20] Pius XI denounced the laws for the unashamed racialism that lay behind them, a racialism made more repugnant in that it was directed at the race which God himself chooses to be the agency of the salvation of mankind, and he kept up to the end his efforts to protect those threatened. On 14 January 1939, less than a month before his death, he addressed the diplomatic corps to the Vatican, asking that visas be made available to the Jewish refugees from Fascist persecution. The 'Alliance Israélite Universelle' wrote on 13 February 1939 that

> we shall never forget the kindness and courage with which the late Pope defended the victims of persecution, irrespective of race and religion, in the name of those eternal principles, whose noblest spokesman he has been.[21]

For its part, the Italian Church in the 1930s was generally ready to go along with Mussolini and his policies, the colonial included. The Holy See remained aloof, meeting the news of the Abyssinian campaign with a warning about the moral indefensibility of wars of conquest. The support of the nationalist cause in Spain was less controversial, since it was seen as a conflict with the evils of communism. Given that, on the whole, the Italian people were ready at least to tolerate the Fascist regime for the benefits it brought, some real, some illusory, and apart from occasional unjust pressure on Catholic Action and the attempt to make the Italians accept the grim racialism of the Nazis, the regime was reasonably benign; many thought it had to be accepted because there was no alternative to it in the circumstances of the time. There was however, no doubt, that confused though it was, it was ultimately at odds with Christianity because of its totalitarian tendency. In theory it claimed the heart, mind and soul of its citizens to the exclusion of any power beyond and above the State; it was also theoretically racialist, and neither of these tenets could be reconciled with Christian belief. The saving grace of Italian Fascism, such as it was, was that except for the hard core of fanatics, it was not as serious as its German counterpart, so that its claimed totalitarianism and racialism escaped the full logical terrors of such a belief.

## 3 The world economic recession 1929–34 and the Church

### (i) The course of the recession

Fascism in Italy and Germany was a rising cause for concern in 1931, but the economic crisis loomed larger for most people, for there was hardly a household in the industrialized world untouched by it, while those in the less industrialized world who supplied raw materials for its industries and food for its people, were also badly hit.[22] Central to the multiple causes of the problem was the shift of economic power away from Europe as a result of its expending its wealth in the recent fratricidal war. Before it, Europe's, and especially Britain's, trade and finance had done more than anything else to create a world economy. It was one which served the needs of British and European capitalism first of all, but it could not do that without developing sinews which helped, as well as exploited, other nations. In particular, Britain's need to invest and sell overseas, and the working of the gold standard in this context, expanded international trade and finance in a manner which, despite periodic slumps, had been consistently self-sustaining and it was on it that the international economy largely depended.

But post-war, many of Europe's industries were either unable or unwilling to adapt to compete on the same scale as before the war and therefore their trade declined. Meanwhile, paying for the war had drained much gold away to America, which was less dependent on international trade and investment and therefore not playing the same role as Europe had in stimulating the international monetary and trading systems. These were still very dependent on London which was looking forward to the return of 'normality', that was, to the pre-war *status quo* and the gold standard. It was a vain hope since the economic strengths and relationships on which that normality had depended were no more.

On top of all this were the political dislocations resulting from the peace settlements that had undermined Europe economically and politically, and the imposition of reparations which did not help rebuild the long-term strengths of the system. It took some time for the full effects of these distortions to produce their full effects, and for much of the 1920s it seemed as if the situation might redeem itself. There had been a boom 1919–20 and though this had given way to slump 1920–1, by the mid twenties the situation seemed set fair. In 1925 Britain had returned to the gold standard, with every major economic power except France following suit within the year, France joining them in 1927; in 1925 Stresemann of Germany and Briand of France had negotiated the Treaty of Locarno which promised peace and prosperity to Europe.

Germany had stabilized after the ruinous inflation of 1922–3; large loans were made available to her, America being the main creditor, and her economy flourished. It looked as though

'normality' had returned; for five years Europe was indeed peaceful and on the whole prosperous, while America enjoyed the
'roaring twenties'. There it seemed that it was upwards all the way.
Population and productivity grew, construction and the new industries, pre-eminently electrical appliances and motor vehicles,
expanded enormously. Closer inspection however revealed that
the pattern was very patchy. Older manufactures were not
booming, nor was agriculture; unemployment remained high and
social security provisions were minimal. No matter: the illusion of
never-ending prosperity had taken hold of the stock market, where
from 1925 there raged a speculative boom which recalled all the
manias from the South Sea Bubble onward.

The idea of stocks and shares soberly valued by the market
according to earnings went by the board. They became commodities which it was assumed would always rise in price and could be
sold on a 'bull', that is a rising market. Every section of that market,
brokers, traders, bankers, financiers, collaborated in ever more
illegal, irresponsible and immoral ways to stoke it while the going
was good. Sober warnings that it could only end in disaster were
being made for those who had ears to hear. The Standard and
Poors agency had always been cautious and sceptical, and the *New
York Times* had tried to keep its readers in touch with reality,[23] but
their voices were drowned in the chorus of boundless optimism
that issued from the press, the academics and business leaders
generally, until on 24 October 1929 the bubble finally burst.

America's problems had been reflecting themselves in the world
economy before 1929; the outflow of capital to Europe had been
checked during the frenzy of the boom, while European capital had
been attracted to the American market, undermining currencies
and weakening industries. Now the USA registered a steep fall in
prices, production, employment and trade; the protectionist Hawley
Smoot tariffs of 1930 made matters worse, and Europe became
protectionist too, magnifying the plunging decline in world trade.
Falling prices meant reductions in production everywhere and
declining production led to rising unemployment as workers were
laid off. Then, just as the unlucky President Hoover was convincing
himself the worst was over in 1931, the collapse of the Creditanstalt
Bank of Vienna,[24] a result of the destabilization of Europe's financial
system following on that of the American stock market, set off a new
round of disaster. Britain's abandonment of the gold standard
marked the end of the old order and helped set off a further spiral of
depression and unemployment which many thought presaged the
end of the capitalist system that Marxists had been predicting.

The international economy therefore had become unstable because the conditions which had made the 1914 structures operate so efficiently no longer existed, and the conditions of the late 1920s in the United States combined to bring out the weaknesses in that economy. The Young Plan agreed in 1929, on which German hopes of long-term economic stability depended, assumed the continuance of those short-term loans which the country had attracted and Dr Stresemann had warned in 1928 that 'if a crisis were to arise and the Americans called in their short-terms loans we would be faced with bankruptcy'.[25] It was precisely that situation which came to be a year later.

The result of the slowing down of German economic activity was a growing increase in the number of unemployed: there were 1.3 million in 1929; a year later that figure had nearly tripled, to 3.14 million. It was no accident that the Nazis for the first time became a major political force in 1930. The number of the seats they held in the Reichstag leaped from 12 to 107. It continued to grow as the crisis deepened, and though they never received a popular majority, they were a very powerful minority and the ruthlessness and uncanny judgment of their leader enabled him to exploit the weaknesses of a crumbling political system to lie, bully and cheat his way to absolute power.

Great Britain had not prospered in the 1920s, mainly because of the poor performance of her basic industries and the effects of the 1925 return to gold at a level which overvalued the pound. Ironically the shock of the depression was somewhat lessened by this unfortunate inheritance. The continuing grimness of life for many and the apparent miserliness of the government's response to the extra social needs of a continued and deepened economic depression further embittered and soured social and industrial relations. In the United States, the depression cut deep indeed. By 1932 stock prices had fallen 83 per cent from their peak, production 40 per cent, wages 60 per cent and dividends 57 per cent; between fifteen and seventeen million were unemployed, money had lost half its value and credit could not be had.[26] Conditions such as these were a challenge and not only to the political stability of the weakened and short-lived German democracy. They were threatening the world's two oldest and most stable democracies, that of Britain and the USA. The attractions of Fascism and Marxism, promising strong leadership in the face of growing chaos, and the advent of a form of social planning that would avoid the wild gyrations of the capitalist system, were becoming attractive. That appeal was always limited but it was real throughout the 1930s and beyond. The lasting legacy in England was the Soviet spy network staffed by so many intellectually able young men of the middle and upper classes recruited in Cambridge University during this time.[27] Fascism had its adherents too, but they did not pose the long-term threat of the dedicated communists. In the United States, the pattern was similar;[28] the shock to the social fabric was stronger there since hopes had been high of perpetual prosperity in the 1920s and the scale of the subsequent recession was greater.

The fundamental assumptions of Western society were in this period questioned more profoundly than at any time since the Enlightenment. The assurance that liberal democracy and capitalism were the only way to run a modern State that had grown up in its wake was no longer so self-confident. Democracy did not seem to be working as it should and capitalism seemed to be fundamentally harsh and cruel, with little place for justice, let alone for brotherhood, charity, or respect for common humanity and its needs. Any attempt at guidance by the Church in these circumstances would have to look to the social foundations of mature capitalism.

The first purpose of *Quadragesimo Anno* ('in the fortieth year') was to celebrate the anniversary of Leo XIII's great encyclical in 1891, but it was also to

> summon to court the contemporary economic regime ... passing judgement on socialism ... [to] lay bare the root of the existing social confusion and at the same time to point the only way to a sound restoration [15].

It came to be subtitled 'On reconstructing the social order'.

## (ii)  Summary of the text of Quadragesimo Anno (QA)(1931)

There is an introduction [1–15] and three main sections to the document.[29]

1. The benefits of *Rerum Novarum* (16–40)
2. The authority of The Church in social and economic matters (41–98)
3. The great changes since Leo's time (99–149)

**Introduction**

Leo's encyclical was written at a time when one class had gained greatly from the advances society had made, but the mass of workers were in poverty [3] and they were consequently tempted to despair and violence [4]. They, and others seeking greater justice, needed guidance [7] and to this need he responded [8–9].

The 'isolated and defenceless workers' faced with 'the inhumanity of employers and the unbridled greed of competitors' were defended [10] by Leo who relied on 'unchangeable principles drawn from ... right reason and revelation' not from liberalism or socialism [11]. The workers were vindicated [12–13] though there were those who doubted the wisdom of his approach [14]. the purpose is of this encyclical is to explain, develop and defend his teaching [15].

## I. Benefits of *Rerum Novarum*

*What the Church has done*
She has continued to encourage her people to study and work for social reform [17–22]. Workers, assured of their dignity, have advanced their cause [23] and the Church has taken its part in organizations and associations for charity and justice in economic life [24].

*The contribution of civil authority*
Leo rejected the narrow liberal conception of the State as merely the guardian of good order. It has rather the task of developing 'public and individual well being' [25] giving chief consideration to the weak and the poor, and States have extended their efforts in this direction, efforts of which the Church approves [26–7]. Labour law has found its place in the affairs of nations [28].

*What has been done by workers and employers*
At the time many, including Catholics, were opposed to unions and Leo helped break down this opposition, encouraging their formation and membership of them [30–1]. They have as their purpose securing for their members 'an increase in the goods of body, soul and property', the spiritual goods being of prime importance [32]. They form Christians to work for justice in co-operation with other classes [33]. Methods used vary from place to place; sometimes they join secular unions; in others Christian unions are preferred [35–6]. Organizations of employers and managers exist but have been less successful [37–8].

## II. The authority of the church in social matters

All the benefits of Leo's encyclical spring from its Gospel origins
[39] yet its teaching has been controverted, and changing conditions require its amplification in some matters [40].

*The role of the Church in secular matters*
While it is not right for the Church to judge secular affairs 'in
matters of technique, for which she is neither suitably equipped
nor endowed by her office' she has the right to do so 'in all things
connected with the moral law' [41]. Economics and economic
science have their own autonomy in their own sphere but it is an
error to say that 'the economic and moral orders are so distinct ...
that the former in no way depends on the latter'. All are subject to
God's law [42–3].

*Private property*
It is wrong to say Leo sided with the rich [44]. According to the
tradition, ownership has a two-fold character, individual and
social. The creator has given man the right of ownership so that he
may provide for his family, but also that the goods intended for all
may truly serve this purpose [43]. Individualism, which minimizes
the social, and collectivism which minimizes the individual aspects,
are to be avoided [47]. The Church has not allowed pagan understandings of the rights of property to infiltrate her teaching here.
The right to own and the right to use are to be distinguished.
Commutative justice governs the right to own; other virtues, which
cannot be enforced in a court of law, ensure its proper use.[30]
Those who seek to define the limits of the right of property and its
use are doing a praiseworthy thing. Not so those who restrict its use
so much that the right itself is denied [48].

*The State and industry*
The public authority 'under divine and natural law ... can determine more accurately, what is and what is not permitted to owners
in the use of their property'. When it brings private ownership into
harmony with the common good 'it does not commit a hostile act
against private owners ... [or] weaken private property rights, but
strengthens them' [49]. Surplus income must be used for almsgiv-
ing, and for the good of the State; for example in providing useful
employment [50–1].[31] It is also permissible for the State to own
productive goods in cases where the industry in question has such
a dominant role in the economy that the common good requires

this [114]. Property is acquired by first occupancy and by labour (or specification). What belongs to no one can be possessed by anyone, but 'only labour which a man performs in his own name and by which a new form or increase has been given a thing, grants him title to these fruits' [52].

*Property ('capital') and labour*
'No nation has ever arisen out of want and poverty ... save by the toil of all the managers and those who carry out the work, yet all these labours are fruitful because of the wealth God has given us'. Right order must be preserved, everything should have its proper owner and it is false 'to ascribe to property or labour alone what has been obtained by the combined efforts of both' [53]. The extreme liberal view that subsistence wages were enough, and those who saw that capital has a right to replacement costs only, are both wrong [54–5]. Private ownership of created goods better serves the needs of all but 'not every distribution of property and wealth' achieves this aim. That distribution of goods must serve the common good; 'by the law of social justice'[32] one class is forbidden to exclude the other from sharing in the benefits of economic and social development. The disparity between the rich and the propertyless is 'the gravest evil'. The norms of the common good and social justice must be applied [57–8].

*Emancipation of the proletariat*
The sufferings of the workers have been much mitigated in the industrialized nations but the New World, and the ancient Far East, are now industrializing and the non-owning poor increase in numbers. The wealth of industrialization is still too badly shared [59–62].

*Just wages and salaries*
The means to redress this maldistribution can only come from paid work; the wage contract is valid but 'must be modified by a partnership contract ... workers thus become sharers in ownership or management or somehow share in profits' [63–65]. Pay must be in accord with justice, although some deny this; others by contrast say labour has the right to the whole product; both are wrong [67–8]. Yet labour is social as well as individual. There is needed therefore a 'truly social and juridical order' watching over the exercise of work 'various corporations ... [which] co-operate and mutually complete one another' [69]. Wages must be enough to support a man and his family; women and children

must not be compelled to work outside the home because of the insufficiency of the father's wages [70–1]. Excessive wages which would ruin an enterprise are unjust, but inefficiency is no excuse for low wages; unjust prices for goods are also an evil [72]. Where businesses collapse, assistance to workers affected must be given. Wage levels affect the common good, especially employment; but they must be sufficient to allow savings for the accumulation of modest wealth: the opportunity to work must be provided for all who are able and willing to do it [73–5].

*Reconstruction of the social order*
The social order also concerned Leo XIII and he called for a reform of social institutions and attitudes [76–7]. Because of the evils of individualism

> the highly developed social life which once flourished in a variety of ... institutions, organically linked with one another ... has been ... all but ruined leaving ... only individuals and the State [78].[33]

It is true that sometimes larger associations are needed to do things which smaller ones used to do yet

> just as it is wrong to withdraw from the individual and commit to the group what private enterprise and industry can accomplish, so it is an injustice ... for a larger and higher organization to arrogate to itself functions which can be performed efficiently by smaller and lower societies ... the aim of social activity should be to help members of the social body ... never to destroy or absorb them [79].[34]

The State should leave to the smaller groups, tasks of less importance which otherwise would distract it [80].

*The labour market: co-operation not warfare*
The conflict between hostile classes in the State must be ended by co-operation in industry and the professions, which is currently lacking [81–2]. The 'hiring and offering for hire in the so-called labour market, separates men into battle lines ... almost into a battle field.'[35] The result is that human society is being threatened with destruction. Labour is not a commodity to be bought and sold; men must be organized

> not according to the position they occupy in the labour market but according to their respective social function ... those who practise the same trade or profession should form guilds or associations' [83].[36]

They must look to the common good of the whole industry [84]. But particular points may involve the advantage or the detriment of employers or workers, in which case the 'two parties may deliberate separately ... as the situation requires' [85]. Those concerned can choose whatever organization best suits them [86][37] and they may join or not join such organizations as they choose [87].

### Co-operation as the key principle in economics

Economic freedom requires that economic life be independent of public authority. But while competition is justified and useful within certain limits it cannot totally direct economic life, as the economic dictatorship which has recently displaced competition has shown. 'Social justice and social charity must be sought ... a juridical order which will, as it were, give form and shape to all economic life' [88].[38] The interdependence of nations indicates the need for wise means to encourage international economic co-operation also, so that a genuine international solidarity develops. Such a pattern is in harmony with the idea of the Mystical Body of Christ [89–90].

Meanwhile a 'special syndical and corporative organization has been inaugurated' which requires some comment [91]. Here the State grants a workers' syndicate (or union) a juridical personality and a monopoly to negotiate on behalf of its members. Membership is voluntary but all pay their dues and must abide by the agreements of the one union. The employers also have their unions and both types are organs of State and co-ordinate the affairs of the industry. Other private associations, which do not have the official unions, status may also be formed [92], but the official organizations of both employers and employed are true organs of the State [93]. Strikes and lockouts are forbidden and the public authorities settle such disputes as the workers and employees cannot end by agreement [94]. There are some advantages in such a scheme but it seems to some that the State is here substituting itself for free activity; 'it savours too much of ... a political system ... serves political ends rather than leading to the reconstruction of a better social order' [95].[39]

The establishment of a corporatist system requires the good will of all [96]. It will need a reform of morality,[40] for there once was such an order which could have been adapted to present need, but it did not happen because men were impatient of authority of any kind [97].

## III. The great changes since Leo's XIII's time

*The unrestricted liberal economy and socialism*
The changes have been great, but the industrial system in which
capital and labour need one another still remains [100]. It is not
of itself vicious, but can be so when it scorns 'the dignity of the
workers, the social character of economic activity and social justice
and the common good' [101]. It is not only the economic system
in being, however. Agricultural economies far outnumber industrial and they have their problems too [102]. Industrialization is
none the less world wide, implosing its advantages and disadvantages on the whole of humanity [103]. Our concern is with both
[104].

*Competition has led to concentration of power*
Individualism and unrestricted free competition has resulted in the
concentration of capital in fewer and fewer hands, often administered by the non-owning directors of invested funds [105]. Those
who control money and credit have the whole system at their mercy
[106]. Only the strongest, who fight most violently and pay least
heed to conscience, survive [107]. There is first a conflict for
economic ascendancy in the State, then a second for control over
the State and finally there is conflict between States [108]. The
result is that 'free competition has destroyed itself; economic domination has supplanted the free market ... the whole system has
become tragically hard, inexorable and cruel' [109].

*Remedies*
The economic system emphasizes the division of capital and
labour, and Christian social philosophy and right reason require
their mutual co-operation

> according to the law of strict justice, called commutative, with
> the support of Christian charity. Free competition kept within
> due and proper limits, and still more economic dictatorship,
> must be brought under public authority in matters which
> pertain to its competence.

Public institutions must make society 'conform to the needs of the
common good ... the norm of social justice' [110].

*Changes in socialism*
Socialism too has changed since Leo XIII's day, there being two
factions within it [111]. The Communist variety preaches class war

and the abolition of private ownership and has laid waste vast
regions of Eastern Europe and Asia. But some still spread the
doctrines, others, who are more to be condemned, refuse to
abolish the evils that cause it [112]. Moderate socialism is very
similar to the Christian tradition, mitigating class war and the
attack on property [113], rightly contending that certain forms of
property carry with them a power so great that they must be
reserved to the State [114].

/But true socialism sees the class war as inevitable and good and
rejects private property in principle.]It 'cannot be reconciled with
the teachings of the Catholic Church' [117]. It holds that human
society exists merely for material well being [118]. Man is totally
subject to society; true liberty is hindered, while the false liberty
which denies social authority's foundations in God is encouraged
[119]. Though there is some truth in this socialism as in all errors,
it is not compatible with Christian belief, and no Christian can call
himself a socialist in this sense [120].[41] It should be remembered
that liberalism was the father of socialism and Bolshevism is its heir
[121–2].

Many Catholics turn to socialism because they say the Church
favours the rich and has no care for the workers [123]. Some
Catholics it is true are 'almost completely unmindful of justice and
charity' but they abuse religion and are not representative of the
Church [124–5]. On the basis of Leo's work all are called to reform
society 'according to the mind of the Church on a firmly established basis of social justice and social charity' [126]. Only
Christianity can remedy the excessive care for passing things which
is the origin of all vices [127–9].


*The root of the social disorder and the remedy*

The whole scheme of social and economic life today is such as to
hinder the mass of mankind from caring for eternal salvation [130].
It is not a matter of teaching the world to use material things better,
if the result is to enslave them to riches [131]. This 'unquenchable
care for riches' has always led to the breaking of God's law through
trampling on neighbours' work. The result is price manipulation,
abuse of limited liability laws, frauds by directors entrusted with
others' savings, irresponsible advertising, ruthless crushing of
competitors [132]. [Strict government watch is needed, but the
modern economy developed when economic teaching and practice
had complete freedom from moral law [133].]Hence wealth-makers

act without regard for others [134]. Since this bad example is given by the leaders of society it is little wonder that workers follow suit, the more so since they are treated like tools by their employers. Young workers and women are exposed to moral dangers at work; housing conditions are shameful; there is disregard for religious obligations; the result is that the production process improves dead matter but degrades those who man it [135].

*Economic life and Christian principles*
Since the order God established in the world directs all our activities to him, including the economic, man must be placed at the centre of all. God 'placed man on the earth to work it and use it in a multitude of ways for his needs'. Gainful occupations dignify man: God willed them in placing us on earth to use it for our needs. Hence

> those who increase the wealth of society by their efforts have the right to increase their fortunes in a lawful manner, for it is only fair that ... he who makes [society] richer should ... be made richer ... provided these things are sought with due respect for the law of God ... and ... the rights of others.

If these principles were put into action, men would be seeking God's kingdom while the temporal goods he knows we need in abundance would be theirs also [136].

*The role of charity*
Charity cannot take the place of justice denied, but 'justice alone can ... never bring about the union of hearts and minds' which is the main principle of stability in society. Without it, rules are futile [137]. Those who work to these ends are commended [138]. Those corrupted by ignorance or environment must be encouraged to have higher aspirations [139]. Many indeed from the ranks of the young workers are mindful of Christ and the leaders of workers' organization are striving for justice, as are many others from different backgrounds and social classes [140]. Bishops and priests should support them in every way.]

## 4 German Fascism and the Church

### (i) Background

The military defeat of Germany in 1918 came as a great shock to the German people, conditioned until the end by their leaders to

believe that victory would be theirs[42] and after the sufferings of the
years of war, the reaction was violent. There were left-wing revolutions in 1918, centred on Kiel, Munich and Berlin, and on 9
November the Kaiser was forced to resign. Friedrich Ebert, leader
of the majority Socialist Party, headed a democratic government
which took power against a background of growing discontent.
The Weimar Republic, as it came to be called – Weimar being the
small town near Erfurt in East Germany where it met – was then
born of this confused period that followed on unexpected defeat,
and to it fell the task of negotiating a peace from enemies who
were not prepared to show enlightened self-interest, let alone
mercy. It was then unjustly blamed for the defeat and the consequences.

The real culprits were of course those military and political
authorities who had misled them; so arrogantly sure were they that
their enemies would fall before them, and this old social and
economic order which had brought Germany to her doom
remained comparatively untouched by events. Imperial officials, by
definition opposed to the new democracy, kept their posts. The
powerful Junker families retained their coherence and influence
and remained hereditary opponents of democracy. The officers of
the new German army were from the old imperial caste and they
did not identify with Weimar. The major commercial, industrial
and financial interests in all sectors were on the whole no true
friends of the new order, and the academic community which had
flourished under the Empire was sceptical about the experiment
and passed this scepticism on to its students. The major professions, the law and the judiciary still sympathized with the old order.
All were oblivious that that order was the reason for their country's
desperate predicament.

The elections for a new National Assembly took place on 19
January 1919, the Ebert Socialists with 163 of the 399 deputies
emerging as the largest party; the Centre Party with 91 was the next
largest.[43] The new Reichstag met on 6 February, and in due course
was compelled to approve the Versailles Peace Treaties which were
signed on 18 June 1919 and ratified on 10 January 1920; the threat
of renewed hostilities was needed before the ratification took
place, so great was the opposition to the terms of the peace in
Germany. They had little to do with Wilson's Fourteen Points,
forgotten during the months after the end of hostilities when
vengeance took over. The Germans were declared solely responsible for the war and were expected to pay its full costs.[44] It is hard
to escape the conclusion that the seeds of the Second World War

were sown by these treaties. Weimar was beset by the problems of
the paramilitary violence of right and left and by the struggle over
the reparations which the Allies had imposed. The uncontrollable
inflation of 1923 was mainly the result of the German government's forcing the closing down of the Ruhr industries in response
to the Allied reoccupation of the region in dispute over the
payment of reparations. With industrial production at a standstill,
the government sought to keep the economy moving by printing
money to the point where one American dollar finally was worth
4200 million marks.[45] It was in the confusion of this situation that
Adolf Hitler[46] first made his mark on German politics. The inflation destroyed the savings and security of many of the lower middle
and working classes and they were alienated from the system;
these, along with those made unemployed by the depression that
started in 1929, were to provide Hitler with his mass support.

In 1919 Hitler had attached himself to an obscure group in
Munich, the NASPD, the German Workers' Party, and had gradually taken it over. In 1923 he believed the time was ripe for a
challenge to the State, but the Munich coup failed and he was
imprisoned for one year. This failure taught him that he had to be
patient; constitutional means had to be found to gain power.

The German economy recovered quickly once the government
took control of it in 1924. The death in October 1929 of Gustav
Stresemann, whose leadership of Germany in the previous four
years had had much to do with its economic recovery, and the Wall
Street crash of that month, brought the prosperity to an end. The
Socialist Chancellor Muller and his Cabinet resigned in 1930 when
President Hindenburg sanctioned the implementation of the
Young Plan, which they thought was too deflationary, the Centre
Party leader Heinrich Brüning being appointed in his place.
Finding it impossible to get his policies accepted by the Reichstag,
the new Chancellor called an election which took place on 10
September 1930[47] and this gave Hitler and his Nazis a chance
which they grabbed with both hands. Already adept at using the
modern arts of propaganda and organizing the Brownshirts (SA),
and the smaller SS, to provide a background of violence, with the
threat of more to come, Hitler's fascinating powers as an orator,
exercised on a people who were deeply disturbed by the confusion
and collapse around them, did the rest. The number of Nazis
elected to the Reichstag rose from 12 to 107.

They now formed the second largest party and a share in government became possible.[48] In the Presidential election of April 1932,
Hindenburg received 53 per cent of the votes and Hitler 36.8 per

cent. In the Reichstag elections of July 1932, however, with unemployment rising to 6 million, the Nazis more than doubled the
number of seats they had held previously; 230 Nazis were returned.
That was the peak of their popularity. After the second election of
that year, their numbers declined to 196[49], and in fact Hitler and
his party never received a popular majority in a free election. That
was to present no problem to his gaining power; the problems of
the government were gradually getting out of hand and he used
recurring crises to ease himself into power, because his nerves were
steadiest, his goals were more clearly defined, and his gangster
mentality saw how to exploit every weakness in his opponents and
to use any chance of the moment to his advantage; unhindered as
he was by any moral scruple or respect for truth or honour, there
was no stopping him.

Chancellor Brüning was forced into resigning by Hindenburg
in May 1932 over his plans to limit the powers of the great
landowners. After several more short-lived chancellorships whose
comings and goings reflected the collapse of the State, Hitler was
finally appointed minority Chancellor on 30 January 1933. Those
who decided on his appointment thought that as the majority of
administration was non-Nazis, they would be able to curb any
possible excesses of the new Chancellor, but it did not work out
that way. The fire that destroyed the Reichstag[50] on 27 February
enabled him to get round this obstacle. Under the pretence that
it had been a signal for a Communist uprising, Hitler suspended
civil, personal and constitutional liberties and announced the
calling of an election on 3 March. But he did not get the full
backing of the German people even with the full powers of State
behind him; only 43.9 per cent of the people supported him.[51]
More was needed for him to be able to exercise the domination
he sought, and he found it.

Most of the Communist members of the Reichstag were imprisoned for their alleged complicity in the plot to rebel and others
were, quite unconstitutionally, not invited to the new session.
Eighty-one votes were thus eliminated from the opposition and
when the Reichstag met on 23 March it had before it an Enabling
Act which Hitler said was necessary to meet the threat to the nation
caused by the discovery of the alleged Communist plot. It provided
for the handing over of governmental powers to the Reich Cabinet
for four years, with the promise that the power of the President
and the position of the Reichstag were safe. Only the Social
Democrats called Hitler's bluff. The leader of the Centre party
naively, or weakly, believed Hitler's assurance that the constitu-

tional rights supposedly only suspended would eventually be restored, and voted with the Government.[52]

Hitler now had the freedom he wanted. One of his first acts was to expel all non-Nazis from state governments and replace them with members of the Party. He also gave himself power to name all state governors, so achieving a centralized Nazi dictatorship; all other parties were dissolved, voluntarily or not, by 14 July 1933. The trade unions were likewise abolished, several of their leaders being killed in the process; the Nazi Labour Front was now the only workers' organization allowed. The schools were gradually brought under State control and Nazi youth organizations enrolled all children from 10 to 18 years old. The press was closely censored and all Jews were progressively purged from the professions. On 30 June 1934 Hitler authorized the 'night of the long knives' when an unknown but certainly large number of enemies of the regime were listed, rounded up and murdered.[53] After Hindenburg's death in August 1934, Hitler merged in his person the office of President and the role of the Commander in chief of the armed forces, whose members took an oath of loyalty to Hitler personally. In 1935, the Nuremburg Laws deprived all Jews of their German nationality, even if they were Christians, but those whose ancestry was less than 50 per cent Jewish could retain it.

There was sufficient in what Hitler and his minions had written and done by 1933 to give warning of things to come, but the enormity of what he proposed prevented his full ambitions being taken seriously by most. Those who were under his power soon knew that he meant what he said; the tactics of terror were used by the Nazis to get where they were, and that made it a gangster, not a political State. It was a question of supporting the party or being, at best, gradually ostracized; at worst it could mean the concentration camp with the possibility of summary execution at any time.[54]

## (ii) The Church in Nazi Germany

Within Germany the Catholic Church had more reason than most other Christian denominations to be suspicious of Hitler. It had crossed swords with Bismarck because of mistrust of state power, and it could not hope to escape the attentions of a creed which had a far more exalted view of the State and its rights than he had ever had. Hitler claimed that he was not anti-Christian; he only wanted to make the churches more German. The Reformed

Churches were used to being controlled by the State; but it was precisely the refusal of Rome to be subject to the State which had been one of the causes of contention with the powers of Europe over the centuries, the Catholic powers included] It was the connection with Rome that was at issue. 'The Catholic Church, united and well organized, must give up once and for all, its allegiance to the man in Rome.'[55] On Sunday 30 September 1930, just two months after the Nazis won 107 seats in the Reichstag and became the second largest party there, the parish priest of Kirschausen in Hesse, with his bishop's full support, told his people that no Catholic could be a member of the Nazi party. During the next few weeks, pastoral letters in other dioceses throughout the country carried the same message and in February 1931 the eight Bavarian bishops summarized the doctrinal errors of Nazism; it puts race before religion, rejects the Old Testament and with it the Decalogue, denies the papal primacy, proposes a German National Church and finally would make 'moral sentiment' the criterion of the moral law.[56]

In the elections of March 1932, that is before Hitler was Chancellor and the constitution and civil liberties had been undermined, the bishops advised their people to vote for the Centre Party because Hitler's version of Christianity was not that of Christ. But it was too late; of the 12.5 million Catholic voters, only 5.5 million took the advice.[57] They were in a familiar and uncomfortable dilemma, that of reconciling their Catholicism with their German nationality, but it was a particularly painful one at this time. They were being bracketed with the 'Reds' as bad Germans; the 'Blacks' were, they were being told, as much enemies of Germany as the Reds. There was also the growing realization that Nazi Party membership, or at least open sympathy with the Party, was the only way to prosper under the new order which was clearly coming. Perhaps detecting that their flocks were drifting away from them, the bishops at their meeting at Fulda on 28 March 1933, with Hitler now Chancellor, withdrew their previous prohibitions on party membership and the reception of the sacraments by uniformed Nazis. Cardinal Pacelli, Papal Secretary of State at the time, expressed the wish that if they had to meet the government halfway, they could have waited a little longer.[58]

The Church had been trying to get concordats with the German states since 1920, and they had been concluded with Bavaria (1924), Prussia (1929) and Baden (1932), and in April 1932, that is under the Weimar Republic, the Holy See had entered into

negotiations, requested by the German government, with a view
to agreeing a Concordat with the whole of the Reich. Because of
the objection of the Left and of some Christian denominations,
it was delayed and the Nazis took it up again. It was signed on 20
July and ratified on 10 September 1933. It has been criticized
since as having given respectability to the regime, but it should
be clear to anyone who knew anything about papal diplomacy,
that dealing with a regime did not mean accepting its philosophy
or policies. The Holy See had tried for as long as it could to get
some agreement with the Soviet Union in the 1920s, only
giving up when it was obvious that there was no possibility of
progress. These persistent efforts could in no way be construed
as giving approval to the regime in the USSR. In like manner,
agreement with the Nazis did not indicate any approval of their
regime.

Nor did the Western world need papal example in dealing with
the Nazis. All it had done was to make an agreement with the
German government which had been initiated by the previous
government, and to which it had responded as part of the same
policy that the Church followed everywhere, and had been pursuing in Germany since the 1920s. The French, British and Italian
governments had on the other hand begun negotiations with the
German government in March 1933 on a four-power pact; it was
initialled on 7 June.

The Pope's opinion of Nazism was on record. In his Christmas
message of 1930 'in a well understood reference to the new
German mythology',[59] he had said that 'if there is in Christianity a
mystery of blood, it is that, not of race opposed to race, but of the
unity of all men in the heritage of sin derived from our first father'.
In January 1931 Cardinal Bertram followed this up; Catholics reject
race religion.

The Vatican had no illusions about the Concordat. It was the
lesser of two evils, a way of hoping to rescue something should the
Church in Germany be put under pressure by the State. It could
have refused to deal with the regime, but those who would have
had to suffer the consequences, the German Catholics, had a right
to expect that the Church's highest authority had taken every step
to try to protect them.[60] Theoretically the Concordat promised
complete freedom for Catholic education, religious practices and
in its internal affairs. In return the Church undertook not to be
involved in politics and to respect the authority of the German
State. The Nazis showed from the start that the Concordat was not
worth the paper it was written on, breaking its terms almost at

once, and the Church found that Hitler and the Nazis were lawless and ruthless in a manner that Bismarck had not been. For all his blood and iron, he had had a basic respect for law and morality. The Nazis had none. Five days after the Concordat was signed they passed a Sterilization Act which struck at the very root of the dignity of man as the Christian tradition understood it, and the rights of man that sprang from it, and which, primarily through Christian influences, had come to be embodied in the right thinking and the laws of all Western nations. Those were fully human who the Nazis decided were so, and the rest could be disposed of in a mad Frankenstein dream of racial purity, the recounting of which today nauseates with its crudity and viciousness.

On the Night of the Long Knives in June 1934 four prominent Catholic lay leaders were among those murdered, and over the following months five hundred priests and religious were arrested, many dying in custody.[61]

> The implacable logic of circumstances doomed to failure every attempt to arrest totalitarianism. The institutions which were too much for Bismarck, the conflicting political forces which had so long pulled Germany this way and that, were all overborne ... political parties ... trade unions ... the States ... only the Catholic Church attempted to resist and, though it was defeated, yet its defeat was perhaps a little less thorough than that of every other organization in Germany.[62]

Among the bishops who tried to do something to stem the tide of evil were Cardinal Faulhaber with his sermons in Munich on the Old Testament, Bishop Preysing of Berlin and Galen of Munster, speaking out against the evils of Nazi paganism; 'a large Catholic Cathedral was undoubtedly the most convenient place in Hitler's Germany to escape from the raucous, vulgar and oppressive hand of dictatorship'.[63] The Protestant Confessional Church was increasingly critical of the evils of the regime, while the tiny band of Jehovah's Witnesses were outstanding for their dedication to Christ's truth. By 1937 it was no longer possible to pretend that any agreement with Hitler meant anything, or to hope that there was any effective way of controlling Nazism by turning the other cheek. Pius XI was prepared 'from then on, undeterred by the danger of collision with the princes of this world' for battle on two fronts 'combating, in the name of individual human rights, the totalitarian ideologies of both the left and the right'.[64]

The events surrounding 'Hitler's Olympics' in 1936 showed that internationally in that year many were too dazzled by the evidence of Hitler's success in getting Germany back to work and in producing an illusion of social peace to ask what lay underneath it all. The Church in Germany knew well enough the evil that it had to contend, with and in 1937 the encyclical *Mit Brennender Sorge* (MBS) ('With burning sorrow') published on 14 March let the world know it. It was initially drafted by Cardinal Faulhaber after a meeting and consultations in January between the Holy Father and his Secretary of State, Cardinal Pacelli, and the other two German Cardinals, together with Bishops Von Galen and Preysing who, as we have noted, were opponents of the regime, and Pius XI gave most credit for its final appearance to Cardinal Pacelli.[65] The reading of the encyclical in all Catholic Churches was the most serious public denunciation to which Hitler's ideas and regime were subjected in Germany during the twelve years he held power.

## (iii) Summary of the text of Mit Brennender Sorge

It is not a long document.[66] After the Introduction [1–6] it sets out the main points of Christian teaching relevant to countering racialism, namely true faith in God [7–13] and in God made man in Christ [14–17], true faith in the Church [18–21], and in the papal primacy [22]. The correct interpretation of Scripture and revelation are highlighted [23–6] as is the proper understanding of the relationship between morality and the moral order [27–31]. It ends with an exhortation to the members of the Church in Germany.

## 1 Introduction

It is with deep and growing surprise that the Pope has followed the trials of the Church in Germany and in the light of them he protests [1–2]. The Concordat was made at the government's request in 1933 in the hope it was offering peace, but it is evident that a war of extermination was always intended [3–4]. The conflict that now exists is the responsibility of those who have acted in this way, yet even now if there was a hope of returning to agreement it would be welcomed; this in spite of the campaign against the Catholic schools, which were supposedly guaranteed by the concordat, and against the free choice that Catholics were to have to determine their children's education, also guaranteed.[67] [5–6]

## 2 Theological truth and the countering of racialism

*Belief in God*
Belief in God must not be warped by ideology [7]. Whoever

> exalts race, or the people, or the State or a particular form of
> State, or the depositories of power or any other fundamental
> value of the community ... and divinizes them ... distorts an ...
> order of the world planned and created by God[8].

Our God 'is personal, one, supernatural, omnipotent, infinitely
perfect, one in the Trinity of Persons, tri-personal in the unity of
the divine essence, creator of all' [9]. He is the sovereign Lord of
all and his commandments apply regardless of 'time, or space,
country or race' [10]. Hence

> only superficial minds can stumble into concepts of a national
> God, or a national religion ... or attempt to lock within the
> narrow limits of a single race, God the creator of the world, king
> and legislator of all nations [11].

The bishops are obliged to keep these truths before the people
[12] and the Pope thanks them for their fidelity in this [13].

*True belief in Christ*
No faith in God can long survive without belief in Christ [14] while
'only blindness and pride' can close the eyes to the treasures of
wisdom which are to be found in the Old Testament [15]. He who
wishes to see biblical history and the wisdom of the Old Testament
banished 'blasphemes the Almighty's plan of salvation' [16]. Nor
may we add anything to revelation; Christ the anointed fulfilled the
work of redemption. No mortal may be placed beside Christ,
regarded as his equal [17].

*True belief in the Church*
Faith in Christ cannot be maintained in its purity without true
belief in the Church which he founded [18] and unless a life that
is worthy of that gift is lived by her members [19]. Whoever is faithful to the spirit of God is guided by the power of Pentecost [20].
The secret and open intimidation that is being applied to her sons
and daughters violates human rights and dignity [21].

*True faith in the Primacy*
Faith in the Church cannot stand without the support of faith in
the Roman primacy. National churches are a seduction and a

denial of Christ who gave the Church a universal mission.]Faith in Christ is linked with faith in his Church and in the papal primacy. The history of national churches, subject as they are to worldly powers, is that of branches cut off from the living Church [22].[68]

### The correct understanding of the Scriptures

Racialism and racialist theories sometimes adapt terms taken from Catholic theology while perverting their meaning for their own purposes. The true meaning of such terms therefore must be clearly restated. [Revelation means God's words to man, not confidence in race and blood divined as evidence in history [23].] Immortality is not to be understood as collective survival here on earth [24]. Christ has redeemed us from the sin of Adam [25] and we look forward to eternal life through persevering in the fight against evil, the cross of Christ being our standard [26]. The heroism of Christians in times past testifies to their humility in the spirit of the Gospel [27]. To give up our adoption as the sons of God in preference to some ideal of the German type is to abuse religion and the sacred [28].

### True morality and order

> To hand over the moral law to man's subjective opinions that change with the times, instead of anchoring it to the Holy Will of the Eternal God and his commandments is to open ... the door to forces of destruction ... the resulting betrayal of the eternal principles of objective morality ... is a sin against the destiny of a nation [29].

It is the fool who says in his heart, There is no God (Ps. 43:1). Natural law is written on the hearts of men by God and can be understood by sound reason, that is, when it is not darkened by sin and passion. [Every positive law can in its turn be judged by this law. 'Nothing can be useful if it is not at the same time good' (Cicero, de Officiis ii 30). 'Man as a person has rights he holds from God and which any collectivity must protect against denial, suppression or neglect' [30].]For example, 'the believer has an absolute right to profess the faith and to live according to its dictates ... laws that impede [these] ... are against the natural law' [31].

### Exhortation to the German Church

To the young, the appeal by the State to abandon Christianity is a powerful one but freedom must be that of the sons of God [32–3]. Human deficiences have disfigured the Church at all times, but the saints and the service to civilization the Church has given are also part of her story. Physical fitness is not to be stressed to the detriment to full human development of mind and soul also. The gaining of eternal life is the highest achievement of which we are capable [34].

Bishops, priests and religious must serve the truth always and use spiritual means to strengthen themselves for the task [35–7]. The faithful generally, and parents especially, are commended and encouraged in the same way in facing the difficulties of the times [38–9].

*Conclusion*

The encyclical ends with the hope that what has been said may help the German people in their time of need. It is one which is marked by the purification of suffering and the Holy Father's hope rests in God that he may defend them in their trials [40–3].

### (iv) Reaction of the Nazis to the encyclical

Special arrangements had been necessary to get the document into Germany without the knowledge of the Gestapo who would have impounded it. Couriers took it across the border secretly, and it was printed under conditions of tight security and then distributed by young priests on foot, bicycle or motorcycle in time for it to be available for reading out on Palm Sunday, 21 March, in all the parish churches.[69] When its contents became known, the response of the regime was angry and immediate. The Nazi press was violent in its condemnation. The German Ambassador to the Holy See was forbidden to participate in the Holy Week ceremonies and the German Foreign Office let its anger be known throughout Europe.[70] But Pius XI did not relent. In the twenty months between the publication of the encyclical and his death, he warned of racialism in 23 allocutions; his message was summed up in the words which became famous: 'it is not possible for Christians to embrace anti-Semitism; spiritually we are all Semites.'[71] When Hitler came to Rome in 1938 Pius pointedly left the city in protest, with and when Cardinal Innitzer with his fellow bishops showed such appalling judgement as to co-operate with the Nazis after they invaded Austria, he was summoned to Rome where it was pointed out to him that he had made a grave mistake. He reversed the policy on the return to Vienna and in retaliation angry Nazi supporters attacked his house and seriously injured his secretary.

# 5  Soviet Communism and the Church

## (i)  The revolution of 1917 and its consequences in Russia

Russia[72] at the beginning of the nineteenth century was ruled by an absolutist Czar, the source of all political power, justice, law and taxation. All, the nobility, the Church, the people at large, were totally subject to him. Some 94 per cent of the people were peasants, most of them serfs; within this class there were many gradations and not all their masters were cruel or unjust, but at best they were considered as baptized property, bought and sold in the market like cattle. Since for the owners they were the only source of income they were on the whole grossly exploited. Change came under the Czar Alexander I (1801–25). Serfs were to be freed and educated, and extended and elected assemblies established, but the programme petered out as the Czar's enthusiasm for it waned. Nicholas I (1825–55) put down with great brutality an uprising by the Decembrists, a group of officers who had been influenced by the ideas of the French Revolution during the Napoleonic wars; he then sought to root out all vestiges of opposition to his rule and all hopes of reform were squashed.

But ideas of it would not go away; the serfs were increasingly rebellious and it was becoming increasingly apparent to many among the privileged that an oppressed and ignorant serfdom was an obstacle to the progress they desired. Alexander II, Czar in 1855, was a reformer; the serfs were freed in 1861, limited home rule was allowed to the provinces through local elected assemblies, and educational reforms were made. This was too little for the radicals; Michael Bakunin and his nihilists, for example, wanted to destroy the State, family and property and the whole existing social order: in 1881 the Czar was assassinated. Alexander III (1881–94) predictably resorted to repression, and Nicholas II (1894–1917) sought to maintain the *status quo*.

Lenin, whose brother Alexander was executed in 1887 for participation in the plot to assassinate Alexander II, was born Vladimir Ulianov in 1870, the son of a senior civil servant.[73] Dedicating himself to revolution, in 1888 he made his first acquaintance with the works of Karl Marx, which broadened his revolutionary horizons and gave him a gospel to preach.[74] The Russian Marxists combined in 1898 to form the Social Democratic Labour Party which in 1903 split into the minority (*Menshevik*) right wing, declaring for a bourgeois, liberal democratic revolution through freedom of speech and assembly, and the majority (*Bolshevik*) left wing, opting for violent revolution, Lenin identifying with the latter. After taking a law degree in 1891, his revolutionary politics resulted in exile in Siberia in 1897, and on his release in 1900 he emigrated. He became leader of the Bolsheviks among the exiled Russian Socialists. Destruction of the old order, the establishment of the dictatorship of the proletariat and a planned economy were his aim; the other subtleties and refinements of Marx's teaching he considered could be ignored.[75] Returning to Russia in 1905, and taking part in the revolution of that year, he went into exile once more when it failed, being smuggled back into Russia from Zurich in April 1917 by the Germans, who hoped that his return would help to end Russian participation in the war.[76] In the February of that year the Czar had abdicated, and the Bolsheviks were co-operating with Kerensky who controlled the Provisional government. Lenin immediately repudiated this policy and by the November of 1917 Kerensky and his government had been overthrown.

Lenin had been demanding elections for a Constituent Assembly but as they approached – they were due on 25 November – it was clear that the Bolsheviks would be beaten in them. They dared not retract their support for them, however, and when their worst fears were realized, with only 9.8 million of the 41.6 million votes cast for them, they had to find a way of cancelling out this disaster. That was only a tactical problem for Lenin. He cynically organized the small hard core of his complaisant military allies to massacre those demonstrating in favour of the Assembly at its first meeting on 18 January 1918; one hundred were shot down without warning. Then, over the protests of the majority, the Assembly was abolished on 19 January.[77]

The Russian revolution of 1917 had been up to this time expressing the frustration and anger of the whole people with Czarism. Now it had been turned, by armed might ruthlessly used, into one man's vision of a Marxist paradise and under his direction it proceeded accordingly. The Soviets abolished private property and nationalized the banks. All the larger estates were confiscated without recompense, and the nationalization of trade and industry went ahead – this against the background of a counter-revolution, the White Russians against the Reds, which had followed the seizure of power. The attempt on Lenin's life in 1918 and the widespread economic and social unrest culminating in the famine of 1920–1, made him realize that his policies needed moderating. The result was the New Economic Policy (NEP) of 1921.[78] He abandoned the objection in principle to private property, agreeing that private initiative was essential for economic well-being, restoring peasants' property rights, but making no political concessions. Only small-scale industry was to be privatized however, basic industries and foreign trade would remain State controlled. To the end Lenin maintained his belief that the abolition of all private economic initiative had been a gross error.[79] He also believed that Stalin, General Secretary since 1921, was not the man to lead the party, but after Lenin's death on 21 January 1924, Stalin did just that.

The NEP was in place from 1921 to 1929; thereafter Stalin's five year plans became the fashion, though, as Alec Nove so succinctly puts it, only divine intervention could have provided the increases in investment, output and productivity they assumed.[80] Gradually, blind to Lenin's experience and warned from all sides, attempts were made first of all to force peasants to deliver their products and then, January–March 1930, to complete the collectivization of farms in the major agricultural regions. The peasants fought back, literally insofar as they could; party officials were assassinated, and they destroyed livestock rather than surrender it. The party was temporarily defeated, but relented only momentarily, to resume the assault more ferociously in 1931–2. Targets for grain production in the main growing areas such as the Ukraine were set unrealistically in the light of the disorganization and inefficiency of collective farming, and the last kilogramme was extracted; the result was that there were grain shortages and severe famines in the growing regions themselves.

This was organized by Stalin 'quite consciously and according to plan'.[81] Altogether some 6 or 7 million peasants died in this famine, some 10 million in all during the collectivization process, a death toll equal to that of the belligerents in the 1914–18 war. Yet no word about the famine was allowed to appear in the press or elsewhere. People who referred to it were subject to arrest for anti-Soviet propaganda, for which the penalty was five years or more in labour camps.[82] Some Westerners were honest enough to accept the evidence of their own eyes; Malcolm Muggeridge gave a graphic account of the famine in the Ukraine.[83] But the average fellow travellers, glorying in the attention being paid to them and wanting to believe the Marxist myth, ignored the evidence, while the West on the whole was not interested in it anyway. The collectivization process was a human disaster on an unimaginable scale. It was also an economic disaster, the ripple effects of which have affected Russian agriculture down to today.

The industrialization process of the same decade was also a human disaster. There was no right of association by workers in their own defence in the workers' State; all that Russian unions had in common with such organizations in free societies was the name. 'Highly centralized party control over the unions' was the Soviet way from the beginning.[84] The unions were an integral aspect of party activity: the loss of union membership meant loss of job; through the unions, the State controlled labour. Though the war against the industrial worker was not a war of extermination as was that against the peasant opposing collectivization, it was a war against the dignity of labour. The only consideration given was to productivity at any cost: the Stakhanovite system, in which the achievements of outstanding workers were made the norm for all, dehumanized the workforce as a whole; the bitterness and hatred it engendered was shown in the frequent murder of Stakhanovites by their fellow workers.[85]

[The new proletariat became more alienated than the old had been, though now the more efficient apparatus of the totalitarian State stifled open opposition. Free movement of labour was forbidden and employment was denied to those who had left their former employ without authorization; unemployment was pronounced to be no more, so unemployment relief was discontinued.]Those who defied the regulations could be imprisoned. There were special penalties for negligence or damage, and the death penalty could be imposed for the theft of State property. The labour camps were a crucial part of the economy under Stalin; their existence was known to the outside world in the 1930s but the reality they represented was not fully brought home to it until Solzhenitsyn was published in the West in the 1970s.

Such labour had many advantages. It was unpaid, it was cheap to feed and house and it could be used for construction and other work which might have led even the exploited free labour to rebel. It was effectively slave labour. The State security organization, the NKVD, contracted to supply it to the government for such projects as the White Sea Canal (1931–3) and the Moscow Volga Canal (1932–7). Construction of whole towns and administration areas was needed to handle the numbers involved in the remote regions where gold and other precious metals were mined.[86] To such camps were sent those who had offended against factory discipline, or who were sentenced under article 58 (for political crimes) or by special boards.[87]

[The trials of those accused of serious offences against the State were the last and the most sinister of Stalin's assaults on the human dignity and rights of his people.]From the mid-twenties the practice of cringing recantation of their errors by the accused had been established.[88] Stalin moved carefully; he was a careful man, knowing he could divide his enemies, real or imagined, terrorize them and get them to incriminate themselves. Those accused had nowhere and no one to turn to. Most of them had dedicated their lives to the cause and when its guardian turned against them, despair made them accept any humiliation. Trotsky, exiled in 1927, seems to have triggered Stalin's paranoia and when the first arrests of sympathizers were made in the early 1930s, their readiness to accuse themselves became notorious. The assassination of Sergei Kirov – one of Stalin's closest collaborators – by a known oppositionist in Leningrad in 1934 confirmed Stalin's worst fears. Scores of those under suspicion were summarily executed. In Leningrad tens of thousands of suspects and their families were arrested and sent to Siberia and political exile; such exile became infinitely more cruel than in the time of the Czars; it became 'an animal-like existence, aimed at depriving the victims of the normal processes of thought'.[89]

From 1936, trials, public and secret, and purges of prominent men too numerous to be listed, multiplied. The remaining members of Lenin's politbureau, were eliminated. Many of the senior military officers were judicially murdered, severely weakening the armed forces for the coming conflict with Hitler. The charges were involvement in plans to assassinate Stalin, or of being enemies of the Revolution from the beginning, or of being agents of Russia's enemies. None was convicted on evidence that would have been verifiable by normal legal and judicial procedures.[90] They were subjected to the combination of physical, mental or psychological treatment which would secure their self-accusation and leave them without a shred of dignity or self-respect. Those who could not be broken were tried in secret so that their defiance went unremarked. Robert Conquest estimated that some 10 million were executed or perished in the camps; taken with the 10 million who died as a result of the forced collectivisation of the farms, the cost of Stalin's terror was 20 million lives and 'the figure is given in the USSR ... the general total of those repressed is now stated in high school textbooks as 40m, half of them in the peasant terror 1929–33 and the other half 1937–53'.[91] There were still some 12 million in the camps in 1952.

## (ii)  The Church and communism in Russia, Mexico and Spain

In Russia the Catholic Church, after the separation of Poland, Lithuania and Latvia from the Czarist Empire in 1918, was reduced in numbers from 13 million to 1.6 million,[92] and this small remnant, like all religions in the communist State, was subject to persecution which became systematic from 1923, with imprisonment, torturings and execution. Despite this, Benedict XV in the first instance had not broken with the regime, but on the contrary sent 12 priests to help with relief work in the famine of 1921–2 and Pius XI in his turn continued to seek to improve relations even after the violent turn of events in 1923, quietly helping to rebuild and reorganize the remnants of the Church there. Three times before 1927 he tried to get formal relations renewed, remarking that if he could save a single soul from harm he would deal with the devil himself.[93] By 1927 however it became clear that there was no further hope; the moment of truth came, as it did with Mussolini and Hitler, over freedom of religious education and from 1930 he became increasingly outspoken in his condemnations of the Soviet persecution of Christians of all denominations.

Marxist influence was also present in the Mexican revolution of 1910[94] and the persecution of the Church that developed thereafter added to that stemming from bitter anticlericalism. The provisions of the 1917 Constitution legalized attacks on many key aspects of church life, and President Callas (1924–8) insisted on its full implementation. From 1926 some Catholic lay leaders were convinced that armed resistance was justified; the *Cristeros* movement that developed was a genuine popular social as well as religious uprising, the bulk of its 20,000 militia being raised from among the students, peasants and workers.[95] Priests had to move clandestinely through the country to minister to the faithful; among them was Fr Miguel Pro, executed and later proclaimed a martyr. Rome was less tolerant of armed revolt than was the local episcopate; though the latter never recommended or countenanced the use of violence, it was less sure that in the circumstances it could be condemned outright as an option open to the faithful. Rome worked in conjunction with the bishops for a peaceful agreement and one was secured in 1929; but so careless of its provisions had the regime become by 1932, that Pius XI issued an encyclical *Acerba Nimis* in which he protested at this. Under President Cardenas (1934–40) the conflict intensified none the less and in 1937 the Pope advised the Church there on the rights and wrongs of resistance.[96] However, by this time it was becoming increasingly evident to the authorities that attacks on the Church were not helping the national interest; they met with too much resistance, which the State exhausted itself in trying to combat. Cardena's successor, President Camacho, therefore tolerated its activities, though not formally recognizing her.

In Spain the historical background was more complex, given the Church's close identification with many aspects of that country's development. The situation in the 1930s was further complicated by the intervention of Fascist Italy and Germany on the side of the Nationalists in the Civil War of 1936–9. That war had its origins in the long struggle of Spain to come to terms with the decline of absolute monarchy after the French Revolution and to face the task of establishing a modern democratic state. Spain had returned to absolute monarchy under Ferdinand VIII (1825–33) and his death had led to a savage civil war for seven years – his younger brother Don Carlos disputing the succession with his niece Isabella, Ferdinand's daughter.

Isabella's cause prevailed, but her reign (1843–68), reflected most of the worst aspects of absolutism and was in turn ended by rebellion which bred further instability until Alfonso II (1874–85) became king. He was a constitutional monarch who restored stability and hope by an initial economic modernization and expansion. Its momentum was lost during the long regency which followed his death, and the economic revival under Alfonso XIII (1902–14) was not adequate to meet the needs of a growing population. Industrial development there was, mainly in the north where Bilbao was the heart of the nation's iron and steel industry and shipbuilding, and Barcelona was a textiles and engineering centre. Coal was mined in Asturias and hydropower, chemicals, cement manufacture and modern light industries developed also. But Spain remained predominantly an agricultural economy which was producing to its maximum, given the nature of the land resources and the practical impossibility, in the short term, of effective agrarian and land reform or modernization.[97] The result was a general rural poverty. Only in the Balkans and Southern Italy did European workers live more frugally than those in Spain in the 1930s.

Alfonso XIII had faced the tensions of the old liberal-conservative divide, together with those of anarchism, socialism, Catalan desire for autonomy, and growing political violence. The latter had begun during a strike in Barcelona in 1909, called by a semi-anarchist group, which had led to a resurgence of primitive and violent anti-clericalism. Churches and monasteries were destroyed, and priests, monks and nuns killed.[98] Neutrality in the Great War 1914–18 produced industrial expansion but also further social tensions. A general strike in 1917 that had revolutionary

overtones was countered by military juntas prepared to act independently on public order issues.[99]

Anarcho-Syndicalists, who believed only in violence and
respected neither authority, life nor property, brought down the
government of the day in 1919, and the assassination of public
figures and general disorder throughout 1921–2 gave the military
an excuse to intervene. After the badly-equipped Spanish forces in
Morocco were defeated by rebels in 1921, further social unrest led
to Primo de Rivera persuading the King to let him act as military
dictator. At first his rule was welcomed, given the felt need for the
restoration of stability and order.[100] But he failed to secure any
long-term legitimacy for his regime, retiring in 1930 when his
handling of economic problems lost him the army's support. King
Alfonso now discredited himself entirely by failing to call a
meeting of the Cortes within three months as the Constitution
required; by April 1931 the traditional supporters of the monarchy
had deserted him, and the Republic was proclaimed in Barcelona
on 14 April 1931.[101]

Not even the army had been interested in saving the King;
national order was its concern and it was unwilling to risk this in
the civil war that maintaining the monarchy would have entailed.
Among the leaders of the opposition to the King were prominent
Catholics like Alcala Zamorra, who became the first Prime
Minister of the provisional Republican government, and Miguel
Maura, Minister of the Interior. Preference for a Republic was
now widespread beyond the ranks of the traditional supporters of
this form of government. Ironically, the events that followed
showed that the greatest dangers to the Republic came from
Republican ranks.[102] When, in May, church and convent burning
spread from Madrid to Andalusia, the Minister of the Interior
called for prompt action by the Civil Guard but it was not forthcoming,[103] and this failure was responsible for the next round of
disasters.

The Constitution for the new Republic was democratically
radical and socially idealistic, which was only to be expected, but a
bitter anti-clericalism was its essential mark and this did not allow
for the compromise that democratic government required; it gave
the extreme Right a cause to which it could rally. Clause 26
reduced clerical salaries, upon which priests depended and which
had been given to them in return for the confiscated Church prop-
erties; the Constitution also paved the way for the expulsion of the
Jesuits in 1932, the exclusion of all religious orders from teaching,
the secularization of marriage, and enforced the removal of cruci-

fixes from schools. This clear and direct attack on the Church was 'political dynamite'[104] and Alcala Zamorra resigned. The anger stoked by these provisions was behind the marked swing to the Right which returned 203 members, against 99 for the Left, in the elections of November 1933. Social tensions in the country meanwhile produced increasing conflict. A general strike in October 1934, a Catalan proclamation of independence, and a rebellion in Alcalá which became a civil war, marked its course; a further rising in Barcelona was quickly controlled by the army. Another in Asturias was so serious that it required a major operation in which Moroccan troops were involved.[105]

The government finally collapsed in 1935 as the old enmities which had accumulated over the centuries boiled up – the hatred of the Church being the most powerful and poisonous of them all. Left and Right in Spain no longer possessed sufficient in common to make a State viable, and civil war was inevitable. The illusive concept of the Popular Front, which was being orchestrated from Moscow[106] where socialist idealism had already soured into a tyranny that was unequalled in modern history, ironically provided a rallying point for the Left. The Front united republicans, socialists, syndicalist, anarchists and communists as well as the anti-clerical diehards, and it won slightly more than half the votes in the elections for a new government. With an absolute majority in the Cortes, the government 'already as we know wedded to direct action, set about the destruction of the bourgeois society that was their real enemy'.[107] The next four months were chaotic as strikes, church burnings, murders, and assassinations of political opponents, multiplied. The Right, led by the Falange, retaliated in kind. The government had no control, and no policy which would ensure it, and the Republic disintegrated.

The attitude of the Church to the changing political situation reflected the complexities of her history in that country. She had always been used by the Crown for its own purposes, even by those monarchs and their friends who could claim to be sincere in their religious beliefs, and the Papacy always had less influence in Church affairs there than canon law and the good of the Church demanded. Since the time of Leo XIII, Rome had been seeking to wean Spanish Catholics from their attachment to Carlism and to resolve their differences on the Constitution of 1876.[108] *Rerum Novarum* had little influence on the Church there, a fact not entirely accounted for by the country being still only 30 per cent industrialized.[109]

Too many influential Spanish Catholics refused to accept the Church's teaching that justice as well as charity to the poor was required. Meanwhile popular misconceptions about the Church abounded. The Jesuits in particular were seen as responsible for every disaster.[110] The anti-clerical provisions of the 1932 Constitution reveal the depth of animosity that existed in influential political and social circles. A final clash between the forces of revolution and the Spanish Church was inevitable but it was not of the Church's choice. After four months of the new Republic, 'its priests murdered and its Churches shut ... subjected to massive persecution',[111] the bishops decided to back the military intervention. They explained in a letter to all their colleagues throughout the world on 1 July 1937 that the Communists dominated the Republicans and were opposed to 'order, social peace, traditional civilization and the defence of religion'.[112]

The choice before the bishops had been between two evils – that of tacitly supporting a regime which had abandoned its duty of protecting the common good, and the armed insurrection which it seemed to some was justified in the circumstances. They chose the latter, but in so doing they also had to accept that its forces were themselves capable of evil. The Fascist Alliance of the Nationalists, particularly when it included the Nazis, was hardly one which could be embraced with fervour. The military under Franco, and his German and Italian allies, together with the Falange who took over the leadership of the Nationalists in October 1936, had their own target groups, and were responsible for 'the political terror which liquidated working class leadership and cowed any middle class opposition'.[113]

### (iii)  Summary of Divini Redemptoris (1937)

[This encyclical[114] on atheistic communism was published on 19 March 1937, just five days after that on Nazi racialism, and it indicates the determination of Pius XI to put on record the Church's opposition to that other form of totalitarianism which was afflicting Europe in this decade.]It has a brief Introduction [1–3] and five sections: I. The attitude of the Church to communism [4–7]. II. Communism in theory and practice [8–24]. III. The doctrine of the Church in contrast [25–38]. IV. A defensive and constructive programme [39–59]. V. Ministers and co-workers in Catholic action [60–82].

## Introduction

The promise of a Redeemer and the hope of salvation has been with the Church throughout its history [1]. The struggle against evil is a part of life and today the Church faces a persecution by Bolshevism and atheistic communism which is greater than she has ever before known [2–3].

## I. The attitude of the Church to communism

The opposition between the Church and communism has been constant since the time of Pius IX [4]. The persecutions in Russia, Mexico and Spain have already been the subject of comment by us [5] but we now need to address the whole Church on the matter, exposing the errors of communism and explaining the teaching of the Church, the hope of civilization and the better service of society [7].

## II. Communism in theory and practice

It offers an illusion of justice, equality and fraternity capable of inspiring the masses because of the economic injustice in the world, but its achievements are the result of brutal methods in exploiting underdeveloped resources [8]. Matter is the only reality according to Marxist dialectic and it evolves blindly. Through class conflict society progresses until the classless society is achieved. Class conflict must then be accelerated; there is no room for God or spiritual values [9].

'Communism strips man of his liberty, robs human personality of its dignity.' There is no recognition of any right of the individual in his relation to the collectivity, no natural right is accorded to the human personality which becomes a 'mere cogwheel in the communist system' [10]. Marriage is a purely artificial and dissoluble civil institution and parents and children are totally subject to the State [11]. This is necessary so that man should reach his earthly paradise, an adequacy of material goods through collectivized production [12]. The classless society achieved, the State will wither away, but until then it is controlled by the Communist Party [13]. Such a system, which is contrary to reason, experience and Divine law, subverts the social order and denies the dignity, rights and liberty of man [14].

Its message, however, also urges 'the removal of the very real abuses chargeable to the liberalistic economic order and demands a more equitable distribution of the world's goods' and these are legitimate aims. Many of the best young members of the community, who reject materialism and terrorism, support it given the present economic problems of the world; it exploits their immaturity as it also exploits racialism and political divisions [15]. Liberal dechristianization hastens its progress among the workers [16]; meanwhile communism uses all the modern methods of propaganda, while there is a conspiracy of silence in parts of the world's press concerning its excesses [17–18]. In Russia, Mexico and Spain it seeks to uproot Christianity and murders clergy and laity for their fidelity [19–20]. These evils are not the effects of primitive violence but the natural result of a system which knows no restraint of natural or divine law [21–2].

The system however defeats itself. Economic aims require some morality, some sense of moral responsibility, but communism knows only terrorism, as we see in Russia today where former comrades are exterminating each other [23]. The fault is not that of the Russian people but of the system to which they are subject [24].

### III. The true doctrine of the Church in contrast

The true understanding of society is that put forward by reason and revelation through the magisterium [25]. God is the ultimate reality, creator and judge of all [26] and man has a spiritual and immortal soul, gifts of mind and body, by grace raised to the dignity of son of God, incorporated into his kingdom in the Mystical Body of Christ. This is the foundation of his human rights – to bodily integrity, to the means of existence, to follow the path marked for him by God, to the right of association, to possess and use property [27], to marry and found a family [28], to live in civil society which is a need of his nature [29] and to whose authority he is subject, provided it enhances and does not diminish his rights; all things being ordained to man as a person [30]. Human labour is of its nature dignified, and relations between employer and employed should be marked by justice and charity according to the true principles of a sane corporative system [31].

Catholic teaching vindicates the State's dignity and its role of defender of human rights. There is a lawful social hierarchy, but the enslavement of man, the denial of his rights and transcendental nature of the State which communism asserts, are contrary to the will of the creator. Both man and civil society derive their origin from God; they cannot reject their responsibilities nor can they diminish each other's rights. Communism, however, arrogates to itself the right to enforce, in place of divine law, a partisan political programme which derives from the authority of human will and is replete with hate [32]. The Church's teaching by contrast balances love and justice, harmonizes rights and duties, and has a proper regard for man's temporal well-being. Not concerned with the technicalities of social systems because she has here no competence, it is her role to provide moral guidance on these matters [33]. The wisdom and supreme utility of her social teaching is widely understood [34]. It was the Church which first affirmed the universal brotherhood of man,[115] contributing to the abolition of slavery, and it was she who raised manual labour to a new dignity. Cicero for example despised those engaged 'in sordid trades; there can be nothing ennobling about a workshop' (*de Officiis* Bk 1, c 42) [36]. She gave new life to society through charitable works, and some today look to the guilds she fostered as a model; similarly Leo XIII defended the right of association for workers faced with liberal capitalism [37]. 'There would be neither socialism nor communism today if the rulers of nations had not scorned the teachings and ... warnings of the Church' and embraced instead liberalism and laicism [38].

## IV. A defensive and constructive programme

The social doctrine of the Church must be put into practice. The fanaticism of the sons of darkness may stimulate the sons of light to this [39–40]. There is much which has been and is being done [41–2]. Yet many Catholics still ignore Christ's exhortation to worship in spirit and truth, and so bring the faith to ridicule [43]. The rich should have the right attitude to riches so that they do not become their downfall: the poor, lest they become too impatient in improving their conditions [44–5]. Charity is needed more than ever [46–8] but 'charity will not be true charity without justice'. The wage earner is not to receive in alms what is due in justice [49]. Unfortunately some Catholic industrialists in particular have at times acted in ways which shake the faith of the working classes in the religion of Jesus Christ. Some have prevented the reading of *Quadragesimo Anno* in churches. Some deny to workers the right of association or use the right to private property as 'a weapon to defraud the working man of his just rights' [50–1].

Social as well as commutative justice is required. The common
good cannot be preserved unless the worker has what is needed for
him to exercise his social functions, a wage which will enable him
to support his family and improve his standard of life, with insurance, public or private, during sickness, unemployment and old
age [52]. Unfair competition which makes it impossible to pay a
just wage must be countered by joint action, and the workers must
deal fairly with employers [53]. Corporative organization is the
best way of achieving justice and charity in social-economic relations [54]. There must be wider study of social problems in the
light of the Church's social doctrine [55] and the Catholic press
has a role here [56].

Communist tactics must be countered. Communists pretend to
be the leaders in the desire for peace while at the same time stirring up class war which threatens bloodshed, and they dishonestly
seek the co-operation of Catholics, while they do not relent in the
war against God [57]. No Christian can work with them [58]. A
world-wide crusade of prayer and penance is needed to counter
the evil [59].

## V. Ministers and co-workers in Catholic social action

It is the duty of priests to keep alive the flame of faith and to be
close to the poor. Unless they do this those in need are easy prey
for communism, and the most effective way of helping the poor is
the practice of a humble, poor and unselfish way of life. An avari-
cious or selfish priest will be a hindrance rather than a help to his
people [60–3]. The laity have a crucial role here both in their daily
occupations and through Catholic Action, and through their
professional and industrial associations [64–8]. Even where the
State has taken right initiatives in these matters, private action is
still needed through new institutions [69]. The efforts of Catholic
working-men are particularly recommended [70]. Unity is needed
within the Church in all this, and those who try to undermine it
bear a terrible responsibility before God [71]. Belief in God is the
foundation of the social order and all must work to see that it is
secured on this basis [72].

The Christian State should co-operate with the Church in building society on these foundations and in particular in resisting the
efforts of atheists to destroy them. No authority, no treaty, can
stand unless it is founded in God [73–4]. It must take particular
care to create the material conditions for a sound society, especially in ensuring there is adequate employment, and be an

example of sound administration in national and international affairs; in the latter encouraging the abolition of economic barriers between nations [75–6]. Spiritual values are essential; purely economic and political aims are not enough and the Church's role here should be respected, especially in the light of the threat of communist materialism [77–9]. Those who have fallen for the lure of communism are exhorted to return to Christ [80].

## 6 Summary analysis of the social teaching of Pius XI

### (i) Ethics and civil society

The true understanding of society is that of reason and revelation. God is the ultimate reality, creator and judge of all; man by grace raised to the dignity of a son of God, created in his image and likeness, with an immortal soul and gifts of mind and body, is incorporated in God's kingdom in the mystical body of Christ [DR 26]. This is the primary solidarity of man and society, the union of all in the body of Christ. This is the foundation of those human rights that society must respect – first of all to live in society according to his social nature, to bodily integrity, to the means of existence, to the self-development according to the path marked out for him by God, to the right of association, to the possession and use of private property, to marry and raise a family [DR 27–8].

Racialist and communist theories which deny the human dignity given to man by God, cannot be the foundation of society; man's dignity and his rights are God-given and cannot be taken away. Man has duties to society imposed on him by God, and society cannot deny him the rights given him by the same God [DR 30]. To exalt race and divinize it and to hold other races in contempt is to distort the order given by the creator [MBS 8, 10]. A sound society is one built up on a proper understanding of the rights and duties of all men and classes, with a particular respect for the needs of the poor [QA 11–14]. In fact society is disfigured by class injustices, threatening, if not actually producing, class war [QA 1–10, 82–3], and the way to overcome these injustices is by peaceful reform [QA 18–22]. This requires building on the person's, the family's, and the private association's capacity for self-help. The help of the community and the State may be needed in order that these private and intermediate groups may attain their ends, but it must never supplant their initiative, only

facilitate it. This principle of subsidiarity is fundamental to sound
social organization [QA 79].


## (ii) Ethics and political society

National and international politics need to be inspired by the influence of the true Christian spirit, to bring about justice and peace
in charity [UAD 48–9, 55–7]. The narrow liberal conception of the
State is rejected; it is more than a means of preserving public
order; it has the positive task of developing individual and social
well-being, giving chief consideration to the poor and the weak
[QA 25–8]. It must respect the right of association and harmonize
the rights of property owners and the common good [QA 49]. It
must also act in accordance with the principle of subsidiarity in
dealing with persons, families and intermediate associations [QA
79]. It does have a role in their support when they cannot achieve
their ends without its help, but this role is subsidiary, aimed at
making them capable once more of doing that. Democracy is a
reasonable and just system in itself but is prone to factionalism
[UAD 12]. The State has an important role in human life but it
must not be divinized, worshipped, made the ultimate source of
truth and values [NAB 44, MBS 7–13] and the natural law and
divine revealed law are the norm of all positive law. Man has rights
he holds from God, and the State may not deprive him of them
[MBS 30–1, NAB 44–52].


## (iii) Ethics and economic society

God placed man on earth to work it and use it to supply his needs
[QA 136]. Those who serve society in this economic process are
entitled to increase their fortunes in a just manner, provided the
laws of God and the rights of others are respected and property is
used in accordance with faith and right reason. Private property
has its origin either in first occupancy, that is, taking what is owned
by no one, or by labour (specification); there is also a right to
inherit property [QA 52, 49]. Private ownership of productive
goods must be the basis of the economy. Liberal capitalism, out of
which the modern economy grew, was based on economic freedom
and private ownership of productive goods. It warped that institution with its excesses of freedom and lack of respect for the social
responsibilities of private ownership, but capitalism itself cannot

be dismissed as by nature vicious [QA 101]. Its evil came from the liberal ideology of the time which made it deny the workers their dignity and neglect its social responsibilities.

Free competition in economic matters is in itself a good thing but it must be subject to social justice and charity; it cannot be governed and controlled by itself. A just social order must be the framework within which free competition operates [QA 88]. [The State has the duty to see that markets work in accordance with the common good] They do not in themselves contain a principle of direction superior to that of right reason and the common good. As it is, many are convinced that any means are good if they increase profits, and unchecked speculation leads to reckless manipulation of prices. Limited liability is abused, frauds and injustices are committed by boards of directors who violate the trust placed in them. The lowest human instincts are pandered to by those who think of nothing but profit, forgetting that the purpose of economic life is supplying real human need [QA 132]. Free competition has destroyed itself. Vast wealth was concentrated in the hands of the few, particularly of those who control finance and credit and therefore control production; those prevail who are least troubled by the promptings of conscience [QA 105–7].

[The right to own private property therefore is one thing, the right to use it as one wishes is another.] The first is an individual right, the second implies a social aspect and has obligations accordingly [QA 45]. Commutative justice, enforceable in a court of law, determines the right to own: other virtues, beneficence and munificence determine use [QA 50]. These are not enforceable at law [QA 47]. But that does not mean that it is entirely up to the individual as to what he owns or how he uses what he owns. The State has the duty of seeing that property laws and their application are in conformity with the common good; it cannot use this right as an excuse for undermining the institution in itself, although the State can own productive goods which are so crucial to the economy that it would not be right to leave them in private hands [QA 48–9 and 114]. Neither does every distribution of property that exists in a given situation meet the needs of social justice [QA 57]. Throughout the world it is in fact grossly unjust [QA 58]. The right of ownership is not then undermined, but strengthened, when the State acts to bring it into harmony with the common good [QA 49].

In industry the rights of capital and labour are to be respected within a context which encourages their co-operation [QA 110].

The wage contract is morally acceptable but it must be a just contract [QA 64–6]. Labour cannot claim the whole value of what is produced, any more than can capital, but it is desirable that the wage contract be modified so that employees become sharers in management, ownership or profits, as already happens in various ways [QA 65]. Workers who support themselves and their families by their work should be able to earn enough for this purpose [71]; such a wage must take into account the state of the business and the economy, though the wage earner should not be penalized for the inefficiency of management or unjust prices [QA 72]. If a business fails it is none the less the duty of all concerned to see that alternative work is found by the public authority for those affected, employers and workers [73]. The common good requires that wages allow the worker the opportunity to save and acquire modest wealth [74]. There is a social as well as a personal aspect to work [QA 69] and there should exist social and organic bodies which can ensure that the social aspects are in harmony with personal needs and those of society. Corporations should be formed of those working in a particular industry or profession – workers and salaried staffs, managers and owners. These corporations would provide a means by which all can work together to better the performance of industry and improve mutual relations [QA 81–2]. In this way the labour market, which currently resembles a battlefield, will be changed for the better for the persons concerned and for society [QA 83–4]. These organizations must be such as to allow workers and employers to deliberate separately on those issues which seem to them to require it, and all such organizations should be established by the parties themselves as a result of free choice [QA 85–7]. There exist some forms of corporative organization which owe their origin to political and state initiative and are controlled by it so that they serve political ends rather than the presentation of a better social order [QA 95].

# 19

# Pius XII (1939–58)

## 1 Pius XII and his Pontificate 1939–45

Eugenio Pacelli, elected Pope on 2 March 1939,[1] was born in Rome in 1876, the son of a lawyer, and was educated at the Lyceum Visconti, the State school. An able student and good musician, he at 18 confirmed an early desire to be a priest by entering the Roman diocesan seminary at Capranica after which he went on to the Apollinare Institute and the Gregorian University. His desire had always been to be a pastor and for two years after ordination (1899–1901) he had his wish, but his intellectual, linguistic and other gifts had already attracted notice and he was prevailed on to enter the papal service in 1901, first teaching ecclesiastical law at the Academia Nobile and then assisting Cardinal Gasparri with the revision of canon law; in between whiles he represented the Pope on various occasions; for Leo XIII in 1901 he attended the funeral of Queen Victoria, and for Pius X in 1911 he was assistant to the papal envoy at the coronation of George V.

On the outbreak of the 1914 war, Benedict XV gave him the responsibility for organizing the Holy See's work for the prisoners of war and their families. Then in 1917 he was appointed to replace the papal nuncio to the court of Catholic Bavaria and, since there was no nuncio to the Imperial Prussian court, to put forward the Pope's peace plan to the Emperor. From the first, the young nuncio made a favourable impression on the authorities with whom he had to deal, not least the Kaiser himself. It was not only the legitimate authorities he impressed. After the Kaiser abdicated in 1918 and chaos reigned in Germany, Archbishop Pacelli was the only diplomat who remained at his post in Bavaria's capital, Munich, looking after the needs of the refugees and the

* The notes and references for Chapter 19 are to be found on p. 449ff

poor. The Bolshevik rebels had taken the city over and the delegacy was one of the many buildings machine-gunned by them. On 29 December Mgr Pacelli had to confront armed intruders intent on his assassination, but he did so calmly and fearlessly – and it would seem he made them relent by sheer courage and force of character.

Pacelli's mission as nuncio was transferred to Weimar in June 1920, and concordats were eventually signed with Bavaria in 1924 and Prussia in 1929. His time in Germany was a happy one for him and for those with whom he had to deal diplomatically. His great qualities and abilities did not mask his common humanity, and he was widely appreciated by the people generally and by the politicians, statesmen and diplomats; he in his turn had a great love for the German people and their country, especially for his fellow Catholics there with their thriving Church. Recalled to Rome in 1929 and appointed Cardinal Secretary of State in 1930, he was largely responsible for negotiating concordats with Austria and Germany in 1933. He was papal legate at the Eucharistic Congress in Argentina (1934) when he visited Brazil also; he went to Lourdes and Lisieux as legate in 1935 and 1937 and to Hungary in 1938: he also paid a private visit to the USA in 1936, during which he travelled thousands of miles within the country, visiting and enquiring about all aspects of the American church and of the country's life and culture. He was very much involved with the drafting of *Mit Brennender Sorge*, knowing it would be confiscated if it went through the normal channels. Instructed to ensure it got through anyway, he had it smuggled across the frontier. Cardinal Pacelli, whose nomination was opposed by both the Nazis and Mussolini, secured 48 of the 63 votes on the first day of conclave on 2 March 1939, and his election marked the first time since 1667 that a Secretary of State had succeeded to the papal office.

As with Benedict XV, elected on the eve of the outbreak of the 1914–18 war, the choice of the conclave was much guided by the need to have at the helm one well experienced in diplomatic affairs. The new Pope had been in the papal diplomatic service for close on forty years under Leo XIII, Pius X, Benedict XV and Pius XI, and for twenty-four of those years he had represented the Church at the highest level. He had dealt with the situation in Germany in particular as Pius XI's nuncio in the 1920s and then Secretary of State in the 1930s: he was also at his side in dealing with Mussolini's Fascism and the growing tide of Soviet communist power. Further, his spell as Secretary of State, and his travels, especially those outside Europe, gave him a wider knowledge of the

working of the Church throughout the world than any of his predecessors.

The first six years of his pontificate were overshadowed by war,
during which the Papacy's responsibility for protecting the interests of the Church world wide was more crucial and burdensome
than ever. As the war went on it became ever more apparent that
the Pope had a unique and unequalled role at this time in defending basic human rights and civilized values; making the fullest and
best use of that power was of interest to all mankind. Great
prudence and quiet courage of a special order was needed in the
holder of the office. As the Nazi power grew, so did the possibility
that the Vatican might be invaded and the Pope seized and
silenced; it was necessary not to provoke that power needlessly. On
the other hand, to seek to placate it at any price was to deny the
Church's responsibility before God and the world. Such was the
delicate task of the new Pope. In leading and guiding the Church
throughout this period, and through the next fourteen years, the
Church's social teaching was crucial as part of the Gospel message
Pius XII was protecting and projecting.

It was the deep conflict caused by the social injustices and the
political and economic instabilities and imbalances of the previous
century which resulted in the 1939–45 war, the greatest and most
destructive conflict in man's history.

> The societies which had nailed liberty, equality, fraternity to
> their mastheads had failed to live up to their ideals; the once
> progressive doctrine of *laissez faire* and enlightened self-interest
> resulted in poverty and inexcusable inequalities of wealth and
> opportunity ... the great promises of the eighteenth century
> were not realized. By the time the swastika rose over Germany,
> the theory of progress by evolution was already in ruins.[2]

In their desperation, alternatives had been sought which would
keep the illusion alive. Many found them in Marx. 'Marx had
accepted the optimistic assumptions of the enlightenment and the
utopian socialists' but promised only violence and proletarian
revolution. Aware of the terrible, and true, accounts of the sufferings of the Russian people under Stalinism, the 'fellow travellers',
most of them middle or upper-class intellectuals and professionals
of the comfortable West, while careful to hang on to their privileges, wealth and freedom, insisted in seeing in the Soviet Union
under Stalin, only 'progress, social justice, scientific rationality,
peace, equality and the workers' state'[3] whereas in fact it exceeded
in its hatefulness the worst the Nazis were doing to their enemies

at this time; the latter had only been in power six years and although they were learning fast, the Soviets had a lead of seventeen years on them, and had inherited a tradition of oppression by the State from the Czars.

The late Pope, and the new one, well knew what progress they had made. Never was there a voice more needed in human affairs which could calmly and rationally ask humanity to think about its priorities, and, as the course of the war developed, help to put them in order as the problems of post-war reconstruction arose. Benedict XV had sought to exercise the function of peacemaker in the previous conflict, and the greatness of his contribution in terms of moral leadership is today being better recognized. Pius XII faced a war no less cruel, and of wider reach, than that of 1914–18. The papal office now possessed more authority than it had in 1914, the clash of titans in 1939–45 was more significant on a world scale than its predecessor had been, and the problems of the post-war world even more complex and far-reaching. The responsibilities, for the Church and for the world resting on Pius XII's shoulders could not have been greater.

His first encyclical *Summi Pontificatus* (1939) was on 'The unity of human society'; it did not then deal directly with the industrial and economic issues, the *Rerum Novarum* agenda; it dealt with the ethics of civil society in the most fundamental Christian sense because the implications of Fascist racialism required it. Thereafter Pius XII did not use encyclicals to develop his social teaching. The conditions of war meant that he was constantly addressing social issues in his radio messages and other addresses because that war was a people's war: the social question and its broader implications had been recognized during it as one of its prime causes, just as the struggle with totalitarianism concentrated minds on the importance of a more effective, and reliable, democracy than those that Mussolini and Hitler had abused to gain power. The Universal Pastor recognized and responded to the needs of the people. The situation was constantly changing, and he commented on the current issues. There was neither time, need nor opportunity for longer and more formal social encyclicals.

The motto of his pontificate reveals his interest in the work of the world. It was *Opus Justitiae Pax*, 'peace is the work of justice', and his wartime message to the peoples of the world was a message of peace and justice in Jesus Christ, God made man, whose death and resurrection had raised his brothers and sisters to a dignity which must be recognized in the way they were treated on earth. The fluctuation of the fortunes of the Axis and the Allied powers during the war necessarily conditioned the responses of the Holy See. There were two main phases to the conflict in terms of world wide geopolitics and Pius XII was at all times concerned to face the immediate issues with an eye to the possible outcome of the struggle.

## 2 The political background 1939–45: the war and post-war reconstruction

In the period after Hitler came to power in 1933, he had cynically manipulated the Western Democracies, playing on weaknesses in a manner which did them little credit. The invasion of Czechoslovakia in 1938 opened their eyes, and it was shortly afterwards followed by the brutal attack on Poland on 1 September 1939 which opened the Second World War.[4] The heroism of the Poles in opposing the invader was not enough against the might and tactics of the German army, and they were taken by surprise at the Russian intervention; by 6 October all resistance had ceased. A few weeks' campaigning on the Western Front in the spring of 1940 forced France to surrender and defeated the British expeditionary force. For two years thereafter the Germans, and their allies the Japanese, were triumphant. German armies invaded and almost totally overwhelmed the Russians in the summer of 1941, while the Japanese attack on the Americans at Pearl Harbor in December of the same year caught them totally unprepared and they could not stem the run of Japanese successes which followed in the new year. The British and the other European empires in the East were soon under threat, crippled or destroyed. Yet within eighteen months, the vaster resources of the Allies and their sound leadership was beginning to tell. In June 1942 the Japanese Fleet suffered a great defeat at Midway. Rommel was defeated at El Alamein in October and the German attack on Stalingrad finally stalled in November.

The entry of the Americans into the war made the anti-Fascist forces predominantly democratic and it was possible for a while to imagine that the totalitarian USSR would be more tolerant of democracy when peace came. In the August of 1941, Roosevelt and Churchill had signed the Atlantic Charter which declared the belief of the signatories in the right of peoples to choose their own governments, in equal opportunities of trade and commerce for all nations, economic collaboration between States in order to raise the living standards of their peoples and the denunciation of aggression and territorial aggrandizement. As the war became increasingly international, this democratic appeal brought more peoples to the Allied cause or gave them sympathy for it.

The Pope's general policy was to use his office as impartially as he possibly could so that the Church's works of mercy could continue among all the belligerents. At the same time, from the start he was active in trying to promote the unchanging ideals which would secure a negotiated settlement leading to a peace and reconstruction built on a basis of justice and charity for all. By 1943 it was becoming clear that the Allies would win; it was also becoming clear in Rome that the democratic systems of Britain and the United States of America were better able to provide the right political context for a lasting and just peace, nationally and internationally.

The Papacy's direct experience of modern democratic government on the Continent of Europe had not inspired much trust in it, bringing with it as it did totalitarian violence and weak political and social systems. The French Revolution had sought to destroy the Church, had destabilized Europe and left as its inheritance to France a continuing instability in the subsequent Republics. The weaknesses of democracy in Italy had helped pave the way for the totalitarianism of its brand of Fascism, as they had in Germany aided the accession to power of Nazism. Representative government and the right of peoples to choose their rulers were acceptable to the Catholic tradition in themselves, but that tradition required that democracy, like any other form of government, should operate under just law preserving the rights and dignity of all, and a stable political system which allowed the peaceful transition of power. As it had operated on the Continent of Europe in the recent past, democracy had not been of that sort.

The course of the Second World War, however, revealed the virtues of that older, and more securely founded democracy which flourished in Great Britain and the United States and which was derived from the theories and practices of Western Christendom in the Middle Ages. But the Papacy in the nineteenth and early twentieth century had little contact with the North Atlantic democracies, and was too much influenced by the recent past to enable it to appreciate the difference between the two strains in modern democracy. Pius XII had travelled widely in the United States in the 1930s, and the events of the Second World War and the Papacy's increasing international role during it enabled him to correct the balance. Democracy as it existed in the United States, as in Britain, was either neutral or positive towards religion and religious belief; the deeper prejudices which marked secular liberalism on the Continent were not there, at least not to the same degree.

In looking to the post-war situation, the focus of the Western world's concern as 1945 approached was then mainly with political justice and with the ethics of international law and relations. Pius XII's social teaching (1939–45) reflected these concerns, although the *Rerum Novarum* agenda, with its concentration on the question of solving the social problems of liberal capitalism was not neglected, not least because these also were still very much problems of the democracies.

## 3  His social teaching 1939–45[5]

### (i)  Summary of the social encyclical Summi Pontificatus (1939)[6]

This encyclical, published on 20 October 1939, was subtitled 'On the unity of human society', and since it was the first issued after the new Pope had been elected, that title indicated the theme for the pontificate. As a papal diplomat, he had lived with the problems of Fascist racialism and the growing strength of Soviet communism in the 1920s and the 1930s, both of which indicated the fundamental disunity in human society, a disunity more marked than at any time since the disintegration of Christendom in the late Middle Ages. Once responsible for the direction of the Church's mission when the world was at war on these and related issues, his concern had to be primarily with helping to provide some basis for unity once again. His approach was theological, not sociological or political. To deal with the issues that divide human society and consider the ways that division could be healed, required a return to basics, and for him those basics were Christian basics; as such they included an understanding of the validity of natural law which provided the Christian tradition with a bridge to all men of goodwill, of all beliefs or none.

#### The chaos of today and its causes

Central to the causes of the chaos of the modern world is the rejection of 'a universal norm of morality ... for individual and social life as for international relations' – the natural law founded in God

[28], and the See of Peter as the exponent of Christian truth [29]. To exclude Christ from public life is to surrender humanity to the slavery of sin and abandon the hope of a healthy social order [30–3]. Once Europe accepted the ideal of Christian brotherhood; it was imperfect but it provided the right ideal and the means to achieve it; now it has neither [34].

**Solidarity and charity**

The obligation of human solidarity and charity is 'dictated and imposed by our common origin and the equality of rational nature in all men, to whatever people they belong, and by the redeeming sacrifice offered by Christ ... on behalf of all men' [35]. Scripture tells us how God made us in his own image and likeness and destined man to eternal happiness [36]. This is a marvellous vision, which enables us to see the human race in the one common origin in God, in the unity of body and soul, in the unity of dwelling place – the earth 'of whose resources all men by natural right avail themselves, to sustain and develop life, and in the unity of the supernatural end, God himself' [38]. Christ commanded us to love one another as he had loved us [40]. These supernatural truths form the solid basis and the strongest possible bond of union among mankind [41]. In this perspective individuals are not 'isolated units like grains of sand, but united by the very force of their nature and internal destiny' [42]. That individual nations exist does not destroy this unity 'but rather enriches it ... by sharing of their own peculiar gifts ... and reciprocal interchange of goods ... which can only be possible when a mutual love and lively sense of charity' unite the children of the same Father [43]. The particular characteristics of peoples which each cherishes and retains as a heritage, follow from this [44] and the Church welcomes them with joy, provided they are not opposed to the duties which stem from our common origin and destiny [45].

**Equality of races**

All, 'whatever their origin or speech ... have equal rights as children in the house of the Lord' [47]. 'There is neither Gentile nor Jew ... barbarian nor Scythian. But Christ is all in all' (Col. 3:10, 11). This does not exclude love of Fatherland and one's own people: Christ himself wept over the fate of Jerusalem; but such love is an inclusive love, embracing all men [48–49].

## Attitude to the State

To separate civil authority from dependence on God is to put it at
the mercy of the few [52] and to give to the State absolute autonomy, making it the supreme end in life and the final arbiter of the
moral and juridical order, putting it in the place of God [53]; it
then rests on a purely human foundation and relies on force and
external authority [54]. It destroys the moral foundation of the
State [55]. Some States of this kind can seem, for a while, to
achieve immense success [56] but there comes a time when the
lack of moral foundations undermines it [57]. It was our creator's
will that civil society should be regulated according to unchanging
principles which aid men to reach their supernatural end [58].

The function of the State is to guide all for the common good,
achieving the harmonious development of man's natural perfection according to God's plan [59]. Where man is subject entirely
to the State, however, humanity and mankind suffers [60]. The
family is subjected to the State instead of being supported by it
[61]. Children should be educated not simply to acquire the qualities that make for material success, but also grow in nobility of
character, humanity and reverence [62]. The rights of the family
are above all to be respected [63]. The more that is demanded
of the family by the State, the more respect must there be for
rights of conscience of the parents which are sacred and inviolable [64–6]. Education should not be indifferent to or opposed
to Christianity [67–70].

## Relations between states

To give the State unlimited authority leads to the violation of rights
within nations and between them [71]. The human race is bound
by reciprocal ties, directed to the good of all nations [72]. These
ties the absolutely autonomous State disregards [73]. Only respect
for the natural law encourages the development of the civilized
virtues [74]. 'The indispensable presupposition of all peaceful
intercourse between nations … is mutual trust; the expectation
that each party will keep its plighted word' [75]. But 'to tear the
law of nations from its anchor in the divine law, to base it on the
autonomous law of States is to dethrone that very law and deprive
it of its noblest and strongest qualities' [76]. Private interest and
collective selfishness will dominate over right. While treaties may
need renegotiating after a passage of time, unilateral abandonment of them destroys trust [77].

## The future

The illusion of limitless progress can no longer be maintained [78], but we are promised a new order based on justice and prosperity by the powers that be [79]; it will not, however, come simply from war and its issue, where victory steels the hearts of the conquerors [80]. It must come from the spirit and be based on the unshakeable foundations of the natural and divine laws, not on interest groups and individuals [81–2]. It is true that present evils afflicting mankind come 'in part from economic instability and the struggle of interests regarding a more equal distribution of the goods which God has given man as a means of sustenance and progress'. Yet there are deeper causes too; the perversion of 'religious and moral belief' caused by 'progressive alienation of the peoples from [the] unity of doctrine, faith, customs and morals'. Hence re-education must be 'spiritual and religious ... [and] proceed from Christ as ... its indispensable foundation ... actuated by justice and crowned by charity' [83].

## The Church's role

'There is no opposition between the laws that govern the life of faithful Christians' and those of 'genuine humanitarianism, but rather unity and mutual support'. The Church wishes all men to see the Lord Jesus Christ and his Church in their true light that those in power may 'allow her freely to work for the formation of the rising generation according to the principles of justice and peace' [93]. The masses, and youth, are her particular concern. She does not wish to dominate but to serve.

> She does not claim to take the place of other legitimate authorities in their proper spheres, but offers them her help after the example and in the spirit of her Divine Founder 'who went about doing good' (Acts 10: 38) [101].

She, who civilizes the nations, has never 'retarded the civil progress of mankind, at which on the contrary she is pleased and glad' [102].

## (ii) Radio messages and other addresses

### On international relations and international law

Given the conflict between the nations and looking forward to the hopes of a more lasting and just peace after it, Pius XII made the subject of his Christmas radio messages to the world the Christian understanding of proper order in international relations, taking up points indicated briefly in *Summi Pontificatus.* That of 1939 proposed five points for a lasting world peace.[1] All nations, great or small to have an equal right to their existence and independence.[2] Mutually agreed, organic and progressive disarmament agreements.[3] A 'juridical institution which will guarantee the loyal and faithful fulfilment' of agreements and provide procedures for handling any adjustments in such agreements when changing conditions make them necessary.[4] The addressing of the real needs and just demands of nations, populations and minorities, in Europe especially.[5] Respect for the law of God, both in the Gospel and in the natural law, enjoining justice and charity among nations, informing international agreements and encouraging their observance.[7]

The address of 1940 enumerated the conditions for a lasting new order among nations: overcoming the hatreds of the past, which means abandoning the propaganda which fosters them; removing the mistrust which makes true agreements between States impossible; abandoning an ethic according to which 'utility is the basis and rule of might ... might makes right', and restoring a serious and effective moral sense in international life and relations; reducing extremes of economic inequality reducing so that 'peoples of every class ... have a proper standard of living'; and egotism, glorying in its own prowess, must give way to genuine, juridical and economic solidarity between peoples, a brotherly co-operation guided by the precepts of divine law'.[8]

The message of 1941, issued a few months after the Atlantic Charter was signed in the August of that year, and a few weeks after the Japanese entered the war, listed what it was hoped would be the positive aspects of the new order: the political freedom and economic development of all nations; national minorities having their rights recognized; the right of access for all to the resources of the earth – 'there is no room for that egoism which tends to monopolize economic resources and materials of common use to the exclusion of nations less favoured' – a 'common sharing of the goods of the earth' is a necessity already affirmed by some of the more favoured nations; the need for a solution to a question 'so decisive for the world economy should be reached methodically, gradually and with necessary guarantees'; the outlawing of total war and the arms race, and the overcoming of the lack of trust that produces these evils; there should be freedom from the persecution of religion and of the Church. A living faith in a transcendent

God is the source of an uncompromising and unified moral strength which animates the whole of life. Such a strength will be needed in the rebuilding of Europe.

The year 1942 brought the possibility of the survival and the victory of the democracies, and the theme of the message in this year was concern with the peaceful internal order of States and its requirements. These were: recognition of the dignity of man and his essential human rights; the acceptance that the society and the State are built up by the social collaboration of private groups within it, the family especially; it is an organic unity of mature and responsible persons, not a mere aggregation of individuals to be dominated; the indissolubility of marriage and the fostering of family life is at the heart of that unity; the provision of a just wage for labour and also the maintenance and development of a social order which will render possible a portion of private property for every section of the community; a juridical constitution based on God's sovereign lordship, immune from human caprice, one which will protect man's inviolable human rights from arbitrary human power; a Christian concept of the State, serving society and the person, not dominating either.[9]

By Christmas 1943 there was a danger that, with final victory almost guaranteed, the Allies would cast their future hopes for peace in terms of material prosperity and ease. 'Those who look for the salvation of society from the machinery of the world economic market' will be disillusioned. Such people 'are not the lords and masters but the slaves of material wealth' if it is sought without reference to the higher ends of man. Those who have the destiny of peoples in their hands meanwhile are reminded that peace must be based on justice, on right, not on purely material considerations or on diminishment of that right by a vindictive peace or by hatred.[10] The question of the conditions for peace and of the post-war order was of consuming urgency.[11] The Atlantic Charter had made reference to a possible future establishment of a permanent system of security, and by March 1945 forty-seven Allied nations had accepted the Charter.

At their meeting at Casablanca in January 1943, Roosevelt and Churchill had reluctantly decided that unconditional surrender would be the terms offered to the enemy, on the grounds that ultimately this was the only way to bring them to their senses and prevent them playing for time by trying to divide the Allies on the terms. In the March of 1945, the 'big three' of Roosevelt, Churchill and Stalin met at Yalta with the end of the war now definitely in sight; there were disagreements between the Western leaders and

Stalin over the exact meaning of the term 'democratic means' pledged in the Atlantic Charter as the norm for the government of all liberated peoples; Eastern Europe, Poland especially, was to suffer from Stalin's flagrant disregard of the intentions of the drafters of the Charter in this. It was at Yalta also that arrangements for a new international organization were set in hand; in April 1945 representatives of the United Nations met in San Francisco and on 25 June, the Charter of the Organization was signed; the war against the Japanese had still two more months to run.

In his Christmas message of 1944, Pius XII took into account some of the points that had been widely discussed in this last phase of the war. There must be an organization to maintain the peace 'invested by consent with supreme power, to smother any threat to aggression'. The vanquished States judged responsible for the war must accept the consequences of their actions, but they must also be treated with justice; they must also be given the hope of a return to the community of nations. Despite the passions raised by the war, human solidarity must be the framework of international relationships. Justice must be done concerning war crimes, but whole peoples cannot be punished. That moral principle must rule in international affairs, must surely be the lesson learned from the war and its suffering. The Church will help to establish true democracy based on the Christian dignity of man. She has a

> mission to announce to the world, longing for better and more perfect forms of democracy, the highest and most necessary message there can be, the dignity of man, the vocation of the children of God.[12]

## Democracy

With the entrance of the United States into the war in December 1941, the reach of that war had become truly global, and it was a conflict between the two great democracies and the Fascist dictatorships. The advent of Soviet totalitarianism as one of the Allies caused conflicts throughout the West but Winston Churchill's judgement on the situation, if a little colourfully stated, was the general one: 'If Hitler invaded Hell I would at least make a favourable reference to the Devil in the House of Commons.'[13] The effort to work with sworn enemies for the greater good had acceptable precedent. The Vatican, until finally and irretrievably rebuffed, had tried to keep open its lines of communication with the Soviets in the 1920s despite their persecution of Christians and their declared militant atheism: further, it was the Russian people, albeit led by an alien regime, who were now threatened, and with them and their defence of their homeland there could be no quarrel: only admiration for their courage, combined with a desire to do what could be done to help. Survival, and victory against the more immediate enemy, made it necessary also.

As was to be confirmed most dramatically with the collapse of real socialism in the late 1980s, democracy is the best way for modern States to handle their political affairs, and it was the leadership given by the Western democracies against tyranny which had captured the world's imagination in the 1940s and first brought its advantages to the world's notice. The Church's political ethic allowed of popular sovereignty, the right of the people to choose their own governments; as we have seen above, there was the 'scholastic doctrine ... of the sovereignty of the people in Thomas Aquinas in its beginnings, and fully developed by Francisco Suarez'.[14] Yet this was in a context of assumed social stability where the other corporate entities kept their influence and rights, and all accepted in theory the divine and revealed moral laws, and the ultimate derivation of all political authority from God. Democracy however was reborn in the eighteenth century under Enlightenment and French revolutionary auspices which denied these assumptions, and produced democratic totalitarianism and gross injustice, as well as being actively anti-clerical, anti-Church and to some extent explicitly atheist. The Church was circumspect in principle, while leaving her members to find a modus vivendi with whatever political system people chose for themselves. Italy had been a special case, given that the popes could only act effectively for the international Church if they were independent of any secular political authority, and the unresolved dispute with the Italian state meant that they were not assured of this. From 1929 this problem no longer existed.

As Pius XII became more acquainted with other than Continental democracy, with liberal democracy on the American and British models in other words, and when that democracy defended so many of the civilized and Christian values which Fascism threatened, he became much more ready to accept this version of it in general, while insisting that democracy required a virtuous people, electors and elected, to be soundly based. This the Catholic tradition had always insisted on, and this was built into the idea of representative government as it came to the modern world through the medieval representative government, the seedbed of modern democracy: the American founding fathers, drawing on the same Christian tradition, insisted that democracy if it was to work needed to be founded in a virtuous people. In stressing this then, Pius XII was putting the ancient wisdom of the Church, and the experience of those who had longest acquaintance with effective democracy, at the disposal of a new generation.

In the 1940s peoples who had little or no control over their political destiny found themselves involved in fighting and suffering in a war over the beginnings and course of which they had very little say, and it was a war which involved whole populations. All fit males of military age were conscripted, and the home front was as important as, and sometimes suffered as much as, the military. The importance of propaganda and the growth of the mass media, newspapers, radio, films, made people aware of issues, and ready to pronounce on them, as never before. Inevitably peoples wanted to make sure in future that they controlled their own destiny; they wanted a true popular democracy. It appears, said the Pope 'as a natural postulate imposed by reason itself'.[15] He clearly goes along with this, but adds that to prevent itself being manipulated by others, such a democratic people, electors and elected, needs to be aware of personal responsibilities and rights, and respectful of those of others, tolerating differences that do not challenge basic equality, justice or charity. The high moral qualities this demands particularly need the strengthening that can be given by Christian belief.

## Solidarity and property

The solidarity of all men made in God's image and likeness and redeemed by Christ, establishes them in a unity which includes 'the unity of dwelling place, the earth, of whose resources all men can by natural right avail themselves to sustain and develop life': this was the message of *Summi Pontificatus* [38]. People 'of every class are to have a proper standard of living as a requirement of the just peace all sought' (Christmas message, 1940) and there must be an end to the egoism which 'tends to monopolize economic resources and materials of common use' (Christmas message, 1941) by the rich and powerful nations.

Man's right to private property is one that derives from his nature, is a natural right and hence does not depend on the State.[16] The latter point is repeated in the 1942 Christmas message, where the emphasis is on ownership of land, but the scope and the need was wider than that. The right to private property is an essential element of the social order in the wider sense, affecting all spheres of economic activity. It is

> a necessary presupposition of human initiative, an impulse to labour, the method of achieving the temporal and transcendental goals of life and thus the goals of liberty and of the dignity of man created in God's own image[17]

and the workers should be encouraged to invest their savings in industry, a habit from which they and the nation would benefit. Property was a good that should be shared in by as many as possible, and it was one of Pius XII's criticisms of the system in practice that there was too great a concentration in the hands of the few.[18]

## Capital and labour

Defence of the principle of private property in productive goods was not therefore a defence of the *status quo*. The

> excessive concentration of economic goods which, concealed frequently under an anonymous form, succeeds in escaping its social duties and making it almost impossible for the worker to accumulate a worthwhile patrimony for himself

is condemned.[19] The encroachment of big business, with labour being treated only as pawns in a game, and the social evils of unemployment, were also deplored. The rights of labour were emphasized: the need for a decent wage so that parents could look after their families properly, adequate housing, access to decent education, provision for times of economic difficulty and old age.[20] The role of unions was 'to represent and defend the interest of workers through labour contracts'.[21] Through this role they will have influence on politics and political opinion, but if they ever seek more than this, their nature as organizations of defence is changed. The defence of the rights of labour was combined with an appreciation of the value of the socially responsible private ownership of productive goods, as opposed to the liberal capitalism which did not respect the dignity of labour or the common good. The economy based on private ownership of these goods is the 'living product of the free initiative of individuals and groups'.[22]

## Social welfare

In an address to Italian workers in 1943[23] Pius XII saw the hope of a better life for them and their families not in revolution but in harmonious evolution ... guided by Christian canons of right and justice ... not in the abolition of private property but its promotion and its spreading ... its prudently controlled marshalling ... for the true well-being of the whole population.

This requires that 'we must not aim solely at the greatest possible profit but ... make use of the fruits which we obtain ... for the improvement of the living conditions of the worker'.

The State must see that the activities of parents and labour associations are assisted 'by means of social institutions, such as social security, health insurance and social welfare' but it must not make the citizens dependent on it.

The picture then is redolent of wartime hopes and idealism but it is at the same time realistic. It is gradualist, based on belief in the market economy's ability to provide the wealth society needs and yet aware that the State has a role in complementing private efforts to provide adequate resources for all by social security, health insurance and social welfare. The State has also a right to own or expropriate productive goods where the common good requires it, but this nationalization should be the exception, not the rule.[24] The basic reason for this positive attitude to welfare capitalism, capitalism which has accepted its social responsibilities, is the conviction that private initiative in economic matters is the best way of making the earth yield its riches for the good of all. Unless the principle and practice of the private ownership of productive goods was defended, the springs of wealth which would make it possible to solve the problem of poverty of the wage earners would dry up.

## 4 The Papacy, the Church and the Jews 1939–45[25]

### In German-occupied Europe

As a result of his experience as a diplomat in Germany in the 1920s and as Secretary of State from 1929, the new Pope had no illusions about the Nazis. Now, as he faced up to his responsibilities of his duties as Pope, he had to decide how to handle this evil, rampant from 1940 because of its military successes, in the light of his duty to the Church and to humanity. There are those who have claimed that if only he had spoken out clearly, strongly and often enough in condemnation of Nazism he would have done something to avert the evils of the Holocaust. Even if he had not succeeded in this, it was his duty, some have said, to put his own life at risk in defying Hitler. It needs to be remembered that this charge was only made in 1961, and that until then and during his lifetime, the judgement on the Pope's work for the Jews had been very favourable because of his is strong emphasis on human rights, his attempts to see that human values prevailed, and the silent but effective assistance given to the victims of racial or political persecution by the Church under his guidance; as one commentator pointed out, at no time since 1848 had the attitude to the Papacy been more favourable.[26] It also needs to be remembered that the hue and cry against Pius XII did not stem from the Jewish people or its leaders, or from scholars and historians, but from the tendentious approach of the playwright, Rolf Hochhuth in his play *The Representative*. What might be taken as writer's licence in the context of a play, suddenly became accepted by many as historical fact and uncontestable truth.

As to his putting his freedom, and possibly his life on the line, Pius XII was prepared for this. He had shown in facing the Reds in Munich in 1918 that he did not lack physical courage in the line of duty. We know from the Italian Ambassador to Berlin that he accepted the possibility of being sent to a concentration camp and was prepared for it. In 1944 Hitler had invited him to come to Germany; he told the College of Cardinals he would never willingly abandon the See nor Rome, but he knew that if and when it suited the Nazis to arrest him they would do so and he would have to take his chance.[27] As to condemning Nazism publicly, the truth is that from the beginning of his pontificate he did so. But he was made aware of his responsibilities to those who were suffering under Nazi rule, and he tried to avoid putting them at further risk by speaking out in ways which would lead the Nazis to treat them even more severely. This is no mere conjecture after the event. In 1939 Poland's Cardinal Sapieha appealed to him to stop protesting at the persecution of the church there because the reprisals that followed made things worse; priests in Dachau learned to fear such protests against Nazi brutality; they led to victimization from the guards and complaints from the non-Catholic clergy against the naïvety of Pope and bishops in thinking they could do any good by them. That public protests against Nazi atrocities would only result in greater suffering for its victims is confirmed from many sources. The Archbishop of Utrecht did so protest but the result was that the Catholic Jews who had formerly been left alone were rounded up with fervour and sent to their deaths; they included Edith Stein. Dr Licthen, a Polish Jew working with B'nai Brith asserted that the

Pope would only have made it worse by speaking out. Dr. Kemperer, one of the American prosecutors at the Nuremberg trials said the same; such action by the Pope would have accelerated the death of priests and Jews. Von Kessel, a German diplomat in Rome at the time of the assault on Jews there confirmed this. Hitler would have reacted with cruel violence. The effect of the strong statements of Churchill and Roosevelt on the matter in 1944 according to the testimony of the Secretary General of the World Jewish Congress, was to accelerate the liquidation of the Jews[28].

Instead of using inflamatory language deliberately to provoke the Nazis, Pius XII spoke the truth quietly and insistently. Meanwhile of the 6.3 million Jews in Europe under the Nazis some 1 million survived, and of those the Israelis calculate that over 800,000 were saved by the Church. In *Summi Pontificatus*, he appealed to the natural laws of morality which should protect the human rights of all, whatever nation they belonged to and he expressed his compassion for all the oppressed and persecuted, calling Paul to witness that 'there is neither Jew, nor Greek, nor Gentile, we are all one in Jesus Christ'. The Nazis knew who he was getting at. Reports of the encyclical in Germany, where only what the Nazis wanted to be reported was reported, were accordingly garbled; so much so that the Holy See protested. Meanwhile priests who read the original in their churches were arrested, and when the BBC broadcast the whole of the letter, the German Embassy in Rome complained to the Vatican.

In his Christmas addresses the same message came through, without rant or rhetoric but in plain unmistakable tones. In 1939 he appealed to Christians to love those who do not participate in their faith; in 1940 he rejoiced that he had been able to help so many refugees, especially non-Aryans. On 29 June 1941 he told his hearers that he refrained from revealing the unspeakable miseries of the persecuted, because of his solicitude for them. That his Christmas message of 1941 was confiscated in Belgium and Holland, on orders from Berlin, showed how careful he had to be if he was to be heard at all. It was the constant stress on human dignity and the common fatherhood of God which led Albert Einstein to say in 1940 that 'only the Catholic Church protested against the Hitlerian onslaught on liberty ... the Church alone has had the courage to struggle for spiritual truth and moral liberty'. The Christmas message of 1942, in which he pleaded for those persecuted, so angered the Nazis that they forbade its dissemination and those who printed it were punished. The *New York Times* spoke of his as 'a lonely voice crying out in the stillness of a continent'. In formal documents as well as his addresses he repeated the simple lesson. The encyclical *Mystici Corporis* of 29 June 1943 repeatedly stressed the need for universal love; those not of their faith, he reminded his people, are none the less their brothers in Christ.[29]

The quiet insistence on these timeless truths was accompanied by the orchestration, by the papal representatives throughout Europe, of the Church's efforts to save Jewish lives. The direct action and example of the Pope in Rome and Italy resulted in more effective aid being given to the Jews than anywhere else in Axis countries; in Rome itself 85 per cent of the 9600 Jews were saved from the Nazi roundup of October 1944 and they were hidden by monks, nuns and clerics, with the laity giving them stout support.[30]

In Slovakia, the 25 per cent of the Jews who managed to survive there owe their lives to the Church's protection and in particular to the papal nuncio supported by the Pope. The record of these achievements was creditable everywhere. In Hungary the Jews were protected until 1944 by the Government of the time, strengthened in its resolve by the papal nuncio and the Pope. There were still 755,000 of the original 1 million remaining in the country in 1944 when the Germans took over, the largest Jewish community in Europe, and the nuncio, Roncalli, the future John XXIII, fully supported by Pius XII, was energetic in their defence. He co-operated with the heroic Swedish envoy Wallenberg in his effort which saved the lives of some 25,000 intended victims. Some 200,000 Hungarian Jews altogether survived the vicious Nazi persecution, and in 1944 the World Jewish Congress sent a telegram to the Holy See thanking it for the protection it had given them in their time of suffering.[31]

Of Romania's 350,000 Jews, 250,000 were saved, the largest proportion of a Jewish population to survive in any country where the Nazi writ ran, and the 16 per cent of the population who were members of the Catholic church, backed by Monsignor Casulo, played a large part in this, The nuncio was proclaimed one of 'the righteous of the nations' by the State of Israel in recognition of his efforts. In Bulgaria and Greece the pattern was the same; the local church under the guidance and leadership of the Papal nuncios, with the Pope's full backing, was at the forefront of efforts to help the persecuted Jews. The Spanish and Portuguese governments, influenced by the Holy See, were also generous in admitting Jews needing refuge.[32]

Poland's Jews had been protected by religious charters since 1264 and this protection was maintained by Polish rulers in a country which had the largest Jewish population of any European State until, with the partitioning of Poland and its loss of independence in 1795 alien traditions of anti Semitism took root. In the period 1939–45, the Nazis killed some 5.3 million Polish citizens, of whom 2.9 million were Jews, most of the other 2.4 million being Catholics. As elsewhere, a large Jewish population bred vicious anti semitism in Poland; yet one quarter of the 200 righteous Gentiles of 14 nations honoured by Israel for succouring Jews were Poles; the longer national tradition was still honoured by many.[33]

In France, the Church and hierarchy backed by Rome were also active in helping the Jewish community. Some 75 per cent, 200,000 of them, survived the persecution, and as a result the London *Jewish Chronicle* thanked the Pope for his efforts on their behalf. No Catholic community was more vocal and openly courageous in opposing the Nazi plans for the Jews of its country than that in Holland, but the dangers of being too flagrant in flouting the regime rebounded on those they tried to help. Hitler's minions stepped up their efforts to round up their Jewish victims and they succeeded; 79 per cent were arrested, while it was notable that the 9000 Protestant Jews were left alone because their churches had been more prudent. The Catholic community managed to hide some 40,000 Jews in all, of whom 15,000 were saved. In Belgium, Cardinal van Roey, with the full backing of Rome, organized the Church's total opposition, but more circumspectly. The Pope's denunciations of racialism were read out in the churches and the whole Catholic community rallied to the hiding and protection of the persecuted. Belgium's Chief Rabbi wrote to the Cardinal after the liberation, thanking him for his work; some 65,000 of the original Jewish community of 90,000 there survived the war.[34]

Israel accepted that 700,000 to 860,000 Jews who survived the Holocaust were saved by the Church's efforts, a figure which exceeds by far those saved by all other churches, religious institutions and rescue organizations combined. It is for this reason that Israel dedicated a forest of 860,000 trees to Pius XII's memory and Golda Meier, Israel's Foreign Minister at the time of his death praised him for upholding the 'highest ideals of peace and compassion'. He and the Church he served did this at a time when few others would.

> It is against this background of genocidal indifference ... that the Catholic effort within Nazi Europe must be considered. On the one hand, statesmen, diplomats and generals refused to save Jews ... on the other hand, peasants, housewives, priests and nuns and workers ... unarmed, defied the mightiest juggernaut of modern times in order to save some 800,000.[35]

## In Nazi Germany

The majority of Germans, Catholics included, accepted Hitler with enthusiasm, though in a totalitarian state it is difficult to judge how genuine such enthusiasm was. He consolidated his power quickly. Within a few months in 1933 he had abolished political parties, the trade union movement and the free press. In June 1934, on the night of the long knives, he eliminated his Nazi rivals and won the allegiance of the army. Then President Hindenberg died in August, enabling him to abolish the Presidency and seize its powers, becoming C in C of the armed forces whose members took a vow of obedience to him personally. With the unopposed reoccupation of the Rhineland in March 1936, the die was cast. The German people were at his mercy.

> Hitler was a person of undoubted ... evil genius ... [who] found in the German people, as a mysterious Providence had formed them ... a natural instrument he was able to shape to his own sinister ends ... without Hitler ... [his] demonic personality, granite will and uncanny instincts, remarkable intellect and soaring imagination ... and, until the end when he overreached himself, an amazing ability to size up people and situations, there would have been no Third Reich.[36]

Hitler's perverted personality was then at the heart and centre of Nazism. His mesmeric powers enabled him to dominate individuals and his oratorical gifts gave him the ability to indoctrinate mass meetings, while his indomitable will overcame all difficulties during the period down to the failure to destroy the Russian armies. At the time he took power, no one could have predicted the outcome. No nation deserved such a fate as his leadership had in store for the Germans; but he was their fate, and in his hands all the national weaknesses of their race were grotesquely magnified. One thing stands to their credit, however, and is too often ignored. It is that they never, as a nation, gave him a popular mandate in a free election; even with all the powers of the State at his service, and with the fear of social collapse and Bolshevism well alive, the majority never freely chose him as their leader. Weakened though Weimar democracy was by the early 1930s, it did not give him and his party a majority in the popular vote: the most he could manage was 43 per cent and in his contest with Hindenburg for the presidency he received only 36.8 per cent. That did not keep him from his prize; his malevolent mind enabled him to manipulate events and men in order to get round that detail. But that in freedom the majority of Germans did not trust him needs to be remembered.

Once he had consolidated his power the people cheered him – but as they were to find in the end, they were as much his slaves as were the 'inferior' races they were taught to despise. The Germans under the Nazis do not appear in a favourable light, but historians and commentators who savage them should search their consciences. Are they so sure they would have done better? The sort of totalitarian State Hitler ran, as depicted by Christabel Bielenburg, is one we find difficult to imagine.[37] In it any open opposition, let alone plots, usually led to disaster, the Gestapo's attentions, the threat of the concentration camp, and danger to all one's family and friends. There had been only one chance of getting rid of Hitler once he had taken power, and that was on 7 March 1936 when with astonishing boldness he invaded the demilitarized Rhineland with but four brigades.[38] If France and England had opposed him he would have been finished; but they did not.

He regarded the Christian churches as hindrances to his long-term plans and among them the Catholic Church in particular. The Reformed churches were split by factions; the compact and well-organized Roman Catholic Church was a different proposition.[39] It was the main enemy from this quarter and the majority of the secret service (SD) reports on religious institutions were on it.[40] Though it had been weakened in the first six years of the Nazi regime, it still retained a strong organizational presence and great influence over one-third of the German people who were its members. Dietrich tells us that the Nazis were aware of its successes in opposing them; it was feared by them and they looked forward to the time when, after their expected victory, they would be able to take the revenge they fully intended to take against it.

The Church was totally opposed to the biological racialism of the Nazis, and this is where it locked horns indomitably with the regime. Dietrich is highly critical of the less ideological but deep-seated anti-Jewish prejudice which he finds among members of the Church: he allows, however, that this sort of instinctive social anti-Semitism cannot be interpreted as support for Nazi racism.[41] The set and deepest theological convictions of the Church condemned it; Nazi eugenics insisted that some human beings were in truth less than fully human and could be treated accordingly. Hence

Despite all its shortcomings, the Catholic Church did not fail to resist Nazism. Its very existence and its activities were effective barriers to the realization of the Nazi aims, as long as the Church could preach Christian doctrine and morality.[42]

Some members of the Church acted more in accordance with Christian principles than prominent critics have been willing to concede. Whether it satisfies contemporary scholars or not, the Church did resist Nazi totalitarianism.[43]

Both the genocidal attack on the Jews and the euthanasia programme aimed at eliminating the unwanted members of society stemmed from a biological social Darwinist anthropology which was incompatible with the Christian respect for man and for human life. This is the theme of the bishops, priests and theologians who spoke out. So Otto Schilling, Professor of Theology at Tübingen, pointed out that natural law, not medical eugenics, governed procreation and that the focus was on the person, not the folk. He condemned sterilization, and he insisted the State had the duty to protect innocent life. Karl Frank, Jesuit Professor of Theology at Düsseldorf opposed racialism. All men were rational beings; there were different cultural characteristics among the races but they were accidental not substantial. It was unacceptable that race could determine morality; divine law was superior to all national and racial dogmas. Professors Artweiler from Cologne, and Schmaus and Tillman for example from Münster, insisted that race could not be such a determinant. All men belong to one human race and all political communities derived from God. Human well-being in the community was based on love, not on politics; the true community was one in which the individual gave to those in need since all men are brothers.

So the chorus of theological dissent continued.[44] The Jesuit theologian Peter Lippert argued that the common good of the community could not come before the rights of conscience; values inherent in man came before political considerations. Ziegler, his colleague at Düsseldorf stressed that the individual only became truly human by obeying first and foremost God's law in Christ. The Church's position was the euthanasia was absolutely evil and could in no circumstances be defended, and the protests of the Fulda Conference in 1940 led to the halting of the programme in Germany. It was against this background that Cardinal von Galen gave his famous sermons in July and August, which made the strongest public attack ever made on the Nazi eugenics and on the brutality of the Gestapo.

Individual members of the hierarchy therefore, like von Galen, condemned aspects of Nazism, so Cardinals Schulte and Bertram, and Bishops Bornewasser, Preysing and Weber, while in 1943 the Bishops Conference denounced the eugenics programme. Sadly but not surprisingly some were anxious to show themselves patriotic by praising the regime and its servants. Archbishop Groeber joined the SS as a promotive member in 1933 and in 1936 Bishop Berning reminded concentration camp guards of their duty of obedience to the state, while in 1938 the Bishops Conference welcomed the invasion of the Sudetenland.[45]

Writers such as Zahn, Muller and Lewey insist that the institutional Church did not do enough to oppose Nazi racialism and this of course is true, but even if she had done all that she could have done, it is to be doubted whether she could have prevented the Nazis having their way while they were triumphant in Europe. The effort to make the Pope and the Catholic Church the scapegoat for the Holocaust, or at least for the failure to oppose it when it was at its height is surely not justified. 'If there is room for accusations, they should be directed against the Jews of the free world for their conduct during the years of horror. All of us failed the test,' said Dr. Goldmann, President of the World Jewish Congress while the International Red Cross and the Western Democracies had far greater resources and power than the Church at their command and failed as badly.[46] By contrast as we have seen, Pope Pius XII was judged by Golda Meier to have acted according to the highest ideals of peace and compassion during this period. The efforts of the Church of which he was head, the policies of his nuncios, the national churches and the individuals he encouraged, and which in Rome and Italy he was directly responsible for, resulted in the efforts of peasants, housewives, priests and nuns in the Catholic communities of Europe saving most of the one million Jews who survived.[47]

The Church nurtured 'a significant grass roots critique of the Nazi world view'[48] with its opposition to biological racialism. The Nazis knew this and they also knew that they had to tolerate it since an open assault on the Church on such an issue would rally support to it and would have been counterproductive. The secret police kept records, watched and waited. In victory the regime would take its revenge. The Supreme Court of Israel recognized that it is 'self aggrandisement and sanctimoniousness' on the part of those who had never lived under such a regime 'to criticize those who did not rise to inhuman heights of morality'.[49]

Some few did rise to those heights. Fr Maximillian Kolbe who gave his life to save another, has been canonized, Fr Rupert Meyer for two decades criticised Nazism and was frequently imprisoned. Frs Bernard Lichtenburg and Karl Leisner were executed for their

opposition; all three have been beatified. [50] All told, 4000 priests,
the majority Poles, gave their lives; 'the vanguard of a noble army'.[51]
Many of the Catholic laity were in that army, to which belonged so
many of other faiths and none. A small minority over all but a significant one, showing the greatness of the human spirit in one of its
darkest hours.


# 5  Pius XII's Pontificate 1945–58

## (i)  Background

### The Cold War[52]

The immediate post-war years in Europe, 1945–50, were a time of
anxiety; there was the fear that the experience after the First World
War would be repeated and a brief post-war boom would give way to
an uncertain recovery and later economic collapse as in the 1930s.
The memories of the blighted hopes for 'homes fit for heroes' that
had inspired an earlier generation lingered. The US economy had
expanded healthily in supplying war needs and continued to boom
with the start of peace. Europe's case was quite other; the devasta-
tion of war had shattered the infrastructures of some of its leading
nations and the economies of all, so that the needs of reconstruction were indeed great. The exhaustion of the victors and the
apparently hopeless position of the vanquished threatened to stifle
hope at the start. Europe, its capital exhausted in war, could not
finance reconstruction and re-equip its industries.

If Europe did not flourish then neither would the trading areas
connected with it, and this would have a knock-on effect on the
international economy, slowing its growth and making it even less
able to supply the increasing needs of the peoples of the world.
There was an even greater fear of the might of the Soviet Union,
and the uses to which it might be put in the new post-war order.
The democracies had been able to stifle their reservations about
the Soviet system before 1945 when they were engaged in a war to
the death with the Fascists and needed its help in bringing it to as
successful conclusion. As the end of the war approached they had
to face the question of their future relationship with their ally.
President Roosevelt had been more inclined to trust Stalin's fair
words, and not look too closely at his deeds and long-term intentions; Prime Minister Churchill was more suspicious, but Britain
was the junior partner to the USA in terms of the contribution to

the war effort overall, while many also thought Churchill's attitude was just that of a conservative imperialist. By contrast,

> Roosevelt said and apparently fully believed that, once victory had been won and the forces of Fascist aggression had been trodden into the dust, an era of international peace and prosperity, freedom and justice could be inaugurated and surely would be if men of goodwill strove to that end.[53]

Whatever Churchill's motives, events proved he assessed Stalinism's and communism's long-term ambitions more accurately.

At Yalta in February 1945 it was agreed that Germany would be divided into Russian, British, American and French zones, pending the signing of a peace treaty. Over Poland, Stalin steamrollered his way; 47 per cent of that country's pre-war territory was incorporated in the USSR; eventually he also established the Polish/ German border on the Neisse River. Churchill and Roosevelt, already fearful of a Russian plan to dominate Eastern Europe, insisted that the Poles be permitted to choose their form of government freely and under universal suffrage and the secret ballot. Stalin gave verbal assent but then established a communist dictatorship at the first opportunity. He proceeded in the same way with the other East European countries, despite Yalta's acceptance of the principles of the Atlantic Charter. The fear that the Japanese would not be defeated without a long and bitter struggle, despite the German collapse, had led to Russia being offered very advantageous terms of continuing the alliance against them, so strengthening their position in the Far East.

Within Western Europe there were political and industrial conflicts which reflected the tension between non-communist and communist forces. France and Italy had large communist parties which had basked in the triumphs of Russian arms and the growing strength of the Soviet cause generally, and it was feared that they might be in a position to attempt some kind of a takeover backed by popular if not majority support, given favourable conditions. While Britain had no such large communist political party, many of its members were active in the strong union movement; the 1945 Labour government was constantly being hindered in its economic policies by the activities of such militants.

Communists were fishing in the troubled waters of Balkan politics also, and generally they were acting as a destabilizing influence throughout Europe. With Soviet puppet governments appearing one by one in Eastern Europe in 1946–7, the hope of the ideals of the Atlantic alliance being realized died. As early as March 1946,

Churchill, in a speech at Fulton in the USA, spoke of the 'Iron curtain' that was descending across Europe, dividing the free nations from the unfree. Disowned by President Truman at the time, its analysis was confirmed by events. In January 1947 economic and political problems compelled Great Britain to abandon any hope of containing the communist attempts to Sovietize the Balkans and, alarmed by what looked like another communist takeover in train, the President announced the policy that came to be named after him; America undertook to support any democratic regime threatened by Soviet expansionism.

Realizing that only injections of American capital would guarantee the revival of the European economy and so head off likely communist takeovers, General Marshall announced on 5 June 1947[54] a plan to do this. The USSR and its satellites were given the opportunity of participating; they declined, but 16 of the other countries of Europe submitted proposals and by the end of the year the expenditure of some 17 billion dollars had been approved by the American government. It was enlightened self-interest at its best. Without this far-sighted and humane policy the revival of the European economy and its full participation in the unexampled expansion of the international economy in the next few years would hardly have been possible.

The reality of the Soviet threat to Western countries with pre-war democratic traditions was brought home forcefully by the experience of Czechoslovakia in 1948. Elections in 1946 were comparatively unhindered, in accordance with Stalin's promises; in them the communists did well and formed a majority in a coalition government. The regime was not popular, however, and fearing they would lose the forthcoming elections in June 1948, the communists staged a coup on 20 February; so thorough were their preparations that hardly any opposition could be mounted. The President finally capitulated on 25 February to save his country the civil war that open opposition would bring. The dangers to Italy and France, with their strong and confident communist minorities, were now too obvious for comfort.

Berlin was the next flashpoint. Soviet foot-dragging hindered plans to make the four zones one, and events in Czechoslovakia removed Western inhibitions about unilateral action; in June 1948 they reformed the currency and lifted controls on prices and rationing, except for food and some other essentials. Alarmed at the effect this would have on their zone, the Russians introduced a blockade of allied areas of the city on 28 June, denying them fuel and food. Determined to avoid war and resist blackmail, the allies organized an air supply of the city, soon bringing in 8000 tons of needed supplies a day, and the Soviets had to admit defeat.

The Cold War was now formalized.[55] In March 1948, Britain, France and the Benelux countries (Belgium, Netherlands and Luxembourg) signed the Brussels defence treaty and in 1949 the North Atlantic Treaty Organization was formed, the United States, Canada, Italy, Iceland, Norway, Denmark and Portugal entering into agreement with the Brussels treaty powers. There were parallel developments in the East though they were much less significant in practical terms. It was through the communist parties in each country, orchestrated by Moscow, that control of all political, economic and military matters was ultimately exercised. The Cominform (the Communist Information Bureau) was formed in 1947 in response to Western moves. It was dissolved in 1956 and replaced by the Warsaw pact. The East European Mutual Assistance Treaty established the Comecon (Council for Economic Mutual Assistance).

In August 1949 the USSR exploded its first atomic bomb and international tension increased. The emergence of what was potentially the world's third superpower, Communist China, in 1949 increased it the more and the Korean conflict revealed the dangers to the full. After the Japanese had been expelled from Korea at war's end, the country had been divided into two zones along the line of the 38th parallel, but failure to reach agreement on the future of the country led to the Americans organizing elections in the South in 1948 and the Russians setting up the People's Democratic Republic in the North; both Americans and Russians then withdrew their troops. On 25 June the North launched an attack on the South, and the United Nations forces, mainly American, expelled them by October of the same year. The Chinese then intervened on the North Korean side and in response more UN troops were committed, so increasing the possibility that the war would become nuclear. Fortunately this did not happen; the conflict reached stalemate in 1951 and an armistice was signed in 1953.

The atmosphere and attitudes of the Cold War, and the threat of nuclear war that any hotting up of it entailed, dominated cultural and political attitudes from the 1950s. Fear of nuclear conflict was palpable in the West, and resentment at the way the Russians had reneged on the promises of democracy for all was deep. After Stalin's death in 1953, the evil nature of his regime was gradually recognized by the party but it still reacted to the desperate revolts of Poles, Germans, Hungarians and

Czechoslovaks in 1956 with a violence and ruthlessness which showed that in essentials nothing had changed; at the same time, the success of the USSR in putting into orbit the first artificial satellite, the 'Sputnik', in 1957 seemed to justify the Soviet claims that on the frontiers of modern science and technology it was forging ahead of its capitalist rivals.

Finally, there was within Western society throughout this time a large minority of intellectuals and academics who were prepared to argue that the Marxist-Leninist view of life, as embodied in the Soviet system, was superior to Western liberalism and the capitalist market economy. Keenly aware of the defects, real and imagined, of the latter, they were not prepared to accept any fundamental criticism of the former. The presence of this large minority did not do anything to calm the fears of those who were already convinced that communism represented some kind of unholy conspiracy against the freedoms that Western man had come to take for granted.

## Christian democracy[54]

It was in the years after 1945 that Christian democracy at last came into its own. Don Luigi Sturzo, whose PPI had a brief success in 1919 to 1922 until it came to grief under Mussolini, went into exile after the party was outlawed in 1923. In Paris in 1924, he gathered round him those interested in the Christian democratic ideal; they included the Italian Alcide de Gasperi, the Frenchman Robert Schuman and the German Konrad Adenauer, the Catholic states-men who with Charles de Gaulle were to be the main rebuilders of a democratic Europe after 1945.[57] Already in 1924 they had plans for a Common Market and European integration with the prevention of future wars in mind. Their general philosophy was provided by the personalism of Jacques Maritain, that the individual should achieve his personal development through his responsibility to others in society, the family and the community in general. It was a Christian philosophy, therefore, which rejected both the individu-alism of the liberals and the collectivism of the socialists.

They took the framework of their social theory from the social teaching of the Church, in particular the concept of solidarity which stressed the instinct and the need for all members of society to respect and help each other, and for all organizations and asso-ciations within it to harmonize their functions in the service of their members and the community beyond them. It is a principle which rejects the extreme individualism of the conservative-minded. The second key social principle was subsidiarity, that the person, the family and the smaller associations in society, whatever their function and purpose within a framework of just law, should be free of interference by the larger association, especially the State, unless the help of such organizations is needed for them to obtain their legitimate objectives. This principle marks them off from the forms of socialism which would make the State and its organization superior to person, family and smaller association.

They therefore drew their membership from all social and economic groupings and in particular from both capitalist employers and active trade unionists alike. They were strong on fair but peaceful industrial relations secured by positive-minded unions and employers, and on social welfare policies. The leaders of the original movement were Catholics, but they welcomed non-Catholics to their ranks and it was Ludwig Erhard, a Protestant, who provided them with an economic theory and policy in the 'social market economy', that is strong sound business practice, proper treatment of workers, and social welfare as an essential part of a free enterprise political economy.

The various parties were autonomous and independent of the Church but with the strong anti-Communism of the early period and the majority of their members being Catholic they were tied into it in many respects, however informally. This connection became weaker in the secular 1960s and has continued to weaken. The great period of flourishing of Christian democracy was the 1950s, with Catholic statesmen, politicians, business and trade union leaders in action with those of other faiths and none, basing their policies on philosophic and social theories which were largely in harmony with the Christian ideal. The sectarianism and mutual suspicions of the nineteenth and the early twentieth century were at last largely put to rest, and the foundations of a new democratic Europe were firmly laid.

**Modern capitalism and State welfare**

As the 1950s went on, it gradually dawned on the astonished West that initial post-war fears of inadequate economic growth had not been justified.[58] There had been a fundamental change for the better in basic aspects of economic, social and political life in the free industrialized world. In the nineteenth century, the slowness with which the mass of the people were able to gain a fair share of the riches they had helped to create led to the socialist and anar-

chist reaction of that time, and left democratic politics elsewhere
with a tendency to bitterness and negativism which lived on until
1939. Now, it suddenly seemed that the people were to have their
reward at last. The likelihood of economic recession receded as the
Marshall Plan did its work and the spirit and the fortunes of
Europe revived. The kick-start to the post-war economy it provided
resulted in an unexampled growth in international trade. Peace,
however uncertain in the longer term, came to be taken for
granted in the short term, and the traders of the world busied
themselves with meeting the needs of peoples throughout it.

Western industry, trade and financial services flourished as never
before. By 1950 industrial production exceeded that of 1939 and a
growth rate of 4 per cent per annum meant that by 1959 it was 46
per cent greater than it had been then. Full employment was
almost achieved, and wages had risen accordingly. There were
comprehensive social welfare schemes in place in all but two or
three of the poorest countries of Europe. Health, housing, education, sickness, unemployment, old age, disability, all were catered
for.[59] The working classes in the industrialized Western nations
were never more prosperous than in the late 1950s.

Socially responsible capitalism, democracy, trade unions, and
social welfare schemes, were showing their ability to iron out most
of the glaring weaknesses of liberal capitalism and its legacy. The
Keynesian school of economics and the experience of the 1920s
and the 1930s, followed by the mobilization of economies for war
under government direction, had done much to convince post-war
governments that they had an active role to play in making sure
that a free enterprise, market economy worked for the common
good. Nationalization and State welfare had their place, but it was
the inventiveness and productivity of the private sector which was
at the heart of the economy, the source of wealth creation, and it
was at last giving back to all those who worked at creating wealth
through it a real share in it.

### The new nations[60]

The Atlantic Charter, with its proclamation that all peoples had a
right to their own self-determination, not only inspired the old
world where the right had not existed everywhere before the 1939
war, but spoke also to the old colonial empires where the indigenous peoples were finally preparing to escape their tutelage and
become independent. The role of many of them in helping the
colonial powers to victory in 1945 made their claim finally irre-

sistible. The support given to the British war effort by India, for example, had been particularly valuable and there could be no returning to the old imperialism.

India became independent peacefully in 1947; it was afterwards that the massive bloodshed occurred – as a result of the tension between the Hindu and Muslim populations. In China there was a Marxist-led revolution backed by the grievances of the long-suffering peasants which gained power in 1949. In Indochina, Indonesia and Algeria, the colonial powers did not yield peacefully and so the progress to freedom was violent. Elsewhere, notably in Africa, independence came later towards the end of the 1950s; in 1959 Fidel Castro's victory in Cuba reminded the world that the problems that had been piling up since the end of empires in Latin America in the previous century had still not been effectively tackled.

The problem the new nations found was that political independence did not necessarily bring with it economic prosperity – which required above all industrialization. It was that which had made the Western nations wealthy, and it had been possible for them because of the inheritance of these nations – a large degree of cultural and social homogeneity, a tradition of craftsmanship enabled skilled workers to make major contributions to the development of machinery and new production techniques, there was political stability and economic freedom and the manufacturers were flexible and able enough to respond to the demands of the market at home and abroad. Sufficient capital, financial and banking expertize was available, as were the raw materials of industrial development at the time, coal and iron above all. Transport by road, canal and railway improved or developed. Britain's tradition as a trading nation meant it had access to the markets of the world.

By contrast the new nations were mostly in the less developed world, and their economic and cultural endowments were not such as to equip them to engage in trade or industry on equal terms with the West. It was in manufactured goods that most of the more profitable international trade took place, and most of that was between industrialized nations. The third or less developed world mainly traded in raw materials or commodities, both of which were on the whole less valuable as well as being subject to wild swings in prices and fluctuating demand. Such a dangerously unbalanced world economy was one which the poorer nations were less ready to tolerate passively, and from the 1950s the West became aware that the question of the relationship between it and the third world needed to be addressed, if not from idealistic motives, then from those of self-interest; failure here could endanger world peace. A better international economic order was needed for the good of all concerned.

## (ii)  The social teaching of Pius XII 1945–58

### Communism

During the struggle with the democratic states and Russia and the Fascist Axis powers, Pius XII had not stressed the conflict between the Christian view of life and that of the communist, though he had not ignored it when the issue arose on specific matters.[61] As the threat to freedom from the strong communist parties in Italy and France after the war became apparent, and as the persecution of the Church in the Eastern European countries increased, the issue became a live one once more. It came to a head first in Hungary with the arrest of Cardinal Mindszenty in 1948 and his conviction and imprisonment in 1949 for conspiracy against the State – for which crime there was of course no evidence. Implacable an enemy of the regime as the indomitable old Cardinal was, he did not need to stoop to political intrigue in his struggle with it; his objections were on spiritual, theological and moral grounds. None the less, as in the famous show trials of the 1930s, the Party found ways of extracting a 'confession' from him for his errors. In July 1949 the Holy Office replied to this injustice by stating that anyone who actively supported communist parties was excommunicated. It was the most absolute rejection of that creed which the Church had yet issued.[48]

The strong policy towards communism and its socialist allies had its effect on attitudes to those in the Christian Democrat party in Italy who were in favour of bringing the Marxist Italian Socialist Party into government; this they reasoned would weaken Italian communism as a whole and bring the working class into the political system. This Pius XII rejected because the Socialist Party still favoured the class struggle and revolution as the means to political power. The question of how to treat the communist parties and what the policy of the Church would be was a disciplinary one, not one of faith or morals, and it depended on how one read the signs of the times. The fear engendered by what seemed to be a communist monolith, threatening human freedom and the basic security of the West, was considerable in those early days of the Cold War, and Pius XII was influenced, not only by the historic and fundamentally spiritual and theological reasons for the rejection of Marxism, but by the geopolitical menace the communist powers presented. His successor John XXIII was to read the signs of his times quite differently on this issue.

## Human dignity and the family

Pius XII saw the family as under threat, not only from communism, but from other influences. The individual and the family, the fundamental building blocks of society, were being manipulated by the authorities without regard to the basic human rights of the persons affected; forced emigration, deportation and repatriation showed this disregard, as did the manner in which displaced persons were dealt with after the war.[63] He regarded stability, attachment to territory and historical tradition as essential to man and to the community; the separation of members of the family, and the degradation of individuals regarded simply as masses of the displaced, undermined these values.

People were also having to rely too much on society for their social needs in some States and of course communist totalitarianism regarded this as a good in itself.[64] Where there was greater freedom, on the other hand, there was a danger of an extreme individualism, a determination that man should make his own values, and if he chose, deny his responsibilities to others and so undermine the social fabric. Technological developments were also minimizing human values and rights. Society was regarded as a subject for experimentation, without regard to historical developments, the habits, the customs, and the faith of the people, which were reflected in their cultural and social institutions.[65]

## Capitalism, trade unionism and State welfare

As the 1950s progressed, Pius showed more appreciation of the positive side of socially responsible capitalism, which avoided the old evils of liberal capitalism. As a strong defender of the right of ownership of productive goods, the Church was also a defender of the market economy and its freedom, but within a framework of moral law, given substance by the just laws of the land. *Rerum Novarum* had declared that the first requirement for the solution of the labour question was that the private ownership of productive goods must continue, because without it the springs of the wealth which would enable society to relieve poverty would dry up. *Quadragesimo Anno* had stressed that the system was not of itself evil. Both encyclicals, however, had insisted that it could do evil in the manner of its operation. It had done so in the past and it could in the present and in the future. Liberal capitalism, which thought and thinks that total freedom provides its own correctives, is rejected; capitalism itself is accepted in the context of social responsibility and the universal purpose of created goods.

Since the system was now returning to the workers a fairer share of the wealth they had helped to create, its more positive virtues could be recognized. So Pius XII showed a greater appreciation of the role of banks and bankers than Pius XI. He commended their role in enabling the small saver to secure and increase his savings. They also encouraged thrift, and put money to use in providing capital for useful enterprises; they also facilitated financial dealings between private parties, businesses and States. Capital's role in society in general was valuable – it helped economic development and vitality, and provided employment. In this it fulfilled one of the conditions of moral approval of private ownership of productive goods – that God's gift of the earth to mankind in general should increase the prosperity of all: and that meant offering to all the opportunity to support themselves by their labour. To fail to invest capital because of excessive caution, and so reduce the employment opportunities for others, was in fact sinful. Profits were morally justified and positively good where they were the result of efficient and socially responsible service of real human needs. Because he served society in this way, the capitalist was socially valuable, using his talents to serve the community, and the mechanisms through which he was able to do so, free competition especially, were good also; the latter could no longer be seen as endlessly destructive. Indeed it was to be encouraged.[66] Investment in useful enterprises is a social virtue and it is undesirable that only a small group within society should have the capital, savings, to invest. Workers as well as capitalists should be able to save, and it is one of the evils of the existing system as he saw it that it was difficult for the worker to accumulate property for himself.[67]

The success of the social organization of workers in industry through trade unions was also one of the undoubted marks of progress in the post-war years. In Belgium and the Netherlands for example the Catholic unions grew to rival in size those of the Socialists. In France and Italy, though less strong, they still organized a sizeable number of workers.[68] In the other democracies, in particular those of the USA and Great Britain, participation in secular unions had been the way for members of the Church and continued so to be. Pius XII grew critical of certain aspects of union activity as the years passed.[69] Animosity towards other social classes was one such; another was the attempt to get such control over the workers that they could not find employment unless they were union members, as when there was a 'closed' or 'union' shop. This policy was considered by those who supported it as essential to the effectiveness of trade unions in contexts in which management was unfavourable to them. Such policies however had many critics among those responsible for organizing and administering industrial relations generally, and those writing and teaching on them, and in that context Pius XII's views were not by any means outlandish. To counteract what he saw as these anti-social ways in which unionism was developing, Pius XII began to urge corporatism once again, and he preferred it to the idea of copartnership or some form of worker participation along the lines suggested by Pius XI. Corporatism found no response among those concerned with the organization of labour management relations, however, because it was impossible to imagine the conditions in which it might be put into practice, even if the concept was clear and in theory sound, which it was not. Copartnership, on the other hand, had its supporters because it was clearly practicable. It was also very much in vogue in the early 1950s in Germany, France and the Netherlands. Pius XII had reservations about it insofar as it seemed to subject the enterprise to outside interference.[70]

Finally a unique experiment by the Church in France to close the gap between it and the industrial working classes in that country had been developing after the war in the form of a worker-priest movement – that is, priests who worked full time in industrial occupations. It grew out of the experience of priests and seminarians who had been drafted for forced labour by the Nazis during the 1939 war, and of those who had gone voluntarily to look after the spiritual needs of their fellow countrymen. In peacetime they found a kindred spirit in Cardinal Suhard, Archbishop of Paris from 1940 to 1959, who had founded the *Mission de France* in 1940 to try to rouse Catholics to the need to counteract the dechristianization of the country, and it was with his authority that a first group of six peacetime worker priests began their apostolate. Six were assigned to the work in 1946 and by 1951 the number had risen to ninety-one. By that time the lack of preparation for those who volunteered for this very difficult ministry, the corrosive secularism they encountered, and the extreme left-wing politicization of the French workers, had resulted in serious questions being raised about the experiment, and in 1953 Rome ordered the end of recruitment for it, the bishops and religious superiors concerned being told to recall priests engaged in it.[71] It was eventually continued in a more limited form with priests having a directly pastoral ministry of a more traditional kind as well as a role as workers.

The increasing provision by the State for the social welfare of individuals and families was one of the main characteristics of the Western democracies in the 1950s, and social Catholics in the various countries had had a great deal of influence in the formation of such policies.[72] These were acceptable in principle provided their practical applications did not reduce personal responsibility too much; as the 1950s went on Pius XII was not convinced that they were avoiding this danger. The State should not have complete responsibility for every aspect of life from cradle to grave, as he had warned earlier.[73] If the State cannot be denied the rights which liberals refused to give it, it is not its task to take over 'economic, cultural and social functions which can be handled by other institutions'.[74]

## The new nations

In his encyclical *Evangelii Praecones*[75] (1951) on the Christian missions, the Pope spoke of the social reforms needed in many countries. Warning against the temptation to put earthly prosperity first, as some social philosophies do, he recalls the teaching of *Summi Pontificatus* and its warning that the goods of the world were given to the whole of humanity; in relief of poverty, charity is not enough: justice must be done. It demands that God's purpose in creating the goods of the earth be recognized; the purpose was that the dignity of everyman might be secured by access to property; all have a right of access to what they need to sustain life; economic dependence and servitude is irreconcilable with man's rights as a person [EP 49–53].

In another letter on the same topic, *Fidei Donum* in 1957,[76] he looks at the new Churches in Africa especially, in nations which were just beginning to face the problems of independence, concerned with growing populations, faced with the unequal division of natural resources and the underdevelopment of some regions, and he dealt with this theme in several other addresses in the weeks before his death in 1958.[77] It was towards the end of the 1950s that the imbalance between the industrialized nations of the West and the less developed regions of what was mainly the former colonial world, was being recognized as a challenge to the stability of international economy and community.

## 6  Summary analysis of his social teaching 1939–58

### (i)  Ethics and civil society

The key social virtue of solidarity grows out of our common human nature, our being persons created by God in his own image and likeness, brothers and sisters in Christ who died to redeem all, men and women, young and old, of whatever race, colour or creed. Society is then not to be seen as an agglomeration of individuals but as a unity, a people under God. We all have the same father [SP 42]. It is that unity, this relationship to God and one another, which gives all a right to a share in the wealth of the world to sustain and develop life [SP 38]. It is this which unites nation with nation while each cherishes its own identity and makes its contribution to the world's wealth and culture.

The uniqueness of individual persons, and the basic human society founded by them, the family, gives rights to them and it prior to those of the State [SP 61–74]. Civil society springs from man's social nature, his desire to co-operate and live with others in an organized group to further their social, cultural, economic and other needs. This he does by forming associations of all kinds and it is out of them that the State, the political authority, is formed. Society, and the State, are built up by the family and the social collaboration of groups: an organic unity of mature and responsible persons, not a simple collection of individuals to be dominated by political authority. Man's inviolable human rights must be secure within it [Christmas message 1942]. The family must be protected against manipulation by the authorities and human rights must be served. Stability, attachment to territory and historical tradition were essential for man and the human community.

### (ii) Ethics and political society

The moral foundations of the State therefore rest on its function in guiding society, its individual members and the organizations within it, towards the true common good [SP 55–8], that is, the harmonious development of man's natural perfection according to God's plan [SP 59]. To make service of the State the supreme end of life and the final arbiter of the moral and judicial order is to put it in the place of God [SP 52–4]. Recognition of the dignity of man and his essential human rights is to be the basis of a sound political order, the acceptance that society and state are built upon the family and the private groups within them (Christmas message 1942).

The true social and political order therefore must be founded on sound moral principles, drawn from the divine and natural law [SP 79–81]. It must proceed from Christ as its indispensable foundation, be actuated by justice and crowned with charity [SP 83]. The Church's role *vis-à-vis* the State is to serve and not to dominate; she does not claim to take the place of the legitimate secular authority in its own sphere but, like her founder, to go about doing good. She who civilizes nations has never retarded the civil progress of mankind, at which she is pleased and glad [SP 101–2]. Hers is a genuine humanitarian concern, founded on the desire that all should see Christ and his Church in their true light, working for the rising generation according to the principles of truth and love; the masses and the children are her special concern.

On the forms of government, the experience of recent years confirms the people today in the conviction that democracy is a natural postulate, imposed by reason itself (Radio Message 24 December 1944). Yet democracy is not to be manipulated, the elected and the electors need to be aware of both of their personal responsibility and of their rights, tolerating those differences which do not challenge basic equality, justice and charity. Christian belief, and the high moral standards it inculcates, can strengthen society in this [SP 108]. Recognition of the dignity of man and his essential human rights is paramount.

The relations between States must be built on the right foundation, and the law regulating them likewise. The indispensable presupposition of all international relations is mutual trust, and this can only exist if the divine law is the basis of those relations. Private interests and collective selfishness should not dominate over rights. Treaties may need renegotiating after the passage of time, but unilateral abandonment of them destroys trust [SP 77]. All nations, great and small, have an equal right to existence and independence, and their just demands in this respect must be met. Between them, lasting peace is only possible on the basis of organized and progressive disarmament and the existence of a juridical institution guaranteeing the faithful fulfilment of agreements (Christmas message 1939). All must give their citizens full political freedom and grant minorities their rights; they must also actively develop their economies in a world which ensures that its resources are for the use of all (Christmas message 1941).

There must be an organization to maintain peace, with the power, based on consent, to restrain aggression. In peacemaking those responsible for the war must accept the consequences, but they must be treated with justice and have the hope of returning to the community of nations. Solidarity must be the framework of international relations; war crimes must be punished, but not whole peoples. Above all, the lesson of the war must be the need to rule international affairs by moral principle (Christmas message 1942).

## (iii) Ethics and economic society

The solidarity that stems from all having God as Father of all makes humanity one, and gives to all who share his gift of the earth the right of access to its material resources [SP 38]. The struggle to obtain a more equal distribution of the goods intended for all contributed to the conflict of the Second World War [SP 82–3]. The need for overcoming economic inequality so that people of all classes have access to a decent standard of living was one of the four points stressed in the Christmas message of 1940, and in 1941 the point was stressed again; there is no room for that egoism among nations which tends to monopolize economic resources and materials intended for the use of all to the exclusion of the less favoured. Those who look to the machinery of the market alone for the salvation of mankind will be disillusioned; they are the slaves of wealth sought without any regard for the higher ends of man. In the 1950s Pius XII showed an awareness of the problems of poverty in the new nations of the world and re-emphasized the message of his first encyclical, that all the world's peoples have a right of access to the goods which enable them to sustain life and maintain their dignity as human beings.

The private ownership of productive goods should remain the basis of the economy. It is necessary in order to encourage initiative in economic matters, to encourage hard work, as a means to achieving the temporal and transcendental purposes of life, the liberty and dignity of man created in God's image. That socially responsible capitalism was of positive value to the community was stressed in the 1950s. The role of bankers and financiers was better appreciated than in the 1930s; they helped the individual increase his capital and facilitate, the financial arrangements which could stimulate or stabilize economies, so encouraging socially valuable investment. Competition and profits were positively good when they served the community; such capitalism had to be encouraged rather than reviled. Capital, however, was in too few hands; it should be more widely distributed. A just social order does not exist when a man cannot by his labour get property for himself and his family;[78] This opportunity gives him an incentive to work, and gives him the freedom to attain the spiritual and material ends of life in a manner of one made in God's image. It also helps the economy if property is widely distributed and profitably used.[79]

Defence of the principle of private property therefore should not be regarded as a defence of the *status quo*. Excessive concentration of economic ownership leads to neglect of the social responsibilities attached to it, and makes it more difficult for the worker to accumulate property himself; too often it means that the workers are treated like pawns in a game.[80] The role of unions is to represent and defend the interests of the workers in industry; this gives them political influence, but if they go further, their nature as defensive organizations is changed and their legitimacy is questioned.[81] The hope of a better life for the workers lies in a slow evolution of the system, the marshalling of private property, and its wider distribution for the well-being of the whole people. The activities of private associations in providing social security in its various forms must be supplemented by the State, though not to the extent of encouraging citizens to be dependent on it.[82] The State has also the right to expropriate or own productive goods where the common good requires it, but this is to be the exception not the rule. To make nationalization the norm would reverse the acceptable order of things, since the role of the State is to serve private rights, not to absorb them.[83] In the 1950s, when State social welfare provisions had increased in scope and number, Pius XII's reservations about it increased, though the principle was never challenged. The state cannot be denied the more positive role that the Liberals refused to give it, but it was not its task to take over economic, cultural and social functions which others or other institutions could handle.[84]

He warned about the possibly antisocial nature of some aspects of union activity, such as seeking to make union membership compulsory, and he expressed his preference for corporatism, but did not press it when it received no response. He had reservations about some forms of copartnership in industry which were developing in Europe in the post-war years insofar as they seemed to make the enterprise subject to some extent to outside control. The idea of full-time worker priests as a way of overcoming the alienation of the workers was finally rejected, though a form of such an apostolate on a part-time basis was approved.

# 20

# John XXIII (1958–63)

## 1 The pontificate of John XXIII[1]

Angelo Guiseppe Roncalli, Patriarch of Venice, was elected Pope on 28 October 1958. Born in 1881, he was almost 77 years old on his appointment to the Papacy, and at that age he was seen as simply a caretaker whose brief reign would open the way for someone more capable of handling the responsibilities of the office. In fact, in reviving the idea of calling a council, which had been discussed in the 1950s, he set in train events which mark his reign as one of the great turning points in the history of the Church.

Guiseppe was the third of 13 children of a peasant farmer at Sotto il Monte near Bergamo in Central Lombardy. From the village school he went on to study at the two seminaries in Bergamo and then completed doctoral studies at the Apollinare in Rome in 1901. After a spell as secretary to the Bishop of Bergamo from 1905 to 1914, and then as Professor of Church History at the seminary, he served as a hospital orderly and later chaplain in the Italian army. The experience gave him, among other things, a unique insight into the relationship of the Church to civil society in Italy, and it revealed and confirmed a broadness of vision and a depth of human sympathy which marked his character, and which grew directly out of his profound grasp of the Gospel, the love of the Church and of all men. When peace came, Benedict XV gave him the post of national director of the Congregation for the Propagation of the Faith, and in 1925 Pius XI recruited him for the Vatican's diplomatic service, appointing him apostolic visitor to Bulgaria, and then delegate to Turkey and Greece in 1934–44.

In these latter posts, not easy ones because of the religious and

* The notes and references for Chapter 20 are to be found on p. 452ff

historical conflicts and tensions which underlay the political and ecclesiastical relationships in the region, he developed a genuine and convinced ecumenism which, like the broad human sympathies he placed at the disposal of his fellow countrymen in the war years, were founded in the Gospel and his service of the Church and humanity. He established excellent relations with the Turkish government and the Orthodox Church, while during the German occupation of Greece from 1941 to 1944 he was active in mitigating as far as could be the persecution the Jews were undergoing. From 1944 he was nuncio in France, where among other things he had contact with the worker-priest movement. He also represented the Vatican at UNESCO. In 1953 he was appointed Cardinal and three days later, on 15 January, he became Archbishop and Patriarch of Venice. On 28 October 1958 he was elected successor of St Peter and took the name John XXIII. In 1959 he announced his intention of calling what became the Second Vatican Council; it met for the first time on 11 October 1962 and concluded the fourth and final session on 7 December 1965.

This caretaker Pope then did indeed live on for only six more years, but they were the years in which the Church equipped herself to face the growing problems of the modern world. His service in the First World War, and in the Vatican diplomatic corps in the Balkans and Turkey from the 1930s, through the Second War years, and in the aftermath of that war, meant that he was very much a man of his times and its suffering, and very well equipped to lead it in the modern world. John XXIII was a man in a hurry to get his message of hope and joy across that world and it is significant that he published two social encyclicals in this short period, *Mater et Magistra* in 1961 when the Council was being prepared and another, *Pacem in Terris*, in 1963, when it was in session and he was presiding at it.

## 2 The social, political and economic background to *Mater et Magistra* (1961)

### (i) The Welfare State and modern capitalism

The British Prime Minister in the late 1950s, Harold Macmillan, was quoted as having said, during the General Election of 1959, that under the Conservative Party the British people had 'never had it so good'.[2] He was referring to the booming trade of the 1950s which,

combined with the influence of Keynesian economics, helped
ensure full employment, and the presence of the Welfare State
which provided a full range of social services for all.[3] Yet it was being
realized even then that the prosperity of the whole, or a major part
of society, does not necessarily mean a happier or healthier society,
and this realization was to hit home increasingly with the social
unrest in Western Europe and the United States in the late 1960s.
The related question of developing the Welfare State in such a way
that it did not undermine personal responsibility had been the
cause of growing and increasingly bitter and ideological discussion
in Catholic circles during the pontificate of Pius XII. It was a matter
of some urgency that a more comprehensive response should be
given on the question, and it came in this encyclical.

What we have called the *Rerum Novarum* agenda was still very
much relevant in the industrialized West. The problems of worker-
management relations, the role of the unions in industry, and the
residual problems left by a curbed but by no means eliminated
liberal capitalist mentality in influential circles, were ever present in
one form or another in most countries. There was less major unemployment, and wages and conditions had generally improved;
the question of the alienation of the worker from the system was still
a real one; and so it remains.

## (ii) The third world

Although both Pius XI and Pius XII had shown concern for the
problems of the international economy and what we now call the
third or the underdeveloped world,[4] it was not until the concern
had become vast and world wide, the social and economic issues
had attracted the attentions of experts in the social sciences and of
practical politicians, and the lines of possible solutions in technical
terms had clarified themselves, that the Church could give a fuller
response. She herself has neither the mandate nor the resources to
work out such possible solutions, the finding of which is the
responsibility of those who have care for the common good; only
when they have become clearer can she seek to give her people
help in facing the moral dilemmas the social crises present. As the
1950s merged into the 1960s, the size of the crisis in this field was
being realized.

The contrast between the social, political and economic
prospects of the mainly Western industrialized countries and those
of the non-industrialized, or less industrialized, of the former colo-

nial worlds of Latin America, Africa and much of the East was one which could not be ignored. First because, through the development of the media, even in the less developed societies, the peoples of those countries were aware of their comparative deprivation, and, through the existence of movements for social reform and revolution which an increasingly well-educated and politically conscious international society produced, they were able to register, or threaten to register a protest which tended to violence. Alignment with one superpower or the other became a matter of importance to those superpowers. The latter were therefore prepared, to a certain extent, at least to sit up and take notice of events in this third world as affecting their vital interests.[5] For those from the communist bloc, stoking up revolution where they could do so was part of their understanding of their political role.

One particular region, Latin America, became of particular importance in this regard. Since independence came to the colonial empires of Spain and Portugal in the nineteenth century, the new nations which were formed from them had been plagued by problems of poverty and political instability which frequently led to bloodshed, revolution, and periods of dictatorship. Independence had done little for the mass of the people in terms of improving living standards and the hope of a better life, but the spirit of freedom remained strong and the will was for better democratic systems which would give justice for all, rather than for totalitarianism; the *caudillo* tradition in itself, though frequently brutal and unjust in pursuit of narrow and selfish interests, did not tend to totalitarianism until Fascism and Soviet communism began to exert their influence in the first part of this century.

In the growing demand for a better life for all which was being heard internationally from the 1950s, and in which Russian and Chinese communism was able to pose as the champion of the poor against the capitalist West, the situation became more serious. Democratic capitalist models, previously thought relevant to the Latin American situation, were being challenged and the communist revolutionary economic alternative was being found attractive. In that most of the population of the region were at least nominal Catholics and the Church was consequently strong there, this posed a problem for her; the size and scale of it was to become apparent with the excesses of some forms of liberation theology in the next twenty years. We will have to look at this background more fully in the next two chapters. For the moment it is enough to recall that in 1959 Fidel Castro's revolution, a social democratic one in the first instance, had succeeded, and as it did so it turned communist; the lesson for unjust or incompetent governments and ruling elites in the third world was that they were no longer safe. Communist and revolutionary violence in that world was set to increase, and this had repercussions on international politics: the governments of the West were then involved willy-nilly.

The situation also had implications for the Church internationally; there were moral issues here which transcended national interests. The teaching of *Mater et Magistra* would help to focus on them and clarify them for members of the Church, and hopefully for all men of goodwill. In that it also dealt with the question of justice for the agricultural sector, in both the developed and the underdeveloped world, it underlined the importance of this sector for the economic life of peoples throughout the world. It was in agriculture that most of them were engaged and the question of food supplies in the underdeveloped countries was crucial; improving productivity and the standard of life on the farms, especially the small farm, was on any rational calculation, the first priority in development.

## (iii) Population and resources

The questions of population growth in the poorer countries, and of the adequacy of the world's resources in supplying the needs of potential population increase, were linked with the problems of the third world. The received wisdom of the 1960s and 1970s was to be that population growth would outrun food supplies and other resources unless every possible step was taken to reduce it. Though the panic had not yet reached its zenith when the encyclical was in preparation, the concern was already wide enough to require a response from the Church, and in *Mater et Magistra* it came.

Paul Ehrlich was probably the best known of those who thought the panic justified. He predicted that 'In the 1970s, the world will undergo famines; hundreds of millions will starve to death'.[6] What in fact happened was that new agricultural methods resulted in increases in food production which far outstripped population growth. There were famines, but they were on a much smaller scale than he predicted and were the result of natural disasters or political and economic mismanagement, not population growth. Taking 1951 as a base, world food production increased by 2.75 per cent by 1992 and population by 2.2 per cent.[7] Population did not rocket. 'In the second half of the 1960s, after millennia of creeping upwards, the rate of population growth began to slow'.[8] Fertility fell without exception, and this was not all due to contraception. 'Strong cultural resistance to contraception in some countries [resulted] in delays in marriage and an increase in lifelong celibacy rather than family planning.'[9]

Far from the overall statistics showing a decline in living standards in the underdeveloped world,

> life expectancy rose from 46 years in 1960 to 62 in 1987 ... adult literacy from 43% to 60%. Under-five mortality was halved. Despite the addition of 2 billion people in the developing countries, food production exceeded the rise in population by 20%.[10]

Nor is there any scientific evidence that the growth of population in the future is going to outstrip predicted food production. Since this involves peering into the future and making judgements about trends which can only be speculative, it is not a scientific exercise but an art. Doomsters insist on prophecy, however, and some efforts have to be made to put things in proportion.

It is estimated that by 2050 today's 5.7 billion will be between 9.8 and 12 billion.[11] It is not realistic to look beyond 2050 because of the uncertainties of such forecasts. Estimates of the world potential in terms of food production vary, but they do not justify belief they will be inadequate. Dr Pawley of the FAO estimated in 1971 that the world could increase food supplies by a factor of fifty,[12] Colin Clark in 1977 that it could support 47 billion at US standards.[13] More recently Paul Waggoner, an American agronomist at the Connecticut Agricultural Experimental Station in New Haven, stressed that the limit to future food supply is set by human ingenuity, not physical resources. He estimated that a population of 1,000 billion could be supported if the full array of techniques were to be used; what can be done is only limited by the amount of money spent to develop new technologies, and to provide the credit and technical assistance to farmers in the developing world to use the technologies that already exist.[14]

The fear that other resources, energy and industrial raw materials, for example, would run out were equally exaggerated.[15] There always has been a problem here; it costs labour and capital to exploit resources and sometimes these are not adequate for the task; but the measure of scarcity, which is the cost in real terms of those resources in labour and their prices relative to wages and other goods, suggests that they are becoming less so.

> The costs of raw materials have fallen sharply over the period of recorded history, no matter which reasonable measure of cost

one chooses to use ... these costs are the best basis for predicting the trends of future cost too.

As P. T. Bauer puts it,

> our predictions are firmly based on the way these problems have
> been overcome in the past. And it is only the past that gives us
> any insight into the laws of motion of human society and hence
> enables us to predict the future.[16]

Human ingenuity has never failed yet in developing the world and
its wealth for its purposes or finding substitutes for things in short
supply, and there are no rational grounds for thinking it will not do
so in the future; indeed with the increase of knowledge and technology at our command, power to do this is greater than ever. So too
with the environment; carelessness in development has caused
considerable damage to it in the past and care will be needed to see
it does not do so in the future. But again the problem can be solved
if the political will and resources are there; it was calculated for
example that the cost of putting right the damage being done to the
American environment by all causes amounted to just one year's
rise in living standards.[17] There is now great concern over the
phenomenon of global warming; that it has taken and is taking
place virtually all scientists agree, but what exactly it signifies and
how much reliance can be placed on the computer-based simula-
tions of the warming and the assumptions on which they are based,
is more problematical.[18] There has been concern among environ-
mentalists themselves that some of the predictions of the green
lobby have been irresponsible and inaccurate; the American environmental journalist Greg Easterbrook has listed some: forests have
not been destroyed by pollution in Europe or America, fossil fuels
have not been exhausted, growing population has not caused
world-wide food shortages, wildlife species have not been made
extinct on a massive scale, and using toxic chemicals has not led to
widespread poisoning.[19]

The predictions of the doomsters then do not stand up to examination – but that does not mean that there is any room for
complacency, especially regarding poverty and malnutrition generally. We must constantly press for the use of all possible means that
exist or could be brought into being to overcome them; social and
political will in the exploitation of man's potential power for good
here, must always be sufficiently strong to meet the challenges. In
1990 there were still some one billion living in absolute poverty
throughout the world, 100 million homeless and 150 million seri-

ously malnourished children.[20] The answer does not lie exclusively in population control, although that can be part of the answer where the rapid growth of population in a particular country in which the resources needed to cope with it are short for the immediate future. But the much more important task is to increase the pace of social and economic development because as standards of living rise, population increase slows[21], as the study of demographic transition has shown, and social and economic development depends on a variety of factors.

Prominent among them in the third world is enabling the peasant farmers, in what are mainly agricultural economies, to produce food and raw materials as cheaply and as efficiently as possible. This requires stable and honest government and administration, fully committed to agricultural reform and improvement, ensuring that the farmers improve their efficiency and that the training, advice and encouragement to enable them to do this is available. Financial help where needed is important, as is an equitable tax and land tenure system, together with co-operation between producers, and a firm and clear law of contracts, property and liability.[22] The farmer must also be assured of a fair price for his products and the best way to do this is through a free market, which, however, needs to be fair and seen to be fair to both the producer and the customer, and to the community at large.

If we look at countries which have been badly affected by famine and other natural disasters in the last twenty or thirty years it becomes evident that it is the absence of good government, peace and stability which causes starvation, not overpopulation. Many African countries have been particularly afflicted by famine, drought and disease, but in Ethiopia it was war as much as drought that caused famine, and not overpopulation; an important element in the Communist regime's war against the guerillas was the destruction of the tribal farming system: it was a deliberate State-sponsored atrocity.[23] In Sudan, though food was available after the best harvest of the decade, rival armies cynically starved a quarter of a million people to strengthen their bargaining positions.[24] One report concluded that

> Government policy sets the stage for all famines; if proper policies are in place, natural disaster need not evolve into famine. Poor policies and armed conflict heighten a nation's vulnerability to natural disasters.[25]

Armed conflict coincided with drought conditions in Chad, Angola, Ethiopia, Sudan and Mozambique during the famines. Those who starved did so as a result of these causes, not overpopulation. The African countries most badly hit by famines were among the least populated, having some of the lowest population densities in the world. That for Ethiopia was 109 per square mile, Sudan 25.8, Chad 10, and Mozambique 50.8. All the African famines of the 1970s and 1980s occurred in little-populated countries. That in the Sahel region in the early 1970s affected 20 million people who occupied an area covering 2 million square miles, equivalent to two-thirds of the continental United States excluding Alaska. The Sahel's problem is not overpopulation; it has so little population that it is almost totally undeveloped.[26] Population policy has its part to play in tackling poverty in the short term where population densities are high and resources are therefore under strain, but it is economic and social development which is the priority in the long run, not population policy. The carrying capacity of our planet is determined by politics, by economic factors, technology, social patterns, all of which are within our control. We are not in the hands of blind fate.

Many of the differences of opinion concerning population, resources and ecology arise from the doomster approach of the prosperous Malthusians determined to prove that we are in the hands of forces beyond our control which will eventually destroy the prosperity of the prosperous such as themselves. This so angers them that they then accuse the less prosperous of being the agents of their destruction and presume they have the right to remove that threat by forcing contraception or abortion on them, or by predicting mass starvation – with the implication that it will serve them right because they bring it upon themselves by their fecundity. Morally responsible control of population where it can pose too great a threat to the common good is of course sometimes necessary as a temporary measure until balance is restored, but it is only a small part of the answer and it is becoming less a part of it. The United Nations is now already concerned about the new demographic crisis – which currently affects 51 countries and will soon affect another 37, countries containing two thirds of the world's population. It is the problem not of too many people but of too few. 2.1 children per woman of the population is the fertility rate needed for population stability, whereas in Italy, Germany, Japan and Spain it is much less than this, as it is in Brazil and Thailand and soon will be in Indonesia, India and Bangladesh; only in countries in Africa, where thinly populated territories are recovering from war did population increase between 1963 and 1993. In the Muslim Middle East and Pakistan population is declining less slowly than elsewhere. Countries in which population is falling are up against problems; fewer in the active real economy means there is less wealth available to support the young, the sick, the old and the bureaucracies which keep government in operation. There will be shortages of labour in the less desirable occupations. Only an increased birth rate or immigration will solve these problems.

As to the world's economy and resources being unable to support foreseeable population growth, the pessimists rely on the concept of the physical limits to growth. Assuming that the present methods of production of food and that the exploitation of natural resources cannot be improved, and contemplating the growth of population predicted, they tell us it is all going to end in disaster. But the concept of the physical limits to growth is not valid.

> If we take into account the creative potential of man, there is no foreseeable limitation on the basic natural resources of food production which are space, water, climatic conditions, solar energy and man made inputs. All these resources are either unlimited or can be expanded, better utilized or redesigned to a very great extent. That might be why several experts have denied there is any upper limit to 'production growth'. The notion of 'physical limits to growth is a faulty concept'

There have been and always will be problems of resources and the environment but there always will be answers to them also, if the human will and the political readiness is there to put them into practice

> The carrying capacity of our earth is a problem of political planning, education, social balance, economic restructuring and institutional efficiency. We are far from physical or biological limits if, but only if, we use creativity, social responsibility, economic initiative and political vision.[27]

Man, his creativity and his potential, is man's most important resource but he must use moral means to achieve moral ends, and accept his responsibility for his neighbour's good as well as his own. We do right to be concerned whether man will face up to his responsibilities here, but if he does not he cannot blame anyone but himself.

## 3 Summary of the text of *Mater et Magistra* (1961)[28]

The occasion of the publication of this encyclical was the seventi-
eth anniversary of *Rerum Novarum*; it commemorates that
document and underlines its continuing importance, but it also
takes into account the changing nature of social problems and
responds to key aspects of them, as a consideration of its contents
reveals. There is an Introduction [1–9], and four main sections: I.
*Rerum Novarum* and afterwards [10–50]. II. The teaching of that
encyclical [51–121]. III. New aspects of the social problem
[122–211]. IV. The rebuilding of the social order [212–64].

### Introduction

> Mother and teacher of the nations, such is the Catholic Church
> in the mind of her founder Jesus Christ; to hold the world in an
> embrace of love, that men in every age, should find in her their
> own completeness in a higher order of living and their ultimate
> salvation. She is the pillar and ground of truth. [1].

Christianity is the meeting point of earth and heaven. It lays claim
to the whole man, body and soul, intellect and will, inducing him
to raise his mind above the changing conditions of this earthly existence and reach upwards for the eternal life of heaven, where one
day he will find his unfailing happiness and peace [2]. Though the
church's concern is primarily for souls [3], like her master Christ
she must have 'compassion on the multitude' [4], a compassion
which is spiritual also [5]. For two thousand years, since the minis-
tration of her deacons began, she has followed Christ in this love
[6]. *Rerum Novarum* is an outstanding example of her social teaching and action [7]. It opened up for that Church new horizons in
her mission of championing and restoring of the rights of the
oppressed [8]. The Popes since Leo XIII have drawn upon his
teaching and the legislation of some States has been influenced by
it [9].

### I. *Rerum Novarum* and afterwards

Leo XIII addressed the problems of his time [10]. Economics had
been separated from morality. Market forces knew no restraint.
Personal gain alone mattered; all aspects of economic life were
determined by a purely mechanical working of the market, and the
civil authority was excluded from it as far as possible. Unions were

merely tolerated where not forbidden [11]. The might of the strongest predominated [12]. The few were excessively rich, workers' wages were generally inadequate, conditions of work, including those for women and children, were poor [13], and extreme remedies were favoured by many workers, cures worse than the disease [14]. Leo XIII defended their legitimate rights in what is 'a compendium of Catholic social and economic teaching' [15]. Far from simply preaching resignation for the poor and charity for the rich, Leo defended the legitimate rights of the poor [16] as is well known [17].

*Work*
Firstly he insisted that work was a human and necessary activity, the means of livelihood for the majority, and that wages must be in accord with justice and equity; they cannot rely on market forces alone [18]. Property is a natural right 'but with a social obligation as well'; it must be exercised for the good not only of the owner but of all [19]. The State's care for the common good includes promotion of 'a sufficient supply of material goods, the use of which is necessary for virtue'[29] and also to protect the weak and 'better the conditions of the working man' [20]. The State is to ensure protection of 'the human dignity of workers'; the development of labour law and social legislation by States here is welcomed [21]. There is a right of association of workers alone, or workers and employers together, and workers can work 'freely and without hindrance' to defend their legitimate professional interests [22]. The relations between workers and employers should be those of human solidarity and Christian brotherhood, not Marxist class warfare or liberal capitalism [23]. These principles were correct [24]. Not only Catholics agree with them [25]. Leo's work is the *magna carta* of social and economic reconstruction [26].

## II The encyclical *Quadragesimo Anno* (1931)

Forty years afterwards [27] Pius XI clarified points that had caused problems [28], mainly on private property and moderate socialism [29].

*Private property*
The origins in natural law of private property were reaffirmed and 'its social aspect and the obligations of ownership' enlarged upon [30]. The wage system was confirmed as acceptable but its inhumanities in practice were condemned, and justice and equity

insisted on [31]. Modification of the wage contract so that 'wage earners and other employees participate in the ownership, management, or in some way share in the profits' was recommended [32]. The factors to be taken into account in determining the just wage were also considered [33].

*Socialism*
Some forms of moderate socialism present policies which do not conflict with Christian teaching. But even moderate socialism, if it knows no other purpose for society but material well-being, is incompatible with Catholicism [34].

*Changes in capitalism*
Unregulated competition had led to concentration of economic power in the hands of a few, and for the most part they were administrators of funds rather than owners [35]. 'The whole economic regime had become hard, cruel and relentless in a frightful measure' [36].

*The remedy*
Economic order must be within the framework of moral order secured by independent economic and vocational/corporate bodies, with the public authority procuring the common good. International co-operation is needed for the economic well-being of all [37]. The supreme criterion in economic matters must not be the needs of special interests, of unregulated competition, or national prestige [38]. Justice and charity should prevail nationally and internationally [39]. A national and international juridical order should exist in which economic activity can be conducted for the common good [40].

## Pius XII: on the fiftieth anniversary of *Rerum Novarum* 1941

Pius XII in a radio message of 1 June 1941 [41] stressed three particular aspects of Leo's foundation document affecting property, work and the family [42]. Concerning property, material goods 'the right of every man to use these for his own sustenance is prior to every other economic right, even that of private property'. The latter 'cannot stand in the way of the axiomatic principle that "the goods of the earth which were created by God for all men should flow to all alike, according to the principle of justice and charity"'[43]. Mutual relations at work, work being a duty and right, should be regulated by the State if the parties cannot do so for the common good [44]. Private property has a part to play in promoting family welfare; it is in it that the right to emigrate is rooted [45].

## Changes in the economic climate since the 1940s

These have been many [46]. In the developed nations nuclear power, synthetic materials, automation, modernized agriculture, television, faster travel, interplanetary exploration are among developments that have affected society [47]. Social insurance and security systems have expanded, trade unions have shown aware- ness of major social and economic problems; education and awareness of the world have grown, essential commodities are available to more people, opportunity for advancement and the breaking down of social barriers has increased; there are also glaring discrepancies between sectors and groups in national communities and 'a marked disparity in the economic wealth possessed by different countries' [48]. More citizens are taking part in public life, governments are more concerned with social and economic issues; new nations have appeared in Asia and Africa, and awareness of international interdependence is growing [49]. The purpose of this encyclical is not only to confirm the exist- ing teaching but to determine the mind of the Church today on new problems [50].

## III Developing the teaching of *Rerum Novarum*

*Private property and the economy*

In the economic order, first place must be given to the personal initiative of private citizens working either as individuals or in association with each other in various ways for the furtherance of common interests [51].

At the same time the State has a role [52] in directing, stimulating, co-ordinating, supplying and integrating production in accordance with the principle of subsidiary function. That is, that persons and private organizations should be left to manage their own affairs; the larger organization, especially the State, should only interfere when it is necessary to help them achieve their ends. 'Of its very nature the true aim of all social activity should be to help members of the social body, but never to destroy or absorb them' [53].

Modern developments give the State much greater scope in its role of securing the common good by economic policy, redressing imbalances and providing employment [54], but this must augment, not limit, private initiative in economic matters, while at the same time essential personal rights must be safeguarded, especially 'a man's right and duty to be primarily responsible for his own upkeep and that of his family'. Hence all systems must permit the free development of producing activity [55]. Individuals and the State must co-operate for the common good [56]. Experience shows that 'where private initiative is lacking in economic matters the State stagnates and political tyranny ensues' and the stifling of creative talent hinders spiritual and material development [57]. It also shows that where the State does not use its powers, there is 'unscrupulous exploitation of the weak by the strong' [58].

*The growth of the Welfare State*
One of the principal characteristics of the time is the growing network of social relationships [59].[30] It is a result partly of growing State intervention; it also reflects the human instinct to face together common problems in matters such as health and education, choice of career, the well-being of the handicapped [60]. Communal help to people in exercising personal rights especially to 'the necessities of life, health care, education, housing, work, recreation' clearly has advantages [61]. Insofar as it requires laws and regulations, however, it often conspires 'to make it difficult for a person to think independently … to act on his own initiative, exercise his responsibility' [62]. But these patterns are in themselves the creation of man, though subject to pressures from their environment; they are not just the product of blind forces. They do not then reduce men to being automatons [63] but they must be developed to get the best out of the pattern, and to reduce its disadvantages [64]. Here the public authority is crucial, ensuring that all the agencies of this growing social organization, intermediate bodies and corporate enterprises, must 'present the form and substance of a true community', which they will only do if they treat their individual members as self-reliant persons [65]. Governments must strike the right balance between the State and the autonomous groups [66]. If this is done the growing social organization will help personal development and organically reconstruct society as Pius XI advocated [67].

*Wages, the worker and economic organization*
Throughout the world, millions of workers and their families have wages inadequate for a decent livelihood, usually because of lack of

economic development [68]. At the same time the wealth of the privileged is flaunted. Elsewhere economic development is hastened without regard to justice or equity, or national resources are squandered on arms or prestige [69]. In economically developed countries, financial rewards are all too often unjustly distributed. Hard-working men get too little to support life decently despite their contribution to the life of the community [70]. While economic considerations are important in wage determination, the good of the economy for example, they cannot simply be left to determination by the laws of the market but must take into account human need [71]; they must be just according to the resources available [72].[31]

Where economies are expanding, inequalities should decrease, not increase [73]. The end of the national economy is to secure for the citizens the material conditions for full personal development. 'The economic prosperity of a nation is not so much its total ... wealth ... as the equitable division and distribution of this wealth' [74]. Where firms are prosperous and expanding, some kind of participation in profits for the wage earner should be introduced [75]. Pius XI stressed that neither labour or capital can claim all the profits [76]. It is desirable that 'workers gradually come to share in the ownership of the company' [77]. Any adjustment of wages and profits must take the common good, nationally and internationally, into account [78]. That good includes a high level of employment, justice between various groups of workers, a balance between wages and prices, and between the various sectors of the economy, among other considerations [79]. Internationally, free competition must be fair, and mutual co-operation must be fostered [80]. The common good embraces all of these [81]. The conditions of work should be fully human. 'Man has, of his very nature, a need to express himself in his work and thereby to perfect his own being' [82]. Economic structures which do not allow a man to do this are unjust, no matter how productive they are and how justly their product is distributed [83].

It is not possible 'to give a concise definition' of economic structures which meet the needs of justice, but small and medium firms, co-operatives and those where the wage contract is supplemented by partnership are on the right lines [84] as, in agriculture, are the family farm and the co-operative [85–6]. Such enterprises need to be technically up to date and economically efficient in meeting the needs of the consumer [87–8]. Craftsmen and members of co-operatives preserve important human values for society and the

State should recognize this in enabling them to serve the community effectively [89–90].

In industry in general the need for flexibility makes it impossible to lay down hard and fast rules for participation but 'we have no doubt as to the need for giving workers an active part in the business of the company'. The enterprise 'is a true community'[32] and should be concerned about 'the needs, activities and standing of each of its members' [91]. 'All parties [should] co-operate actively and loyally in the common enterprise', workers should have their say in its running and development, while it maintains 'necessary and efficient unity of direction' [92]. All this accords with the needs of man's nature as well as with progress generally in the economic, social and political spheres [93]. Greater skill is also being required of workers, and they need assistance in gaining it [94] and provision for longer schooling [95]. All these factors favour greater responsibility and contribution to society and the common good generally [96].

Trade unions (workers' associations) have grown in number and mainly work through co-operation in collective bargaining: unions also have a role in the State generally [97]. Public authorities and other institutions make decisions affecting the economy [98]; the workers as well as the employers have a right to representation in these areas to speak for their members [99]. The Pope commends the efforts of all those engaged in professional groups and trade unions throughout the world. They are often up against great difficulties [100–1]. The work of all who operate in this field with respect for natural law and rights of conscience is also commended; especially the International Labour Organization [102–3].

*Private property*
Forms of ownership and its problems are changing. Owners, private or public, hand over control of productive capital to professional managers and such firms have considerable influence on the economy; it is important to ensure that their policies work for the common good [104]. More people find that adequate social insurance is providing the security that possession of property used to provide [105]. Proficiency at trade or profession rates higher too than income from property [106]. This is as it should be: work is the immediate expression of personality, property is instrumental only [107]. Does this mean that man's natural right to ownership, including productive goods, is no longer valid [108]?

By no means; 'the right of private ownership of goods, including productive ... has permanent validity. It is part of the natural order which teaches that the individual is prior to society.' It would be quite useless to insist on free and personal initiative in the economic field while at the same time withdrawing man's right to dispose of the means indispensable to the achievement of such initiative. Further, history and experience testify that 'in those regimes which do not recognize the rights of private ownership ... the exercise of freedom in almost every other direction is suppressed or stifled' [109]. Some who previously denied this are coming to see the value of private ownership of productive goods [110]. In this the Church's position is not mere defence of the *status quo* but 'aims at securing that the institution of private property be ... according to the plan of the divine wisdom and the disposition of nature'. It is a guarantee of the essential freedom of the individual and at the same time an indispensable element in a true social order [111].[33]

The increasing productivity of modern economies should increase wages so that the wage earners may save and become property owners [112]. All classes of citizens should be among them [113] as Pius XII stressed. It is a demand which arises from the moral dignity of work; a secure, if modest property should be available to all classes [114]. The body politic must make this an object of policy, especially in the light of the current rapid economic development of States. They should have an economic policy which encourages the ownership of consumer durables, e.g. houses, and the tools and land of craftsmen and farmers, and shares in companies large and medium [115]. The right of the State to own productive goods remains valid where the true common good requires it [116] in accordance with the principle of subsidiary function [117], and competence and accountability should be expected of those who direct State enterprises [118].

Ownership of external things, property, is given us not for our own use only. St Gregory the Great tells us that those who have received a large share of temporal blessings should use them for the benefit of others [119].[34] The increasing growth of State and public agencies does not outdate the social function of private ownership but makes it more necessary, because the efforts of individuals or groups of them are more effective in promoting charity and spiritual values [120]. The Gospel tells us that it is better for the rich to store up treasure in heaven by giving to the poor [121].

## IV New aspects of the social question

*Agriculture*
It is not only worker/employer relations in industry that need re-establishing on the basis of equity and justice but those between different sections of the economy [122]. The drift from the land to the city is for example a world-wide phenomenon. [123]. Economic development leads to the movement of people into industry from the land, and the city is also attractive in terms of its apparently greater, versus the land's declining, prospects [124].

Reversing this drift must depend on increasing the prospects of rural living [125] and here the State's role is crucial in providing better communications, educational and recreational facilities and better living conditions [126–7]. Agriculture requires to be modernized and to be made more efficient [128–30] with a sound public policy encouraging this; 'tax policies, credit, social insurance, prices, the fostering of ancillary industries and the adjustment of the structure of farming as a business enterprise' [131].

Taxation must be equitable [132] and the special needs of agriculture must be taken into consideration. Farmers have to wait longer for returns and are subject to greater hazards [133]. Credit on moderate terms must be available [134], and the same social insurance as other citizens [135]. This can be a means of reducing imbalances between sectors [136]. Prices established for agricultural products [137] should take into account that they represent returns for labour, rather than on invested capital [138].[35] There should be justice between the prices charged by the different sectors of the economy [139].

> While it is true that farm produce is mainly intended for the satisfaction of man's primary needs, and price should therefore be within the means of all consumers, this cannot be used as an argument for keeping ... farm workers in a permanent state of economic and social inferiority ... depriving them of ... a decent standard of living. This would be opposed to the common good. [140]

A degree of compatible industrialization can be developed in rural areas [141]. The pattern of rural life and society depends on the needs of individual regions but the family farm, if it provides for those who work it a decent living, represents something of a Christian ideal [142]. If it is to survive, however, it needs to be efficient, using the best modern techniques and working in co-operation with others [143].

The farming community must work together to advance its own economic development and way of life [144]; their labour has a dignity all its own, and many branches of industry depend on it [145]. Rural workers, however, require to foster a strong sense of social solidarity, forming co-operatives which facilitate efficiency and give the community a voice in political affairs [146]. If they organize for the common good, their interests can be properly safeguarded [147]. The work of all those who are combining to these ends is commended [148]. Work on the land is a God-given and noble task, which raises those who do it, and others, to a higher degree of civilization [149].

Within the whole political community there is often a considerable disparity between different regions, which it is the duty of the public authority to seek to eliminate or reduce [150]. The common good must always be kept in mind; all three sectors, industry, services, agriculture, need balanced promotion, the less developed being allowed to play the major role in improving their lot [151]. 'Private enterprise too must contribute ... in accordance with the principle of subsidiary function' it must be entrusted where possible with 'the continuation of economic development' [152].

*International problems and the relationship between developed and under-developed countries*

The land and population equation varies in different countries [153]. So too with food production; some produce too little, some have surpluses [154]. Human solidarity demands that these discrepancies be rectified by movement of goods, capital and men between countries [155] and the FAO has done much to facilitate collaboration in this [156]. There is a contrast between the wealth of the developed and the poverty of the underdeveloped nations. Solidarity makes it impossible for the former to regard this with indifference; nor will peace itself prevail if such imbalances exist [157]. This situation should weigh heavily on the consciences of those blessed with the world's goods [158]. The Church wishes her members to remember their responsibilities in this [159] and it is a source of great joy that the wealthier nations are responding to the need [160].

Justice obviously demands that food which is surplus to the needs of the rich nations should be available to those which are poor [161]. Such over-production it is true can be economically harmful, but it also can be used to help others [162]. However, such aid is only a stopgap. The long-term answer is to help the people in the poorer countries to feed themselves adequately, by transfer of skills and knowledge and with economic development [163]. Consciences have been roused in recent years on these matters [164] and the response has been heartening; the generosity and dedication of so many is commended and in the years ahead this work needs to be expanded [165].

*Lessons from the past*
The developing nations would do well to learn from those which have undergone development [167]. One lesson is that the extra product generated must be justly distributed in a balanced economy [168], another that the economic strengths and characteristics of a nation should be built on [169]. Those who would help them develop must respect individuality [170]. Nor must aid be aimed at gaining political control of the aided [171]; this would be a new form of colonialism [172]. Helping the aided nation to achieve its own goals must be the intent [173]. In this way the world community can be built up [174].

Nor must we forget that, important though economic development is, it and its implications are not supreme values in themselves [175]. Carelessness of spiritual values is one of the great defects of the economically developed countries. It should not be allowed to undermine the often sounder attitudes the less developed societies possess [176]. This national integrity is the foundation of true civilization [177].

*The role of the Church*
The Church is universal: she embraces all people and is present everywhere on earth [178]. Christians and the Church have always cared for human dignity and so have always helped improve human institutions and environment [179]. She is one with all peoples because her members are of all peoples, reborn in Christ [180]. She aims at unity in Christ but not human uniformity; each people, each nation, has its own identity and should foster and keep it [181]. Catholics in the newer and poorer States are playing their part in work for their development [182]. Those in the older and wealthier states are doing their part in assisting that development and helping students from developing areas who are studying in their country [183]. To all of them, the Pope's paternal greetings go out [184].

*The Christian response to the population question*
There is concern over the problem of food supplies for a growing world population [185]. We are told that population growth over

the next few decades will outstrip man's capacity to provide food for it, and disaster will follow [186]. Further it is claimed that in the less developed countries, the problem will become increasingly acute because mortality rates are decreasing and birth rates remain high; prevention of conception or birth is therefore necessary [187]. The fact is that such arguments are 'based on unreliable and controversial data' and are of uncertain validity [188]. The resources of nature are almost inexhaustible and man has been given the intelligence to develop them for his needs. The answer to population/ food supplies problem is 'in a renewed scientific and technical effort on man's part to deepen and extend his dominion over nature'. Progress until now opens up limitless possibilities [189]. The very real problems of poorer nations are more often caused by defective social and economic organization and solidarity among the people [190]. Solutions which do violence to the dignity of man are clearly not acceptable [191]. Only on the basis of the value of every individual human life and on international co-operation for the exchange of knowledge, capital and manpower, can they be found [192].

The family is the context in which human life is transmitted by an act 'subject to the all-holy, inviolable, and immutable laws of God which no man may ignore or obey' [193]. Human life is sacred.

> From its inception it reveals the creating hand of God. Those who violate his laws ... degrade themselves and humanity ... also sap the vitality of the political community of which they are members [194].

Parents must secure for their children a sound cultural and religious formation, especially regarding the family and the procreation and rearing of children, and the Church must aid them in this [195]. We were told to fill the earth and subdue it [196], not to destroy nature or life [197]. The contradiction of modern life is the spectre of want and poverty and the use of technology and science to create the means to destroy life [198]. God's providence gives us the means to solve the problems of sustaining human life; only man's perverted mind and will makes them insoluble [199].

*International co-operation and moral values*
Science and technology have increased relationships between nations, and made them more interdependent [200]. Since none can solve its own problems alone, however great its resources and skills, their solution depends on the actions of others also [201],

hence the need for co-operation felt even by the biggest States [202]. At the same time the ability to co-operate is thwarted by lack of trust; men and States live in mortal fear of one another [203], armaments pile up as a form of deterrent, resources and effort being wasted and society disrupted and made fearful [204].

Ideology is the cause of much of the distrust. 'There are some indeed who go so far as to deny the existence of a moral order which is transcendent, absolute, universal and equally binding on all' [205]. Yet without agreement on the law of justice, appeals to justice are meaningless and force and self-interest prevail [206]. Mutual trust must be founded on respect for the moral order [207] 'which has no existence except in God; cut off from God it must ... disintegrate'. So too must society; man is spirit as well as matter and demands a 'moral and religious order' for the society in which he lives [208]. The claim that scientific and technical triumphs enable man to construct a civilization without God is hollow [209]. Science has put vast forces for destruction in the hands of mankind and the need of spiritual and moral values becomes greater, not less [210]. The illusion of an earthly paradise is rapidly being destroyed. Meanwhile the interest in human rights is reminding mankind of its limitations and the need for spiritual values [211].

## V The rebuilding of the moral order

*Foundations in God's moral law*
After all the scientific and technical progress man has made, the problem of rebuilding a new order where national and international communities are more humanely related remains [212]. Such theories as have been floated have had little impact because they fail to take account of human weakness and suffering and the deep-rooted sense of religion that exists in mankind [213]. That sense is not the result of a feeling due to fantasy, but arises from man's deepest needs; God has made us for himself and our hearts find no rest save in him [214]. There will be no peace until man recovers the sense of dignity that comes from being a creature and a child of God, the source of justice, truth and love [215]. The contrast between the dignity of those who suffer persecution for their faith today, often in countries of ancient Christian culture, and the barbarism of their persecutors, shows the truth of this [216]. The tragedy of the modern world is the urge to construct a solid social order apart from God – its only true foundation [217].

*The enduring validity of the Church's social teaching*
'The permanent validity of this teaching admits of no doubt [218]. This teaching rests on one basic principle; human beings are the foundation, cause and end of every social institution' [219]. For men are social beings by nature, yet raised by providence to an order above nature. The Church's social doctrine, particularly as formulated over the past hundred years by priests and laymen, points the way to social reconstruction, providing the 'principles of universal application [taking] human nature into account and the varying conditions in which man's life is lived' [220]. It is essential that this teaching be understood and put into practice [221]. It is 'an integral part of the Christian conception of life' [222].

It must continue to be studied, especially in schools and seminaries, parishes and associations of the lay apostolate; it must be publicized in every way possible and its relevance to modern needs demonstrated [223]. The laity can do much to diffuse it [224]. It can be used to demonstrate the truth and provide answers to modern difficulties [225]. It must be translated into practice [226]. Our people must be educated in it [227] so that it fosters an awareness of their economic and social responsibilities [228]. There are difficulties in translating theory into practice [229] which only the demonstration of the manner of practical application will overcome [230]. 'Formal instruction must be supplemented by the students' active co-operation in their own training' [231]. They then need to become involved in social action [232]. The lay apostolate is then crucial [233]. It must be remembered however that the Christian conception of life demands a spirit of moderation and self-sacrifice [234] whereas around us we find a spirit of hedonism which sees life as nothing more than a quest for pleasure, which is totally opposed to the Christian view of the purpose of that life [235].

In putting social principles into practice, the method of 'see, judge and act' is useful [236]. Knowledge acquired in this way does not remain abstract, but becomes active [237]. When differences of opinion on the practical application of principles occur among Catholics, they should not lose their respect for one another but see what points of agreement there are [238]. In dealing with those who do not share their view of life, while doing nothing which will compromise religion or morality, they should seek for points of agreement on practical action, to do the good that can be done. Where they decide it is necessary, however, the hierarchy still has the right to decide on the matter of the practical application of principle [239].

The laity, whose role it is to take an active part in the temporal affairs of society, have a noble role to play [240] by being well qualified in their trade or profession in accordance with its own laws, but also in a manner compatible with the Church's social teaching. They must respect ecclesiastical authority; if they fail in this they may fail in justice to others, as well as bringing discredit on the Church [241]. While having ungrudging admiration for modern man's achievements in mastering the world, we know he is in danger of destroying himself [242].

He can be master of scientific and material progress but spiritually a pygmy [243]. He admires his own works to the point of idolatry [244]. Christians by contrast must keep good consciences [245]. While respecting all man's achievements and material improvements, these must be kept in their context; they should be so used as to make men better men in the natural and supernatural order [246] lest they gain the whole world and lose their souls [247].

Keeping the Sunday holy [248] is a way of safeguarding man's dignity by reminding him of the things of heaven [249] and underlining his right to rest from work [250], in this establishing the connection between his moral and physical well-being [251]. The disregard of this law is deplored [252] and all concerned are called on to respect it [253]. The Christian does not disdain this world [254] it is only the evil that is in it that he rejects; a life of activity in it is entirely compatible with Christian life in itself [255]. Man perfects himself through his daily work, and in doing it to the best of his ability he serves both God and man [256]. He seeks first the things of God, but knows that in doing this he can better serve society in its human affairs, he makes the needs of others his own, and his activity in every field is enhanced by his love of Christ [257].

We are living members of the Body of Christ [258] and men are united with their master when they are engaged in work for the world; it becomes his work, so leavening human civilization [259]. There is hope as well as deadly evil in the world [260] and courageous co-operation with the Church's teaching will help realize Christ's kingdom in it [261]. The Church is mother and teacher of the nations, ever watchful for the good of man [262]. May the redeemer God reign and triumph [263].

# 4  Background to *Pacem in Terris* (1963)

This encyclical was published on 11 April 1963, just a little less than two years after *Mater et Magistra*, and over six months after the

Second Vatican Council opened on 11 October 1962. The appearance of two social encyclicals in such a short space of time, and the second while the Council was in session, reminds us how eager John XXIII was to ensure that the whole of his guidance to the Church on social ethics was put across.

The two encyclicals blend into one another. The first had surveyed the whole field, considering the degree to which the *Rerum Novarum* agenda had been completed, and then looking at the main issues which had arisen in the first half of the twentieth century, especially the fact that concern with the social problem in its various forms had become world wide. *Pacem in Terris* goes on to deal with the question of political ethics, national and international, the framework within which mankind had to work. Aware as never before of the physical limitations of the earth, and the dangers of mankind's destroying itself if men did not learn to work together in justice and peace, humanity had the most compelling reasons for finding the means to these ends. Two world wars, the Cold War that followed the second one, and the growing awareness of the lunacy of the arms race, especially as a result of the Cuban missile crisis in 1962, concentrated minds on the need for a new world order. The realization that human solidarity demanded more concern to improve the conditions of life in the third world, not least because injustices on such a scale were a threat to the security of all, reinforced this conviction.

## (i) *International politics and international relations*

International politics and relations since the end of the Second World War, both regionally and internationally, have been marked by a growing awareness of the interdependence of nations despite, or perhaps because of, the Cold War. The United Nations Organization was set up in 1945 in the light of post-war needs in this field.[36] It succeeded the League of Nations, established after the First World War, but not accepted by the United States and in the end ineffectual. The post-1945 situation was quite different; there was an awareness among the Western Allies of the need for an effective international organization or nations that had not been there at the end of the First World War. The attitude of Russia to it was ambiguous but it participated anyway.

A *Declaration* by the 26 United Nations was issued on 1 January 1942, pledging their governments to continue the fight against the Fascist powers, and proposing a United Nations Organization.

Plans for it were produced at the Conference between the USA, the USSR and the UK at Dumbarton Oaks, in Washington DC, in September 1944. They were accepted, with certain amendments, by a Conference at San Francisco on 25 and 26 of June 1945 and 50 founder members signed its Charter, the Organization coming into existence officially on 24 October 1945. Membership was open to all nations, and the 50 founder members had become 159 by 1991. Its aims were international peace and security, and the development of international co-operation in economic, social, cultural and humanitarian problems. It has in consequence developed new institutions and agencies, as well as adopting old ones; the International Court of Justice for example was a product of the League of Nations, as also was the International Labour Office.

The main institutions are the General Assembly, attended by all nations, the Security Council, which has a membership of 15. China, France, the Soviet Union, the UK and the USA are permanent members, while the other ten are elected for two-year terms by the General Assembly, only the permanent members voting. The secretariat consists of the Secretary General, the UN's chief administrator, assistant secretaries and an international staff. The Secretary General is an important figure internationally but the effectiveness of the office depends on the character of the holder and his capacity to use his office to enable effective policies to emerge and be acted on; this is not easy in an organization in which the big powers inevitably have more clout and require careful handling. Perhaps the failures of UNO outweigh its successes, and aspects of its organization require radical overhaul, but its survival in spite of all indicates that the world community is convinced an international political organization is necessary and that the UNO, faults and all, is the best we have and deserve until the nations are prepared to trust one another, and the UN, better.

The International Monetary Fund was established as a result of an International Monetary Conference held at Bretton Woods in New Hampshire, USA in July 1944 under the chairmanship of Henry Morgenthau, Secretary to the US Treasury, with Lord Keynes leading the British delegation. The Fund was established on 27 December 1945 to facilitate international monetary co-operation and multilateral systems of payments, and to provide funds to help nations with balance of payments problems while they took steps to remedy those problems. Initially it was an independent organization but from November 1947 has worked in co-operation with the UN. Its members contribute to the Fund on a quota basis and can also borrow to meet its needs; it lends to both developed and underdeveloped countries. The same Conference established the International Bank for Reconstruction and Development (IBRD), sometimes referred to as the World Bank, to provide funds and technical assistance to help the underdeveloped countries; the International Development Association was set up by the IBRD in 1960 to help the poorest nations, and the International Finance Corporation, which dates from 1956, an affiliate of the IBRD, invests in and provides loans for companies in the developing world.[37] The success of the United Nations in countering the exigencies of the Cold War was inevitably limited, but events were concentrating minds more and more on the dangers of the international political system being at the mercy of the rivalries of the superpowers. This was made clear by the Cuban missile crisis in 1962.

## (ii) The Cuban missile crisis 1962[38]

The United States and Cuba had developed into bitter enemies after Castro turned to Marxism and the Soviet Union once he had successfully ousted the American-supported President Batista in 1959. President Kennedy, who took office in 1960, inherited from the previous administration a plan for the overthrow of Castro and in April 1962 unwisely allowed it to go ahead as it had been, badly, planned; the landing in the Bay of Pigs was a total disaster and only deepened the animosity between the two governments. In the wake of it, the Russian leader Khrushchev, already giving economic and technical aid to Castro, decided to gamble and make Cuba a missile base directed at the USA, sending surface-to-air missiles, fighters, nuclear bombers and surface-to-surface (i.e. offensive) missiles there in 1962. The increased military build-up alarmed the Americans although they did not initially realize its true purpose; Cuba protested that the war materials being imported were purely defensive, but on 15 October aerial reconnaissance photos showed clearly a launching pad with an offensive missile in place.

The President was determined to see the complete removal of nuclear weapons from the island, but was at the same time fearful of escalating the conflict needlessly, and so it was decided to block-ade the island to prevent the missiles still on the way being landed, and to bring the maximum diplomatic and other peaceful pressures to bear for the removal of those which were already there. Carefully giving Khrushchev room to manoeuvre out of the difficulty without too much loss of face, his plan succeeded. The ships carrying the missiles turned back and the immediate crisis was over; by 27 October 1962, Russia had also agreed to remove the missiles already there.

The awareness of all parties that the world had come close to nuclear war over Cuba helped to clear minds about the need for effective arms negotiations. There had been attempts made to achieve agreement on arms control on several occasions since 1946 but they had made little progress because of the differing perspectives of the superpowers, and when in 1949 the USSR exploded its first nuclear bomb, hopes of coming to any agreement faded further. Not until after the end of the Korean war, the death of Stalin and the explosion of the first Russian hydrogen bomb, was more progress possible. Technological and strategic developments, combined with the intensive testing of new weapons, had raised new fears. Some progress was made towards at least clearing the ground for negotiations, although the question of German rearmament delayed matters. Finally, in 1957, a cessation of nuclear testing was agreed.

There were, however, still problems to be resolved before such formal agreements could be signed, and when the shooting down of an American spy plane over Russia in 1960 intervened, the hostilities of the Cold War were once more renewed. A proposed summit conference was cancelled and tests were resumed by the Russians in September 1961. The shock of the Cuban missile crisis in October of the next year caused a rethink all round and a more extensive test-ban agreement was reached which provided for the installation of a direct and permanently open hot line between the White House and the Kremlin in 1963.[39] When *Pacem in Terris* was published on 11 April 1963, these events were still fresh in the mind. The human race had been saved from what could well have been a disaster, which even if it had not ended civilization as we know it, could have led to suffering and the collapse of whole societies ravaged by atomic, bacterial, and chemical warfare, the terrifying new ABC about which humanity was learning.

## (iii) Summary of the text of Pacem in Terris[40]

There is an Introduction [paras 1 to 7] and five sections. I. The order between men [8–45]. II. Relations between individuals and the authorities [46–79]. III. Relations between States [80–129]. IV. Relationships of individuals and political communities with the world community [130–145]. V. Pastoral exhortations [146–173].

## Introduction

Peace depends on the observance of the divine order which has
been established in things [1–2]. The progress of scientific knowledge and technology reveals both how great the works of God are,
and the marvel of man, made in God's image, who has been set
over this world [3]. The disunity among men contrasts with this
divine order [4]. God however 'has stamped man's inmost being
with an order revealed to man by his conscience ... the law written
in their hearts' [5] despite erroneous opinions arguing otherwise
[6]. This law determines the principles governing relationships
between individuals, between individuals and States, States and
States, and individuals with the world community [7].

## I. Order between individuals

Man is a person

> endowed with intelligence and free will. As such he has rights
> and duties, which together flow as a direct consequence from his
> nature. These rights are universal and inviolable and therefore
> altogether inalienable [8–9].

As redeemed by Christ, man's personal dignity is incomparably
increased [10].

*Human rights*
The rights are: to life and the means to sustain and develop it; to
food, clothing, shelter, medical care, rest, social services, the right
to be cared for in ill health, after accidents at work, and unsought
unemployment [11]; the right to be respected; to a good name,
freedom to seek the truth, freedom of speech and publication
(within the limits of the common good); to choose a profession
and to be informed about public events [12]; the right to share
in the benefits of culture; to general, and technical/professional
training and advanced studies according to talent and the ability
of society to provide the means [13]; the right to worship God
according to conscience and to profess religion privately and in
public, according to the freedom which the apostles and martyrs
claimed 'which most truly safeguards the dignity of the human
person' [14]; the right to choose family life or to embrace priesthood or religious life [15]; the family, founded on freely chosen
marriage, one and indissoluble, is the primary cell of society and
must be protected by it [16]; the support and education of chil-

dren is the right primarily of parents [17]; the right to work and
to personal initiative in it, under conditions which respect human
dignity and development, of adults and juveniles, male and female
[19]; the right to economic freedom and to rewards according to
responsibilities. For the wage earner supporting a family this
means a wage adequate for this [20]; the right to ownership of
private property including productive goods; ownership allows the
assertion of personality, an opportunity for the exercise of responsibility, security for the family, and ensures peace and prosperity
for the State [21]; the right to private property, which brings with
it social obligations [22]; the right 'to meet together and form
associations with their fellows', and give them the purposes and
organization needed to suit their aims [23]. Such intermediate
groups or societies are essential for freedom with responsibility
[24].

There are rights also to freedom of movement and residence
within States, and of emigration where there are just reasons for it,
because all are members not only of a particular State but of the
whole human family [25]; to take an active part in public life and
make one's own contribution to the common good; men and
women are the end and purpose of the State, not inert elements
within it [26]. They are also entitled 'to legal protection of their
rights, effective, unbiased and just' [27].

*Human responsibilities*
Natural rights are bound up with duties [28]. So the right to live
imposes the duty to preserve one's life; the right to a decent standard of living, the duty to live becomingly, and the right to seek the
truth, the duty to search for it ever more widely [29]. To claim
rights and ignore duties is to build with one hand and tear down
with the other [30]. Society being natural to man, recognition and
acceptance of both rights and duties is therefore essential to the
good of the social order [31]. The right to the necessities of life
should be accompanied by the readiness to see they are possessed
by all [32]. It requires the collaboration of all in the many enterprises of our civilization in order that this may be done [33] and
this collaboration must proceed from free initiative, not coercion.
'There is nothing human about a State that is welded together by
force.' Each man should act on his own initiative, conviction and
sense of responsibility in pursuing his rights and accepting his
obligations as a free man able to choose to do right by himself and
to others in society [34].

*Social life in truth, justice and freedom*
Society must be based on truth, guided by justice and animated by
a love which makes men 'feel the needs of others as their own'. It
must also be based on freedom, each assuming responsibility for
his actions [35]. Human society must then be regarded 'primarily
as a spiritual reality' through participation in which men can share
their knowledge of truth, can claim rights and fulfil duties, can be
encouraged to aspire for spiritual goods and 'share their enjoyment of the wholesome pleasures of this world' passing on to
others all that is best in themselves [36]. Such an order is founded
in 'truth ... brought into effect by justice and animated by love'
[37]. But such an order 'universal, absolute and immutable ...
finds its source in the one true personal and transcendent God'.
Human goodness, according to St Thomas 'depends much more
on the eternal law than on human reason [38].[41]

*Characteristics of modern society*
Three things mark our modern age [39]. First there has been 'the
progressive improvement in the economic and social condition of
working men' [40]. Secondly, women are now playing a greater part
in political life. Both in public life and domestic, they are demanding 'the rights and duties that belong to them' [41]. Thirdly,
peoples have attained or are on the way to attaining political independence [42]. Nations are no longer content to submit to foreign
domination. Class domination is also fading [43]. All are aware they
are equal in dignity, hence the rejection of racial discrimination
[44]. When society is based on a sense of rights and duties, a grasp
of spiritual and intellectual values comes easily, leading to a better
knowledge of the true God [45].

## II. Relations between the individual and the public authorities

Legal authority is needed to preserve the State's institutions for the
service of its members, and, as St Paul teaches, that authority
comes ultimately from God, though not in the sense that all rulers
are appointed by him – as St John Chrysostom pointed out [46].[42]
But that authority is limited. It derives its force from the moral law
which has its origin in God. This law protects the rightful autonomy of man, the subject of duties and rights and the origin and
purpose of human society. Without this order being founded in
God, the State lacks an ultimate authority. It is without life. With
State officials sharing in some way in the authority of God which
validates legitimate State power, they and their offices possess a

moral authority, vivifying the State [47]. Hence a State which rules by threat of force or hope of reward is offensive to human dignity. Rulers should appeal to conscience, the needs of the common good; and that conscience cannot be forced [48]. The State must have its authority from God if it is to bind conscience [49]. The obedience of the citizen is then homage to God; his dignity is thus preserved [50]. Hence laws which are contrary to the moral order have no binding force. Human law must be in accordance with right reason which derives from the eternal law of God. As St Thomas teaches

> human law has the rationale of law insofar as it is in accord with right reason and as such it derives from eternal law. A law which is at variance with reason is to that extent unjust and has no longer the rationale of law ... it is an act of violence [51].[43]

The fact that authority comes from God does not mean that men have no power to choose those who are to rule the state, or decide 'the government they want ... determine the procedures and the limitations of rules in the exercise of their office ... [this] teaching is consonant with any genuinely democratic form of government' [52].

*Purpose of the State's authority; the common good*
The State's role is to oversee individuals and groups, according to justice and within the limits of its competence for the common good, as they make their specific contribution to the general welfare. Such groups and individuals harmonizing 'their own interests with the needs of others', offering 'their goods and services as their rulers direct' [53]. The attainment of the common good is the purpose of the State [54]. The human person is to be taken into account at all times [55]. Each has a right to share in it 'though in different ways depending on his tasks, merits and circumstances'. No individual citizen or category of citizen may be favoured, save the weaker members who are less able to defend their own legitimate interests [56], and the common good affects the whole man, body and soul. The State then must foster the spiritual as well as the moral good of the people [57] as was stressed in *Mater et Magistra* [58]. Since man is body and immortal soul, the measures taken for the common good must help him to eternal salvation; in his mortal life he cannot attain perfect happiness [59].

*Ensuring the common good: human rights*
This good is best secured where personal rights and duties are guaranteed

> The chief concern of civil authorities must therefore be to ensure that these rights are recognized, co-ordinated, defended and promoted and that each individual is enabled to perform his duties more easily [60].

A State which refuses to recognize human rights or acts in violation of them not only fails in its duty but 'its decrees are wholly lacking in binding force' [61].

Rights must be exercised in such a manner that others are not obstructed in the exercise of theirs, or in the discharge of their duties; the rights of all are to be safeguarded, and restored if disturbed [62]. States must secure citizens in the freedom to exercise their rights and fulfil their duties also, and public policy should be such as to make this possible, providing adequate social and economic development and social services, otherwise inequalities continue [63]. The public administration therefore must care for social as well as economic progress: communications, housing, medical care, religious and recreational services, social insurance, provision of employment, fair pay and conditions for workers, encouragement for intermediate groups, access to cultural opportunities [64]. Care must be taken however that excessive State action does not limit freedom. 'State care must augment freedom while guaranteeing the protection of everyone's rights' [65]. This must hold in all departments of life [66].

*Forms of government and citizen participation*
It is not possible to give a general ruling on the most suitable form of government or the most effective discharge of its legislative, administrative and judicial functions [67]. The needs of different peoples and situations will determine them but it is desirable that the law should be precise on the functions of government and the mutual relations of citizens and public officials [68]. Justice, respect for the moral law and the common good and support for individuals and subsidiary groups within the State is at all times crucial [69]. The right functioning of the judicial system is necessary for the common good [70] though given the complexity of social life, inadequacies in such systems inevitably arise [71]. The relations of citizens, of intermediate groups and the public authorities frequently seem to defy the law; it is therefore necessary for the authorities to have a clear idea of their legitimate spheres of action [72].

It is 'a natural consequence of men's dignity' to 'take an active part in government' depending on 'the stage of development reached by the political community of which they are members' [73] and such participation gives a new vitality to political authority [74]. A charter of human rights [75], a public constitution [76] and the need for clear understandings of the respective rights and duties of public authorities and citizens are necessities in a well-ordered and just society [77] although the idea that the will of the individual and of the group is the primary source of rights or, the government's authority is to be rejected [78]. People are, however, growing in awareness of their dignity, are entering government service and seeking constitutional recognition of their rights [79].

### III. Relations between States

States and heads of States are, like private individuals, the subject of reciprocal rights and duties, and their relationships must be harmonized with truth, justice and freedom [80]. They are bound by natural law when acting in their country's name [81]. They do not lay aside their humanity and its obligations on their appointment to public office. The qualities which lead to their being given office mark them as outstanding representatives of the political life of the people [82]. Their authority is essential for ordering civil society, and God in the Old Testament has warned that it is subject to his law [83]. The authority that regulates the relations of States must in their relations with one another also promote the common good [84] and one of the principal imperatives of that good is that it must be founded on moral law, the natural law [85].

Truth is the first requirement in interstate relationships, for the equality of States, the repudiation of racialism, the right of each to its good name and the responsibility and means for its own development [86]. Individuals differ in knowledge, virtue and wealth but all must be treated properly by those in power [87]. So between nations, the more powerful should not seek to dominate but rather help the less strong to progress [88]. States, like individuals, are equals in their natural dignity [89]. Nations are not denied the right to urge their own virtues but they must not denigrate other nations [90]. Between nations then there should be justice and mutual acceptance of rights and duties [91].

States have the right to their own development but they must not harm others in so doing; they have the right to play the leading part in their own development [92] and clashes between States on such issues must be settled peaceably [93]. Conflicts between ethnic groups seeking autonomy are particularly difficult to resolve [94]. To want to check the vitality of such groups is wrong [95]; justice is best served by fostering them [96], but the opposition such groups meet often leads them to exaggerate their claims, whereas they should seek close association with those among whom they live [97].

States collaborate with one another in social, political and economic matters as the common good demands [98] and judicious pursuit of their own interests must be combined with such co-operation [99]. The universal common good requires this; ethnic differences are real and important, but that all peoples have much in common should provide the basis for such co-operation with others [100].

## Population, land and refugees

Economic imbalances between resources and population exist in some countries and nations should collaborate in redressing them by the circulation of goods, capital and manpower [101], with as little displacement of the latter as is feasible [102]. Political refugees are a particularly painful problem [103]; some rulers of States forget their duty is to safeguard the community and its freedom, and they oppress their people, driving some of them into exile [104]. The world must recognize that these refugees are persons and their rights must be respected [105]. One of them is the right to enter countries where they may seek a better life for themselves and their families and it is the duty of officials to accept them, so far as the good of their own community, properly understood, permits [106]. Those who work to relieve the need of refugees are much to be commended [107–8].

## The arms race

The contest in armaments between the developed countries results in the waste of resources needed for social and economic development [109] and at the same time it produces an atmosphere of fear: deterrence may have worked temporarily [110], but the knowledge that even testing nuclear weapons could lead to disaster beyond imagining is ever there [111]. An end to 'the arms race ... [and] general agreement on ... a disarmament programme with an effective system of mutual control' is a demand of justice, right reason and the dignity of man; a third world war cannot be contemplated [112]. Given the desire to avoid this calamity there is no reason why the steps to this end should not be taken [113].

There are therefore three reasons for disarmament. The first is that disputes between nations must be settled by reason and not by force [114]. The second is that there is a craving for peace [115], and the third is that all will benefit from it [116]. The nations are urged to take heed [117]. Sincerity in negotiations based on mutual trust and faithful fulfilment of obligations would solve the problem [118] and the Pope prays that this will be achieved [119]. Relations between States must be based on freedom, respects for the rights of others and a sincere desire to help others [120].

### The developed and the underdeveloped nations

Because all men are brothers in Christ and form one family, the richer nations must help the poorer [121]. Much has been done [122]. They in their turn must 'be conscious that they are playing the major role in their economic and social development; they are themselves to shoulder the main burden of it' [123]. As Pius XII reminded us, a new order founded on freedom is the surest defence against the violation of their rights. The more powerful nations economically can bring pressure to bear on the weaker, but the latter must control their own political destiny and can exercise neutrality in international conflict. They also have the right of assuring their own economic development and must be assured of this right [124–5].[44]

### Signs of the times

There is a growing awareness that negotiation, not force, must settle international conflicts [126] and that it is fear of the destructiveness of modern weapons that brings this about [127], while at the same time, the desire to deter aggression produces the arms race [128]. It is to be hoped, however, that men will become more aware of the ties that link them and that love, not fear, will predominate in their relationships [129].

### IV. The relationships of men, individuals and political communities with the world community

Developments in science and technology, growing ease of travel and communications, the organization and growth of national economies, are among the factors which have extended international co-operation and interdependence [130]. No longer can one State pursue its interests isolated from the rest; its progress depends on the progress of all [131]. Nothing can destroy the unity of the human race; aware of the dignity of man, it will always tend to seek to promote the common good of all [132]. Old-fashioned diplomacy is giving way to the far-reaching changes that have developed in international relationships. But no meetings of rulers can solve the increasingly complex problems facing the international community; they do not have the authority [133–4] to serve the common good of that community [135]. There must be a true public authority with the means to secure the common good for which it exists [136]. 'Consequently the moral order itself requires the establishment of some form of public authority' internationally [137]. That does not mean that nations can or should accept an authority forced on them [138–9]. The principle of subsidiarity which governs the relations within States must apply internationally [140]. No public international authority can limit the authority of those States, but it can establish the conditions in which the citizens and the intermediate groups in each State can carry out their tasks [141].

The United Nations Organization was established with the purpose of maintaining and strengthening friendly relations between States, based on equality and mutual respect; to it were later added subsidiary organizations concerned with specific functions, economic, social, educational, health and so on [142]. Its *Declaration of Human Rights* was typical of the farsightedness of the Organization [143]. Not all of the points of the *Declaration* are satisfactory but the document is a step in the right direction, asserting the personal dignity of everyone, the right to seek the truth, to follow moral principles, to practice justice and to lead a fully human life [144]. The hope therefore is that the UN may be able 'progressively to adapt its structure and methods of operation to the magnitude of its task' [145].

## V. Pastoral exhortations

Christians should work for the good of their own social, political and economic communities and for the benefit of all humanity, seeking man's betterment in both the natural and the supernatural order [146]. For this they need to be fired by enthusiasm for the Faith [147] and also competent and committed in the practice of their own professions [148], seeking to base relationships on truth, justice and love [149]. The need is above all for recognition of the moral order and spiritual values [150]. There is little of Christian faith and practice informing civil institutions today [151], even where those who helped create and still largely staff those institutions were and are Christians [152].

The reasons for this lie partly in an inadequate education in

Christian teaching and morality, and we must seek to overcome this in training our own people [153]. There is also the difficulty of understanding clearly

> the relation between the objective requirements of justice and concrete situations ... to what degree and in what form doctrinal principles and directives must be applied in the given state of human society [154].

Yet given the pace and complexity of modern activity and the opportunities it opens up, the need for each to contribute to the common good and the search for justice does not diminish but increases [155]. It is an age which has almost limitless horizons [156].

*Christian collaboration in the work of reform*
As pointed out already in *Mater et Magistra*, in putting these mainly natural-law principles into practice, Catholics must necessarily work with others who do not share their faith, co-operating with them on objects which are good in themselves [157]. 'It is always possible to distinguish between error as such and the person who is led into error.' The person in error retains his human dignity [158].

> It is perfectly legitimate to make a clear distinction between a false philosophy of the nature, origin and purpose of men and the world and economic, social, cultural and political undertakings, even when [they] draw their origin and inspiration from that philosophy.[45]

The undertakings themselves may have in them elements which conform to right reason [159]. Prudence should determine whether the moment for co-operation based on this reasoning has arrived for 'the attainment of economic, social, cultural and political advantages'. For Catholics, the decision rests with those taking a leading part in the life of the community in these specific fields; they must however act in accordance

> with the principles of the natural law and the directives of ecclesiastical authority. For it must not be forgotten that the Church has a right and a duty, not only to safeguard her teaching on faith and morals, but also to exercise her authority over her sons by intervening in their external affairs whenever a judgement has to be made concerning the practical application of this teaching [160].

Reforms must come slowly and from within, they must not be tackled impetuously like some political revolution [161]. Hot-headedness was never constructive; rather it destroys everything [162]. Truth, justice, charity, freedom, at all levels from personal relationships up to the international relations of States, must be the hallmark of those who would establish true peace in accordance with the divine order [163]. Many are proceeding on this basis and we take this opportunity of recognizing and thanking them [164]. There will never be lasting peace until peace is found in the heart of everyman [165]. The Pope's teaching is inspired by the desire that peace be established on earth [166]. As the Vicar of Christ, the Prince of Peace, it is the Pope's duty to bend his efforts to secure it, a peace founded on truth, built up on justice and animated by charity, issuing in freedom [167]. It cannot be achieved without God's help [168].

## 5  Summary analysis of the social teaching of John XXIII

### (i)  Ethics and civil society

The person is the purpose, cause and foundation of human society [MM 218–219] and it is in the family that human life is transmitted, sacred from its inception by the all-holy laws of God. Those who violate those laws degrade themselves and humanity, and sap the vitality of the community. Parents must secure for their children a sound cultural and religious formation, especially regarding the family, and the Church must aid them in this [MM 193–7].

Man has been created in God's image and likeness in being given intelligence and free will [PT 3] and he is accordingly the lord of creation. God has stamped on man's conscience a sense of the order has created in him and his world; he is not moved by blind elemental forces; the laws that govern man indicate how he must behave towards others in civil and political society [PT 5–7]. Society must embody the principle that man, a person with free will and judgement, has rights and duties which flow from his nature and these are universal and inalienable. He has been redeemed by Christ, and grace has made mankind friend and heir of God [PT 8–10].

The person must be free and able to act on his own initiative in society, and in his turn each person must act with a sense of personal responsibility towards others and to society [PT 34]. Man, being social by nature, must learn to consider the interests of others, and must recognize the rights and duties that order in society requires [PT 31]. That order must be based on truth, guided by justice and animated by a love which makes men feel the needs of others and as their own. Freedom implies assuming responsibility for one's actions. Society is primarily a spiritual reality; through it men share their knowledge of truth, claim rights and fulfil their duties, can be encouraged to aspire for spiritual goods and share the enjoyment of the wholesome pleasures of this world. These spiritual values should inform culture, social institutions, economic life, political structures, laws and life [PT 36]. They have their source in the true, personal and transcendent God. Human reason derives from the eternal reason [PT 38]. Societies based on recognition of rights and duties grasp the spiritual and intellectual values that are involved and can come to a recognition that God is the foundation of their lives [45].

Society therefore is natural to man [PT 31], and it must be based on freedom, not coercion [PT 45–71]. The citizens possess natural rights which society and the State must recognize, and with these rights go responsibilities. There is a right to life and the means to sustain and develop it, to physical needs, to food, clothing, shelter and medical care; a right to marry or not to marry, to work at a fair wage and in conditions which respect human dignity; a right too to private property and economic freedom, responsibly exercised. Cultural rights include the spiritual and the intellectual: to worship God according to conscience, to education according to ability and the resources of society, to participation in public life and politics, the right of association, to freedom of speech and information [PT 11–25]. These rights carry with them responsibilities; the right to life, for example, imposes the duty of living becomingly. To claim rights while ignoring responsibilities is to build with one hand and pull down with the other [PT 28–35]. The rights of ethnic minorities and refugees must be recognized [PT 97–108] and Christians are to work for the good of the whole of society, seeking necessary reforms by peaceful means. In working for that reform, it will often be necessary to co-operate with others, some of whose fundamental views are not shared; but that should not prevent co-operation on those issues where practical aims coincide [PT 158].

The need for more social provision for families and individuals has been recognized and a growing network of organizations has developed to meet it [MM 59]. Health care, education, housing, work, recreation, are all the concern of the State or other groups; this is good insofar as it helps in the exercise of personal rights and responsibilities, but there is a danger that initiative might be stifled, and this must be guarded against. If this is done, and the rightful autonomy of individuals and groups is preserved, society will have been organically reconstructed as Pius XI advocated [MM 59–67]. The numerous intermediary bodies and corporate enterprises are the main vehicle of society's growth; they have their own autonomy, co-operating in seeking their own good and the good of all. Collectively they form the substance of society, the community, treating their members as persons and encouraging them to take an active part in the ordering of their own lives [MM 65–7].

## (ii) Ethics and political society

The purpose of the State is to secure the common good, the good of each and the good of all, and the authority to make laws binding on its members is necessary to this end. All legitimate authority comes ultimately from God, though not in the sense that rulers are directly appointed by him. [PT 46]. Such authority as it does have is limited by the force of the moral law, natural and revealed, which is founded in God. The law has to protect the rightful autonomy of man, the subject of the rights and duties of the citizen, the person who is the end and purpose of all social organization. Unless the social order has its foundation in God it lacks an ultimate authority. It is without life. Only if State officials are seen to be sharing in that God-given authority can their power be validated, and can they expect to bind the consciences of the citizens concerning obedience to just and necessary laws [PT 47]. A State which lacks this moral authority can only rule by force or bribery, and neither is worthy of human dignity; an appeal to the common good is an appeal to conscience; it implies the exercise of judgement and free will which are the prerogatives of persons, and demonstrate and guarantee their dignity. Obedience to just and necessary laws pays homage to God, and laws which are contrary to his laws have no binding force [PT 48–51].

That authority comes from God does not mean that the people cannot choose their government or rulers and determine how authority is exercised; the teaching on the origin of political authority in God is consonant with genuine democracy [PT 52]. Citizens must make their contribution to the general welfare and do so under the proper authorities which work within their limits of competence, seeking the common good [PT 53–4]. The

measure of the achievement of the common good is the degree
to which the human rights of all are secured and their responsibilities accepted [PT 60–6]. Forms of government are for the
people to decide; they cannot be imposed [PT 67–8]. It is a
natural consequence of man's dignity to take an active part in
government. A charter of human rights, a public constitution and
need for clear understandings of the respective rights and duties
of public authorities and citizens are necessary [PT 73–7]. The
principle of subsidiary function must always be preserved; the
function of government is to recognize, respect and co-ordinate,
safeguard and promote the individual citizen's rights and duties
and to do the same for the family and other subsidiary groups
within the State, not to seek to replace them [PT 65–9].

The relations of States and heads of State are, like those of
private individuals, the subject of reciprocal rights and duties
based on truth, justice and freedom according to the natural
law and the demands of humanity [PT 80–2]. Not all States
are equal in resources, stages of development, wealth and
power, but this does not mean the powerful should dominate;
justice should prevail in all things. No State may defend its rights
by injuring others, and clashes between States should be settled
by negotiation, not by force of arms [PT 91–2]. The common
good of each nation depends on others: what a nation cannot
achieve of itself it needs to co-operate with others to achieve
[PT 98–102].

Developments in science and technology, economic prosperity,
ease of travel and communications are among the factors that have
extended international co-operation and independence. No State
can pursue its interests isolated from the rest, and the older
methods of handling international relations through diplomacy
and treaties are not enough. There is needed a public authority
with the power, organization and means adequate to the situation
world wide. It must embody the principle of subsidiarity, creating
the conditions in which individual States can co-operate to these
ends [PT 130–41]. The United Nations has done much, and the
hope is that it will be able to adapt itself to meet the magnitude of
its task [PT 145]. The arms race between the developed countries
is wasteful of national resources and produces an atmosphere of
fear. Deterrence may work temporarily but the only long-term
answer to the problem is an end to the arms race based on effective agreements backed up by effective systems of mutual control
[PT 109–11].

## (iii) Ethics and economic society

The national economy is built up by those in the community and the State who seek to satisfy the material needs which must be met if the life of the citizens is to be adequately developed. When these needs are satisfied on a permanent basis the people are economically rich in the best sense because the general well-being is secure: the personal right to the use of worldly goods accords with the will of the creator [MM 74]. The basis of the economy and economic life must be the private initiative of individuals and associations formed by them to this end; the State also has a role in directing, stimulating, co-ordinating and integrating production in accordance with the principle of subsidiary function [MM 51–3]. Of its nature the State exists to facilitate the activity of its citizens, not to destroy or to absorb it. Modern developments have given the State greater scope in economic policy, redressing imbalances and providing employment, but it must always maintain its first function, to facilitate private initiative. State and citizen must co-operate for the common good; experience shows that where economic initiative is muzzled, the State stagnates and political tyranny ensues. At the same time, however, experience also teaches that where the State does not act for the common good, the strong exploit the weak [MM 57–8].

The economy then should be based on private economic initiative, but that initiative should operate to produce justice for all. In fact, throughout the world, millions of workers have wages inadequate for a decent livelihood. Economic development is carried on with no thought for justice, and national resources are wasted on prestige projects or arms. In economically advanced countries rewards are often apportioned unjustly; the laws of the market cannot be left to operate unhindered; wage earners should have a just share of the economic resources available. It is not so much a country's total wealth but the equity of its distribution which indicates true economic prosperity. The workers should somehow have a share in management, ownership or profits; they need to express themselves in work in some way [MM 68–77]. The demands of the common good must always be kept in mind when the question of the determination of wages or profits arises. On wages, the level of employment, prices, and many other factors must be taken into account [MM 78–9]. International factors also impinge on the common good, the level of trade [MM 80] and the demands of the common good are relevant in determining the return to management and shareholders [MM 81].

Wages cannot be left simply to the market. They must be just according to the resources available [MM 71–2]. Where firms are prospering, some kind of participation in profits should be introduced, and it is desirable that workers come to share in the ownership of the company [MM 75–7]. The conditions of work should be fully human; man has a right to express himself in his work and so perfect himself [MM 82]. Craft businesses and co-operatives must be encouraged [MM 85–90]. Ways in which it can be done vary, but there is also no doubt that workers should be given an active part in the business or companies they work for, private or public: they must be true communities, all parties co-operating in service of their fellow men [MM 91–2]. The workers also should participate in decision making by public authorities and institutions which influence the well-being of industry [MM 97–9].

Forms of ownership and the means of providing security for oneself and one's family have changed. Professional managers control large amounts of capital on behalf of its owners, and government is concerned to ensure they do so for the common good also. The ownership of productive goods by individuals as a means of security can also appear to be of less importance than social insurance; proficiency at one's trade or profession certainly rates higher than property; the latter is instrumental only, while work is an immediate expression of personality as well as being a means of livelihood. But the right to private property is part of the natural order which establishes the person and his rights as prior to any right granted by the State. Where the right to property does not exist, the exercise of freedom in other directions is more easily suppressed or stifled [MM 105–9]. This makes it more imperative that those, the mass of the wage earners, who do not own property, should have access to it as industry becomes more productive and their increased wages make it possible for them to save [MM 112–15]. The right of the State to own productive goods remains, in accordance with the subsidiarity principle; competence and accountability should be demanded of those who direct State concerns [MM 120]. The State also has a major role in establishing justice between the different sections of the economy, particularly in redressing the disadvantages suffered by the agricultural sector in so many ways [PT 122–152].

The solidarity of the human race demands that the discrepancies that exist between the wealth of the developed and the poverty of the underdeveloped nations be redressed [MM 157]. There are two aspects to the question; firstly, that of meeting emergency shortfalls, for example in food supplies, by giving emergency aid;

for instance by transferring surplus food stocks to needy countries. More important in the long term is the need to help the countries concerned to produce their requirements out of their own resources by transfers of capital, skills and technology [MM 161–3]. The developing nations would do well to learn from the experience of the developed countries. It is the economic strengths and characteristics of a nation that should be built on, and those who would help them must remember this; helping the new nations to achieve their own goals should be the aim [MM 169, 173]. Underdeveloped countries must carry the main responsibility for their own development. It is only the nation itself which can guarantee to its people that the common good can be achieved, and those who would help them must respect this [PT 123–4].

The population question, the ability of the world to provide adequately for its people, at present and in the future, is important in this context. This problem is not excess population; it is one of organizing the technical and scientific effort to exploit the riches of the world, and improving the defective solidarity and social and economic organization of the countries in question [MM 185–92]. The conviction of the value of every human life and the co-operation between nations in the exchange of knowledge, capital and manpower is needed if the challenge is to be met. This international co-operation cannot be achieved without mutual trust, which can only be based on a morality founded in God and inspiritual values [MM 200–8]. Man's forgetfulness of these facts results in his self-destruction [MM 242–57].

# 21

# The background to the social teaching of the Church 1962–78

## 1 The cultural revolution in the Western world

In *Pacem in Terris* John XXIII pointed out the positive characteristics of modern society, greater recognition of the rights of workers and women, nations gaining their freedom, racialism being challenged. That was in 1963, but as that decade went on more negative aspects made themselves evident. Fuller employment, higher wages, better educational, health and social services did not impress the post war generation. Their benefits were taken for granted, their defects inflated out of all proportion.

Many groups seem to have been beyond the reach of what came to be called the Welfare State, and to have gained little during a time of fuller employment and higher wages. Such were the families of the less skilled workers, or of socially inadequate parents, those living in decaying inner-city areas, racial minorities, those working in traditionally badly-paid jobs for example. Nor were there lacking fundamental critics of the whole project. In France the intellectual scene had been set by left-wing intellectuals such as Jean-Paul Sartre whose social influence was almost entirely negative, with its confused and often contradictory Marxist existentialism, bearing down in hard criticism of bourgeois society, at having confused and corrupted the working classes and duped them into abandoning their Marxist vocation. Towards the real socialism of the Soviet variety he was ambivalent to say the least. He did not deny the existence of the Gulags but refused to allow them to tempt him into counter-revolutionary attitudes. Albert Camus, less political than Sartre, regarded political commitment as at best a necessary evil; he was also more realistic about Stalin's crimes, finding it less easy to explain them away by seeing them as 'the

---

* The notes and references for Chapter 21 are to be found on p. 456ff

wave of the future' than did Sartre. Followers of such masters as these could hardly be anything else but nihilistic and against the established order.

In Germany the economic miracle and the need to come to terms with the recent past produced a more contented but yet sombre mood until the late 1950s. In the immediate post-war years there was little or nothing which could be seen as a literary or cultural movement of any kind in a country in which cultural leaders had not been the conscience of the nation in the grim Nazi years. The past had to be purged; the question of how Nazi Germany could have happened was the main theme dealt with by many writers who had survived the Hitler years. From the late 1950s, however, a new literary intelligentsia had appeared; it was bitterly critical of the bourgeois society which, in its turn rejected its members as mere spoilers.[1] The emergence of the Baader-Meinhof gang in the early 1970s revealed how soured and violent a section of the middle class and university-educated population had become.[2]

In Britain the rejection of accepted standards was less ideological and violent, being centred on a group of writers and dramatists, the 'angry young men' who sneered at the conventional post-war literature and the political consensus; Kingsley Amis, John Osborne and John Braine are the names that stand out.[3] In the United States in the 1950s and early 1960s the situation was different. The virulent anti-Communism of the McCarthyites ruffled the waters, but this was in support of the anti-Communist *status quo* and the consensus on which it rested, rather than being critical of it. The Civil Rights movement which began stirring in 1955 and became national under the leadership of Martin Luther King, particularly after the march on Washington in 1963, was a crusade to get basic rights from society, not a rejection of it for denying them until then. With the Vietnam War and the Black Power movement in the second half of the decade, however, things changed.[4]

They did so in the context of a much more fundamental cultural revolution which challenged the basic moral premises upon which Western society had been built, and applied that challenge to attitudes and institutions which really did support the social order. The key word and idea was 'permissiveness' – not being judgemental of any personal preference in action or lifestyle which people freely wanted to adopt; the only limitation was that if others were involved, their preferences and manner of life should not be harmed or hindered by one's own. The social implications of this selfishness were not considered. Where anything goes, it is the

ruthlessness of the greedy, the strong and the wealthy which
prevails; the weak, the less pushful, the respecters of the rights and
needs of others are overridden. No man is an island; the illusion
that in doing my own thing I hurt no one provided I allow others
the same freedom is based on the false premise that all values and
lifestyles are equal. Some enhance man's dignity, some degrade it:
social mores must protect the former and penalize the latter, or
else there is soon no civil society to speak of, but only a hedonistic,
atomistic individualism in which the weakest, the very young and
the very old in particular, go to the wall.

But everything could now be questioned; no institution was
sacred, no person, idea or ideal could command automatic and
assumed acceptance. The signs were there in the late 1960s: the easy
tolerance for divorce on trivial grounds, for premarital sex, the
contraceptive pill, the social acceptance of abortion, of homosexual
relationships as on a par with heterosexual as a choice of life-style,
the growing pressure on the traditional family and its values, all
indicated abandonment of social norms long respected, with no
consideration of the long-term effects of their abandonment with
which we are now living. The fact is that the moral foundations of
Western democratic society are Christian. There was a time, and it is
not so long ago, that it could be said that 'Christianity ... sets the
way Westerners think ... even those who would hate to think of
themselves as Christians'. The individual 'endowed with an immortal soul of priceless value is a free moral agent' and as such 'once he
is mature knows, by the grace of God and the teaching of the
Church, right from wrong'. He can then choose to do wrong and
'plead physical coercion and to a limited extent ignorance, but he
cannot plead irresponsibility'.[5] It was the idea of the moral responsibility for one's own human actions, the choices which man freely
and knowingly makes, and the respect for the Christian moral law
according to which those choices should be made, which underlay
the Western idea of personal freedom and so ultimately its political
tradition. The respect for law that was the cornerstone of those freedoms was ultimately for the law of God; this is shown in the oath still
tendered in our courts, the attestation to 'the truth, the whole truth
and nothing but the truth, so help me God'. The right to representative, and ultimately democratic, government, and the freedom of
the citizen under the law, are ideas we inherited from the Christian
tradition and they both assume the moral responsibility of the
person, made in God's image and likeness in being given intelligence and free will. As such he is free to choose between good and
evil, but he is aware from the Christian tradition that defiance of the

moral law, divine and natural, undermines human dignity and the social order.

The destruction of the view of the world which made such reasoning possible has been in process gradually over a long period: what prevented it having its catastrophic effects earlier was the strength of the ideas and institutions which kept the ideal before us; they were embodied in the Christian churches as a whole, in the institution of the family which was still based on the sacramental understanding of marriage and its obligations, despite the acceptance of divorce in practice, and in the laws which framed our society. Western liberalism had rejected this Christian tradition, but its ideals still provided society's structures with the cement that held them together. That liberalism emerged from the Renaissance and was confirmed by the Enlightenment, and its central belief was the absolute autonomy of the individual, independent of any obligation to a transcendent power. Man does not need authoritative guidance; he is of himself capable of fulfilling his potential.[6] Initially many liberals kept their belief in objective moral law, the natural law as the Christian tradition knew it. Hugo Grotius (1583–1645) was an example of the principled liberal. He and those who thought like him 'were not able to disregard the Christian tradition of which they were part'. They believed there were certain objective values, eternal truths, which were independent of individual will and interest; they were part of the order of things, limitations on individual liberty evident in the natural law which guides conscience. There were, in other words, merging contradictory concepts, the idea of absolute human autonomy, and an idea of the natural law as objective, binding and perceptible by right reason, preventing freedom becoming licence.[7]

As we have seen, to the Enlightenment natural law meant something quite different; it was modelled on physical law, an in-built morality which had to be freed from any external restraint, any objective natural law to which the human mind had access, or any revealed moral law or authoritative church interpreting it. Their God, for those who accepted his existence, was not involved in the affairs of the world; it, including its human element, had been wound up like a clock and would run on of itself in complete social harmony if only left alone. Liberalism and Enlightenment also inevitably encouraged scepticism on all matters, and another school of thought, the positivist, which emerged in the nineteenth century, finally dismissed any idea of moral law and its application as a mirage. Only that which could be measured and weighed, which was material, physical, had reality. There was no natural

moral harmony in things provided by the God of the Deists, as
there were no eternal truths perceptible by reason, as many principled liberals had believed.

Secular liberalism, having rejected absolute moral truths and
unchanging principles, inevitably degenerates into intellectual
and moral anarchy or into a form of cultural totalitarianism.
Where the liberal political system is so weakened by events that in
effect it collapses, as in inter-war Italy and Germany, the totalitarian State emerges. Where the society in which it is embedded is
initially stronger, in time it falls into the former, as its strength is
slowly sapped by scepticism and relativism, as it has been sapped in
the Western democracies, and permissive selfishness takes over.[8]
The effects of this undermining of moral principle were staved off
until the middle of this century by the continuing vitality of the old
hierarchies of society, the paternalist family, the Church, the
school, the law, the State. But the anarchy became more marked
from the 1960s and has continued to gnaw away at the essential
cultural code, any effective sense of right and wrong in the objective order, which any society needs to hand on to its children if
they are to be formed into socially responsible citizens.

The crime figures indicate an overall trend to greater lawless-
ness. In England for example, the rate per 100,000 of the
population in the twentieth century until 1954, in peace and war,
slump and boom, was less than 1000; by the 1970s it was 3200[9] and
it was beginning to show in social behaviour at every level. The
most significant change in social mores has been in the conditions
set by society for the family, marriage and the conception and
rearing of children. Until the 1960s, the sacramental idea of
marriage, which our culture had received from its Christian inheritance, still influenced attitudes to it. That ideal was of a lifelong
commitment to an exclusive union between man and wife who, in
the normal course of things, would raise a family to whose care
they would be committed, and that ideal was backed up by the law
of the land, the law of the Church, by most educational institutions, by most families and individuals and by society.

In this model, the role of the father was one which it has become
fashionable to decry as 'patriarchal', and this is an attitude which
has its origins in Marxist-Leninist thinking.[10] It proposed that
there had at one time been forms of family based on mother right,
but that as civilization developed, and with it forms of private property, the family came more and more under the control of men,
and matriarchy was replaced by patriarchy. The emancipation of
women then depends on their being given access to socially

productive work and so becoming financially independent of their husbands. Like many aspects of Marxist ideology there was a core of plausibility about this; the theory seemed to be confirmed by experience as more and more women have been able to find financial independence by paid work outside the home.

Yet the theory as elaborated by Lenin had no basis in fact. Matriarchy was posited of prehistorical times, and what is prehistory is beyond proof or verification. That of course means nothing to the ideologue. It is now widely accepted that all patriarchy in some way is by definition oppressive of women, and the idea of a strong father responsible for his family in a manner that differs from the way a strong mother is responsible for it, is seen as unacceptable. New men should be gentler and caring, more womanly, not concerned if their wives are better providers than they, ready to play the role the wife was traditionally called upon to play as homemaker, and 'mothering' the children while the stronger female is called upon to play the father's traditional role as well as the mother's when necessary. The trouble is that the new man and the new women may be figments of the imagination of the minority of ideologists who think they stand to benefit from their appearance. But the readjustment of thinking and acting that is required if they are to have their way requires social engineering on a massive scale. One would have thought that the experience of such engineering over the last two hundred years would have cured us of the taste for it; the excesses of rampant liberalism in the French Revolution and its aftermath, liberal capitalism and its inheritance, and of the appalling brutalities of Nazism and Soviet Communism were all examples of it.

The experience so far does not seem to support the ideology. Even the societies which have done their best to foster the new men and women have not had much success[11] while that a healthy society requires a stable patriarchal one, has been urged not only by theologians but by anthropologists and psychologists[12]. The cultures which have endured longest and made the greatest contributions to civilisation have been based on marriages of this kind. It is a lesson that a civilisation which was so built up should keep in mind when confronted by the popular clamour against them.

One of the responses of the modern male to the new social pattern, for example, is to avoid marriage and have relationships which often result in fatherhood on a casual and irresponsible basis. Another is to divorce more easily, an option which, for those who have children means that they become less fatherly and do not give their offspring the support they need in growing up to be good citizens; this is particularly true of the young boys. Neither alternative to stable patriarchal marriage is then healthy socially. Children need responsible caring mothers and fathers.

Most men in fact see their role in the family as being the patriarchal provider as the 1993 British social attitudes survey showed. This was true especially of the least educated, whose ambitions in this regard are severely undermined by the likelihood they will be in low paid jobs or unemployed. They do not therefore make good marriage prospects and for that reason often remain unmarried. From the point of view of the males therefore it would appear that the marital and paternal instincts which would fit them to be supporters of the patriarchal marriage style which has served Western civilisation so well is being undermined not by the ideals of role-changing but by poor employment prospects and low wages.

This new way of looking at the responsibilities of men and women in the context of the family, has developed at a time when society has failed to fulfill adequately the hopes and promises which seemed on the point of fulfillment in the near full employment and higher wages which the Western nations experienced in the 1950's and 1960's. Enough of this achievement has remained however for us to remark it – for the first time in modern history and probably in all history, the vast mass of ordinary people had at least an adequate wage, security against the foreseeable disasters life can bring and possibility of advancement through better education; and they achieved all this at a time when easy travel and all the ordinary conveniences of life were available to all. But it is not clear how a theory of role reversal helps in this context; accepting lower or lesser certain male earnings on the grounds that women are now expected to make up for them, is unsatisfactory from every point of view.

It has also developed at a time when the ideal of parents freely contracting through marriage to spend their whole lives together and to raise a family, support their children and bring them up to be responsible citizens in their turn was under pressure. The pressure had been there from the time of the Matrimonial Causes Act of 1857, which allowed divorce on very limited grounds, subsequently in 1923 and 1957 considerably relaxed. Divorces increased from 10,000 annually in the 1940's to 110,000 in the 1970's, and since then marriages are down by half, divorces have trebled and the number of illegitimate children has quadrupled[13]. Selfish secular liberalism is destroying the traditional family, the basic unit of civil society and the state.

Until the 1950s, social pressures supported the traditional family and sought to ensure that couples accepted it as the natural context of their love for one another. But in the next twenty years this changed; influential opinion, particularly as projected by the mass media, began to insist that the single-parent family was as good as the traditional, and still basically Catholic, model.[14] At first there was an attempt to show that this represented simply a change in the type of family that society supported: it did not mean a deterioration of family values and virtues, despite the universal experience that children reared by single parents were generally disadvantaged in comparison with those of the traditional family.[15] Between them, the statistics which reveal a rising tide of crime, and the breakdown of the traditional family which alone provides for the adequate socialization of the young, show that more than increasing overall prosperity and the care of the State for its people's welfare is needed if the human condition is to be improved. There is need for a respect for moral values that are accepted as binding on all, so that society can hand on to the present and future generations its experience in the art of living.

This undermining of basic moral values which had served Western society well coincided with and was partly responsible for serious social unrest. In 1967 the USA was deeply divided over the Vietnam war, while the social conditions in its own inner cities were inciting the mainly black population there to increasingly violent protest. There was discontent in the universities also.[16] The number of students had been increasing steadily since 1945 and the system had proved unable to cope adequately with their needs; administratively and academically the old university system and the attitudes of those who operated it had been found wanting. The volatility of student populations had been a fact of life since universities began, and the combination of the students' own problems and their identification with political protest provided a potent focus for discontent. They were now reflecting the concerns of society generally in some matters, notably on the American role in Vietnam.

The summer of 1967 saw outbreaks of violence in the cities. In New Jersey eight blacks were shot dead by the police and the army; later in Detroit thirty-seven more died. 'Black power' began to exert itself, demanding the blacks form a separate nation from the whites. In 1968 the unrest continued. On 4 April, Martin Luther King, the civil rights leader, was shot dead in Memphis, and the threat of insurrection seemed to rear its head in some states in the wake of his death. On 5 June, Robert Kennedy, a Presidential candidate, was also shot dead in Los Angeles while on campaign, and the tensions within the Democratic party on racial matters and on Vietnam resulted in violent picketing and barracking of the Democratic Convention on 26 August, provoking what was later described as a police riot.

In 1968 students in France began what at one time looked to be the beginning of a genuine revolutionary movement. It had been assumed that the events of the 1930s and the experience of the Second World War would make any open advocacy of violence and social revolution impossible, but the generation which reached the stage of political awareness in the early 1960s, had no direct experience of these things and started their analysis from their own standpoint. Many had already been radicalized. Groups of student Trotskyites, Maoists, Guevarists and Castroites had been discussing revolution from the early 1960s, and it was only a matter of time before the movement became more widespread. The strike of sociology lecturers and students at Nanterre in November 1967 gave it the impetus it needed. In February 1968 Paris students followed suit, with Daniel Cohn Bendit from Germany being prominent in leading it. In early May demonstrators tried to seize university buildings and the police, surprised by the violent turn of events, reacted too vigorously, so adding to the protestors' rage. Sympathy strikes by trade unions and street demonstrations by thousands of Parisians objecting to Gaullism followed. Student soviets appeared in most universities and the revolutionary expectations seemed to rival those of Petrograd in 1917. By 17 May, ten million workers were out on strike also with demands of their own to be met. President de Gaulle, breaking off a visit to Bucharest to face the crisis,[17] had his first efforts to negotiate an ending of it rebuffed and he changed tack. First assuring himself of the loyalty of the officer commanding French troops in West Germany in the event of further widespread violence, he announced new elections for 23 June; he also called for civic action against the threat of Communist revolution. What genuine public support there had been for the disturbances faded and the elections duly returned the party of order, all left-wing groups losing votes.

In Germany, Italy and Great Britain there were student-led demonstrations and protests of varying degrees of intensity, none of them rivalling that in France. In Berlin in June 1967 there were demands for, among other things, student participation in government of the university, demands which were escalated by increasingly radicalized students after every concession. Street fights broke out, and in the same month one student was shot dead by police, many more joining in the protest as a result. Later Rudi Dutschke, one of their leaders, was shot by a mentally deranged youth. In the February of 1968, backed by many liberal elements in society at large, a campaign was launched against Axel Springer, Germany's largest newspaper owner, and vocal critic of the student movement. The latter was highly ideological, influenced by Herbert Marcuse[18] among others, and identified more and more with the hopes of revolution in the third world. Yet despite its impact, or because of it, it drew little general support; its main base remained the universities.

Italian students rioted in Rome in April-May 1966, and in November 1967 there was a more widespread outbreak of protest which affected the country at large: starting with demands for better grants and facilities, they went on to attack bourgeois society generally. In Spain the students were prominent in the struggle to overthrow Franco: Barcelona University was closed in April 1966, and by 1968 their action had spread throughout the country. In Britain there were student protests also, but they were less violent. Only one demonstration, that in central London against the Vietnam War in October 1968, threatened more general violence.

When they had subsided it became plain that the series of disturbing and violent episodes and the endless innovation of revolutionary slogans had not amounted to serious revolutionary intent. The movement was too confused and incoherent, and its leaders were never seriously committed to anything but short-term gains, causing confusion and instilling what fear they could into the targets of their anger, the powers that were and those who served them. It was a sign of cultural discontent, much of it superficial and contrived, not a serious threat to the whole social order as, for example, the anarchists and the threat of Marxist-inspired violence had been in the late nineteenth and early twentieth century. Meanwhile, in Czechoslovakia in 1968, twelve years after the attempted openings up in East Germany, Hungary and Poland, Alexander Dubček sought to make life a little less oppressive for his people without breaking with, or even inconveniencing, the other Warsaw Pact countries. On 21 August, a Russian invasion crushed his hopes, emphatically demonstrating that the dictatorship of the proletariat was less tolerant of its social dissenters than the bourgeois society of the West.

## 2  The Church and social justice in Latin America[19]

The Church in Latin America slowly grew to maturity as it shrugged off the influences of its colonial background. The clergy

both in Spain and in Latin America had been divided over the
Church's role in society, before the nineteenth-century independence movement in that region, growing from the 1820s, gradually
succeeded in freeing the former colonies. Was that role to be to act
as the support of royal power and absolute monarchy, conceived as
God ordained, whatever its defects in practice, or should it be
unambiguously defending the rights of the people, and especially
of the poor? After independence in Latin America, the Church's
position was then complicated by the anti-clericalism among many
leaders of the new States, generally strongly opposed to the
Church as an organization, and to its clergy in particular. They
were influenced by European ideology, its liberalism, its positivism
and its belief in capitalist economics and incentives, competition
and materialism, all of which strengthened their anti-clericalism.
The conservatives, on the other hand, in theory rejected these
ideals, preferring the cultural values of the colonial period, spiritual rather than material rewards for the people generally,
industrial guild organization and the traditional land-holding
structures.

The waves of revolution had led to the establishment of formal
democracies on the American Presidential model which in practice were oligarchies, usually militaristic in nature, representing
the conservative and liberal political interests. After 1848 a new
generation of liberals surfaced, inspired by the events in Europe,
and pushed their agenda more vigorously, gradually gaining
control of most countries, save those of Central America. Many of
the clergy, who had originally been convinced that, with reservations, the liberals could be supported, now changed their minds
because of the breakdown in morality and the political confusion
their policies seemed to produce. Their adhesion to the conservative cause had the effect of strengthening the liberal conviction
that ecclesiastical organization and immunities were incompatible
with democracy; it also confirmed the conservative conviction that
religion and liberalism could not be reconciled.

Liberalism particularly targeted the Church's wealth and the
support of charitable works which it saw as encouraging idleness;
capitalistic values were what the masses needed to produce
economic progress. Not until the Church's wealth was in more
responsible and economically-motivated hands would progress be
possible. The truth was that they and men like them wanted the
Church's lands and property for themselves; the appeal to efficiency was a means to make their ambitions respectable at least in
their own eyes. The conservative political agenda, and the clergy's

insistence that the attacks on the Church's hierarchical structure would result in a general levelling down throughout society, now converged and the alliance became more marked.

Initially the social philosophy of the conservatives was paternalistic. The lower classes were not to be encouraged to rise above their station since this would threaten the natural order of things; they were not to be despised, however, being equally called to eternal salvation along with their betters. They should live in reasonable comfort therefore, protected by paternalism. By contrast the liberals wanted the lower classes to improve their status and make themselves economically independent. Liberal administration would offer greater educational opportunities, access to the vote, and employment to make this possible. But it was an illusion. Opportunities for ordinary people to better themselves were not there in the numbers and kind needed, yet ideology blinded the liberals to this fact. Convinced that those who did not better themselves were feckless and should be left to their own devices, they and the administrations they controlled felt absolved of all concern for the suffering of the poor. In time this attitude became evident among the conservatives also, despite their ostensible paternalism; they also decided that charity was wasted on those who lacked economic virtue. The result was that, as population growth and industrialization increased towards the end of the nineteenth century and into the twentieth, social conflict intensified and threatened to become revolutionary.

However, the beginnings of change were detectable; the industrialization that occurred in the late nineteenth century, limited though it was, bred a labour movement, and the occasional employer who saw the need to treat industrial workers more justly, if only for the sake of self-interest.[20] Catholic Action groups along the lines of those established in Italy provided social activists within the Church with a context in which they could commit themselves to peaceful social reform. By the 1950s most of the positive developments in the Church over the next twenty years had already been outlined in one way or throughout the region. They were fed from many sources. The Cursillo movement ('Short courses in Christianity') flourished in the 1950s; these were three-day events which immersed the participants in a prayerful examination of the Christian way and what it meant to them. They were a means of assisting many to rededicate themselves more fully to Christ, and to practical work for others. The influx of missionaries from other countries in the 1950s introduced new ideas and linked Latin America more closely to the international Church, while the formation of the Latin American Episcopal Council (CELAM), which met for the first time in Rio in 1955, was the first time the Church in the region had co-operated and worked as one. It was structurally weak because of difficulties of communication and lack of a tradition of inter-regional contact, but it helped the development of both, preparing the Church for the approach to the Second Vatican Council, enabling clerics and lay workers to collaborate more freely.

The transnational character of the Church, evidenced in the papal nuncios in each country, also helped. Though of their nature non-political, it often happened that the nuncios were approached for help on important disputes locally when there seemed to be no other recourse, and they also acted as mediators, seeking to lessen the oppression of governments and to help with human rights problems; their work in arranging settlement of disputes between nations had been significant, and they were also important channels of communication between the churches, nationally and internationally. Finally there were the informal networks established by those involved in work for the Church throughout Latin America, priests, nuns, journalists, academics, and lay activists generally. Through them they kept in touch and co-operated on joint enterprises. The existence of these organizations became of extreme importance as the Council approached.

In the secular social thinking of the early twentieth century in Latin America, several factors were favourable to the Church. The leaders of the reaction against positivistic and utilitarian philosophies – de Figueiredo of Brazil was one – saw the need for a theological and supernatural basis for their humanism and were consequently drawn to her; the Church also remained the most powerful defender of the cultural values of the masses – the mestizos and the Indian communities.[21] The appearance of radical theorists supporting class war also resulted in some liberals having second thoughts about capitalism and egalitarian democracy, and they allied themselves with conservatives and the Church against the threat of sweeping change. Catholic Action was seen as a way of supporting moderate trade unionism and ameliorative work for the urban poor, so reducing the threat of violence.

The support by some Catholics of a form of corporatism, overcoming the alienation of the masses from society by breaking down its structures into their natural subdivisions, organisms or corporations, and involving the masses in their governing, was however, an unhelpful development.[22] That support implied that the Church should have more direct political influence through this system and this was of course not acceptable to the secular liberals. The more far-sighted saw also that this form of organization, even if it were desirable and possible, would prevent the emergence of the truly pluralistic institutions which were the only hope of the long-term and successful political and economic developments which would stabilize society. Unfortunately, some well-intentioned clerics could not see the dangers of identifying the Church with what was a confused right-wing initiative, defensible perhaps as part of the secular search for a more ordered society, however badly thought out it was; but it was at best, and in theory, provisional, and as it had been proved, was quite impractical. Inevitably such support left the Church tainted with the suspicion of sympathy with Fascism.

After the Second World War the concern of the Church for the poor became more marked and priests were active in encouraging social reform: their minds were concentrated by awareness that if the traditional forces in society did not respond, new ones, especially Marxism in some form, would do so; the events surrounding the fall of the Arbenz regime in Guatemala revealed how conflict on this matter, and over-reaction to real or imagined communist menace, could thwart needed democratic reform.[23] Some thought that all that was needed was more effective charitable work for the poor. Others saw the need for fundamental changes but could not agree on the means to that end. The forced redistribution of wealth, or increasing the productive powers of the people through credit, consumer and agricultural co-operatives, were some of the remedies suggested. Paulo Freire's theory of conscientization, that is, making people aware of class solidarity and the potential power of the poor in shaping events if they organized themselves, also had considerable influence.[24]

The hope of economic development, which was the hope of meeting the needs of the poor, lay mainly in the export market. The export sectors of the Latin American countries in colonial times expanded after independence. Precious metals and sugar had been the original leaders, but now minerals and agricultural products generally became important, and Chile, Argentina, Uruguay, Venezuela and the São Paulo area of Brazil for example became dynamic centres of growth, mainly through supplying Europe and North America.[25] The problem was that concentration on exports of primary products left the supplying countries very much at the mercy of the volatile international markets where demand, and consequently prices, fluctuated considerably. At the same time Latin American economies depended heavily for manufactured goods on imports from the more developed countries, and prices for these goods were higher and more stable. The result was that when their earnings from their cheaper exports slumped they borrowed heavily to pay for their imports of manufactured goods, or simply printed money for internal use, and both inflation and foreign imports increased accordingly. There was the further problem that the export industries were, in the main, run by foreign interests and it was they who gained most during the times of prosperity. Initially those foreign interests were mainly British who took the place of the former colonial powers as the link with the international economy; by the turn of the century however the North Americans were beginning to overtake them in this. It is therefore not to be wondered at that the citizens of the new States considered that they were being exploited by foreign interests.

From the 1950s, the problem of how to free these countries from their dependency was increasingly being discussed. It was claimed that since foreign interests controlled their economies or dominated them, governments were not able to act for the good of the people at large but had to follow policies that favoured their masters. They could not for example industrialize sufficiently, because the profits taken out of Latin American economies deprived them of needed investment. The injustices existing in Latin America were then caused by this dependency. This theory was favoured by Marxists, it being an extension of the Lenin-Hobson theory of capitalist development, according to which international trade by the Western nations was undertaken exclusively for their own interests and was by definition a form of exploitation.[26]

That the investors in Latin America enterprises sought primarily their own profit is of course true. It is the nature of market forces to respond to the lure of such profit. In that sense the Lenin-Hobson thesis simply states the obvious. The countries in question, however, were in no position to modernize their societies and economies at the time because they had neither the resources nor the educational, social or economic infrastructures, nor the political will that would have made that possible. Their social structures were riddled with the relics of their colonial class consciousness, the mestizos and the natives not only poor but despised and with little or no education, and the entrepreneurial spirit generally underdeveloped. A modern State needed railways, good roads and communications, technical, commercial and business skills, and the resources to provide them were limited or lacking.

In this context any capital and technological input, whatever the

motives behind it, would benefit the country concerned in important ways, and it is now accepted that not a little economic
development did take place as a result of the long export boom in
the nineteenth century; larger export earnings meant increased
incomes and a growing demand for local manufactures and products, and the means to import machinery which would help
improve the domestic industries. There was large-scale railway
building, and steamships linked previously isolated regions; the
larger cities adopted the new gas lighting. The effects must not be
exaggerated; overall impact on the economies of the countries
concerned and on the lives of the majority of their people was
limited. Most improvements affected the lives of the comparatively
few who lived in the big cities, and the exporting sector did not
stimulate the growth of a risk-taking economic class, the entrepreneurs who would find new ways of making profits and building new
industries or developing new agricultural techniques and products. The creole grandees were merely exploiting the near-
monopoly of the commodities, food and minerals which could be
worked cheaply because natural resources and labour were there
in abundance. With few exceptions, neither the economic structures, nor those who owned and controlled agricultural and
industrial life, were adaptable and alert enough to readjust and
face the economic and the political demands of the new century.
It was the internal weaknesses of the social, political and economic
structures of Latin American society and national states which
prevented them addressing the question of development in the
broadest sense, to which economic development is crucial, and the
major responsibility for this failure must rest with those who were
leaders in society at all levels, including those who controlled the
productive forces. Foreign interests simply exploited the situation:
they did not create it.

The new century brought no relief. The export sectors which
had developed relied on a favourable balance of trade which had
favoured competitively-priced Latin American food and raw materials in supplying industrializing Europe. From the end of the First
World War, however, the demand for its products gradually
declined, as competition from alternative sources of supplies of
primary products emerged and the pattern of demand and trade
internationally changed. America replaced Britain as the region's
major trading partner, and her large agricultural sector meant she
needed to import less, while the preference for the countries of the
British Empire reduced exports to Britain.[27] The great depression
of 1929–34 made things worse at a time when increasing United

States involvement in Latin American affairs roused nationalists against America and everything American. The relations of the rest of the world generally, and North America in particular, with Latin America, in the inter-war years were then not of the best. It felt that it had been exploited and then rejected.

The 1939–45 years brought a moderate recovery but by the 1950s there was a general crisis of development in practice as well as in theory; the policy of import substitution, which it was hoped would enable demand for manufactured goods to be met from home resources, so reducing expensive imports and employing local capital and labour, faltered at the same time as the impoverished peasants moved into the cities to try to find there the means to live and perhaps prosper.[28] With the success of Castro's rebellion in Cuba in 1959 and its subsequent turn to Marxism, it was inevitable that the demand for social justice throughout the continent in the 1960s would become distinctly revolutionary, and the first world's social unrest in the 1960s, with the fashionable Marxism that it fostered, encouraged this trend. This was the background as bishops, priests, religious and laity from Latin America were involved in the process of preparation for the Second Vatican Council.

# 22

# The Second Vatican Council

## 1 Introduction

Two of the decrees of the Council dealt specifically with social issues, the one on Religious Freedom, namely *Dignitatis Humanae* (DH), and that on the Church in the Modern World, *Gaudium et Spes* (GS). They had been under consideration since the first session which started in October 1962, but because of the difficulties that attended their evolution, both were finalized only during the fourth and last session which took place in the last three months of 1965.

The reason for the delay in getting them through lay in their novelty and in the problems which attended their drafting. It was the first time that major documents of an ecumenical council had dealt in depth with such issues, and cultural factors did not make it easy for what was still a mainly European-based Church to rethink them. The attitude to religious liberty – a Gospel value – for example, had been coloured first by the Church's involvement with the social order in the Middle Ages, then by the violent reaction against it in the Reformation period, followed by the experience of the Enlightenment, the French Revolution and nineteenth-century liberalism. To absorb the lessons of all this, to rethink the matter in depth, and to produce a document which was true to the apostolic tradition and relevant to the modern world was an exhaustive, lengthy and often heated process.

As for a document on the Church in the Modern World, the pitfalls besetting its way were manifold; there were social encyclicals responding to specific circumstances and issues, but such an open-ended commitment to cover the whole range of topics dealing with 'the world', however the concept was defined, was another matter. Yet these two documents were crucial in the task of enabling the Church in the twentieth century to continue in its central mission of evangelization. The pre-Vatican II Church was not a ghetto deliberately closed against the world and the idea of religious freedom, but the cultural pressures and assumptions under which she had to work in the previous centuries had produced a mind-set that made it suspicious of many aspects of the more open societies, for better and for worse, of the second half of the twentieth century. The suspicion was more than justified in many respects, but those societies were the context in which she had now to work, and as in previous generations she had now to look at the more positive aspects of that context and build on them. When she did she was in many respects pleasantly surprised.

But the Council had the difficult task, in a few short months, of deciding what was perennially valid in the older attitudes, and what was historically-conditioned response which could and should change in order to make its work for souls more effective as the second millennium drew to a close. Inevitably the evolution of these documents was surrounded by controversy.[1] As they stand, however, they represent the mind of the Church through the Council and, in that they do, they are in many ways the most remarkable of its many achievements.

*Gaudium et Spes* does not deal specifically with the Church's social teaching but uses its insights; it is on it which it mainly draws, as the footnotes to the text attest, and it specifically says that the Church

> in the course of the centuries has worked out, in the light of the Gospel, principles of justice and equity demanded by right reason for individual and social life and also for international relations. The Council now intends to reiterate those principles in accordance with the situation in the world today and will outline certain guidelines [GS 63].

The very thoroughness with which the popes had developed the social magisterium on the social and economic issues that constituted the *Rerum Novarum* agenda over the previous seventy years or so, meant that the Council had very little to do in its general survey in these areas, beyond restating and drawing out its implications. However, there were areas, such as political ethics, which had not been on that agenda and on which the modern social teaching had had less to say: it needed filling out and consolidating, while the whole relationship of the Church, its organization and teaching, to human culture was a field practically unexplored. *Gaudium et Spes* then, was, broader in scope than the individual social encyclicals, concerned as they were with responding to specific social issues or situations. Here the proposal is to restate in outline the relationship of the Church with every aspect of man's life in society at the present day in order to make its guidelines as comprehensive as possible.

## 2 Summary of the social teaching of *Gaudium et Spes*[2]

There is a Preface [1–3], an Introduction [4–11] and two Parts. The first has four Chapters [1] 'The dignity of the human person' [12–22], [II] 'The community of mankind' [23–32], [III] 'Man's activity in the Universe' [33–39] and [IV] 'The role of the Church in the modern world' [40–45]. The second Part deals with five specific questions [I] 'The dignity of marriage and the family' [47–52]. [II] 'Proper development of culture' [53–60]. [III] 'Economic and social life' [63–72], [IV] 'The political community' [73–76] and [V] 'Fostering of peace and establishment of a community of nations' [77–93].

### Preface

This expresses first of all the solidarity of the Christian community with mankind, 'the joy, the hope ... grief and anguish of the men of our time, especially those ... poor and afflicted ... are the joy, the hope, grief and anguish of the followers of Christ as well' [1]. The Council therefore addresses all men, since God sustains all things and Christ has died to redeem all [2]. 'It is man therefore, who must be saved; it is mankind that must be renewed ... body, soul, heart and conscience, mind and will' [3].

### Introduction

The Church has the responsibility of 'reading the signs of the times and interpreting them in the light of the Gospel'. Man's intelligence and creativity have brought him increased power but also increased uncertainty about how to plot his course. Many are wealthy and free today as never before, yet poverty and new forms of slavery still flourish. International solidarity grows but so does ideological bitterness and threat of total war. Mankind oscillates between hope and fear; permanent values are under threat [4].

Man's intellectual powers and scientific knowledge have changed former static concepts and replaced them by those which are dynamic and revolutionary [5]; the social order of older societies, family, clan, tribe, village, is changed as industrialization and urbanization grow. Man is becoming more socialized through contacts with his fellows, while personal development and relationships do not flourish as they should [6]; moral and religious standards are also evolving; children are frequently 'rebellious in their distress' and the search for a more personal religion goes hand in hand with a decline in religious practice [7]. The multiple imbalances in levels of personal development, and the opportunities open to different peoples, persons and classes produce distrust, conflicts and hardships [8].

> Meanwhile there is a growing conviction of mankind's ability and duty to strengthen its mastery over nature and of the need to establish a political, social and economic order at the service of man.

For the first time people are not afraid to think that cultural benefits are for all throughout the world [9]. Yet man is torn between his awareness of his shortcomings and the feeling that he is destined for higher things. The Church offers Christ its Lord and master as the answer to these questionings [10].

**Part One: the Church and man's vocation**

The Church is moved by the belief that 'the events, the needs, the longings' of the times reveal signs of 'the presence or purpose of God' and reveals itself as human in being religious [11].

**I. The dignity of the human person**

*Man, the image of God*
Most people believe that man is the centre and summit of things. Christianity teaches that mankind was made in God's image, a social being, male and female [12]. Though through the Fall wounded by sin and divided against himself he yet, with Christ's saving grace, can chose the good [13]. He is a unity of body and soul and therefore respects his body while he must not allow it to serve evil [14].

*Reason, wisdom, and morality: the excellence of freedom*
'Man, as sharing in the light of the divine mind, rightly affirms that by his intellect he surpasses the world of mere things' and this intellect should be fulfilled in wisdom, and knowledge of the

true and the good [15]. In his conscience 'man discovers a law which he has not laid upon himself, but which he must obey ... a law inscribed by God' which prompts him at the right moment to avoid the evil and do the good. Moral standards are therefore objective: a conscience blinded by sinful habits is not the same as one suffering from unavoidable ignorance [16]. Freedom is not freedom to do as one likes but exists in 'freely choosing what is good', and, weakened as we are by sin, it is only through God's grace we can do this. By this standard, 'to each one according as he has done either good or evil', we will eventually be judged [17].

*Death and denial of God: atheism*
Bearing as he does within himself the seeds of eternity, man shrinks from gradual decline and death, but Christian teaching answers our fears and queries; we will live again in our original wholeness [18]. The dignity of man consists in his call by God to communion with him, yet many today reject him. There are many kinds of rejection. Frequently atheists are reacting against evil in the world, but those who ignore their consciences and 'try to drive God from their heart ... are not free from blame'. Neither are some Christians whose behaviour is such 'as to conceal rather than to reveal the true nature of God and religion' [19]. Systematic atheism on the other hand insists on human autonomy to the point of denial of any dependence on God [20]. 'The Church holds that to acknowledge God is in no way to oppose the dignity of man.' She rejects atheism but she is prepared to work with all men of good will for right order in the world, demanding freedom therefore for her mission; her message responds to the deepest needs of the human heart since it champions man's dignity [21].

*Christ, the new man*
Christ 'the image of the invisible God' is the new man, the perfect man who has restored man to God's likeness. He took our human nature. We are his brothers and sisters, called to the hope of the resurrection. Christ died for all men of goodwill [22].

## II. The community of mankind

This Chapter looks at some points from recent Catholic teaching on human society and relates them to revelation which the Council puts before us [23].

### God's design, man's communitarian nature

God desired that all should be one family and treat one another as brothers; made by the one God, given the commandment to love, we are to be one [24]. Life in society is a necessity for man, not an option; through it he develops. He forms societies naturally, the family, the political groupings, the intermediate associations through 'socialization'. Some social environments are of course inimical to virtue, only countered by the life of grace [25].

### The common good and respect for the person

The common good, 'the sum total of social conditions which allow people, groups or individuals, to reach their fulfilment more easily', reaches its fullest realization when all have their human rights protected, the good of the person coming before the good of things [26]. Crimes against the person debase the perpetrators as well as the victims – such crimes as murder, abortion, genocide, euthanasia, wilful suicide, mutilation, subhuman living conditions, arbitrary imprisonment, deportation, slavery, prostitution, treating workers as tools for profit [27]. We must respect those who differ from us politically; in religious matters we love the one who is in error but reject the error [28].

### The equality of all men: social justice

Though men differ in capacity and powers, all are created in God's image and have the same basic rights, which forbid discrimination on grounds of sex, race, colour, class, language or religion; women too often do not have the same cultural benefits as men. Extreme economic and social disparities are 'a source of scandal and militate against social justice, equity, human dignity ... peace' [29]. All must respect the social good, paying taxes, obeying the law, accepting social responsibilities; many make light of these things but they are among the primary duties of modern man [30]. Education, and opportunity to participate 'in public life in genuine freedom' are essential to these ends. We need not only those with refined talents, we need greatness of soul, among the educators. Man grows in strength in facing the responsibilities of life, the demands of partnership and the service of the community, though these things demand of him sacrifice [31].

### The Incarnation and human solidarity

God did not create men to live as individuals but as social beings, and willed to save them as a holy people. 'This communitarian character is ... fulfilled in Jesus Christ.' He shared in the life of an ordinary man of his time. His message is to all peoples, his Church a brotherly communion in love, where all serve all according to their gifts. 'This solidarity must be constantly increased until the day it is brought to fulfilment' [32].

### III. Man's duty in the universe

*The purpose and value of human activity*
Man's immense mastery of things through science and technology is now raising questions of its purpose [33]. The mastery in itself is according to God's plan; he was told to conquer the earth and all that is in it. Men and women who work to provide for their families and serve the community can rightly look upon their work as a prolongation of the work of the creator, 'not a challenge to it' [34].

*Human activity, sin, redemption*
Man 'when he works transforms matter and society [and] fulfils himself'. This growth is more valuable than wealth or technical progress; man is precious for what he is, not for what he has. Material things are good in so far as they foster brotherhood, and a more humane environment; they can supply the means for human progress but cannot of themselves bring it about [35]. Man's rightful autonomy in exploring the laws and values of matter and of society is not in conflict with religion. Material reality and faith derive from the same God; but claiming an autonomy that involves denial of God who is creator of all is false; when God is forgotten, it is impossible properly to understand the creature [36]. History shows that man's progress is beset by terrible temptations in the 'world' of vanity and malice of which St Paul warned us. Redeemed in Christ, however, we can use the earth's riches in a spirit of poverty and freedom [37].

*Human fulfilment and the kingdom of Christ*
'Constituted Lord by his resurrection, and given all authority in heaven and on earth, Christ is now at work in the hearts of men by the power of the Spirit.' He gives them the desire for eternal life and also the desire 'to make life more humane and conquer the earth for this purpose' [38]. Yet, distorted by sin, this world is passing away; there is a new earth where all our desires will be fulfilled. Earthly progress and the kingdom of Christ are therefore to be distinguished, but the better ordering of human society is of vital concern to the kingdom of God. For after we have sought to foster on earth the values of human dignity we will find them

again, transfigured, when Christ's kingdom of holiness, love and justice comes [39].

## IV. The role of the Church in the modern world

*Their mutual relationship*
A visible organization and spiritual community, the Church shares and seeks to leaven the lot of human society; strengthens it, humanizes it. The good done by other Christian and ecclesial communities and by the world to this end, in preparing the ground for the Gospel, is recognized by it [40].

*The Church, the individual and society*
Man today seeks self-development and his rights, but God alone can satisfy the deepest yearnings of his heart. That God is creator and saviour restores and consolidates man's rightful autonomy. The Gospel and the Church secure man's rights [41]. The union of the human family is consolidated by that which Christ established among his people.

> Christ did not bequeath to the Church a mission in the political, economic or social order; the purpose he assigned it was a religious one. But this religious mission can be the source of commitment, direction and vigour

in establishing community. She must initiate such action where circumstances require it, especially on works of mercy, and she sees the good in and welcomes the increasing concern for healthy social organization and civil and economic co-operation today. Though 'by its nature and mission, the Church is universal and not committed to any one culture or to any political, economic or social system' she can work with various such systems provided they give her freedom to carry on her mission. She desires to work for all men under any regime which recognizes the basic rights of the person and the family [42].

*The interaction of the Church and Society*
Christians have a duty to be good citizens. 'It is a mistake to think that because we have here no lasting city we are entitled to shirk our earthly responsibilities', we are to fulfil them the more as Christians. 'It is to the laity, though not exclusively to them, that secular duties and activity properly belong ... for guidance and spiritual strength let them turn to the clergy' who cannot be expected to have ready answers to every problem. They should

rather 'shoulder their responsibilities under the guidance of Christian wisdom and with eager attention to the teaching authority of the Church'.

Christians will disagree on practical matters and 'no one is permitted to identify the authority of the Church too exclusively with his own opinion'. The clergy are to shed the light of the Gospel on the activities of the faithful as they engage in their task. By the power of the Holy Spirit, the Church is the faithful spouse of the Lord and 'will never fail to be a sign of salvation to the world' though some of her members, clergy and lay, in the past 'have been disloyal to the Spirit of God': we must combat such weakness today [43]. The Church as a social reality has profited from the history of mankind and the wisdom of the philosophers, and she will continue to do so today. She also understands social life more fully in that Christ established her as a visible social structure, which promotes human community from the family to the national and international level [44]. Her aim is only to further the kingdom of God and the salvation of souls [45].

## Part Two: problems of greater urgency

The document identifies five, namely (1) marriage and family, (2) culture, economic and social life, (3) politics (4) the solidarity of peoples, and (5) peace. Light for dealing with all these must come from Christ's teaching.

## I: the dignity of marriage and the family

'The well-being of the individual person and of both human and Christian society is closely bound up with the healthy state of conjugal and family life' [47]. Marriage is rooted in the contract of the partners, their irrevocable personal consent, confirmed by divine law and society, for the good of the partners, the children and society itself. 'God himself is the author of marriage and has endowed it with various benefits, with various ends in view.' The institution of 'marriage and married love is ordained to the procreation and education of children' and its intimate union requires total fidelity. Christ blessed this love abundantly. 'Authentic married love is caught up into the divine love.' The family is the 'path of truly human training, of salvation and holiness' for everyone, parents and children; it is an image of the partnership of love between Christ and his Church, showing forth its authentic nature [48].

*Married love and respect for human life*
Married love 'the acts of marriage by which the intimate and chaste
union of the spouses takes place are noble and honourable' and
enrich the spouses. Their love, by Christ's sacrament, 'excludes
adultery and divorce'. Equal personal dignity must be accorded to
man and wife in mutual affection. Their vocation requires courage,
and grace is needed in its living. The dignity of married love must
be inculcated in the young, especially in the heart of the family
[49]. Without underestimating the other ends of marriage, that
love is directed to 'disposing the spouses to co-operate valiantly
with the love of creator and saviour, who through them will
increase and enrich his family from day to day'. Parents decide the
size of their family, with respect for God, their own good, spiritual
and material, and that of their children, society and the Church.
They should be guided by conscience 'conformed to the law of
God according to the teaching authority of the Church, which is
the authentic interpreter of divine law'.

Marriage is not only for the procreation of children: mutual love
demands that the love be shown even if the partners cannot have
children of their own [50]. Where the partners cannot increase
their family for the time being there can be no conflict between
God's law and authentic married love. 'Abortion and infanticide
are abominable crimes', and on birth control 'the sons of the
Church are forbidden to use methods disapproved of by the teaching authority of the Church in its interpretation of divine law'
[51].[3]

*Fostering marriage and the family*
The family is a school for human enrichment for all its members
and each member, within and between the generations; civil
authority, the Church and all social influences must help it in its
task [52].

## II: the proper development of culture

Culture is here understood in the broadest sense, that is, all the
influences which refine and develop 'man's diverse and mental
and physical endowments' [53] by work and play, by the practice
of religion, study and education, the arts and sciences, the skills of
workers in all fields.

*The cultural situation today*
The advances made by man today in all fields are evident to us all;

man is more fully aware of his potential [54]. A new humanism exists; people are the craftsmen and moulders of their communities [55]. The question is how to preserve what is best in the traditional wisdom and cultural patterns, while encouraging the dynamism of the new cultural influences [56].

*Principles of a sound cultural development*
Man's achievements bring him closer to God, although they can also breed agnosticism and belief that man is sufficient of himself [57]. The Church meanwhile is at home in all ages and cultures, renewing and purifying them through the good news of Christ [58]. Culture should be related to 'the integral development of the whole person', of community and of mankind. Faith and reason are complementary; the latter, in the sciences or the arts, has its own autonomy. While he must respect the moral order and the common good, man can seek the truth in any field of knowledge. Human culture is determined by the needs of man's nature, and has its own autonomy subject to the needs of the common good. The public authority has no mandate to determine cultural forms, but should provide the proper environment for their development [59].

*Some more urgent problems of culture*
Man now has the power to free the majority of the human race from ignorance; all must have access to basic culture and to education up to the level of higher studies for those capable of this [60]. Integral cultural development of the person is to be the aim, the person who by the Creator's plan, is possessed of intellect, free will and conscience, and aware of human brotherhood [61]. Culture and faith can be difficult to synchronize, and theology should look for new ways of presenting old truths 'provided the meaning and understanding of them is safeguarded ... for the deposit of faith is one thing, the manner of expressing them is quite another'. Clergy and laity alike must keep abreast of new ways of thinking and feeling [62].

**III: economic and social life**

Man is the source, the centre and purpose of all economic and social life. Recently

> increased efficiency in production and ... methods of distribution and in the exchange of goods and services have made the

economy an instrument capable of better meeting the growing needs of the human family.

The disparities in wealth, however, are disturbing, and people feel that modern techniques can rectify this, through the greater technical and economic resources available world wide. And this requires a change of mentality and attitude by all.

It was for this reason that the Church in the course of the centuries has worked out in the light of the Gospel, principles of justice and equity demanded by right reason for individual and social life and also for international relations. The Council now intends to reiterate these principles in accordance with the situation in the world today and will outline certain guidelines, particularly with reference to the requirements of economic development [63].

*Economic development*
Today proper attention is being given to the increase of production to meet the needs of growing world population and the desires of the human race. 'We must encourage technical progress and the spirit of enterprise ... the eagerness for creativity and improvement ... [and] all the elements which contribute to economic progress.' But economics is not to be primarily concerned with increased production, profit or prestige, but with the service of man, the whole man, his material needs and those of his intellectual, moral, spiritual and religious life. It must be carried out 'in accordance with techniques and methods belonging to the moral order' so that God's plan for man will be achieved [64]. Economic development cannot be left 'to the almost mechanical evolution of economic activity, nor to the decision of public authority'. It needs 'voluntary initiatives of individuals and free groups integrated with state enterprises'. Private owners of resources are reminded they must be used for the common good [65]. Excessive economic inequalities must be ended, and provision made for those affected by needful change [66].

*Principles of economic and social life, work and working conditions*
Human work, in all branches of the economy 'surpasses all other elements of economic life; the latter are only means to ends'. By work, man puts his seal on the things of nature. Christ was a manual worker, hence the dignity of labour, the obligation to work loyally, the dignity of work and the rights of workers; it must never enslave or dehumanize but develop talents and personalities [67].

Without weakening executive unity, active participation of all in the business enterprise is to be encouraged and in some way, in economic and social decisions made at higher levels outside the business. Workers have a right of association, and the right to strike as an ultimate means of defence in the context of the desire for negotiation and reconciliation [68].

### The universal purpose of created things

'God intended the earth and all it contains for all men and all peoples so that all created things would be shared fairly by all mankind under the guidance of justice tempered by charity.' Private property is not exclusive to the owner; ownership is to be respected but its use has social responsibilities. Every man has the right to sufficient of the world's goods for himself and his family; the Fathers and Doctors of the Church teach that men are bound to come to the aid of the poor, and not merely out of their superfluities. In extreme need each has the right to take what is needed out of the riches of others.[4] Social insurance schemes can be one way of seeing that the universal purpose of created things is achieved, but they must not encourage social passivity in recipients [69].

### Money and investment

Those who have money to invest (individuals, association, public authorities) should do so with the good of individuals and the community in mind, remembering that all are entitled to the necessities of life, balancing the needs of consumption and investment for future generations. The needs of the underdeveloped regions must be remembered and the need to maintain the value of money.[70]

### Ownership, private property, expropriation

Ownership should be fostered because it helps the 'expression of personality and provides ... the opportunity of fulfilling a role in society and in the economy'. It is an expression of freedom, stimulates a sense of responsibility and is one of the conditions for civic freedom. Public ownership, in the light of the common good can be justified. Far from the State having no right to regulate private ownership, prevention of its abuse protects it, because such abuse leads to questioning of it in principle. So where rural estates are badly, if at all, cultivated, and the need of the majority for land is great, expropriation, with just compensation, might be justified; if so, adequate support must be made available to the smallholders to become and remain efficient [71]. Christians in economic and life and in the struggle for justice and charity, contribute to the prosperity to mankind and true peace; they should maintain a right balance in loyalty to Christ and the Gospel, seeking first the kingdom of God [72].

## IV: The Political Community

The profound changes in the structures and institutions of peoples have great influence on the life of the political community. In many places better politico-juridical structures are emerging, protecting the rights of individuals and encouraging political participation with respect for the rights of minorities and those of other religions. At the same time, in other systems these positive developments are lacking. The basic characteristics of the true political community therefore need stressing [73].

*The nature and purpose of the political community*
The State arises because individuals, families and the various groups 'which make up the civil community' realize that there is need for a wider society to foster the common good, 'the sum of those conditions in which men, families and associations ... perfect themselves'. In such communities 'an authority is needed to guide the energies of all to the common good', acting as a moral force based on freedom and a sense of responsibility. The political community and the public authority are then founded in human nature and therefore they belong 'to an order established by God ... the choice of the political regime and the rulers are left to the free decision of the citizens'. Legitimate political authority which acts in accord with the moral order binds in conscience; where it is abused, citizens can defend their rights within 'the limits of the natural law and the law of the Gospel' [74].

*Participation in public life*
Political systems which allow citizens full participation in 'the election of leaders' and the choice of constitution and its administration are fully consonant with human nature, and those who have the vote should use it for the common good. Those who devote themselves to the public good for the service of men should be esteemed for this. The rights and responsibilities of rulers and ruled must be defined and understood and individuals and groups are to be encouraged in their lawful activities. The modern situation requires the intervention of State authority in social,

economic and cultural matters in order to give more effective help to citizens and groups in achieving their ends. The balance between socialization and autonomy must be kept. Citizens should be patriotic but should also keep in mind the welfare of the whole human family.

They must be dedicated to the common good, reconciling 'personal initiative with solidarity' and recognizing 'the legitimacy of differing points of view about the organization of worldly affairs'. They should show respect for their fellow citizens with whom they disagree. Political parties must never put their own before the common good. Civic education is vital for all, especially the young, and those who have the talent for active politics should prepare themselves to participate in it. They must oppose injustice and tyranny, the arbitrary domination of one individual or party, being dedicated to the service of all [75].

### The Church and politics

The Church, by reason of her role and competence, is not bound up with any political community ... or political system. It is at once the sign and safeguard of the transcendental dimension of the human person

and the political activities of Christians should not be seen as representing the Church. The distinction between the two powers should not be absolute; they both deal with the same persons and they will do this better if they co-operate. The Church teaches the Gospel truths of charity and justice and encourages political freedom and the responsibility of citizens, but those who preach the Gospel must use the ways and means of the Gospel only. Using temporal realities as its mission requires, the Church does not place its hopes in privileges accorded it by civil authority.

At all times and in all places ... [it] ... should have true freedom to preach the faith, to proclaim its teaching about society, to carry out its task among men without hindrance and to pass moral judgements even in matters relating to politics, whenever the fundamental rights of man or the good of souls requires it.

The only means she may use are those which accord with the Gospel and the welfare of men. The Church is uncommitted to any system; she is the sign of the transcendence of the human personality; and there is a distinction between the personal political commitment of the laity and their action with pastors in the name of the Church. She will co-operate with the secular authorities for the common good,

> in fulfillment of its mission in the world, the Church, whose duty
> it is to foster and elevate all that is true, all that is good, and all
> that is beautiful in the human community, consolidates peace
> among men for the glory of God [76]

## V: The fostering of peace and the establishment of a community of nations promoting peace and the community of nations

*Peace the work of justice*
The growing awareness of the unity of mankind demands that we
look again at the question of peace and war [77] peace being not
mere absence of war but the fruit of justice (Isa. 32:7) based on the
love of our fellow men [78]. The binding force of 'universal
natural law' is recalled in the light of the increasing savagery of
modern war, which threatens barbarities unknown in previous
conflicts; international agreements to try to make it less so need
consolidating and extending. The right of conscientious objection
is to be protected, but those who serve their country in the military
make a contribution to establishing peace. 'Governments cannot
be denied the right to legitimate defence once every means of
peaceful settlement has been exhausted' but the means must be
just [79].

Total war, and the indiscriminate destruction of 'entire cities or
extensive areas along with their population is a crime against God
and man' [80]. There is controversy over deterrence, but whatever
may be the facts behind the arguments for it, the arms race is not
a safe way of keeping the peace;[5] further, it diverts resources that
are necessary to succour the poor [81]. The necessity is for war to
be condemned by consent of all nations. Enmities and hatreds
must be put aside and firm and sincere agreements for universal
peace concluded [82].

*Avoiding war and bringing justice: the need for an effective international
community*
To remove the causes of wars, the community of nations must
organize for the common good [83]. International and regional
organizations have already made progress, laying the foundations
for an international community [84]. 'The present solidarity
of mankind also calls for a revival of greater international co-
operation in the economic field.' New nations are still not free
economically. Aid, human and financial, is needed and with it a

profound change in trading relations; loans, grants and investments must be made generously and received honestly [85]. In
this the following norms are relevant. Developing nations should
bear in mind that progress arises and grows above all out of the
labour and genius of the nations themselves, based as it is on
utilization of their own resources, especially their human and
cultural resources. The help of developed countries is also very
important, and it should not exploit the economic weaknesses of
the poorer States. In accordance with the principle of subsidiarity, economic relations throughout the world should be
reorganized so that the inequality of power between the nations
is redressed. Finally, economic and social structures in the underdeveloped countries in many cases need to be reformed, but
valuable cultural traditions must be preserved [86].

*Development and population*
Governments undoubtedly have rights and duties, within their
proper competency, regarding the population problems in their
countries' but solutions which are against the moral law must be
avoided. The size of family is for parents, not States, to decide [87].
Christians in the nations accounted wealthy must co-operate in
building an international order which respects rightful liberty and
the obligation to help the poor. Charitable work of all kinds must
be organized efficiently [88] and the church should foster co-operation among men, collaborating with those who are working in
these areas [89]. Some organization within the Universal Church
should be set up so that 'the justice and love of Christ towards the
poor may be developed everywhere' [90].

   The Conclusion to the document points out that it is addressed
to all men of our time, that it is very general and will need specification according to circumstances. The Church's wish is 'to shed
on the whole world the radiance of the Gospel message, and to
unify under one spirit all men of whatever nation, race or culture'
and seeks sincere dialogue to that end [91–3].

# 3 Summary of the social teaching of *Dignitatis Humanae*[6]

The decree was issued on 7 December 1965 and deals first with the
question of the right of the person and communities to social and
civil liberty in religious matters; there are two chapters: the first on
'The general principle of religious freedom' and the second on
'Religious freedom in the light of revelation'.

The opening statement notes the interest of contemporary man in the dignity of the human person, and the insistence that he has full freedom to make his own decisions uncoerced by anyone. In the light of this, the Council declares first that it believes that Jesus Christ founded the one true Church, Catholic and Apostolic, and sent it to teach the truth to all nations. But 'truth can impose itself on the mind of man only in virtue of its own truth' which wins over the mind with gentleness and power. Hence 'the traditional Catholic teaching on the moral duty of individuals and societies towards the true religion and the one Church of Christ' is left intact [1].

**Chapter 1** declares that the human person has a right to religious freedom, within due limits; it is based on man's dignity as known through revelation, and this should be a civil right, one recognized in the constitutions of States. Men, possessing reason and free will, are by nature bound to seek the truth and adhere to it; the right is an objective one, not founded on subjective attitude; as long as the just requirements of public order are respected, those who do not live up to their duty of seeking the truth, however, may not be coerced into so doing [2]. The existence of the divine eternal law, objective and universal, which man participates in, makes this freedom clear. Through his conscience man sees and recognizes the demands of the divine law. He cannot be forced to act contrary to conscience; the practice of religion consists primarily in voluntary and free acts which human authority cannot command. These acts, private and public, transcend the temporal order and the State cannot control them. To deny man the right freely to practise his religion, the just requirements of public order being observed, is an injustice to the person and against God's order [3].

Religious communities therefore, provided the just requirements of public order are not violated, 'have a right to immunity so that they may organize themselves according to their own principles'. They must be free to preach the word of God and instruct their members in it. They must also be free to train their own ministers, erect buildings for religious purposes and acquire and use property. In bearing witness to their beliefs they must avoid any appearance of coercion. They must not be prevented from teaching; their beliefs help to a better organization of human society and they must be free to form educational, cultural, charitable and social organizations [4].

The society which is the family has a right, under the control of the parents, to organize its own religious life. It cannot be denied the right to choose a religious context to the education of children, one which excludes anything contrary to the beliefs of their parents [5]. There must be legislation to these ends and conditions favourable to religion and its practices. All religions and their members must be treated equally by the law [6] but civil society has the right to protect itself against possible abuses committed in the name of religious freedom in so doing it must act in accordance with objective moral standards and legal principle. Settlement of conflicts of rights must be peaceful and must respect the integrity of freedom in society. Freedom should only be restrained when and in so far as it is necessary [7]. Man today is subject to pressures which hinder freedom; others use freedom to reject all authority. Educators must be careful to incubate a respect for the moral order which enables man to act with greater responsibility towards others and society [8].

**Chapter 2** bases the right to religious freedom on the dignity of the human person. Christ respected that dignity in that he called man to fulfil his duty of believing in God in freedom. Religious freedom in society is in harmony with the Christian faith [9]. Man must accept God and his law with a faith that is 'reasonable and free'. Religious freedom produces the situation in which he can be invited to accept the Christian faith [10]. Christ acted patiently in attracting and inviting his disciples. He denounced the unbelief of his listeners but left vengeance to God on judgement day. Christ had no political ambitions; he recognized civil authority and its rights, but warned that the higher rights of God must be respected also (Matt. 22:21) He achieved salvation and true freedom for man by his sacrifice on the cross. He bore witness to the truth not by violence but by his sufferings. His disciples sought to convert by God's power, not by coercion, and showed respect for the weak even when they were in error (Rom. 14:12). They despised earthly weapons, recognizing the civil power as did Christ (Rom. 13:1–2) but were prepared to 'obey God rather than men' (Acts 5:29) [11].

Faithful to the Gospel, the Church recognizes the principle of religious freedom as in keeping with man's dignity and divine revelation. Although at times in history the people of God have seemed to act contrary to the Gospel, the Church always taught that no one should be coerced into believing.[7] The Gospel has helped the growth of the conviction that the human being must be free from coercion in matters of religion [12]. The Church claims freedom for herself in human society so that she may preach the word of God, and she claims freedom for herself as a society of men living in accord with the demands of the faith. The Christian faithful, along with the rest of men, have the right to live their faith in society [13].

In forming their consciences, however, the faithful must pay careful attention to the Church's teaching, for it is by the will of Christ the teacher of the truth. They also must be faithful in announcing that truth without having recourse to methods contrary to it [14]. Today religious freedom is accepted as a civil right in most constitutions. On the other hand there are States which have such constitutions but in fact hinder religious bodies in practice. Closer unity among cultures has produced a growing sense of individual responsibility. Man's highest rights and duties, those concerning religion, must be respected [15].

## 4 Summary analysis of the social teaching of Vatican II

### (i) Ethics and civil society

Individuals, families and intermediate groups constitute society [GS 74] and since man is the source, focus and end of all social organizations, that society must develop in a manner worthy of his dignity [GS 12, 25, 63]. Man is communitarian by nature; it is natural and necessary for man to live a social existence [GS 25]; he is born into that society which is the family, the cornerstone of the civil order. The family is the first stage of man's education in the ways of social life: its well-being therefore is essential to the person and to society at large, the civil, the political and the economic [GS 47]. Marriage is rooted in the contract of the partners, confirmed by divine law and society, for the good of the partners, the children and society itself. The procreation and education of children is central to marriage, though where the partners cannot have children the marriage remains [GS 48–50]. Christian marriage does not allow of methods of family planning which contradict Christian teaching, or of adultery, abortion and divorce [GS 49–51]. The family is a school for human enrichment for all its members and for each of its members, and the Church, civil authority and all social influences should co-operate in its support [GS 55].

The common good of society is achieved when all, individuals, families and groups, reach their fulfilment [GS 26]. Mutual relationships and interdependence in civil society give rise to a variety of associations in a process of socialization for the strengthening and betterment of human qualities and human rights; these inter-mediate organizations are part of the communitarian nature of man which is God's plan [GS 25]. Individualistic morality is not good enough and must be transcended; the good of society should be the care of all of us, and we should respond to its needs by respecting the law of the community and fostering public and private organizations devoted to bettering the conditions of life [GS 30]. Solidarity and communitarianism stem from our life in Jesus Christ [GS 32]. All should look after their neighbours as themselves [GS 27].

Man, made in God's image, a social being, male and female, is a unity of body and soul and therefore must respect his bodily needs. Born for freedom, and having intelligence and free will, this freedom is not a freedom to do as he likes; it consists in choosing the good according to God's law [GS 12, 16, 17]. He must do this freely; truth cannot be imposed, it must be freely accepted [DH 1]. Acknowledging and obeying God does not diminish man's dignity [GS 21]. Successful in exploring all realms of knowledge, his intel-lect finds its last perfection in wisdom which draws the mind to the true and the good [GS 15].

Given their dignity in being made in the image and likeness of God, people yet differ in capacity and power, but they all have the same basic rights, which forbid discrimination on grounds of sex, race, class, language or religion [GS 29]. People are conscious that they are the craftsmen and moulders of their communities, and it is necessary to preserve what is best in the traditional values while benefiting from the dynamism of new cultural influences [GS 54–62], culture being understood as all that develops man's mental and physical skills, at work and play, and the institutions which embody them [GS 53]. Everyone should have access to basic culture according to endowment and opportunities [GS 60].

## (ii) Ethics and political society

The State comes into being because civil society requires it; it is necessary to man in order that the common good, the condition in which all individuals and groups in the State have access to the means to fulfil their aims, may be achieved. It requires an author-ity to this end, acting as a moral force based on freedom and responsibility. As essential to man, therefore, political society is God-ordained. The citizens may choose their own form of govern-ment and rulers, and laws which accord with the moral order must be obeyed; the citizens however can defend themselves against the abuse of power, by means in accordance with the natural law and the Gospel [GS 74].

Citizens have a right and a duty to vote and those who devote themselves to political life for the public good are to be held in esteem. The rights and responsibilities of government and citizens are to be clearly understood, and while it is necessary for the State to intervene for the well-being of some groups, needless dependence is to be avoided. Patriotism is a virtue, but only in the context of the whole human family. Christians will often differ on the solutions to political problems, and legitimate differences of opinion are to be respected [GS 43], but they must put the common good first [GS 75]. Political education is essential especially for the young.

There must be freedom of religion; the State cannot deny it though it can regulate excesses [DH 2]. The Church is not bound to any political community or system but is a sign of the transcendence of the person who has an eternal destiny. Church and State are autonomous and independent of each other but since they deal with the same human beings, their co-operation is desirable. The Church does not want special privileges from the State. It should always be free to do its work and to pass moral judgements on politics where human rights and the good of souls requires it [GS 76]. In international relations, the question of peace and war has to be faced. Governments are not to be denied the right of self-defence when all means of peaceful settlement fail, but the means must be just [GS 79]. The right of conscientious objection remains, but citizens who serve in the armed forces are also to be commended. Modern weapons have changed the way we look at war, and any use of them against civilian populations is a crime against God and man. Whatever the value of deterrence, the arms race is inimical to peace. The nations must work to avoid war and, secure the firm and sincere agreements which are needed to assure international peace [GS 81–2]. An effective international community is required in order to remove the causes of wars and organize international relations, especially on economic matters for the common good. Human solidarity demands action to improve the economic prospects of the poorer nations.

### (iii) Ethics and economic society

Man has increased economic efficiency to the point where it is possible that economies can meet the growing needs of the human family, but the disparities of wealth, and the knowledge we have the means to overcome them, is making people uneasy. For this reason it is necessary to recall the relevant principles of justice and equity [GS 63].

It is technical progress and the spirit of enterprise, the creative and ever-improving agencies of the economic order, which enable society to meet the material and cultural needs of mankind, but these agencies must operate in accordance with moral order. Neither a mechanistic view of economic activity, nor one controlled by public authority, is acceptable. Private and public enterprise must be integrated; economic resources must be used for the common good, excessive inequalities ended and the needs of those affected by change provided for [GS 66].

God intended all created things to be shared fairly by mankind under the guidance of justice tempered by charity, and property should not be possessed exclusively but benefit others too [GS 69]. Ownership of private property is to be fostered because it helps to express personality and freedom and is one of the conditions for civic freedom: it also stimulates responsibility, and fulfils a role in society and the economy. Public ownership is also lawful, but where it involves transfer from private ownership it must be done in accordance with just law, and with compensation. In the case of the transfer of land, where the need of the majority requires it, adequate resources must be provided to make the new owners efficient. The State may also prevent anyone abusing his property when it offends against the common good; not least because such abuse calls into question private ownership itself. Those who have money to invest, individuals or organizations, should do so with the common good in mind; consumption and investment need to be balanced, and the need of underdeveloped regions kept in mind [GS 70].

Regarding labour conditions, human work is the most important element in economic life; all others are means to ends, but man by his work puts his seal on nature; Christ himself was a manual worker. Work must develop the talent and personality of the worker, who should work loyally. There is a right of association, and to strike, the latter as an ultimate means of defence in the context of negotiation and reconciliation. While executive unity must be preserved, all should participate in the enterprise and have a say in decisions made outside the business [GS 67–8].

Solidarity calls for greater co-operation internationally in the economic field since the political freedom of nations does not guarantee economic freedom. Aid can take the form of experts giving their help; it also can be financial, in loans, grants and investments. The labour and genius of a nation, based on its own culture and resources, is however is to be the main agency and the road to development. Peoples have the prime responsibility for their own development [GS 85]. But richer ones should not exploit the weaker. Keeping in mind the subsidiarity principle, the inequality of economic relations should be redressed. There must be profound change in trading relations. Economic and social structures in the underdeveloped countries may need reforming, but valuable cultural traditions must be safeguarded [GS 86].

# 23

# Paul VI [1963–1978] and the Second Meeting of the Council of Latin American Bishops [CELAM II] Medellín, Columbia, 1968

## 1  Paul VI: background[1]

Paul VI, Giovanni Battista Montini, was born in 1897, his father being a successful lawyer, political editor and parliamentarian; his mother, Guiditta, had been the ward of the radical Mayor of Brescia at the time she met her future husband when she was nineteen years old. Giovanni began his studies for the priesthood in 1916 and was ordained in 1920; further studies in Rome followed and two years later he began his work in the Papal Secretariat of State, serving in Warsaw for six months before his health failed him and he returned to Rome. There he combined his work in the Secretariat with being chaplain to the national union of Catholic students (FUCI) from 1924, at a time when Mussolini's Fascists were growing in strength and disputing the Church's rights in the education of the young. He became a domestic prelate to the Holy See in 1931 and assistant to Cardinal Pacelli, Secretary of State in 1937. From his family background he had absorbed much of the experience of the Catholic social movement and the enthusiasm for the PPI, the Catholic Popular Party of Don Sturzo, which flourished briefly in the early 1920s.

After Cardinal Pacelli's election to the Papacy in 1939, Montini remained close to him, taking charge of internal Church affairs in 1944. Appointed as Pro-Secretary of State in 1952, he did not accept the proferred cardinalate in the next year, but was appointed Archbishop of Milan in 1954. The diocese was faced with consider-

* The notes and references for Chapter 23 are to be found on p. 460ff

able problems, particularly those affecting the industrial working
class, and he came before his people as the worker's Archbishop,
setting to work with a will to improve matters. John XXIII appointed
him Cardinal in 1958 and he worked closely with the Pope in the
preparation for the Council. He had visited Hungary in 1938, the
USA in 1951 and 1960, Dublin in 1961 and Africa the following year.

Giovanni Battista was elected Pope Paul VI on 21 June 1963 on
the fifth ballot and in September the Vatican Council entered its
second session. Pope Paul visited the Holy Land in January of 1964
and India in the December, and he followed this with a visit to New
York and the United Nations in October 1965: the last session of
the Council ended on 8 December 1965. *Populorum Progressio* (PP)
was published on 26 March 1967, just fourteen months after
*Gaudium et Spes*. Paul VI had been deeply impressed and affected
by his visit to India, seeing the problems of poverty in a developing
country for the first time. In writing the encyclical he had been
much influenced by Louis Lebret OP who had been summoned to
the Council as a *peritus*.

## Summary of *Populorum Progressio*[2] (1967)

There is an introduction [1–5] and two sections. I. Human development and economic development [6–42] and II. Economic
development and collaboration among the nations [54–87].

### Introduction

The development of peoples concerns the Church, especially that
of those suffering poverty in all its forms and who are trying to attain
to a more human life. The Council called attention to this problem
[1] and contemporary social questions have been dealt with since
Leo XIII [2]. From the time of John XXIII it has been clear that the
social question has become world wide [3]. The Pope's own travels
have enabled him to see problems at first hand; the United Nations
were addressed on the matter and he is seeking ways of fulfilling the
Council's wishes on it [4]. The International Commission on Justice
and Peace will see that they are kept before the Church [5].

### I. Human development and economic development

Today men are striving 'to do more, learn more in order to be
more' but many new nations find that political freedom is not

enough [6]. Colonizers were 'sometimes concerned with their own interests' and left the local economy exposed, but 'the structural machinery they introduced', although imperfect did help to reduce ignorance and disease [7]. These structures however are now inadequate and the imbalance between rich and poor nations grows [8]. There is social unrest throughout the world in consequence [9]. Traditional cultures clash with modernization attempts [10] and easy deceitful solutions beckon [11]. The Church fostered human progress in the former mission lands, building 'hospitals, sanatoriums, schools and universities'; sometimes missionaries were too conscious of their own culture for the good of the Gospel, but they did protect the indigenous peoples [12]. The Church has had a long experience of human affairs; she rejects political ambitions, the Gospel vision guides her in encouraging the aspirations of peoples [13].

*True development*
Development must primarily be [14] part of that self-development obligatory on man to whom God gives intelligence and free will, making each man responsible for his self-fulfilment as he is for his salvation [15] which leads us to union with Christ, the highest goal of human life [16]. We owe much to previous generations; we must then make our contribution to the inheritance of future generations. 'The reality of human solidarity brings us not only benefits but obligations' [17]. Our scale of values must be correct. Material goods are necessary for human life and we are duty bound to work for them, but excessive desire for them is to be avoided [18]. All progress is two-edged and goods can enslave man [19]. But true development is humanistic, and makes man more truly human [20]; material deprivation, injustice and oppression of all kinds of dehumanizes [21].

*Obstacles to development: the abuse of private property*
God intended all to enjoy a good life from the earth's wealth; 'under the leadership of justice and in the company of charity, created goods should flow fairly to all'. All other property rights are subordinated to this [22]. When 'private gain and public needs conflict' it is 'for the public authority to seek a solution ... with the active involvement of individuals and social groups' [23]. Expropriation may be justified in some circumstances. Capital may not be invested in foreign countries contrary to the interests of one's own [24].

Industrialization was necessary for economic growth and human progress.

By dint of intelligent thought and hard work, man gradually uncovers the hidden laws of nature and learns to make better use of natural resources ... he is stimulated to undertake new investigations and fresh discoveries, to take prudent risks and launch new ventures, to act responsibly and give of himself unselfishly [25].

But

profit as the chief spur to economic progress, free competition as the guiding norm of economics, and private ownership of the means of production as an absolute right [with] no limits nor concomitant social obligations

is 'unbridled liberalism, it paves the way for a particular kind of tyranny, condemned by ... Pius XI ... the international imperialism of money', whereas economics is supposed to be in the service of man. This sort of capitalism has caused injustice and conflicts down to today, but it must not be taken as a condemnation of the process of industrialization in itself; it has played a major role in the task of development [26].

Work, which is willed and approved by God, develops human creativity, personality and brotherhood [27]. Yet it also promises money, pleasure and power and makes some selfish and others rebellious, it threatens 'man's dignity and enslaves him'. On the other hand, professionalism, a sense of duty and love of neighbour are also fostered by it. There is need then to restore the dignity of the worker where this is offended. Man must be made a partner in the enterprise. It must become a true human community, concerned about the dignity of all who are involved. Work is, after all, directed to the establishment of a supernatural order on earth [28].

Meanwhile too many are suffering; hasty industrialization and agrarian reform may produce greater evils [29]. Whole nations lack the bare necessities of life and suffer oppression. The temptation is to use violence [30] yet

everyone knows that revolutionary uprisings – except where there is manifest, long-standing tyranny which would do great damage to fundamental personal rights and dangerous harm to the common good of the country – engender new injustices, introduce new inequities and bring new disasters. The evil situation that exists, and it surely is evil, may not be dealt with in such a way that an even worse situation results' [31].

At the same time the present state of affairs demands bold initiatives, especially by those in authority [32].

*Conditions for effective development*
Individual initiative and competition alone are not enough, but are an essential part of development; public authority should determine goals and plan accordingly, along with 'private initiative and intermediary organizations' protecting human rights [33]. All economic and technological programmes should have the aim of enabling people 'in the sphere of temporal realities to improve their lot', at the same time furthering their 'moral growth and ... spiritual endowment'. Economics and technology must serve man and not enslave him [34]. Basic education is a condition of social progress, and economic growth; it is a primary agent of development [35].

While family influences at times have resulted in the denial of human rights, the natural family, stable, monogamous, as fashioned by God and sanctified by Christianity, is the basis of society [36]. Population growth is a cause of concern in some regions and the authorities can intervene in this matter, but only in accordance with the moral law and the rightful freedom of couples who, their consciences informed by God's law authentically interpreted, are to decide the size of their family [37]. The family is the first and most important element in the social structure; professional organizations often supplement it and help its development [38]. Social action needs a doctrine, and only those which deny human freedom and are atheistic and materialistic in their nature are unacceptable. Variety in intermediate organizations is essential to help freedom in society by their friendly rivalry. All those who work in them are commended [39]. Cultural institutions also have great influence on development, and those which embody a people's tradition must be preserved [40]. The excessive worldliness and the materialism of the richer nations must be rejected and only their noble and good values embraced [41]. True development is open to God because 'man infinitely surpasses man' [42].

## II. Economic development and collaboration among the nations

*The duty of solidarity*
All humanity, the children of the same God, must have the opportunity for self-development in economic as in other matters and work together for the future of human race [43] and the wealthier nations have a threefold obligation in this. [i] In mutual solidarity

they should give aid. [ii] Social justice must rectify trade relations between strong and the weak. [iii] In charity they must seek to build a more human world community [44]. Hunger and basic needs of all kinds demand a response [45] and such response has been forthcoming [46]. But these efforts, and those involving gifts, loans and investments are not enough. It is not a matter of simply improving conditions, though this is necessary; a true international community must be built in which men can live fully human lives free of oppression of any kind. It requires self-sacrifice, the readiness to accept higher taxes, to pay more for imports if necessary, to emigrate to help emerging nations [47].

Nations as well as individuals must promote solidarity. While the rich nations are entitled to enjoy their national good fortune, they must also share to help the less fortunate countries [48]. It is in their interest, for their avarice otherwise will 'arouse the judgement of God and the wrath of the poor' [49]. Co-ordination of effort is needed [50]. Military expenditures should be cut and the resources saved be used to relieve the needs of the poor [51]. Bilateral and multilateral agreements must be free of any form of neocolonialism or economic pressure [52]. Excessive military expenditures are wasteful, as are many of the lavish displays of wealth by nations or individuals [53].

*International co-operation; justice in aid and trade*
A dialogue between nations is needed on this matter so that the generosity of the developed and the real needs of the underdeveloped countries can be matched; the latter must not be swamped by debts they cannot repay, while donor nations have a right to insist that 'there is no question of backing idlers or parasites'; the recipients for their part must have their sovereign rights respected [54]. In countries where the struggle for subsistence absorbs energies, every help must be given to the people to 'take steps for their own betterment and seek out the means that will enable them to do so' [55]. Much is being done to help the poorer nations financially and technologically, and trade relations must be made just [56]. The more fully industrialized nations on the whole export expensive and profitable manufactured goods whose value increases. The less industrialized nations, on the whole, export basic foods and raw materials whose prices are too often low and unstable [57]. Free trade must be fair trade [58]. Contracts must be fair to be morally defensible, as *Rerum Novarum* insisted [59]. How this is done is a matter for the nations to decide; to some extent they do compensate or protect some sectors where the common good

requires that purely market considerations be counterbalanced. The same principles should be applied internationally [60]. Competition is necessary but must be made to operate fairly; there must be equality of opportunity. The mechanisms by which this is done can be established only gradually; here international agreements can help [61].

*Solidarity as the answer to extreme nationalism and to racialism*
Nationalism and racialism are enemies of solidarity. Honest pride in one's nationality should not demean that of others [62] and love of one's own people must not be made the basis for racialism. Racism is found in young and old nations, in clan and political rivalry, and it is a hindrance in the battle against injustice [63]. The answer is a heightened sense of solidarity; geographical proximity should help nations to grow in this, regional organizations gradually drawing them together [64].

A more effective world solidarity should allow people to become makers of their own destiny, and it must be the basis of international relations [65]. It is not so much depleted resources or their control by the few which threaten society as the weakening of brotherly ties [66]. Christian charity demands solidarity with immigrants – helping them to face the problems which confront them in new lands [67]. They run the risk of losing respect for their own cultural heritage [68] and are often subjected to inhuman conditions [69]. Those dealing with the new nations must be respectful of their hosts, seeking to advance indigenous workers, proper contracts spelling out the duties and rights of superiors and subordinates [70].

*The need for a new international juridical order*
The number of experts helping in the developing countries is encouraging [71]; but such experts must show respect for the cultures and feelings of the people they help [72]. Dialogue between cultures and respect for different traditions is the key: 'then the bonds of solidarity will endure, even when aid programmes are past and gone' [73]. The generosity of the young laity in assisting missionaries in various social programmes is particularly commended [74]. Each must do 'as much as he can, as best he can' [75].

The fight against poverty furthers man's spiritual and moral well-being as well as the material; it also brings peace, which stems from 'the establishment of the ordered universe willed by God, with a more perfect form of justice among men' [76]. 'Nations are the architects of their own development, and they must bear the burden of this work; but they cannot accomplish it if they live in isolation from others' [77]. This need for international collaboration involving all the nations of the world requires 'institutions which will promote, co-ordinate and direct it, until a new juridical order is firmly established and fully ratified'. The hope is that the United Nations will enjoy ever-growing authority [78]. These hopes are not unrealistic, but fulfilling them demands sacrifice [79]. Once again the seriousness of the issue is called to mind [80].

In the developing nations, the hierarchy interpret the moral law on these issues; the laity have the duty of improving the temporal order in practice. In the developed nations, individuals are encouraged to offer their skills to those working to solve the problems of the underdeveloped nations [81]. All Christians should work together on this task, and they should co-operate also with non-Christians [82]. All who have influence in society have their role to play in constructing the new world order [83]. Governments should draw their communities 'into closer ties of solidarity with all men' [84]. The need is great [85]. Those who have come to the aid of the needy nations are the apostles of genuine progress and development and they are blessed [86–7].

## 2  CELAM II at Medellín, Columbia (1968)

The second meeting of CELAM, which is the acronym for the Council of the Bishops of Latin America [Consejo Episcopal Latino Americano], took place at Medellín in Colombia, in 1968. That meeting became increasingly important to the Church internationally because of the significance of the Latin America's Church's struggle for social justice. It was a crucible of new social thinking and action, in particular of the liberation theology movement throughout the world. In that the general conclusions of CELAM II, modified somewhat by those of CELAM III [1979], were accepted by John Paul II into the corpus of the social magisterium, they have significance for the whole church. There were sixteen sections of the Final Document at Medellín:[3] of these three were of particular significance because of their relevance to current problems and the controversy and questions they raised. These were those on justice, peace and poverty.

## (i) Summary of the text of the document on justice

The misery in which so many of the poor of the continent live, cries out to heaven. Families, education, equal rights, especially for women, the rewards of labour, the expectations of the middle classes, all are affected by it [1] and the lack of socio-cultural integration leads to the imposition of other cultures, meeting the needs of the wealthy only; the result is political instability and purely formal institutions. There is a lack of national solidarity, combined with injustice in social structures [2]. Whereas

> God ... in the fullness of time sent his son in the flesh so that he might come to liberate all men from the slavery to which sin has subjected them, hunger, misery, oppression and ignorance, in a word, that injustice and hatred which have their origin in human selfishness.

Hence

> for authentic liberation, all of us need a profound conversion ... the uniqueness of the Christian message does not so much consist in the affirmation of the necessity for structural change, as it does in the insistence on the conversion of men which will in turn bring about this change.

We must be people who know how to be truly free and responsible according to the light of the Gospel [3]. This is why the Church emphasizes liberation in Christ, in 'love, the fundamental law of human perfection' [4]. This is the manner in which the Church desires to serve the world, bringing about a greater respect for human dignity and social unity. 'With the second Vatican Council [GS 38–42] we repeat that temporal progress is of vital concern to the kingdom of God though not identified with it' [5].

The pastoral role of the bishops is to help educate the conscience of the believer on social justice in the light of the documents of the magisterium [6]. Intermediate structures between the person and the State, the family, workers' organizations, professional organizations, should be fostered as a vital network of society [7]. The family here has a key role in helping the process of change, organizing their economic and cultural potential so that they influence decision making [8]. So too have the workers, especially the peasants, struggling to humanize and dignify their work [9].

In the organization of production, human dignity comes first. Business enterprises, industrial and rural, are the dynamic bases of the economy, and such enterprises should not be identified with the owners of capital but with all who work. Persons cannot be the property of individuals, society or the State.

> The system of liberal capitalism and the temptation of the Marxist system would appear to exhaust the possibilities of transforming the economic structures of our continent. Both systems militate against the dignity of the human person. We must denounce the fact that Latin America sees itself caught between these two options and remains dependent on one or other of the centres of power which control its economy.

The Bishops appeal to businessmen and all responsible authorities to follow the guidelines of the Church's social teaching: 'social and economic change in Latin America ... a truly human economy ... will depend fundamentally on this' [10]. Many workers feel effectively enslaved by their condition; they should instead be allowed the fullest possible participation and development of their human powers, assuming the 'necessary unity of direction' of the enterprise [11]. Their unions should also possess a responsible strength and power [12]. 'Socialization' as a socio-cultural process should bind Latin America in justice and brotherhood to liberate it from new colonialism [13].

'An authentic and urgent reform of agrarian structures and policies' is needed to give the peasants justice.' More than the redistribution of land is called for; it must be done in a way which ensures it will be effective for the peasant and the national economy [14]. Industrialization is necessary for economic independence and integration into the world economy 'preserving legitimate autonomy' and respecting the rights of persons and intermediate structures [15]. Political reform, however, is a precondition of all else. Political authority exists for the common and not the private good and too often this is in practice not the case.

> The lack of political consciousness in our countries makes the educational activity of the Church absolutely essential ... participation in the political life of the nation is a matter of conscience ... the practice of charity in its noblest and most meaningful sense' [16].

'Conscientization' and social education, forming social consciences and realistically assessing the problems of the community in all strata of society is to be integrated into pastoral action [17]. National episcopal conferences will assist in this process, encouraging the participation of all, clergy, laity, religious [18]. Commissions on social action will support courses for 'technicians, politicians, labour leaders, peasants, managers and educated men of all levels of society' [19].

> It is necessary that basic small communities be developed ... the Church, the People of God, will lend its support to the downtrodden of every social class so that they might come to know their rights and how to make use of them [20].

The Commission on Justice and Peace must be supported in all our countries at least at national level and should be staffed by people of high calibre [21]; other necessary organizations are to be set up also or, if already operating, do so within the joint pastoral plan [22]. The media also have their place in the programme of social education and full use should be made of them [23].


## (ii) Summary of the document on Peace

There are several internal challenges to peace in Latin America [1]. The marginalization of different groups [2], the extreme inequality between social classes [3], the growing frustration that these tensions produce [4], the insensibility of the privileged [5], the power unjustly exercised by the dominant groups [6], the growing awareness of the oppressed [7].

There are external challenges also [8]. The first is the economic, and there are several aspects to this. a) The growing distortion of international commerce. *Populorum Progressio* pointed out that those whose main products are raw materials are at a disadvantage in world trade because those products are decreasing in value while manufactures increase in value. b) In the search for security, much capital and many well qualified people leave the less prosperous countries, so further weakening economics. c) Companies, including foreign ones, evade taxes and send profits and dividends abroad, so depriving the home country of investment. d) International debt tends to become progressive, repayment becoming excessively burdensome because the realities of the situation are not taken into account. e) The 'international imperialism of money' condemned by Pius XI and Paul VI is the real cause of Latin American dependence [9].[4] The imperialism of any ideology which influences Latin America is rejected [10].

Finally there are tensions between individual countries in Latin America. They have historico-political causes; more integration is a necessity for the region and is not solely an economic process but social, political and cultural [11]. Exaggerated nationalism [12] and arms races between different countries increase the tensions [13]. The Christian approach to peace is, firstly, that it is the work of justice. Without the removal of injustices which challenge it, lasting peace is impossible. Secondly, peace keeping and making is a permanent task. The tranquillity of order requires constant effort. Finally, peace is the fruit of charity, of love of God in Christ the Prince of Peace. Peace with God must be the foundation of peace with man [14].

Latin America is a violent place and the Conference reaffirms its Christian preference, not for pacifism, but for the state of peace [15]. But the patience of those who have suffered much and are still suffering in being denied necessities and a chance for development should not be abused. Peace can only be assured by justice [16]. The wealthy should not take advantage of the position of the Church 'in order to oppose either activity or passively the profound transformations that are so necessary'. If they do they could be 'responsible to history for provoking "explosive revolutions of despair"' [17]. 'Also responsible for injustice are those who remain passive for fear of the sacrifice and personal risk implied by any courageous and effective action' [18], while those who are tempted to violence must remember that though it is sometimes morally justified, the danger is that it will produce greater evil. Considering

> the totality of the circumstances ... the Christian preference for peace ... the difficulty of civil war ... the atrocities it engenders ... the risk of foreign intervention ... the difficulty of building a regime of justice and freedom while participating in a process of violence ... we desire ... the organized community be put at the service of peace [19].

To further the cause of peace in circumstances which encourage violence, the Christian conscience must be educated, and the injustice which destroys peace denounced [20]. Through the mass media Christians will seek to [21] defend the rights of the poor and eliminate injustice, venality, insensibility [22], to favour integration by denouncing excessive inequalities [23], and give a social dimension to their work for the Gospel [24]. They will also encourage in education a critical sense concerning society and foster a sense of service to the community [25], co-operate with other communities to these ends [26], encourage grass-roots organizations for justice [27], seek to correct defects in administering justice [28], urge the ending of arms races between nations in the region [29], invite Church and other leaders in the developed nations to seek justice in trade with them [30], interest universities to look into the human rights record in Latin American countries [31], denounce and seek decisive procedures to prevent world powers which encourage war and invasion of weaker countries [32], and support all who are seeking for a new world order [33].

## (iii) Summary of the document on the poverty of the Church

The bishops cannot remain indifferent to the cry of the poor in Latin America [1] and the charge that the hierarchy, clergy and religious are rich. The great church buildings, luxurious cars, and attire inherited from earlier days, and the taxes to support clergy and education, all encourage erroneous opinions on money received, while secrecy concerning church finances magnifies and distorts the situation [2]. The reality of the greater number of poor dioceses and parishes, and those who work in them, is ignored, leaving the false image in place. Yet the clergy have economic security while the poor lack it, and that the people feel at times they do not identify with them [3].

Three kinds of poverty must be distinguished. [i] The poverty which makes it impossible for human beings to live worthily and which is an evil. [ii] Spiritual poverty, total dependence on God, breeds detachment from worldly possessions, and is the ideal of the poor of Yahweh. [iii] Freely chosen poverty commits the individual to sharing the hardships of people who suffer from want, which is an imitation of Christ who became poor for our sake [4]. The Church must denounce the first, preach and live the second, and is bound to material poverty [5]. All members of the Church are called to live in evangelical poverty, but in different ways [6]. The example of the Church, bishops, priests, religious and laity must reflect the spirit of poverty according to the charism of each and their state of life [7].

The clergy have to relate their lives and words to the demands of the Gospel [8]. They must give 'preference to the poorest and most needy sectors and to those segregated for any cause whatsoever' [9], sharpening their 'duty of solidarity with the poor' to which charity leads them. 'The solidarity means that we make ours their problems and their struggles, that we know how to speak with them' [10]. 'Human advancement must be the goal of our action on behalf of the poor man ... [we must] respect his personal dignity and help him to help himself' [11]. The practical witness of a modest life style by the clergy, and in general a commitment to the poor, will present to the world a sign of the poverty of Christ [12–18].

## 3 *Octogesima Adveniens*: Apostolic Letter of Pope Paul VI, (1971)

This Apostolic letter was sent to the President of the Justice and Peace Commission set up by Paul VI. Its authority being derived from the ordinary magisterium of the Pope here exercised, it is no less authoritative than an encyclical. Its oneness with the Papal tradition is revealed in that it was issued to mark the eightieth anniversary of *Rerum Novarum,* as the title, 'The eightieth anniversary' itself tells us.

### (i) *Background to the letter: liberation theology of G. Gutiérrez*

A complex phenomenon, liberation theology contains many elements and there are many forms of it. The nucleus of its theory was already emerging in 1968 but it was not widely influential at that time: the documents of CELAM were framed by the Church's social teaching and reflect its social ethic, as the summary of it given above reveals. Liberation theologians who see Medellín as in some way being formed by that theology are not supported by the texts; some of the ideas which have been made familiar to us by liberation theologians, for example the 'option for the poor' which is evangelical, were embodied in those texts because those ideas were not new but part of the Christian tradition on which it drew. In that sense the sound elements in liberation theology were in some way formed by Medellín.

The most distinctive characteristic of that theology as it has come to be known, however, is that some forms of it embrace Marxist social analysis of, and remedies for, social injustices. However, Marxism is rejected specifically by the Conference, along with the socially irresponsible form of capitalism which is liberal capitalism. The liberation of which Medellín speaks is liberation in Christ leading to personal conversion which then imposes the obligation of working for justice, along with charity and the other virtues, and not exclusively for it. In so far as liberation theology was developed by Medellín, it was not then a theology that required the abandonment of the traditional understanding of theology. Quite the contrary; it follows from that tradition and its understanding of the nature of salvation.

Liberation according to Medellín is primarily liberation from sin, which is the source of injustice as of the other moral evils in the world, and the way of liberation is through return to the Gospel; it is liberation in Christ, in love, elevating the dignity of man. By extension of this idea, social structures need to be changed if they are sinful, but this will only be done when the personal sin that is embodied in the structures, and causes the social sin, is corrected. Personal conversion to the Gospel is the core of liberation, personal and social. In looking to the reform of society and its structures therefore Medellín kept within the guidelines of traditional theology: it does not try to invent a new one. Medellín on social issues, takes its inspiration from the social teaching of the Church. The bishops' duty is to enlighten the believer on social ethics in the light of the documents of the magisterium. The social teaching of Pius XI and Paul VI is specifically mentioned.

Liberation theology as developed by its main sponsors was taking a rather different direction. It had its roots in European theology as it was developed in the universities and theology departments of France, Germany, Holland and Belgium in the 1950s and 1960s. Gustavo Gutiérrez, whose *A Theology of Liberation* is its basic text, studied at Louvain 1951–55 and then at Lyons, before being ordained in 1959 and returning to Lima in Peru to be Professor of Theology at the University there.[5] When liberation theology emerged in Latin America in the 1960s, therefore, it was aided by insights from the theologies of revolution, of development and of hope, dialogue with the Marxists, and political theology, which were European and North American in origin, and from an ecumenism which was far more radical than that envisaged by the Council.

Cleary considers that the first formulation of liberation theology was made at a meeting organized by Ivan Illich at Petropolis in 1964 at which Gutiérrez developed the theme of theology as a reflection on praxis; this was later reworked for other gatherings in Montevideo, Montreal and then at Cartigny in Switzerland over the next three years. His *Notes on Liberation Theology* were published after the Cartigny meeting of SODEPAX in 1967 and 1971; *A Theology of Liberation* was published in Lima in 1972.[6]

Theology, Gutiérrez tells us, was initially a theology of wisdom encouraging people to sanctity; then in the high Middle Ages it became a rational, intellectual discipline under the influence of Thomas Aquinas, before declining into an ancillary discipline of the magisterium in the context of the Counter-Reformation. Modern theology is by contrast a critical reflection on ecclesiastical practice and as a result 'charity has been rediscovered as the centre of Christian life'[7] while the Church which formerly 'did almost nothing to better the world'[8] has come to concern herself with orthopraxis, right practice that is, not only orthodoxy or right belief. Liberation theology is a new way of doing theology, which in fact can only be done when engaging in the struggle for justice; the theologian 'will be engaged ... where nations, social classes, people struggle to free themselves from domination and oppression'.[9]

In effecting this change, Marxism was one of the influences, because Marxist thought was focused on praxis and geared to the transformation of the world; Sartre's opinion, 'that Marxism, as framework of all contemporary philosophical thought, cannot be superseded'[10] is quoted approvingly. Certainly 'it is to a large extent due to Marx's thought' that contemporary theology has begun to reflect on the meaning of the transformation of this world and the action of man in history. Concerning the relationship of the concepts of liberation and development, the 1950s and 1960s belief that the latter would solve the problem of poverty has been challenged because it implied reformist processes and did not attack root causes. To do that a radical break with the *status quo* was needed: 'a profound transformation of the private property system, access to power of the exploited class and a social revolution which would allow a change to socialist society' or the possibility of it. Marx has constructed a 'scientific understanding of historical reality. He analysed capitalistic society in which were found concrete instances of exploitation'. Pointing the way to a time when man can live humanly he 'created categories which allowed for the elaboration of a science of history'.[11]

In view of this, Gutiérrez thought little of the social encyclicals, especially in so far as they advocated developmentalism and stressed peace. He would have preferred something which allowed the poor to take control of their own destiny. He suggested that as a result of Medellín, the emphasis has changed to liberation as he understands it, though in fact it rejected any form of Marxist analysis and specifically insisted on the social teaching of the Church and peaceful development, as we have seen. The Second Vatican Council missed the point, we are told by Gutiérrez, which is that the 'social praxis of man is reaching maturity' and is determined to wrest power from those who think they have the right to rule. It is the great revolutions of France and Russia which orient this modern social praxis.

Reformism is not enough, as support for the social revolution means abolishing the *status quo* and building a just society on the new relationships of production. The political arena is necessarily conflictual. Previously Christians disregarded 'structural knowledge of socio-economic mechanisms and historical dynamics'[12] and stressed the conciliatory aspects of the Gospel, not the political and the conflictual. The latter must now be faced. The option before the Latin American Church is clear; it must reject the developmentalism of the 1950s and accept the dependency theory, which is basically sound, though it needs to be shorn of its less scientific elements. Class analysis is the only guide; Latin America is experiencing a full-grown revolutionary ferment, mainly socialist, and it needs to be given a Latin American flavour. This is where Cuba's influence is important, as are Mariategui's theories also, and Che Guevara's[13] call for a new socialist man.

The Church in Latin America is in process of liberation in which some bishops and priests and others have specifically advocated socialism as the only viable option, meaning at base 'the social ownership of the means of production'. The case of Allende's Chile is evidenced.[14] The Church should be united only with the disinherited, though Medellín only recommended denunciation of oppression; the revolutionary thrust of the Gospels must be recognized. 'The Church must place itself squarely within the process of revolution amid the violence which is present'.[15]

Salvation is linked in the Bible with creation and the link is the liberating experience of the Exodus. The liberation of Israel was a political act in the long march to a society free from misery and alienation. Christ brings this to fulfilment; his work is a liberation from sin and all its consequences. Exodus remains vital because of the similar historical experiences the people of God undergo. To struggle against misery and exploitation is to be part of the saving action. But the texts of the magisterium do not really throw light on the proper relationship between the temporal order and the progress of the kingdom. Temporal progress is to be seen as a continuation of the work of creation; in the third world this means political liberation and the will to revolution. Sin has produced oppressive structures to which the Church belongs; sin is not to be seen as private: it is in these structures. The *Magnificat* sums up the spirit of liberation. The future of history belongs to the poor and the oppressed and their liberation will be their own work.

The Church's role in this context is not 'to save in the sense of guaranteeing heaven. The work of salvation is a reality which occurs in history'[16] and the reality of the class struggle in society raises the question of Christian brotherhood; the division of humanity into the owners of the means of production and those who are denied the fruits of their labours produced the class struggle, and if the Church rejects this struggle it is defending the privileges of the few. To speak of the priest as a man of unity in these conditions is to make him part of the unjust system; we must opt for the oppressed. The bond which unites God and man is recalled in the Eucharist, but

> without a commitment against exploitation and alienation, and for a society of solidarity and justice, the eucharistic sacrifice is an empty action lacking any genuine endorsement by those who participate in it'.[17]

Such was the analysis and policy favoured by Gutiérrez in a book which has had enormous influence on the Latin American and the international Church. Gutiérrez' thinking has developed since then, but the ideas set out in the first edition of this book were those which have been most influential, the ones for which it will be remembered. There is no doubting the author's personal goodness and dedication to the cause of Christ's poor, but any rationalization of the Christian commitment to the cause of social justice along the lines it suggested was misguided in theory and in practice. To reduce theology to the role of handmaid in the struggle for social justice is to deprive it of all objectivity, and to reject the mind of the Church he is ordained to serve concerning the nature of her theology is also to come dangerously near to worshipping the proletariat in their struggle, rather than the God who made all things. To speak of the scientific socialism of Marx as the answer to all the ills of society revealed a naïvety which the collapse of real socialism has made painfully apparent. To claim that the commitment to socialist revolution, the class struggle and the new dawn when the social ownership of the means of production would solve all problems, was the way that Latin America was going and which the Church had also to go, was totally to misunderstand the sociology and politics of the region. Finally, to reduce the Church's work for salvation to working for salvation from earthly injustice, and to deny the brotherhood of man and access to eucharistic worship to those who were not committed to revolution and the class struggle such as liberation theology recommended, was to reject the Church's sacramental theology, secularize the Church and make it the appendage of one social group.

## (ii) Summary of Octogesima Adveniens[18]

There is an Introduction [1–7] and three main sections. I. Urbanization and related problems [8–23]. II. Politics, ideologies and Christianity [24–41], and III. Seeking answers [42–51]. The Introduction refers to the event it commemorates – the eightieth anniversary of *Rerum Novarum* [1], and notes that the spirit of the Lord is still working in the hearts and minds of men to raise up true apostles of Christ's Gospel in the modern world [2]. There are difficulties facing Christians in many and various parts of the world as they try to put it into practice [3]. It is then difficult to propose universal remedies; it is for the Christian communities to analyse their different situations, to apply to them Gospel insights, and to draw principles, norms and directives from the Church's social teaching, having confidence in the Christian tradition in these matters [4].[19] The conditions of the workers in industrial society was the first focus of the church's social magisterium in modern times; now the social question is world wide [5]. The forthcoming synod of bishops would be considering the question of justice in the modern world; the occasion of the anniversary of Leo's great encyclical gives the Pope the opportunity to confide his preoccupations in this field to the Pontifical Commission on Justice and Peace [6] by drawing to its attention several important issues [7].

### I. Urbanization and related problems

This is a characteristic of the industrialization process and it has led to cities with tens of millions of inhabitants becoming commonplace [8]. Unfortunately, the 'megalopolis' often does not provide work for its population nor can it provide them with the goods and services the people need [9]. Urban civilization in general then can bring a new loneliness and new forms of poverty and alienation as the old structures of family, neighbourhood and Christian community are broken up; decent housing for the young working class is lacking and this produces its own moral problems [10]. It is the weakest who suffer most. Community and parish centres of all kinds are needed to help rebuild a sense of community [11] and this is a task in which Christians must share [12].

Youth must be catered for and women given full recognition of true personal equality and participation in cultural, economic, social and political life, not the false equality which denies the importance of her role at the heart of the family [13]. For the worker, the right to work, to personal development, and to adequate rewards must be safeguarded and the importance of unions recognized, together with the right to strike as a final form of defence. Yet where the good of society as a whole may justify the judgement that demands are excessive, or political, or affect public services seriously, there is a 'limit beyond which the harm caused to society becomes inadmissible' [14].

Much has been done in securing greater justice in human relationships but much remains to be done. Egoism and the desire for domination are permanent temptations. Victims of industrial change, together with those on the margins of society, the maladjusted, the handicapped, the old [15], those discriminated against by reason of race, origin, colour, culture, sex or religion – all are entitled to justice. A country belongs to every one; all should be equal before the law, find equal admittance to economic, cultural, civil and social life and benefit from a fair share of the nation's riches [16]. Migrants and foreign workers are also entitled to justice for their contribution to their new land; their integration and advancement should be favoured. Christians especially must work for the establishment of universal brotherhood [17].

Demographic growth calls for a sense of solidarity which will enable humanity to meet its challenges, instead of the growing fatalism that leads the authorities to accept contraception and abortion as answers. As *Populorum Progressio* stated, governments have a right to concern themselves with limiting population growth in certain circumstances, provided moral means are used [18] but the real answer to the social and economic problems of the countries concerned lies in imaginative policies and application of the same capital and resources to solutions of these problems as have been devoted to armaments or technological developments [19].

The improvement of modern communications makes it possible to spread information, education and culture ever more widely to the great advantage of humanity, but 'those who hold this power have a grave moral responsibility with respect to the truth of the information they spread, the needs and reactions they generate and the values they put forward'. The public authorities cannot avoid their responsibility for protecting the common good in the face of those influences which undermine essential values [20]. Man is also suddenly becoming aware that by an ill-considered exploitation of nature, he risks destroying it and becoming in his turn the victim of this degradation. It is a wide-ranging problem which must concern the Christian, taking responsibility with the rest of mankind [21].

The aspiration to equality and to participation grows stronger [22]. Progress in securing human rights has been constant, but much remains to be done. Discrimination still exists. Further, legislation must be backed up by respect for persons, by a charity which goes beyond the law and seeks a preferential respect for the poor and a readiness to give up rights in order to place goods more generously at the service of others. Over-emphasis on equality can give rise to individualism in which each one claims his own rights without wishing to be answerable for the common good; a renewed awareness of solidarity is needed to counter this. Christianity stresses the need of love, and makes love, brotherhood, the prime value of the earthly order [23].

## II. Politics, ideologies and Christianity

Equality and participation are the marks of a democratic society and various forms are tried; the Christian has a duty to participate in the organization of the life of political society. Rights and duties go together; duty itself is conditioned by self-mastery, the acceptance of responsibility and the limits placed on freedom [24]. It is for cultural and religious groups to develop freely in society, in a manner appropriate to each, the ultimate convictions on the nature, origin and end of man and society. It is not 'for the state ... or political parties ... closed unto themselves ... to impose an ideology ... a dictatorship over minds' [25]. The Christian cannot accept ideologies which radically or substantially go against his faith and his concept of man. Among these is the Marxist atheistic materialism, its dialectic of violence and its absorption of the individual into the collectivity. Also among them is liberalism, which so exalts individual freedom as to withdraw it from every limitation, by stimulating it through exclusive seeking of interest and power and by considering social solidarities as more or less automatic consequences of individual initiatives, instead of being an aim and a major criterion of the value of the social organization [26]. Christianity relates man to God, transcendent and creator, who calls on him as endowed with freedom and responsibility [27]. Ideologies can become man's new idols and enslave him [28].

On the other hand there are signs that ideologies are in retreat, and John XXIII noted that movements based on ideologies can grow away from them and represent lawful human aspirations

[30]. But Christians who are attracted to socialist movements because of their will for justice, solidarity and equality, can fail to recognize the limitations of historical socialist movements which remain conditioned by the ideologies from which they originated. Distinctions must be made between the various levels of expression of socialism. A genuine aspiration for a more just society is one, but there are others linked with historical movements, and political organization and aims which possess an ideology claiming to have a complete and self-sufficient picture of man [31].

Marxism, it is sometimes claimed, is so ideologically splintered and weakened that rapprochement with it is possible [32]. For some, Marxism is essentially the class struggle; for others it is the collective exercise of economic and political power under a single party, or a Socialist ideology based on historical materialism and the denial of the transcendent. Finally, it can be seen as scientific activity, a rigorous method of examining social and political reality which links history with theoretical knowledge and the practice of revolutionary transformation. Through selectivity in its presentation and interpreting reality in the light of ideology it furnishes some people with a certitude and a spur to action, and the certitude preliminary to action: the claim to decipher, in a scientific manner, the mainsprings of the evolution of society [33]. However

> it would be dangerous to accept elements of Marxist analysis without recognizing their relationship with ideology ... to enter into the class struggle and its Marxist interpretations while failing to note the kind of totalitarian and violent society to which this process leads [34].

Liberal ideology, meanwhile, is undergoing a revival. Certainly personal initiative must be maintained and developed, but Christians who embrace liberalism as a social philosophy should remember that philosophical liberalism erroneously affirms 'the autonomy of the individual in his activity, his motivation and the exercise of his liberty ... hence the liberal ideology likewise calls for careful discernment' [35]. For his commitment to society, the Christian will find inspiration rather in the sources of his faith and the Church's teaching than in such ideologies [36]. The weaknesses of ideologies are showing themselves in bureaucratic socialism, technocratic capitalism and authoritarian democracy, and the rebirth of Utopias is upon us as a consequence. The latter can be escapist; they can also be useful in so far as they can help to sustain a vision of the future, and it is here that Christianity can meet them with its faith in the Spirit of Jesus Christ and its involvement in building up the human city, peaceful, just and fraternal, as an offering to God [37].

The modern understanding and analysis of man through the human sciences runs the risk of imprisoning him in his own rationality, making it impossible to understand him in his totality [38]. Man can also become the object of manipulation; to build a new society for the service of man it is necessary to know what man is [39]. Christians involved in those sciences which can and do deepen and enrich our knowledge of man, can enter into fruitful dialogue on human liberty and social conditioning; but these sciences cannot solve the mysteries of the human heart or meet the desires of his inmost being [40].

Indefinite progress as an end in itself has become a modern ideology also, but today there are doubts about it. Quantitative economic growth, for example, is of little value if true quality of life suffers. The growth of moral consciousness, solidarity, being open to others and to God, is a more genuine progress, and all progress must take into account the mystery of death and its implications, which for the Christian is taken up into the death and resurrection of Christ [41].

### III. Seeking answers: the Church's social teaching

Faced with what seem to be ever more urgent social problems, the social teaching of the Church seeks to guide man in the search for solutions. It neither authenticates structures nor offers ready-made models, but neither does it limit itself to recalling general principles.

> It develops through reflection [on] the changing world under the driving force of the Gospel ... a disinterested desire to serve and pay attention to the poorest ... it draws upon its rich experience of many centuries continuing its permanent preoccupations' [42].

Greater justice is needed in the sharing of goods, both within nations and between them. Each country should have the freedom to develop itself, but a revision of international economic relations is needed also, on the division of production, the structure of exchanges, the control of profits, the monetary system. The models of growth in the rich countries and the people's outlook need to be challenged [43]. New economic powers are emerging, multinational companies whose scale of operations is largely independent of political authority, and therefore of control for the common good [44]. Men today are yearning for freedom from oppression, but unless they embrace true interior freedom they run the danger of adopting ideologies which mean they simply change masters. They opt for technological, economic and military power, and the inequalities and injustices accumulate with the struggle for justice forgotten [45]. Economic activity at its best serves and furthers the brotherhood and dignity of man. Yet it can be over-emphasized and must be subject ultimately to the political order which has care of the common good. All individuals and groups within the State must be subject to it, while it must use its power to help them to exercise their freedom for the common good. Politics 'are a demanding manner, but not the only one, of living the Christian commitment to the service of others'. Nor does politics represents an absolute value. Christians should work 'in the framework of a legitimate plurality' [46].

Politics also accommodate the modern man's desire to share responsibility and decision making. That desire has its reflections also in the economic sphere, in industry especially where some form of shared responsibility is required. Human groups should develop a community awareness based on shared responsibility and leading to a real solidarity among men. For the Christian, it is losing himself in God that gives him true freedom [47]. The task of renewing the temporal order belongs to the laity and they should use their initiative accordingly; it is for the hierarchy to interpret the norms of morality to be followed. The knowledge that Christ is working in the world should give us courage to work for justice within it [48]. Each must decide what he is called on to do, avoiding selfish particularism or oppressive totalitarianism [49]. We should be aware of the legitimate variety of options open to Christians in this matter; the bonds which unite the faithful are greater than the differences which may divide them [50]. They give witness to their faith by working for a more just society [51].

## 4 *Evangelii Nuntiandi* of **Paul VI (1975)**

This apostolic exhortation,[20] published to mark the end of the Holy Year and the tenth anniversary of the close of Vatican II, was related to the Third General Synod of Bishops (1974) which had discussed evangelization in the modern world but had been unable to agree on a major statement; it therefore gave its findings to Paul VI so that a document could be published eventually: its English title, 'On announcing the Gospel' indicates it is a response to those findings.

Strictly speaking, therefore, it is not equivalently a social encyclical, but since it reflects on the theme of liberation and liberation theology and comments on the growth of base communities, and both were controversial in the Church's work for the world especially in Latin America, it touches upon important aspects of the Church's social teaching, placing work for justice in the context of evangelization of spreading the Gospel, and it must be part of the work for the salvation of man as the Church has always, in the apostolic tradition, understood it.

## (i)  Summary of its key texts on social ethics

The Introduction [1–5] considers the Church's task of proclaiming the Gospel, and the document has seven main sections or parts. Only those sections which are relevant to the development of the social teaching will be referred to. Parts VI to VII are therefore not examined and other sections are foreshortened.

### Introduction: proclaiming the Gospel

Proclaiming the Gospel to the people of today, who are buoyed up by hope yet often oppressed by fear, is a service to all humanity [1]. This is the tenth anniversary of the closing of the Council and it is also one year after the close of the Third Synod of Bishops [2]. The importance of this theme of evangelization has been frequently mentioned, and the Christian message must be presented so that 'modern man can find the answer to his questions and the energy for his commitment to human solidarity' [3]. We must transmit this message living and intact [4]. It is unique, irreplaceable, admitting neither difference, syncretism nor accommodation [5].

### Part I: The example of Christ

Christ announced it as his task to proclaim the kingdom of God, bringing the good news especially to the poor [6]. What meaning did this imperative have for Christ? [7]. First, he stressed that compared with the gaining of this kingdom, all other things in life are secondary [8]; salvation is the good news, the great gift of God which is liberation from everything that oppresses man, but which is above all liberation from sin and the evil one [9]. The kingdom and salvation are open to all through radical conversion, a profound change of mind and heart [10]. He won the approval of all by his teaching [11] and confirmed his mission by his signs, to one of which 'he attaches the greatest importance ... the humble and poor are evangelized' [12]. The community which is the Church is formed by believers [13] and she knows that her essential mission is to evangelize [14–15] ... hence those who today claim to love Christ but not the Church are misguided; Christ himself said, 'Anyone who rejects you rejects me'. Christ loved the Church and sacrificed himself for her [16].

## Part II: The meaning of evangelization

Partial and fragmentary definitions of evangelization deprive the concept of its fullness of meaning [17]. It means bringing the good news of salvation to all humanity [18]. It implies upsetting all criteria which are in contrast with it [19]. The testimony of witnesses proclaiming it is to permeate society in its very roots [20]. All Christians are witnesses by their very being [21], but active proclamation of the Gospel is always necessary [22]. It only reaches full development when it is accepted and assimilated, and acceptance means membership of the Church and receiving its sacraments [23]; the person evangelized then goes on to evangelize others [24].

## Part III: The content of the message

There are many secondary elements in the message [25] centred on its clear proclamation that Christ, the Son of God made man, came to witness that God loved the world and sent his son who died to save it, and rose again [26–7]. It looks then to the future life; it proclaims the hereafter [28], but at the same time it takes account of man's life here on earth, and contains a teaching on human rights, family, peace, justice, development, and liberation [29]. The Church has a duty to proclaim liberation to the millions who are marginalized [30].

'Between evangelization and human advancement – development and liberation – there are in fact profound links.' Man who is evangelized is pressured by adverse social conditions and in its message there is concern for justice and charity [31]. Some however 'are ... tempted to reduce the Church's mission to a simply temporal project, to reduce her aims to a man-centred goal ... to material well-being' [32]. The liberation brought by evangelization embraces the whole man, his social, political, economic and cultural life certainly [33].

Nevertheless she affirms the primacy of her spiritual vocation and refuses to replace the proclamation of the kingdom by the proclamation of forms of human liberation ... her contribution to liberation is incomplete if she neglects to proclaim salvation in Jesus Christ [34].

The Church 'links human liberation and salvation in Jesus Christ but never identifies them' because 'not every notion of liberation is compatible with the evangelical vision of man and further, all political liberation ... even if it pretends to be today's theology ... fails, if its final goal is not salvation in God' [35]. Those who live and work in unjust structures must undergo a conversion of heart if these structures are to be humane [36]. Nor is violence the path to liberation: 'violence provokes violence ... engenders new forms of oppression' [37]. Liberation guided by her social teaching is the way [38]. Human rights are fundamental to it and among those rights is one to religious freedom [39].

*Basic communities*
*Comunidades eclesiales de base,* basic or small church communities, have developed in solidarity with local Churches in areas where priests are few – as a result of the desire for a more intense life of faith, prayer and fraternal charity. Or, still in union with the local churches, they grow out of a sense of shared mission in particular groups drawn together by age, culture, occupation, charitable or other work for the poor. In other places they grow up in opposition to the 'institutional' Church, and proclaim themselves based on the Gospel and opposed to the hierarchy, so cutting themselves off from her. Those which are in sincere communication with the pastors of the Church and the magisterium and have the other marks of a true Christian community are of real value to the Church [58].

## 5 Summary analysis of the social teaching of CELAM II

### (i) Ethics and civil society

In Latin America, the socio-cultural integration of society is often lacking because of the absence of a national sense of solidarity, and whatever structural changes are needed, conversion of heart is the first requirement [Justice 1–3]. The intermediate societies, the family, the workers and professional organizations, the vital network of society, need to be fostered, especially those of the peasant seeking recognition of their dignity and all responsible authorities are urged to follow the guidelines of the Church's Social teaching [Justice 7]. Socialization as a socio-cultural process should bind Latin America in justice [Justice 13]. Conscientization and social education, forming social conscience and assessing the problems of the community is necessary [Justice 17]. Basic communities must be used to support the oppressed and help them know their rights and make use of them [Justice 20].

Tensions between classes exist because of internal colonialism and marginalization [Peace 2]. The suffering of the poor makes the appeal to violence attractive but peace is the way of the Church. The long suffering of the poor should not be exploited by the wealthy taking advantage of peace. Nor is passivity in the face of social evils justified. Profound transformations are needed to stave off revolutions of despair [Peace 14–18]. A critical sense regarding society is needed and the service of the community must be fostered, with encouragement for grass roots organization [Peace 25–27]. The Church in Latin America proclaims its identifications with the poorest members of society; solidarity makes their struggle, its struggle [Poverty 4–10].

## (ii) Ethics and political society

Political authority, which exists for the common good, in Latin America is too often in fact used for private good. The Church in her educational activity must therefore emphasize that participation in the political life of the nation is a matter of conscience, the practice of charity in the noblest sense, because political reform is a necessary precondition of all reform [Justice 16]. Latin America is a violent place; there are tensions between nations in the region that have historico-political causes and lead to exaggerated nationalism and arms races. Social, political and cultural integration is necessary to overcome them [Peace 11–13].

The Christian approach to peace is that it is the work of justice and that it is a permanent task; the tranquillity of order requires constant effort. It is the fruit of charity also; peace with God must be the foundation of peace with man [Peace 14]. Those who remain passive for fear of the sacrifice and personal risk involved in courageous action are responsible for the injustices that result from their inactivity [Peace 18]. Those who are tempted to use violence in the face of injustice are reminded that though this may sometimes be morally justified, the danger is that it may produce worse evils than it abolishes. The Christian preference must be for the peaceful way [Peace 19]. The systems of liberal capitalism and the temptation to Marxism seem to exhaust the possibilities of transforming the structures of Latin America; both militate against the dignity of the human person and are to be rejected [Justice 10].

## (iii) Ethics and economic society

The process of industrialization is irreversible and is a decisive factor in raising the standard of living. It is therefore necessary to plan and reorganize for this [Justice 15]. Business enterprises, rural and industrial, are the dynamic bases of the economy and such enterprises should represent all who work, not only the owners of capital; in the productive process, human dignity comes first. Both liberal capitalism and Marxism militate against the dignity of the person. There is an appeal to all businessmen and responsible authorities to be guided by the Church's social teaching. Many workers feel enslaved; they should participate in the running of the enterprise, saving the unity of direction it requires [Justice 10–11]. Workers' organizations should be able to participate at all levels, and they should train those who can accept these responsibilities for their exercise [Justice 12]. An authentic and urgent reform of agrarian structures and policies is needed to give the peasant justice; redistribution of land is called for, but it must be done in a manner which ensures it will be for the good of both the peasant and the national economy [Justice 14].

External colonialism still hinders Latin America's economic development. Its main wealth is in agricultural and related products which decrease in value in comparison with the manufactures it still needs to import. In search of security or better prospects, many qualified people and much capital leaves the region. Companies, home and foreign, evade taxes and send profits and dividends abroad, depriving it of investment. International debt becomes progressive, its repayment burdensome; the international imperialism of money accounts for the region's dependence [Peace 8–9].

## 6 Summary analysis of the social teaching of Paul VI

### (i) Ethics and civil society

Today men are striving for a fuller human development, seeking to do more and learn more in order to be more. True development is humanistic, with more human conditions embracing all that frees man from any kind of oppression and enables him to appreciate the dignity of the higher values and of God himself [PP 20–1]. The natural family, stable and monogamous, is basic to this development; population policies when necessary must conform to the moral law and respect the freedom of the couple [PP 37]. Professional organizations supplement the family, and cultural traditions which embody the tradition of a people need to be safeguarded [PP 38–40]. Full humanism, open to God, is the aim of development, for 'man infinitely surpasses man' [PP 42]. Racism is an enemy of the just social order and the answer to it is a heightened sense of solidarity [PP 63–4].

Modern urbanization brings to man a new loneliness [OA 8] for the poor and the alienated, and community and parish centres can help to overcome this [OA 11]. The young need catering for, and women should be allowed full equality in cultural, economic and social life, an equality which should not impair their importance at the heart of the family [OA 13]. The marginalized, the maladjusted, the handicapped, the old, need special care as do those discriminated against by race, origin, colour, culture, sex or religion [OA 16]. Human rights make progress but much needs to be done. It is the cultural and religious groups which develop the social body and it is not for the State or for the political parties to impose ideologies [OA 24–5]. Marxism absorbs the individual in the collectivity while liberalism removes all limits from individual freedom, stimulates it by power-seeking, and considers solidarity to be an automatic consequence of individual initiative, not a major criterion of social organization; by contrast Christianity relates man to God who calls on him as free and responsible [OA 26–8]. Marxist analysis cannot be separated from the class struggle and the totalitarian society to which it leads [OA 34]. Neo-liberalism likewise is still rooted in the error of the absolute autonomy of man. Such ideologies subject man to bureaucratic socialism, technocratic capitalism and authoritarian democracy. Christianity seeks to build up a human city on Christ, peaceful, just, fraternal and offered to God [OA 37].

The human sciences tend to imprison man in his own rationality; they can also manipulate him. Useful though they are, they cannot solve the mysteries of the human heart or satisfy the desires of his inmost being. Genuine progress is found in the development of moral consciousness which leads man to wider solidarity and to open himself to others and to God [OA 40–2].

## (ii) Ethics and political society

Christians have a duty to take part in the organization and life of political society according to their understanding of its nature, origin and end. It is not for political parties to impose ideologies, and the Christian cannot accept those which are incompatible with their faith and understanding of man [OA 24–5]. Marxist and liberal capitalist ideologies are both inimical to those understandings. Bureaucratic socialism, technocratic capitalism and authoritarian democracy are the fruits of such ideologies. So too are Utopias: these can be escapist; they also can help sustain a vision of the future, and here Christianity can meet them with its faith in Jesus Christ [OA 37].

Political commitment accommodates man's desire to share responsibility and decision-making, and Christians involved in politics should be aware of the legitimate variety of opinions open to them [OA 47–50]. Politics are a demanding manner, though not the only one, of living the Christian commitment to the service of others. Nor does politics represent an absolute value; it allows of a plurality of opinions [OA 46].

The pressure that some countries in the underdeveloped world are under as their people suffer from a lack of the bare necessities of life, is threatening revolutionary uprisings. But while long-standing tyranny, which would do harm to fundamental rights and the common good, could justify such a course of action in some circumstances, an evil situation should not be dealt with in such a way that greater evils result, bringing new injustices and disasters. The problems in question must therefore be dealt with vigorously but by developmental means. [PP 30–2]. In development efforts, public authority should determine plans and goals but must see that private initiative and intermediate organizations are involved, avoiding both collectivism and damage to human rights [PP 33].

## (iii) Ethics and economic society

God intended all to enjoy a good life from the wealth of the world, giving it to all to use in justice and charity; all property rights are subject to this proviso and when private gain and public good conflicts, it is for the public authority, in consultation with individuals and social groups, to seek a solution [PP 22–3]. Expropriation may be justified, with due compensation, where private property does not serve the common good; the Second Vatican Council pointed out that where extensive, ill-used or poorly-used estates impede general prosperity this may be the case. Nor is it permissible for those who have profited from economic activities within their own country to deposit a large part of their funds in foreign countries for their own gain while taking no account of the national interest [PP 24].

Industrialization is necessary for economic growth and human progress. Through his intelligence, his prudent judgement in launching new ventures, and his hard work, man has discovered the laws of nature and has learned to make use of the world's resources, by acting responsibly [PP 25]. Such industrialization has benefited mankind, including the underdeveloped world; though the foreign interests often involved were seeking gain, they also helped local economies in some degree by their activities, in the reduction of ignorance and disease for example [PP 7]. But any understanding and practice of economic life which makes profit the chief spur, free competition and the absolute rights of the property owner the norm, with no limits or social obligations, is the unbridled liberalism that Pius XI condemned. Economics must be in the service of man. Liberal capitalism has caused injustice in the past and does today [PP 26].

In advancing the cause of economic development, individual initiative and the interplay of competition is not enough. The public authorities must be involved in laying down the desired goals and stimulating activity, but they must see that private initiative and intermediary organizations are involved so that they avoid collectivism and the dangers of a planned economy which threatens liberty and human rights [PP 33]. The developed nations have a duty in justice to help the poorer in the task of development; mutual solidarity, social justice and universal charity demand it [PP 44], but it must be remembered that nations are the main architects of their own development and it is they who must bear this burden primarily, but they cannot bear it alone; they need help [PP 77].

Charitable organizations have an important role to play and are playing it, but public and private gifts, loans and investments are essential [PP 46–7]. Bilateral and multilateral agreements between nations are also helpful, but they must not be neo-colonialist, but examples of true solidarity [PP 52]. The superfluous goods of the rich nations must also be placed at the disposal of the poorer. If the former are only conscious of their own advantage, they will incur the wrath of God [PP 49]. The expenses of nations on armaments are excessive; they and the superfluous expenditures of individuals and nations generally should be cut back, so that what is saved is used to the benefit of the poor [PP 53].

Developing nations should not be burdened with debts whose repayment cripples their economy, and that repayment needs to take this into account. Donors for their part are entitled to ask for assurances on how capital transfers will be used; idlers and parasites are not to be encouraged [PP 54]. Trade relations must be just, because ultimately it is by trade that the less developed nations will prosper. Free trade must be fair trade. The advanced nations accept this in their internal affairs, as with the support given to agriculture [PP 56–60]. The division of production, the structure of exchanges, the control of profits, the monetary system, all may need examining in the light of the call for a new order [OA 43].

The organization of labour and the productive process which industrialization has brought are vital to development. God willed that man should labour in completing the work of creation [PP 25, 27]. Every man has the right to work, to express his personality through it, to earn a just wage and by these means to lead a worthy life, materially, socially, culturally and spiritually. He has the right of association in trade unions and the right to strike, though the limits to the latter may have to be set by the State if the common good suffers [OA 14]. All workers are to some extent creators; they leave their imprint on their work and develop their own powers by so doing; when it is done in common it has it in its power to unite the hearts of men. However, it has its negative side; it can threaten man and enslave him. Every effort then must be made to see that the enterprise is a true community, concerned with the needs of all its members [PP 27–8]. In the course of development in the past man has often exploited the riches of nature in an irresponsible way so that the environment has been seriously threatened. The effort of the whole of humanity is necessary if the problems are to be faced effectively [OA 21].

# 24

# John Paul II and CELAM III at Puebla, Mexico, 1979

## 1 John Paul II: background

John Paul I, who was elected to succeed Paul VI on 26 August 1978, died suddenly a month later on 28 September, and in the subsequent consistory seven ballots failed to produce an Italian Pope. A group of Cardinals thereupon decided to look for one from further afield and Cardinal Carol Wojtyla, a Pole who had become very widely known in clerical and academic circles outside his own country because of his work in the Council and after, came under scrutiny. He had travelled widely, visiting France, Belgium and West Germany and had given conferences in Rome, Paris, Milan and Louvain; he had also been to Australia, Guinea and the Philippines, attended the Eucharistic Congress in 1976 and had lectured at the Harvard Summer School. He had also become known as a writer, especially through his book *Love and Responsibility*, published in 1960. Yet to the world, and to the Church at large, he was unknown and the surprise when he was elected was great. At 58 he was young for the job, and he was also the first non-Italian Pope for some four hundred years and the first son of Poland to hold the office.[1]

His father, also Carol, had been a retired commissioned quartermaster of the Austro-Hungarian army, and his mother Emilia a schoolteacher. They had two sons, Edward and Carol, Emilia tragically dying in 1929 in giving birth to the third child, a girl who did not survive. Carol was then ten years old. Three years later Edward, newly qualified as a doctor, died in a scarlet fever epidemic. The sadness of losing his mother and sister when he was ten, and his

* The notes and references for Chapter 24 are to be found on p. 462ff

admired elder brother when he was thirteen, could not but have a profound effect on the young boy – but he did not repine. At school he showed himself an outstanding pupil; he also participated enthusiastically in games and sports. He loved soccer and hockey, and above all he loved to walk and camp and canoe, and in the winter to ski in the Tatra mountains. As he grew up, literature and the theatre were his favourite intellectual and cultural interests; he was a poet, a good actor and he had set his heart on studying literature and philosophy at the famous Jagiellonian in Cracow which was the oldest University in Central Europe. His father had moved their home to the suburbs of that city in 1938 and Carol junior launched himself with gusto into student life. The invasion of Poland by the Nazis on 1 September 1939 ended all this. Within a month the Polish forces had been crushed and the country's new masters designated the Slavs a servile race; they were to be deprived of all but menial roles in the new order. The University was closed and most of the faculty put in prison camps to die there. Students were also in danger: it was advisable for them to register as manual workers and so Carol did, becoming a labourer in the Solvay company's stone quarry in Cracow.

The student body kept in touch with one another, meeting secretly to continue their studies and to take part in clandestine poetry readings and theatricals. Many, like Carol, were also engaged in underground activities, helping among other things to succour the persecuted Jews. The deep faith of his father, the simplicity of his upbringing, and the shocks he had had to absorb because of the death of first his mother and then his brother before he was thirteen years old, had marked and helped mature him early, rooting his natural integrity of character ever more deeply in a manly faith – but he had no inkling of a vocation to the priesthood in his teens.

Towards the end of his high school years he tells us

> people around me thought I would choose the priesthood. As for me, I did not give it a thought. I was quite sure that I would remain a layman, committed to be sure ... but as a priest certainly not'.[2]

Gradually however it came to him that it was precisely the priesthood to which God was calling him and there could be no question of his refusing the invitation; he was helped in responding to it by the influence of a lay mystic, Jan Tyranowski, a tailor by profession, who was steeped in the theology of St John of the Cross and it was to the contemplative life that he, Carol, was increasingly drawn. As a first step he joined the clandestine seminary of Cardinal Sapieha, the aristocratic, profoundly spiritual and spirited Archbishop of Cracow. It was he who divined that the young man's vocation was to the active apostolate as a diocesan priest and not to the contemplative as a Carmelite friar. In 1944, fearing that the few seminarians who had survived would dwindle further as a result of the wholesale and unpredictable sweeps to which the Nazi subjected the people, Cardinal Sapieha decided they should be hidden in the episcopal palace. There Carol and his companions stayed until the Russian 'liberation' took place. It was of course not a liberation, but the replacement of one mortal enemy by another.

On 1 November 1946, at 26 years of age, Carol Wojtyla was ordained and sent to Rome to prepare a doctoral thesis on St John of the Cross; this he finished in 1948, after which he went to France for a period, and there he became familiar with the Young Christian Workers' movement. Back in Poland he worked as a curate, first in a country parish and then in Cracow; in both he had a tremendous impact. A philosophy doctorate at the Jagiellonian followed, Max Scheler's philosophy being the subject, and he then lectured on ethics and social ethics at the Seminary and the University of Lublin from 1952 to 1958; he was appointed auxiliary Bishop of Cracow in 1958 and Archbishop in 1964. These were years of conflict between the Church and the Communist regime, interspersed with periods of comparative calm.

In the wake of Khruschev's condemnation of Stalinism in 1956, the Polish workers were among the first to react; 50,000 of them demonstrated in Poznan on 29 June 1956, defying the Soviets and demanding bread and freedom; Marshal Rokossovsky, the Red Army officer who was also Poland's defence minister, suppressed the demonstrators with tanks, and seventy of them were killed. 1956 also saw the first peaceful mass protest by the Polish people. On 15 August, the Feast of the Assumption of Our Lady, one and a half million defied the regime in assembling at Jasna Góra, the shrine of Our Lady at the hilltop monastery of Czestochowa, to celebrate the anniversary of the day 300 years ago when the Poles had survived the onslaught of the Swedish invaders. They now prayed for an end to the tyranny under which they suffered. It was a display which compelled the regime to be more conciliatory; the Church reciprocated, the bishops encouraging the people to vote in the elections of 1957.

Bishop Wojtyla was a formidable adversary of the regime, but he was politically shrewd, never seeking needless confrontation; while always being prepared to oppose those responsible for injustice, he did this in the most patient and peaceful way open to him, however long he had to wait; it was more difficult to encourage his people to persist peacefully. The clash with the authorities over the right to build a new church at the new steel town, Nowa Huta, which was constructed in the early 1950s near Cracow was a case in point. It had been thought that the provision of a church for the families of the new socialist man was not necessary, but the people disagreed and reluctant permissions for its construction was given in 1957 – only to be withdrawn again in 1960. The new bishop had to handle this delicate situation, and he used every peaceful and spiritual means to get the authorities to change their minds; he organized petitions and goaded by sermons, and at last permission was given once again in 1967 for the building to go ahead. It was ten more years before the voluntary labour of the people, financed by funds from home and abroad, completed the task, but completed it was.[3]

In the meantime the regime was not improving its standing with the Polish people; indeed its relations with them were getting worse: when Mr Gomulka, the party leader, announced in December 1968 that food prices were to be increased by 25 per cent, there were riots in the Baltic ports and, according to official figures, 12 were killed and 1200 wounded in Gdansk alone, with other deaths and woundings in the other cities along the Baltic coast. The unthinkable had happened, Pole had killed Pole; Gomulka had to resign on 19 December and was replaced by Edward Gierek. The new leader, realizing well enough that he needed the co-operation of the people at large if he was to govern, withdrew the threatened increases and also sought a new relationship with the Church; it was accordingly agreed that she would not actively oppose socialism if her religious and educational role in society was respected.

Difficulties in implementing the agreement soon arose. For example, the Church had been so hindered in her work in the past that it was calculated that three thousand new churches were needed to cater for the spiritual needs of the urban areas; for such a vast building programme the regime claimed it did not have the resources, and it had ideological objections to it anyway. Nor was Christian education allowed to flourish: rather it was restricted the more. Cardinal Wojtyla, as he now was, preached against the inhumanity and the impossibility of imposing atheism on a country which had been vibrantly Christian throughout its history. Meanwhile the regime was as clumsy and brutal as ever; it announced an increase in food prices once more in June 1976, and more protests were met by more repression. During this time Cardinal Wojtyla was encouraging the workers to seek a living wage and insisting on human rights, but he also urged realism; surrounded as they were by Warsaw Pact countries they had to tread cautiously, but that did not mean they had to surrender. The State exists for the people and the nation and not vice versa; that nation desired to be free and independent, and the people had the right to defend their rights and aims by peaceful means, no matter what the Party or the State said or did.

It was this combination of a clear grasp of the fundamental moralities of social life, and an absolute refusal to surrender them by default, combined with infinite patience and persistence in the face of repression and brutality, always without resorting to violence, which was the recipe for toppling the Soviet monolith, already seriously weakened from the inside. The Church was united under her bishops, and closely identified with the worker-based movement for freedom, because she was rooted deeply in the peasantry and the urban working class. The intellectuals on the other hand were not united because of tensions caused by anti-Semitism in Poland, and being mainly middle class they were distanced from the popular movements of the workers; they also had a strongly liberal anti-clerical element among their number. But these problems were being seen as less and less relevant in the light of the need to oppose the regime, and the brutality of the workers' state in 1976 provided the occasion for greater unity among the intellectuals and also with the workers and the Church; it was given expression in the formation of the Committee for the Protection of the Workers (KOR).

The Church had formed the fulcrum of the peaceful opposition for change; the Soviet State was opposed by her moral and spiritual strength and it was clear she spoke for the Polish people. In the words of the former Marxist Leszek Kolakowski, the repressive State could not destroy 'the most powerful crystallizing force of moral authority to resist the Sovietization process ... the Catholic Church'.[4] The clubs of the Catholic intelligentsia were able to link their peers with Solidarity in the struggle against a State which had become separated from the people. The Church's role now became secondary, supportive in what became a struggle for political power in civil society, led by the workers and the intelligentsia.

Gierek was seeking some way of calming the situation, while blandly denying that there was any rift between Church and State. He was anxious for this to be demonstrated in some way and he took his chance when he visited Rome in October 1977. He had a private audience with Paul VI and after it affirmed the greatness of the man. But the fuse was still smouldering back home. The students of Warsaw formed their own 'Flying University' to enable people to study free of the deadening and distorting view of reality imposed on them by Communist orthodoxy. By now, Cardinal Wojtyla had become a national symbol, appealed to by all, atheists and non-believers alike, in the demand for human rights and greater freedom: he supported the Flying University and offered five of Cracow's churches as lecture halls for their meetings at a time when few were available for them because of State action.

At this point, however, events beyond the frontiers of Poland were overtaking him; on 6 August 1978 Paul VI died and there was a conclave to attend; in fact there were two, one in August which elected John Paul I, and one in October out of which Cardinal Carol Wojtyla emerged as John Paul II. From now on, what part he played in helping his countrymen to achieve their freedom peacefully had to be played as part of his wider role in rallying the Church in the face of her many problems throughout the world. One of them was dealing with the exuberance of the Church in Latin America.

## 2  CELAM III at Puebla, Mexico 1979

### (i) Background

When John Paul II came to office in October 1978, the third Council of the Latin American Bishops to be held at Puebla in Mexico was pending, having been postponed because of the death of the last two popes; it was rescheduled for late January 1979. The question of liberation theology had become ever more pressing in the region throughout the 1970s and things were coming to a climax as John Paul II made his way to the meeting. The climacteric had much to do with the growing success of the Sandinista rebellion in Nicaragua.

This small Central American republic[5] was potentially wealthier than most in the region in natural resources, but had suffered the fate of many Latin American countries dominated since independence by a few wealthy families who either could not or would not face their responsibilities of trying to build up a viable political economy. The result was primitive turbulent politics and an economy tied to the industrialized nations which took its agricultural products and provided its main investments. The conservatives requested American help in their difficulties in 1910, and United States Marines were stationed there intermittently until 1933, establishing a national guard before they withdrew; three years later its Commander, Anastasio Somoza, seized the Presidency, to rule until 1956, when he was assassinated. His elder son who had succeeded him had sought to legitimize the regime, but on his death in 1967 the younger son, Anastasio junior, steamrollered his way into the office and continued in his father's tradition, but with none of his father's comparative prudence in his policies. 'Tachito' Somoza embodied in himself all the worst aspects of military dictatorship. He was cruel, greedy, shortsighted and totally without scruple and so mismanaged every crisis he faced that, in a region beginning to be touched both by the hopes of moderate social democratic change, and, more threateningly, by Marxist ideologies, he gradually lost the support of every section of Nicaraguan society apart from the Guard and his cronies; in the circumstances he made revolution inevitable. Prominent among his enemies was the Marxist Sandinista Liberation Front (FSLN).

The Sandinistas were Marxists of the Castro, Che Guevara and Ho Chi Minh schools but the cooler heads among them realized that, given their limited following, it was only by co-operating with the non-Marxists in opposition to the dictator that the revolution could succeed; the assassination of the social democrat Joaquin Chamorro on 10 January 1978 provided them with the opportunity to forge such an alliance. They formed a group, including two priests, which became the centre of national resistance; there were also some Catholics in the base communities who were linked to the Sandinistas; others who were not Marxists were prepared to take up arms against the regime, and some of them had the support of the Archbishop of Managua, Mgr Obando y Bravo. On 2 June 1979, in the period before the insurrection became general, the bishops as a whole distinguished between acts of violence which were lawless and those which were aimed at overthrowing a tyranny.[6] The distinction was sound theology; its practical application will always be a matter of nice judgement. Most commentators would probably agree that at the time the bishops' decision was justified.

The final assault of the rebels on the Somoza forces took place in the period May to July 1979 and, led by the Sandinistas whose ideology and discipline had made them the most coherent and effective element in the armed opposition to the dictator, they were victorious and entered Managua in triumph on 9 July. Their programme at this stage was social democratic; an independent judiciary, an apolitical army, and a Council of State on which all political groups were represented along with business interests. In practice the clearer headed and better organized Sandinistas slowly took over, and one by one their former allies resigned from the Council in 1980, aware that their participation had become meaningless.

The participation of every section of society in the Nicaraguan rebellion, and the specific contribution made to it by several priests and Catholic groups, some of them proclaiming themselves liberation theologians, was what had aroused interest, enthusiasm and general approval of many in the Church throughout Latin America and in the international Church generally, though there were strongly discordant voices also, and all this was the background to the Puebla Conference assembling in January 1979. The Pope spoke of one of the growing problems for the Church in this context, that of the direct involvement of priests in political action, when he addressed the priests and male religious of Mexico on 27 January in the basilica of Our Lady of Guadalupe. Quoting *Lumen Gentium* [10] of Vatican II he reminded them that the ministerial priesthood is specifically different from the priesthood of the faithful, and that in the Church the centre of unity is the bishop to whom they owe obedience; only the bishops are the authentic teachers of the faith. Witnesses themselves to the love Christ has for men, 'that love is not partisan ... excludes no one, although it is expressed preferably for the poorest'. Those who lived in habitual contact with God do not give way to

> socio-political radicalisms ... you are priests and not social or political leaders or officials of a temporal power. Temporal leadership can often be a source of division while the priest must be a sign and agent of unity and brotherhood.[7]

### (ii) John Paul II's address to the bishops

The conclusions of Medellín would be the meeting's starting point

> with all the positive elements contained therein but without disregarding the incorrect interpretations that have sometimes resulted and that call for calm discernment, opportune criticism and clear cut stances.[8]

The bishops had a threefold role. They were teachers of the truth, signs and builders of unity, and defenders and promoters of human dignity.

## Teachers of the truth

Their duty was to guard purity of doctrine: it is truth that will make us free, it must never be betrayed out of desire to please or to shock; quite the contrary, it is to be defended at whatever sacrifice. The truth was first truth about Christ. It is from a solid Christology that light must be shed on doctrine and pastoral practice. Christ is the Son of the Living God, the Messiah; but misreadings can obscure his divinity, project him as a political activist, involved in the class struggle, a revolutionary. 'The conception of Christ as a political figure, a revolutionary, as the subversive from Nazareth, does not tally with the Church's catechesis' [4]. It is faith in Jesus Christ, the Word and Son of God, which has informed history, including the history of Latin America.

Secondly, there is the truth about the Church, which is born out of a response in faith to Christ, and we are in turn born of the Church. She begets and nourishes us by the sacraments; she is our mother. In St Cyprian's words, 'one cannot have God for one's father if one does not have the Church for one's mother' [5]. To love Christ is also to love his Church, and that love requires fidelity and trust. Without a well-grounded ecclesiology we cannot have respect for the magisterium which preserves the authentic word of God, and guarantees effective evangelization. In some of the documentation for this Conference, however,

> and particularly in the contributions of many Churches, one sometimes notices a certain uneasiness in interpreting the nature and mission of the Church ... the separation that some set up between the Church and the kingdom of God ... that we do not arrive at the kingdom through faith and membership of the Church but rather merely by structural change and sociopolitical involvement'

It is a view which forgets that 'the Church receives the mission to proclaim and establish among all people the Kingdom of Christ and of God. She becomes on earth the initial budding forth of the kingdom (*Lumen Gentium* 5)' [6]. The Church of the poor is also preferred to the institutional Church. Where there are such conflicts our evangelizing work suffers.

Thirdly, there is the truth about human beings. It is a paradox that in an age of various humanisms and of anthropocentrism, 'human beings have been debased to previously unsuspected levels ... human values have been trodden underfoot as never before' [7]. The paradox is explained by atheistic humanism, which severs people from the Absolute which is an essential dimension of their being. 'Only in the mystery of the incarnate word does the mystery of man take on light' (*Gaudium et Spes* 22). The Gospel gives the Church its anthropology, its theory, its truth about man. Its

> primordial assertion is that man cannot be reduced to a mere fragment of nature or to any anonymous element in the human city. The human being is single, unique and unrepeatable, someone thought of and chosen from eternity, someone called and identified by name.

This 'truth about human beings is the basis of the Church's social teaching and of all authentic liberation' [8].

**Signs and builders of unity**

The bishops should be united among themselves, inspired by the love of the Church. There must be unity too with priests, religious and faithful; parallel magisteria are to be avoided [9].

**Promoters of human dignity**

They must remember that in the history of the Church, the bishops have promoted human dignity, though it is true her role is not primarily social or political. Christ himself said that it was whether we cared for the needy which will mark us out as his friends (Matt. 25:31ff.); alien ideologies are not needed in order to justify Christian liberation. At the heart of the Christian message is the inspiration for justice and peace. Standing aside from opposing systems, the Church teaches that it is not through violence or the power plays of politics that one comes to a better future, but through the truth about human beings. Hence in defending the institution of private property [10] which she has always done, she insists on the social mortgage on it. It is this which results not only in a more just and equitable distribution of goods, but also enriches the whole of man's life; this is the teaching of the Fathers, of St Thomas, of John XXIII, the Second Vatican Council and Paul VI [11]. Justice and love must have their place; economic needs and mechanisms are not enough.

Human rights are also defended; the right to life and full human development, to freedom from all kinds of oppression. But liberation is liberation above all from sin. As Paul VI reminded us in *Evangelii Nuntiandi*, liberation must be

> in the framework of the Church's specific mission, it cannot be

reduced simply to the restricted domain of economics, politics, society or culture ... sacrificed to the requirements of some particular strategy, some short term praxis or gain' [12].

Attention to the social teaching of the Church, even though some tried to sow lack of confidence in it, is the guarantee of an authentic Christian commitment to work for justice. Above all it is the laity who have the vocation to make their contribution to the political and economic areas, safeguarding and advancing human rights [13].

### (iii)  Puebla, the bishop's statement on Evangelization in Latin America

There are five parts to this 160-page document, the core of its social teaching being in parts 1 and 2, which are summarized here.

**Part 1: Pastoral overview**

*Chapter 1: Historical overview*
Despite the mistakes of the past, the Church's record overall [39] attests that the spirit of evangelization has been more powerful than human weaknesses; the challenge before Christians today is to live up to past achievements.

*Chapter 2: Evangelization*
Hopeful signs are: the generosity in sharing, especially among the poor [41], the growing sense of the dignity of everyman, the respect for indigenous cultures, significant economic progress, the growth of the middle class and educational advances. Yet so much remains to be done. The mass of the people must be freed from need and oppression, from poverty in all its aspects [42], from the unjust structures of society, national and international, abuses of power by government, guerilla violence, terrorism, kidnapping, denial of human rights, over-politicization of unions [43]. Curtailment of political freedoms, and excessive reliance on market forces has brought injustice; the prosperity of the few contrasts with the poverty of the many. Marxist violence and ideology and the excesses of National Security States[9] threaten, as do technocrats who apply development models with no thought of the poor [44].

Indigenous peoples suffer, materialism and consumerism spreads, the family is undermined, public and private integrity suffers, hedonism fosters gambling, drugs, sexual laxity. Though education and social communications have made great strides, there is manipulation by power groups and their ideologies. The media are being misused to undermine Latin American and Gospel values [45]. Underlying causes of these problems are several: unjust economic systems, lack of co-operation between Latin American States, waste of resources on arms, lack of agrarian reform, poor moral standards in public and private life, materialism and sinfulness. The background is population growth not matched by the opportunities and the services to cater for it, and at the same time pressure for immoral forms of birth control grows [45–6].

*Chapter 3: The ecclesial reality*
The problems of a secular age are to be faced, while the lack of vocations to the priesthood reduces the Church's ability to serve her people adequately [46–7]. Other problems of the Church are, for example, internal disputes over social action, and confusions on faith and morals; yet she is aware the Holy Spirit is working within her [48–9]. She is attentive to justice and aware of the conflicts that facing it arouses; many of her children are suffering, even dying in witness to her mission. The basic ecclesiastical communities have matured, though in some places political interests separate them from their bishops [48–51].

*Chapter 4: Present tendencies, future evangelization*
The rapid changes in all areas of social life will continue and we want society to be more humane and just. The Church must therefore become more independent of secular powers, more spiritual, capable of responding to the needs of the people [53–6].

**Part 2: God's saving plan for Latin America**

*Chapter 1: the content of evangelization*
The truth about Christ is that he proclaimed his kingdom, founding a Church whose visible head was Peter [59]. Not a revolutionary nor merely a prophet, his message was for all. God planned and created the world in Jesus Christ, creating mankind to live in fraternity and happiness together in active transformation of the world; man's rebellion brought evil, death, violence and hatred into the world. Yet God did not abandon man. The history

of Abraham, Moses and the election of the people of Israel shows God the Father beginning the liberation from sin and its consequences [60]. In time he sent his Son, born of the Virgin Mary by the power of the Holy Spirit; God, one with humanity in our human nature. Born poor and living poor, he preached 'reform your lives and believe the Gospel', bringing liberty to captives, sight to the blind, liberation to the oppressed. The forces of evil rejected him; he gathered a few around him from 'various social and political strata' to form the foundation of his Church by 'disinterested self-giving and sacrificial love'. She embraces all human beings, giving a privileged place to the weak and the poor 'in a new fraternity capable of opening the way to a new history'; though the kingdom he proclaims 'came to pass through historical realizations it is not identified with these or exhausted by them' [61].

After the resurrection, the exalted Jesus lives on in his Church, those who gather in his name, in his pastors and the poor especially. In this way the kingdom of God is implanted in history. The renovation of human beings and of society depends on the action of the Spirit who gives life; those who exclude others from it do not have the Spirit themselves. The Spirit inspires the hierarchy and the institutional Church; there are charisms in her today as always; genuine renewal of this kind is welcomed but deviations are to be avoided. The Spirit also reaches to those who do not know Christ, for the Lord wishes all to be saved and come to the truth [62–3]. Evangelization is a summons to participate in communion with the Trinity, in communion with the Spirit who wishes to liberate all creation [64–5].

The truth about the Church is that she cannot be separated from Christ; she was founded by him, with Peter at her head, and Jesus points to his Church as the normative way; it is not something left to the discretion of each as an inconsequential matter. The core of Jesus' message is that of the kingdom; it transcends the Church's visible bounds for it is found 'in a certain way wherever God is ruling through his grace and love ... but that does not mean that membership of the Church is a matter of indifference'. The Church received the mission to announce and establish the kingdom; she becomes on earth 'the initial budding forth of the Kingdom' [66]. In this context the Latin American church is a people, the family of God presided over in love by the hierarchy; its pastors, through the Eucharist, constitute her visible centre, exercising a ministry of service. She is a holy people, demanding social as well as personal virtue all that violates the human body, the living temple of God, is to be rejected – homicide, torture, prostitution, pornography, adultery, abortion, every sexual abuse. She is a pilgrim people, a social entity, presided over by the bishops, successors of Peter and the apostles, who were appointed by Christ: basic communities must accordingly be part of the hierarchical order if they would serve the Church; popular churches or parallel magisteria are not acceptable [67–71]. Those who are against all change in principle, and those who want continual change for its own sake are equally in error. There are not two churches, one old one new, in conflict, there is one Church which as she moves through history 'must necessarily change but only in external and accidental ways' [72].

The Church has a prophetic role, announcing the Lord and denouncing injustice, and all the evils which prevent her children entering in to a fraternal society [72–3]. Her people are a servant people, all contributing to evangelization in their own way. She is a sign of communion and should be a model of living together in freedom and solidarity, where authority is exercised as Christ taught. She is a school for the makers of history. There is tension between those who are totally passive, wanting to leave everything to God, and the activists who believe that he is so remote that we are completely responsible for everything. They should study Jesus' attitude, total trust and total commitment and co-responsibility. This is Jesus' praxis; docile hearts who can make their own way guided by providence, their sorrows and those of their people transformed through the pasch to conversion, initiative and creative imagination [73–4]. The Church finally is an instrument of communion. The sin that will always be an obstacle to her can be overcome through the inspiration of the Spirit, guided by Mary's *Magnificat* and by the Sermon on the Mount [75–8].

The truth about man is that Christ came to restore his dignity from within. This is essential to both evangelization and liberation. Determinism, man as controlled by occult forces, has its influence in Latin America as does psychologism, man as responsive to stimuli, particularly the erotic, so that he is devoid of freedom. Economist views are also present; man as a mere object of production, consumption, power and pleasure, the common good and social justice ignored. The classical Marxist view was of man as constituted essentially by social existence, without freedom or values other than those the system provides, therefore without human or religious rights. The National Security State sees the citizen solely in terms of the struggle to eliminate social, political and economic strife in the name of communism; hence personal rights count for nothing [79–81].

By contrast the Church stresses the inviolable dignity of every individual human being that has to be respected at every stage in life from the time of conception. It is only in Christ that the dignity is fully illuminated, but Christians unite with all other clear-sighted human beings who follow the light of the Spirit. Man's dignity requires freedom; 'to be our own person, act on our own initiative' [82]. The love of God, the root of our dignity, 'necessarily becomes a loving communion with other human beings and fraternal participation' and today must become a labour of justice for the oppressed [83]. Sinfulness produces injustice at every level; it is sin which undermines human dignity and Jesus Christ who redeems that dignity [84].

*Chapter 2: what does evangelization entail?*
Evangelization has a universal dimension and the Church's mission reflects this [85–93]. Latin American culture is pre-Columban, African, Spanish and Portuguese in origin; from the nineteenth century urban industrial civilization began to have its impact on it, and it came imbued with rationalism, and inspired by liberalism and Marxist collectivism leading to secularism, as the transition from agrarian to urban economies and societies progressed [94–5]. The Church accepts the legitimate autonomy of the secular order, but the ideology of secularism which separates man from God is rejected [97]. Social and economic structures which owe their origins to liberal capitalism, transformed in some cases by Marxist collectivism, are the product of cultures alien to the faith and 'a new conversion is called for that new structures of social life may then be imbued with the spirit of the Gospel' [98].

The task of the Church is one of evangelizing the people's religiosity once again. Here the shift from an agrarian to an urbanized industrial society is subjecting that religion to a crisis, and the Church must organize to meet it [101]. Pastoral groups since Medellín have made great progress, and the difficulties they have encountered should not discourage but inspire the search for new paths [102–3]. The social teaching of the Church, based on the Scriptures, the Fathers and major theologians of the Church and the magisterium, especially the recent popes, has a dynamic character, the laity contributing their experience and their professional scientific competence. Its primary object is the personal dignity of the human being, the image of God, and his inalienable human rights [103].

Liberation in Christ is liberation from all forms of personal and social sin, leading to progressive growth in being through communion with God and other human beings. Culminating in heaven, it is being gradually realized in history, in personal, social, political and economic forms, but always makes its own specific and distinct contribution. It does not resort to violence or class struggle but relies on the action of Christians moved by the Spirit to respond to the needs of others [104–5]. Worldly goods and riches are meant to serve human progress.

> Each and every one has a right to share in the use of these goods ... there is a social mortgage on all private property ... right of ownership must primarily be a right of use and administration [which] does not rule out ownership and control, but denies these are absolute or unlimited [106].

Both Liberal capitalism and Marxism are to be rejected, as are all forms of idolization of goods and uncontrolled industrialization, reckless depletion of our resources, and pollution of the environment [107]. Political totalitarianism is a form of State idolatry which is too prevalent in Latin America. In its stead there should be equality for all citizens, the right to exercise freedom, self-determination and justice 'effectively implemented in practice by institutions that are operative and adequate' [108].

The Church is concerned with the political order: her task is to look to the common good and spell out the fundamental values of the community. She hopes to foster the values that should inspire politics and interpret the aspirations of the people, politics in the practical sense, in the hands of concerned citizens who seek and hold political power to solve economic, political and social problems 'according to their own criteria ... ideology [or] party politics' [110]. Pastors on the other hand must not identify with partisan political ideology but remain centres of unity; men dedicated to the Absolute must not run the risk of absolutizing a political ideology [110–11]. Even when inspired by the Church's teaching, 'no political party can claim to represent all the faithful'. Party politics is properly the concern of the laity, guided by Catholic social teaching. The hierarchy's role is spiritual and supportive. 'Pastors ... must be concerned with unity [divesting themselves of] every partisan ideology that might condition their criteria and attitudes.' Relying on the Gospel without any ideology or partisanship following the example of Christ, they will have far more impact. This was the teaching of Medellín also. A close relationship with God and a consequent lifestyle is the way they give testimony, following a poor, chaste and obedient Christ [111].

Violence by the authorities charged with the common good, in the form of torture, kidnapping, persecution or exclusion of dissidents, defiles those who act in this way. Terrorist and guerilla violence when unleashed becomes uncontrollable and cruel and cannot be justified as the way to liberation; it is an attack on life and it reveals its own weakness and inadequacy [112]. Political ideologies have their positive aspects, motivating people to action. They also have their negative aspects, and the task of the social teaching of the Church is to help the faithful to discern the good and the evil in them. That social teaching is based not on any ideology but on the Gospel message and its implications. The power of the State can be and has been abused, but this should not lead us to forget the necessity of the State's functions properly considered and operating. Liberal capitalism has achieved much in releasing man's creative abilities in the economic sphere; it also absolutized the rights of property and led to gross injustice; mitigated in many places by social legislation and government action, it can still be found in its original cruel form [113–14].

Marxism took its origins in the criticism of capitalism but it has failed to go to the root of the latter's idolatry, its rejection of the God of love and justice. Marxist class struggle results in the dictatorship of the party and it is naïve to think that elements in its creed can be used independently of its philosophy: that philosophy leads to a totalitarian society. Both liberal capitalism and Marxist communism are closed to the transcendent perspective, the one through militant atheism, the other in practice. The National Security State is unacceptable because it claims to defend Christian civilization while denying effective participation to the masses and subjecting them to military and political elites; at the same time it encourages and increases social inequalities [114–15]. The Church must maintain her freedom from manipulation both by integralists wanting a new Christendom, a close alliance between Church and State, or radicals wanting such with Marxism. Both tendencies are incompatible with the Church's true role [116].

## Parts 3–5

These are entitled, 'Evangelization in the Latin American Church; communion and participation', 'A missionary Church serving evangelization in Latin America' and 'Under the dynamism of the Spirit; Pastoral Options'. As their titles imply they are concerned with internal organization and the spirit of the Church in her task. There are one or two points from these chapters that are crucial to the Christian social ethic.

*The family*
The family is central to the life of the Church and society and the problems it has to face in Latin America today are surveyed; social injustice, poor quality of life, manipulation, inadequate rewards for work, secularism, moral confusion especially in family planning, all have had their impact. On the positive side, there is the evidence of the great faith of families, the care that goes into preparing couples for marriage, the help that families give to one another [118–19]. Pastoral care must be constant, with every effort made by education and action to help them live their lives in Christ more fully [122–3].

*Base level ecclesiastical communities (CEBs)*
These communities are the hope of the Church (*Evangelii Nuntiandi* 58) and complement the work of the parish and of the diocese where the bishop is the guardian of the faith and its unity above all with Rome and the Pope. It is for the bishop to discern the charisms and promote the ministries of the evangelizing community [123–7] and there should be proper care for the training of the pastoral agents involved in them; their work should also be co-ordinated with that of other diocesan organizations [128].

*Preferential option for the poor*
Despite some who distort the spirit of Medellín in this matter, the bishops reaffirm emphatically the Church's preference for and solidarity with the poor. It is a fact that the vast majority of people live in poverty and the bishops' attempts to help redress this situation have caused tension within the Church [178]. They keep in mind that service of the poor is a privileged, but not the exclusive, measure of the service of Christ, and that the best way they can help the poor is by evangelizing them; this will assure them of their dignity, liberate them and lead them to communion with God and their fellow human beings who live a life of poverty [179]. For the Christian, poverty does not mean simply material deprivation. The 'poor of Yahweh' (Zeph. 2:3, 3:12–20. Isa. 49:13) were those whose lives were models of the ability to use the good, of this world without absolutizing them. Evangelical poverty combines trusting confidence in God and an austere life which rejects greed and pride. It is also generous in sharing spiritual and material goods. Committed to the poor, they condemn as anti-evangelical the extreme material poverty that affects so many, and declare they will work to create a more just world. They defend

the right of the poor to organize to promote their interests and make responsible contributions to the common good [180–1].

[Note: John Paul II's teaching is further considered in Chapters 25–28 and summarized overall on pp 378ff. That of CELAM IV is examined in Chapter 28 and it, together with the social teaching of CELAM III, is summarized on pp 387ff]

# 25

# John Paul II's social encyclicals 1979–81

## *Redemptor Hominis* (1979)[1]

*Summary of text*

John Paul II was elected on 16 October 1978 and this encyclical – on Christ the Redeemer of Man – was published on 4 March 1979, after he had attended the CELAM III. Though not strictly a social encyclical it is concerned with the connection between man's dignity and the Incarnation, and that dignity is central to its social teaching. It is no accident that it was issued by the Pope who had experienced the degradation of man under Nazism and Communism. There is an Introduction and three sections to it: I. Inheritance [1–6], II. The mystery of the Redemption [7–12], III. Redeemed man and his situation in the modern world [13–17], and IV. The Church's Mission and Man's Destiny [18–22]. We examine the paragraphs with particular reference to the dignity of man.

### I. Inheritance

This section looks to the year 2000 and what it implies for the Church, and considers the inheritance that John Paul II received from his immediate predecessors in office as he faces up to his own pontificate and its programme [1–6].

### II. The mystery of the redemption

Christ has the words of eternal life [7.2]. The Second Vatican Council tells us that only through the Incarnation does the mystery of man take on light.

* The notes and references for Chapter 25 are to be found on p. 463ff

Christ is the perfect man ... who has restored in the children of
Adam the likeness to God ... by his Incarnation, he, Son of God,
in a certain way, united himself with each man. He worked with
human hands, he thought with a human mind, acted with a
human will and with a human heart he loved. Born of the Virgin
Mary, he has truly been made one of us, like us in all things
except sin [8.2].

Man fully reveals man to himself; he must take to himself the whole
reality of the Incarnation and redemption in order to find himself,
to realize how precious he is in God's eyes – who gave his only Son
in order that man may not perish but have eternal life [9.2].

The mystery of Christ is the basis of the Church's mission and of
Christianity, and the true missionary attitude always possesses a
deep concern for what is in man, for what man has worked out in
the depth of his spirit concerning the most important problems, by
the Spirit which blows where he will. The mission is never one of
destruction but of building up, fresh building by God's grace
[11.2]. The Council stresses that the truth revealed to us by God
imposes on us the obligation to respond to it as the truth that
comes not from men but from God [12.2]. The words 'you shall
know the truth and the truth shall make you free' warn us of the
need to be honest in regard to the truth, to reject illusory forms of
freedom which do not recognize the whole truth about man and
the world [12.3]. When Christ came before Pilate he affirmed that
'for this I came into the world, for this I was born ... to bear witness
to the truth'. For all her weaknesses the Church does not cease to
follow him who said that those who worship God must do so in
spirit and in truth [12.4].

### III. Redeemed man and his mission in the modern world

Because by his Incarnation, the Son of God in a certain way
'united himself with each man' the Church wishes to ensure that
each person may be able to find Christ and walk with him. Jesus
Christ is the chief way for the Church as he is for every man
[13.1]. She cannot fail therefore to serve man's well-being. As the
Second Vatican Council said, the world should be conformed to
man's dignity in order to make life more human; the Church
however is not bound by any political system, being the sign of
man's transcendence [13.2]. Her concern is not with man in the
abstract but with each man, here and now, and the whole man,
who was made in God's image: the only creature willed by God

for himself, chosen by him, called and destined for grace and glory [13.3].

Each man, intellect and will, conscience and heart, man, a person with his own history of life and soul, which he writes through his links with others in society, is the Church's concern [14.1]: man in whom so many conflicting elements wrestle with one another [14.2]. Such is man redeemed by Christ, and the Church must be aware of all his problems and potentialities, all that helps and all that hinders him [14.3]. Man seems to be under threat today from the result of his work by hand or brain. He is capable of unimaginable self-destruction, of wholesale damage to the environment [15.2]. 'Yet it was the Creator's will that man should communicate with nature as an intelligent and noble master and guardian, not as a heedless exploiter or destroyer' [15.3]. Progress in technology and civilization should go along with progress in morals and ethics but does not. Does progress then make life on earth more human, more worthy of man? [15.4]. Does it foster a growth of social love or breed selfishness, the desire to dominate? [15.5]. Christ the king has given us dominion over things [16.1]. All things must then be judged according to whether they enable men to 'be more'; he cannot be allowed to become the slave of things, as modern material civilization tends to make him [16.2].

Man does not accept the demands of the objective moral order today; there is lacking both justice and social charity. Consumerism, the superfluities of the rich nations, and the deprivations of the poor reveal that [16.3]. The fever of inflation and the plague of unemployment exist along with the excesses of the privileged [16.5]. The principle of solidarity should inspire the search for answers [16.6], but true change of heart is needed. Freedom is too often confused with selfishness; the programme set out in *Populorum Progressio* will assure man's true freedom. Yet new nations are too often offered modern weapons for wars that are not of defence but chauvinistic adventurism; meanwhile the people starve for lack of the investment that would provide for their needs [16.7]. The Church must urge the importance of the task of respecting the dignity and freedom of every man [16.11].

This has been a century of calamities for him, mainly self-inflicted. The effort of the United Nations Organization to make human rights effective in member states, however, has been a sign of hope while the Church has made known support for them [17.1].

The essential sense of the State, as a political community, consists in that the society and the people composing it are master and sovereign of their own destiny. This sense remains unrealized if, instead of the exercise of power with the moral participation of the society or the people [there is] the imposition of power by a certain group.

Hence this participation

is essential in the present age with its enormous increase in people's social awareness and the ... need for the citizens to have a right share in the political life of the community, while taking account of the real conditions of each people and the necessary vigour of the public authority [17.6].

The purpose of the State being the common good, that good is secured when the rights of man are respected [17.7]. Among the rights are included those of freedom of religion and conscience [17.8].

## IV. The Church's mission and man's destiny

Since Christ united himself with every man the Church 'lives more profoundly her own nature and mission by penetrating to the depths of this mystery' [18.1]. For man 'it is the spirit that gives life, the flesh is of no avail' (John 6:53). The body is given life by the Spirit [18.2]. There is in him a search for truth, the need for the good and the beautiful [18.3]. By concentrating on the dignity of man in Christ through the grace of the Holy Spirit, the Church then makes herself better fitted for the service of man [18.4]. The Church was made responsible for teaching the truth of God; Christ promised her the Spirit of truth, the gift of infallibility as confirmed by the first and second Vatican Councils [19. 1–2].

The Christian vocation to service and kingship builds up the Church as the people of God. The dignity of this kingship that we share is expressed in the readiness to serve [21.1]. Membership of the Church, the mystical body of Christ, emphasizes that we are his disciples, and as such are subject to this kingly service. Fidelity to one's vocation in this is of particular significance to those engaged in work which has more direct influence on society [21.4]. The full truth about human freedom is inscribed in the mystery of the redemption, and the Church truly serves man when she guards this truth [21.5].

# 2 Dives in Misericordia[2]

This encyclical was published on 30 November 1980 and complements its predecessor in revealing to us the central inspirations
of John Paul II's pontificate. Its theme is God the Father of
mercy, rich in mercy [*dives in misericordia*] and in Christ the
mercy of God made visible through his living and dying for
man. Like its predecessor it is not strictly a social encyclical,
but it elaborates the theology that lies behind basic concepts
of that teaching – the connections between mercy and charity,
and between charity and justice, and so is very relevant in our
context.

## Summary of the encyclical

There are eight sections to the document. I. Who sees me sees
the Father [1–2], II. The messianic message [3], III. The Old
Testament [4], IV. The parable of the prodigal son [5–6],
V The paschal Mystery [7–9], VI. Mercy from generation to
generation [10–12], VII. The mercy of God in the mission of
the Church [13–14], and VIII. The prayer of the Church in our
time [15].

### I. Who sees me sees the Father

In Christ and through Christ, God becomes especially visible in
his mercy and gives the word definitive meaning. In him
God becomes visible as the Father who is rich in mercy [2.2].
'The present day mentality ... seems opposed to a God of mercy
... the word and concept of mercy seems to cause uneasiness'
[2.3]. The Pope wishes this document to be an appeal by the
Church for that mercy which the modern world needs so much
[2.4].

### II. The messianic message

Christ announced that he had been sent to bring the good news to
the poor, the blind, the captives, the oppressed [3.1] and he called
these works to witness when questioned by John's disciples [3.2].
Christ reveals God as rich in mercy, as St Paul says (Eph. 2:4), and
Christ recommends this virtue to his followers [3.4]. Christ, the
fulfilment of the messianic prophecy, has become the incarnation
of love [3.5].

### III. The Old Testament

In deeds and words the Lord revealed his mercy [4.7–8]; the Old Testament encourages those suffering from misfortune to appeal for mercy and enables them to count on it [4.10]. Mercy is contrasted with justice and is shown to be more powerful and profound than it. Love, so to speak, conditions justice, and justice serves love; it is through mercy that this is achieved. Love excludes hatred. It links justice and mercy [4.11]. God has chosen his people and he loves them everlastingly [4.12].

### IV. The parable of the prodigal son

Though the word 'mercy' does not appear in the parable, it expresses the essence of divine mercy [5.1]. Similarly the word 'justice' does not appear, but the prodigal's readiness to work for his living as a hired servant in his father's house is what justice demanded [5.2]. The father of the prodigal is faithful to his father-hood; he not only receives his son back as his son, not as his servant, but does so with joy, giving him a welcome which makes his elder son angry [6.1]. 'He had compassion on him, ran to meet him, threw his arms around his neck and kissed him' [6.2]. Good has been achieved by truth and love, and the evil done is forgotten [6.3]. Mercy is manifested. It not only shows compassion but restores to value, promotes and draws good from evil [6.4–5].

### V. The Paschal mystery

The reality of the redemption in its human dimension is that it reveals the greatness of man; so much so that reclaiming man for God 'gained for us so great a redeemer' [7.1]. Man was created in God's image in the beginning but then our creator went further; God sacrificed his own Son to redeem him [7.2]. For our sake God made him to be sin who knew no sin; it is the ultimate and definitive revelation of the holiness of God. Justice sprang from love and was achieved through love [7.3]. And God's love goes further; he grants participation to man in his very life, Father, Son and Holy Spirit; he who loves desires to give himself [7.4]. Belief in the crucified Son means seeing the Father [7.5] and believing that love is present in the world and is more powerful than any kind of evil; believing in this love shown in mercy means belief in mercy [7.6]. This love is more powerful than death and more powerful than sin [8.1–7]. Mary at the Visitation spoke of the mercy that is 'from generation to generation' [9.3].

## VI. Mercy from generation to generation

The modern world knows it is privileged in benefiting from progress that only a few years ago was beyond the imagination. Man's creative activity, intelligence and application has extended his power over nature and has seen obstacles to progress disappear; he has also seen the mutual dependence on solidarity and looked beyond geographical or racial barriers [10.1–2]. Yet there is a sense of unease; he knows he often does the very things he hates and does not do what he wants; in the words of the Council, he is divided against himself [10.3–5]. The sense of justice in the world has been awakening on a vast scale and the persistence of injustice therefore becomes less acceptable [12.1]. The Church shares this hatred of injustice [12.2] yet it notes that

> very often, programmes which start from the idea of justice ... in practise suffer from distortions ... they continue to appeal to the idea of justice ... nevertheless experience shows that negative forces have gained the upper hand, spite, hatred and cruelty.

The desire to annihilate the enemy, to deny his freedom or independence, becomes the aim, whereas justice tends to establish equality and harmony. In the name of an alleged injustice the neighbour can be stripped of fundamental human rights. 'Justice is not enough ... it can lead to the negation and destruction of itself if that deeper power which is love, is not allowed to shape human life in its various dimensions.' '*Summa jus, summa injuria*' (the highest justice, the greatest harm) is a saying to which historical experience has given substance [12.3].

This does not make the order of justice any less important but only reminds us to condition it with the more profound powers we possess. Justice without spiritual values, without love that produces mercy, is destructive; the growth in interest in justice, while at the same time basic moral values are being undermined, is disturbing. Especially is this true of the respect for human life from the time of conception, as also for indissoluble marriage and the stable family. There is also a lack of truth in human relationships, and of a sense of the common good, while at the same time a process of desacralization is in train which becomes in effect one of dehumanization [12.4].

## VII. The mercy of God in the mission of the Church

The Church in our time must become more conscious of her need to bear witness to God's mercy, above all in the example of Christ and his apostles, and the tradition [13.1]. She lives an authentic life in so far as she does so [13.3]. True mercy is the most profound source of justice [14.4]. It enlightens the way to it. Mutual relationships cannot be regulated solely by justice; love and mercy are needed [14.5]. The civilization of love will not be built otherwise [14.7]. Society can only become more human when forgiveness demonstrates the presence in the world of love more powerful than sin [14.8] and Christ's teaching insists on that forgiveness [14.10]. Justice always enters into the sphere of mercy, and mercy has the power to confer on justice a new content – forgiveness [14.11]. So the Church must guard this teaching [14.12] and give witness to evangelical poverty, bearing witness to the mighty work of him who is rich in mercy [14.13].

### VIII. The prayer of the Church in our times

We must have recourse to God through Christ for his mercy on the present generation the more it moves away from God and becomes secularized [15.1]. We must work and pray, desiring the true good for each individual in every community which is the practice of love, without difference of race, culture, friends and enemies, young, old, men and women: love for every individual human being [15.4]. The stronger the resistance of the world, the more that it refuses to accept God, the greater must be the Church's closeness to the mystery of God in Jesus Christ and in his mercy [15.7].

## 3 Laborem Exercens[3] (1981)

This, the first strictly social encyclical of John Paul II, was published to commemorate the ninetieth anniversary of *Rerum Novarum* in 1891, and like it is specifically concerned with the problems of industrialization in the modern world. However, *Laborem Exercens* reflects more deeply on the philosophy and theology of work, as well as on the specifics of the employer/employee relationship and organization of that relationship, which were the predominant concern of its predecessor. Besides bringing to the preparation of this encyclical his expertise as an academic who had spent many years teaching social ethics, John Paul had direct experience of manual work. *Laborem Exercens* is then, like *Redemptor Hominis,* a very personal encyclical. The latter owes much to the author's experience of indignities with which humanity was treated under the Nazis, and in Auschwitz in particular, which was in John

Paul's Archdiocese of Cracow. The former owes much to the time he spent as a quarryman, a manual worker, threatened in his human dignity in some respects by this status because of the liberal capitalist tradition still marking so many attitudes to those who toil.

*Summary of the text*

There is an Introduction [1–3] and four main sections: I. Work and Man [4–10], II. The conflict between labour and capital in the present phase of human history [11–15], III. The rights of worker [16–23], and IV. The Spiritual Significance of Work [24–27].

**Introduction**

The first paragraph, not numbered, presents work as that activity through which 'man must earn his daily bread', contributes to the advance of science and technology, and improves the cultural and moral level of society. It means 'any activity by man ... manual or intellectual ... any human activity that can and must be recognized as work, in the midst of all the activities of which man is capable' and to which he is by his nature disposed. Man made in God's image is placed in the world to subdue it, to work it. Work is the mark of a person within a community of persons and this personal mark determines its characteristics.

**I. Human work on the ninetieth anniversary of *Rerum Novarum***

This document is devoted to human work, to man in the context of work, man being the primary and fundamental way for the Church [1.1]. Man's life is built up every day from work and from work it derives its specific dignity; yet it means toil, suffering and often injustice [1.2]. Automation, the cost of energy and materials, questions concerning resources and the environment, the new nations and peoples and their need for a place in the sun all affect work. Readjustments will cause problems, among them unemployment. 'It is not for the Church to analyse scientifically the consequences ... these changes ... may have on society': it is hers to defend the human dignity of the worker in the process of change [1.3].

*Organization and development of the Church's social action and teaching*
Since *Rerum Novarum* the Church's teaching has been concerned with this question and no break with previous teaching is intended

here [2.1]. At the same time the general situation of man in the modern world calls for 'the discovery of new meanings of human work' [2.2]. The Church's concern with the social question has been constant, and since *Quadragesimo Anno* the concern has switched increasingly from the problem of industrialization in individual nations, to that of international social justice [2.3]. The situation today requires further clarification [2.4].

*The question of work: the key to the social question*
The social teaching of the Church 'finds its source in the sacred scripture ... the Book of Genesis ... the Gospel and the writings of the Apostles'. It was part of her teaching from the beginning, her concept of man and life in society, and social morality developed according to the needs of different ages. On this patrimony, Leo XIII and his successors drew [3.1]. The teaching on man and work is probably 'the ... key to the whole social question' [3.2].

## II. Work and Man

*The book of Genesis*
The Church is supported by many scientific disciplines in its belief in work as fundamental to man's existence [4.1]. Genesis tells us that after God had created man and woman in his own image, he told them to be fertile, to fill the earth and subdue it. This latter command, while not specifically about work, indirectly implies it. Man is the image of his creator, partly through the mandate to subdue, to dominate the earth, reflecting the very action of the creator of the universe [4.2]. Work is a transitive activity 'an activity beginning in the human subject and directed to an external object'. Implicitly the command is to subdue the whole earth insofar as man requires it to meet his needs [4.3]. Through his work man becomes more and more the master of the earth and at times this mastery seems to accelerate. Work embraces all generations and people, but it remains the action of individual human beings [4.4].

*Work in the objective sense: technology*
Work is objective also: it tells us what sort of work is done, work in agriculture, in industry, providing services and in research [5.1]. Technology has taken much of the toil out of some kinds of work [5.2] but the proper subject of work remains man [5.3]. Technology in general is his ally, though it can work against him if it supplants him [5.4]. The biblical injunction to subdue the earth

includes the technology which is the fruit of man's genius [5.5]. At the same time, technological advance raises important ethical questions [5.6].

*Work in the subjective sense: man the subject of work*
Work as subjective, work as personal, is the biblical perspective [6.1].

> Man has to subdue the earth because as the image of God he is a person ... a subjective being capable of acting in a planned and rational way ... deciding about himself, with a tendency to self-realization.

As a person

> man is the subject of work ... as a person he works ... performs various actions belonging to the work process ... independently of their objective content, these actions must all serve to realize his humanity [6.2].

The dominion spoken of in the biblical text in a certain sense

> refers to the subjective dimension of work ... more than the objective one ... this dimension conditions the very ethical nature of work ... human work has an ethical value all of its own ... linked to the fact that the one who carries it out is a person, a conscious and free subject ... that decides about himself [6.3].

It is the heart of the Christian teaching on work [6.4].

> The ancient world [divided] people into classes according to the class of work done. Work that demanded physical strength ... muscles and hands was considered unworthy of freemen and was given to slaves.

Building on the Old Testament tradition, Christianity brought about a fundamental change, for the Gospel tells us that 'the one who, while being God, became like us in all things, devoted most of his life on earth to manual work at the carpenter's bench'. The dignity of work then lies in its human agency, not in the type of work done [6.5]. Hence work is for man and not man for work. Different kinds of work can have a different objective value and work will be rated and qualified in that way, but in the last analysis it is always man who is the purpose of work, however humble the work is [6.6].

*Threats to the right order of values*
However, employers, especially those in the early nineteenth

century, looked at work as a form of merchandise to be bought and sold accordingly, the worker selling it to the capitalist who owned all the means of production. The worst excesses of this kind have gone but the idea of materialistic economism which lay behind it, of labour as merchandise, remains [7.1]. This results in neglecting the subjective dimension of work, work as personal, so making man an instrument of production and reversing the Genesis role [7.2].

> Everyone knows that capitalism has a definite historical meaning ... opposed to socialism or communism ... the error of early capitalism can be repeated wherever man is treated on the same level ... as the material means of production ... not as a subject and maker [7.3].

This analysis of human work is crucial to the solution of the social problem within nations and also internationally [7.4].

*Worker solidarity*
The subject of work, the human being, remains the same, but objective work changes radically, as it has done over the last 90 years. Civilization is enriched in this way, though some forms of work disappear, and there are undesirable developments in the process [8.1]. One such was the degradation implied in the concept of 'the proletariat', the exploitation which bred a worker reaction in solidarity during the process of industrialization [8.2]. As *Rerum Novarum* and subsequent documents of the Church noted 'it must be frankly recognized that the reaction against the system of injustice ... and harm that cried to heaven for vengeance ... was justified in terms of social morality'. The circumstances of the time had favoured economic initiative by the capitalist but treated the workers as only instruments of production [8.3]. Workers' solidarity since then has brought many changes and workers' rights are better recognized. They share in running businesses, influence pay and conditions and social legislation [8.4]. Yet injustices remain in industrialized and non-industrialized countries. 'Movements of solidarity in the sphere of work – a solidarity that is never closed to dialogue and collaboration' are therefore still needed. This is required now also for those white-collar workers affected by problems of proletarianization [8.5]. For this reason also the continued study of the subject of work is required [8.6].

*Work and personal dignity*
There are some problems that more closely define the dignity of work [9.1]. God's fundamental intention for man made in his

image and likeness was not withdrawn when he was told he would earn his living in the sweat of his brow. All who work, by hand or brain, feel the effect of this penalty to a greater or lesser extent; it is familiar to women who work hard, at caring for the home and family, often without recognition from that family [9.2]. But work is still a good for man: not only good in the sense of useful and enjoyable, but as corresponding with his dignity. Through it he becomes more human.

> It bears the marks of a *bonum arduum* [a difficult good] ... through work man not only transforms nature ... but he also achieves fulfilment as a human being and indeed, in a sense, becomes more a human being' [9.3].

This gives a meaning to industriousness, makes it a virtue, a moral habit which makes man good, as man. Work can of course be used against man, as punishment, as exploitation. Industriousness needs to be linked with the moral and social order of work [9.4].

*Work and society – family and nation*
Work is a condition for enabling a family to be founded, providing for its material support.

> Work and industriousness also influences the whole process of education in the family ... everyone becomes a human being through, among other things work, and becoming human is the main purpose of education [10.1].

'The family is simultaneously a community made possible by work and the first school of work, within the home, for every person' [10.2]. Work is also the basis of cultural and historical life which incorporates the work of previous generations. In this way work adds to the whole human heritage serving the peoples of the world [10.3]. These three spheres of human existence therefore demonstrate the importance of subjective work which takes precedence over work as objective [10.4].

## III. The conflict between labour and capital in the present phase of history

*The dimensions of the conflict*
The Bible-based and traditional teaching of the Church on work has had particular significance since *Rerum Novarum* [11.1]. This will be returned to later [11.2]. For the moment it is noted that throughout this period the capital versus labour struggle found its

expression in the 'ideological conflict between liberalism, understood as the ideology of capitalism, and Marxism understood as the
ideology of scientific socialism and communism' [11.3]. The latter
professes

> to act as the spokesman for the working class and the world-wide
> proletariat ... a systematic class struggle conducted not only by
> ideological means but also and chiefly by political means ... the
> philosophy of Marx and Lenin sees in the class struggle the only
> way to eliminate class injustices in society and eliminate the
> classes themselves ... the collectivization of the means of
> production so that through the transfer of those means from
> private hands to the collectivity, human labour will be preserved
> from exploitation [11.4].

In the meantime the political struggle continues under the
Marxist 'dictatorship of the proletariat' exercised by the
Communist Party. According to the principal ideologists, the aim
of this programme is 'to achieve the social revolution and to introduce socialism and finally the communist system throughout the
world' [11.5]. The whole fabric of international life has been
affected by these issues [11.6].

*The priority of labour*
The tension in the modern situation stems from a variety of causes,
among them the technological changes and the prospect of
nuclear war. The Church's response is to recall

> a principle that has always been taught ... that labour has prior-
> ity over capital. The principle directly concerns the process of
> production ... in this process labour is always the efficient cause,
> capital the instrumental cause [12.1].

From Genesis we see that the earth which man has to subdue will
give him the resources he will need, but he has to work them, and
to do this he has to take possession of part of the earth's surface
[12.2]. God's creation, the riches that man finds there, are used by
man in the productive process. 'At the beginning of man's work is
the mystery of creation. This is the guiding thread of this document' [12.3].

'Capital' then includes not only natural resources but the whole
of the means by which man appropriates them, and the latter are
the products of labour. All the factories, plant, machines, tools,
instruments, techniques are of man's making [12.4].

It remains clear that every human being sharing in the production process, even if they are doing the kind of work for which no special training or qualifications are required, is the real efficient subject in the production process, while the whole collection of instruments, no matter how perfect they may be in themselves, are only a mere instrument subordinate to human labour [12.5].

The primacy of man over things is part of the Church's social teaching. 'Man as the subject of work and independent of the work he does – man alone is a person' [12.6].

*Economism and materialism*
Capital and labour therefore cannot be separated from or opposed to one another. A labour system which overcomes the opposition between labour and capital, through being shaped in accordance with the principle of the priority of labour, is therefore morally legitimate [13.1]. The production process itself emphasizes that capital and labour are interlinked rather than opposed. By work man enters into the inheritance of the resources given us by nature, and the work done by others that produced the instruments of production in use.

In working, man ... enters into the labour of others ... it is a consistent image, one that is humanistic as well as theological. In it man is master of the creatures placed at his disposal ... it is dependence on the giver of all the resources of creation and also on other human beings [13.2].

This image was broken.

Labour was separated from capital and set in opposition to it ... as though they were two impersonal forces. This way of stating the issue contained a fundamental error, what we can call the error of economism, that of considering human labour solely according to its economic purpose.

A materialist philosophy brought this about [13.3], the same philosophy which at the other end of its spectrum produced dialectical materialism. Since neither form of materialism makes man first and foremost the subject of work and the efficient cause of the production process, neither can provide a sound philosophy of work [13.4]. These errors were rooted in the whole economic and social practice of the time, causing the just reaction of the workers spoken of above. It recurs today where primitive capitalism and liberalism exist [13.5].

*Work and ownership*
The question of the ownership of capital is crucial in considering the labour question [14.1]. The Church's teaching here differs from that of the Marxist and the liberal capitalists. Unlike the Marxists the Church accepts the moral legitimacy of the private ownership of productive goods, but unlike liberal capitalism she 'has never held this right ... absolute and untouchable'; rather, 'the right to private ownership is subordinated to the right to common use, to the fact that goods are meant for everyone' [14.2]. The social conflict with labour is avoided by this analysis. 'Property is acquired first of all through work in order that it may serve work.' Property in the form of the means of production cannot be isolated in opposition to labour because

> the only legitimate title to their possession ... private or public/collective ... is that they should serve labour [so achieving] the first principle of this order, the universal destination of goods and the right to common use of them.

This means that social ownership of some of the means of production is not excluded when conditions require it. The Church's modern social teaching, drawing on the older tradition, reaffirmed this [14.3].

Rigid capitalism, the idea that private ownership of productive goods is an untouchable dogma of economic life, is rejected. The respect for work demands that this idea undergo a revision in theory and practice, for capital is increasingly being created through work by all at the great workbench 'not only ... manual labour but ... including white-collar work and management', labour by hand and brain [14.4]. Proposals for joint ownership, sharing in management and/or profits, labour shareholding, etc., therefore take on special significance. Certainly the worker's place in the production process requires adaptations and changes [14.5]. Yet abolition of private ownership itself solves nothing if the means of production are simply administered by managers for the community [14.6]. Workers must be in some way part-owners [14.7].

*The personalist argument*
The 'principle of the priority of labour over capital is a postulate of social morality'. For 'when a man works ... he wishes to be a sharer in responsibility and creativity through his work' [15.1]. He desires 'not only due remuneration for his work ... he also wishes to know that in his work, even on something which is owned in common, he is working for himself'. Bureaucratic centralization prevents

this happening; he knows he is a cog in a machine and not a true subject of work, an instrument rather than a person with initiative. The Church has always felt that the economic system and the production process should benefit the personal values. In the mind of St Thomas[4] it is the value these personal considerations have for the production process which makes private ownership preferable. Even where social ownership is desirable it must ensure that the person can be aware he works for himself [15.2].

## IV. The rights of the worker

### In the context of human rights

To work is an obligation, and it is also a source of rights [16.1]. Man must work because the creator commanded it, his own humanity requires it and others need his work: his family and the whole human family [16.2]. In considering the rights of workers, we think first of the relationship with the employer, direct or indirect [16.3]. The distinction is important [16.4]. The former is the person or institution for whom the individual agrees to work; the latter is anyone affecting the work contract or the relationships arising from it [16.5].

### Indirect and direct employers

The responsibilities of the indirect and the direct employer differ [17.1]. The State is an indirect employer, and must have a just labour policy [17.2]. Links between States, however, make them all interdependent and the advantages of the industrialized nations can force the direct employer in the less industrialized to pay his workers poorly [17.3]. The right order, however, gives the objective rights of the worker precedence [17.4]: economic systems should reflect this [17.5].

### The right to work

This is the first and basic right of workers. Indirect employers must ensure against unemployment as far as possible, and supply unemployment benefits where they cannot; the common purpose of created goods demands this [18.1]. This responsibility implies the need for forward planning to prevent or limit unemployment [18.2]. Co-operation between nations and international bodies is an extension of this [18.3] and here *Populorum Progressio* had guidelines to offer [18.4]. Proper organization of and use of labour is also essential [18.5]. Throughout the world vast resources are

unused; there is also considerable unemployment, which argues
there is something wrong with the organization of work and
employment [18.6].

## Wages and social benefits

Of the other rights, that to adequate rewards for work done is
fundamental: nothing does more to secure a just relationship
[19.1]. It is through wages that workers have access to the goods
destined for all; hence wage justice morally justifies the whole
socio-economic system [19.2]. Family needs are here crucial, met
either through a family wage or through family allowances or
grants, in accordance with need, to mothers devoting themselves
exclusively to their families [19.3]. It will pay society if, without
inhibiting or penalizing them in any way compared with other
women, it enables mothers to devote themselves full-time to their
children. They should not have to put their role as mother at risk
in order to take paid work outside the home [19.4]. If society
needs them to do that work it should reorganize it so that she can
combine them [19.5]. Apart from wages, the worker can claim
social benefits for health and other needs [19.6].

## The importance of unions

The right of association in trade unions is vital for defending the
interests of workers [20.1]. History teaches that they are an essential element in social life [20.2]. From one angle they are
organizations for justice in a class struggle necessary to secure just
rights but this should not be part of a struggle to eliminate the
opponent.

> It is characteristic of work that ... it unites people. In this
> consists its social power, its power to build a community. In the
> final analysis both those who work the means of production, and
> those who manage or own them, must in some way be united in
> this community ... Even if it is because of their work needs that
> people unite to secure their rights, their union remains a
> constructive factor of social solidarity and it is impossible to
> ignore it [20.3].

Therefore 'union demands cannot be turned into a kind of group
or class egoism' though they can and should aim at correcting –
with a view to the common good of the whole of society – everything defective in the system of ownership or management [20.4].

Union activity therefore 'undoubtedly enters the sphere of politics' but 'unions do not have the character of political parties',

should not be subject to them or have too close links with them [20.5]. They have an important task in meeting the specific professional education needs of their members [20.6]. There is a right to strike, but it must not be used for political purposes; it should only be invoked as an extreme means, and the authorities have the duty to keep essential services going in spite of strikes [20.7].

*The dignity of agricultural workers*
All these rights belong to the agricultural worker also [21.1] although frequently not so much appreciated by society as his urban counterpart. In many areas of the third world they are unjustly treated by large landowners; even in the developed world they are frequently not allowed just advancement [21.2]. Changes are accordingly needed to promote the dignity of work in and for workers on the land [21.3].

*Disabled persons and work*
Much has been done recently to ensure that the disabled have the right to work [22.1]. It is a complex and difficult task, but a proper understanding of subjective labour will make it possible to ensure that, increasingly, disabled people are not cut off from the world of work and so can make their contribution to society according to their capacities [22.2–3].

*Work and emigration*
Man has a right to leave his native land to seek better conditions, but there are difficulties for his country, himself and his new land [23.1] and all possible help should be given him [23.2]. He should not be exploited or denied his rights [23.3].

## V. The elements of a spirituality of work

*A particular task for the Church*
As subjective work is always personal, the whole person, body and spirit is involved in it, and it is to that whole person the living word of God is directed [24.1]. The Church then sees it as her duty to bring out the human and moral value of work, to form a spirituality of work so that through it we may come closer to God [24.2].

*Work as sharing in the activity of the creator*
Vatican II spoke of the mandate given to many by God to govern the world with justice [25.1]. Man, made in God's image, shares by

his work in the activity of the creator who is depicted as working in his creation of the world [25.2]. Man then imitates God in both working and resting, as God rested on the seventh day [25.3]. In working also man provides for himself and his family, and for society [25.4]. Modern man, far from seeing the works produced by his talent as opposed to God, should see them rather as a sign of God's power [25.5]. That we share in God's creative work in our working is the most profound reason for undertaking it [25.6].

### Christ the man of work

That Christ was known as the carpenter of Nazareth, that he warned against too much anxiety about work and life, but that his own way of life was that of a worker, should be for us especially significant [26.1]. He used many illustrations from working life in his preaching [26.2]. Paul echoes this also, boasting of his own trade and telling people to work for a living [26.3]. His approach complements that of Christ [26.4]. From this the Church understands that man develops himself through work, and this is more valuable than mere riches, harmonizing as it does God's plan and human good [26.5]. Man is more precious for what he is than for what he has, so all that is done for greater justice has greater worth than technical advances in themselves [26.6]. This teaching forms the 'gospel of work' [26.7].

### Human work in the light of the cross and the resurrection of Christ

All work is linked with toil. Genesis also tells us we will earn our living in the sweat of our brows [27.1]. The cross of Christ is the final answer to this [27.2]. The difficulties we experience in work offer us a way of following [27.3] and sharing in Christ's work [27.4]. His cross leads on to the resurrection and is therefore our hope also [27.5], the promise of the new life beyond, spurring us on to look to earthly progress here at the same time. For such progress is of concern to the kingdom, though distinguished from it [27.6]. Our work then is significant for the kingdom through the better ordering of human life [27.7].

# 26

# Liberation Theology
# Congregation for the
# Doctrine of the Faith 1984–86
# John Paul II 1986

## 1 *Libertatis Nuntius*: Instruction 'On certain aspects of the theology of liberation' (1984)[1]

### (i) Background

The Congregation in question is entrusted with the task of ensuring that the teaching of the Church on faith, morals and discipline is presented accurately by theologians, lecturers and others in its official teaching institutions, or by any who teach in its name. When the CDF's theologians have finished their investigation on any matter they lay their conclusions before the Pope and he approves of them and gives permission for publication; they are a valid expression of his teaching office in the Church.

Paul VI as we have seen, dealt with aspects of liberation theology in the documents he issued, but he did not deal with it comprehensively; it was still a very live topic in 1978 when John Paul II took office. He touched on aspects of it in his Puebla address, but since doctrinal issues of some complexity were involved, there was a need of a more measured consideration of the whole question. This document of the CDF, the first of two on the matter, together with the Letter to Brazilian Bishops given below, provides it.

The Church in Nicaragua was, as we have seen, caught up in the popular revolution there against the Somozas; the bishops had initially and guardedly accepted the revolution's moral legitimacy,

---

* The notes and references for Chapter 26 are to be found on p. 463ff

while many in the Church in the country, and some basic communities, were actively engaged as partisans in its cause. But conflict
between the bishops and the regime grew as the Sandinistas in
power consolidated their position after 1979. John Paul II had
made plain that he did not accept the way the Church had been
treated nor the way in which several prominent priests had actively
participated in the regime as Ministers of State; and he got first-
hand experience of the tensions created by the situation when he
visited the country in 1983.[2] Support for the regime continued in
many sections of the Church there, however, and sympathizers in
the international Church were numerous.

## (ii)  Summary of the text

After an introductory few paragraphs there are eleven sections: I.
An aspiration [paras 1–9], II. Expressions of this aspiration [1–4],
III. Liberation as a Christian theme [1–4], IV. Biblical foundations
[1–15], V. The voice of the magisterium [1–8], VI. A new interpretation of Christianity [1–10], VII. Marxist analysis [1–13], VIII.
Subversion of the meaning of truth and violence [1–13], IX. The
theological application of this core [1–13], X. A new hermeneutic
[1–16], XI. Orientations [1–18], and a brief Conclusion.

The document is subtitled in English 'Instruction on Certain
Aspects of the Theology of Liberation' and its purpose was 'not
to deal with the vast theme of Christian liberation in its own
right'. This it intends to do in a subsequent document which will
detail in a positive fashion the great richness of this theme but its
purpose here is

> to draw attention ... to the deviations and risks brought about
> by certain forms of liberation theology which use, in an insuf-
> ficiently critical manner, concepts borrowed from various
> currents of Marxist thought.

This present document is not intended to disavow in any way
those responding generously to the 'preferential option for the
poor' and it should not be used as an excuse for indifference in
the face of the problems of injustice.

## I. An aspiration

The universal aspiration of mankind for today is for liberation [1].
Human dignity is seen to demand the rejection of all forms of

oppression [2] and the Gospel itself supports this aspiration and its consequences [3]. Consequently mankind no longer passively accepts injustice and deprivation [4]. Through the achievements of science and technology, even the poorest know that the world can provide them with the basic requirements of a decent life [5]. The gap between rich nations and poor is no longer tolerable [6]; injustices between nations in their trading relationships [7], the defects of colonialism living on [8], the arms race [9], all press on mankind.

## II. Expressions of this aspiration

This yearning for justice requires guidance [1], because many who claim to speak for the poor advocate violence [2] and such systematic violence does not accord with man's dignity [3]. We must therefore read the signs of the times in the light of the Gospel [4].

## III. Liberation – a Christian theme

Liberation itself is at the heart of the Christian message [1] and liberation theology was born of Latin America's Christian heritage [2]. It reflects a special concern for the poor which leads to a commitment for justice, but there are many kinds of liberation theology, understanding Christianity in different ways [3]. Liberation in itself

> repeats a theme which is fundamental to the Old and New Testaments ... the term theology of liberation is a valid term ... a theological reflection on the biblical theme of liberation ... and the urgency of its practical realization.

It can only be properly understood 'in the light of the specific message of revelation, authentically interpreted by the magisterium of the Church' [4].

## IV. Biblical foundations

The theology of liberation encourages the deeper understanding of the meaning of central biblical themes in the light of the yearning for liberation [1]. Most fundamentally, the Christian experiences liberation as freedom from sin because sin is the most radical form of slavery, hence liberation is not to be confused with licence [2]. Its theologians stress the significance of the exodus, 'a fundamental event in the life of the chosen people, representing freedom from foreign domination and slavery'. Yet

> the specific significance of the event comes from its purpose ... ordered to the foundation of the people of God and the covenant cult celebrated on Mt Sinai. That is why exodus cannot be reduced to a liberation which is principally or exclusively political in nature. Moreover it is significant that the term freedom is often replaced in Scripture by the very closely related term redemption [3].

In the definitive liberation, God is recognized as Liberator and he will enter into a new covenant with his people [4].

It is also to be noted that the suffering from which the Psalmist appealed for help was not only poverty or political oppression but also 'the hostility of one's enemies, injustice, failure and death', and the 'poor of the Lord' rely entirely on him [5]. The prophets on the other hand stress the theme of justice and solidarity with the poor oppressed by the rich; the covenant demands that God's people act with justice and faithfulness to it, and it cannot be imagined without that justice [6].

These requirements are more radical in the New Testament; the beatitudes require conversion of heart [7], while the commandment of brotherly love extends to all [8]. Poverty for the kingdom of God is praised. Christ himself became poor for the love of us, and when he comes again it is by our love of the poor that we will be judged [9]. Those who suffer for justice's sake are identified with Christ himself [10] and the rich are reminded severely of their duty to the poor in their need [11]. Sin is the greatest evil since it strikes at the heart of personality [12]. It is precisely because the New Testament demands are so radical that they do not need to deal with political or social change; yet freedom obtained by the grace of Christ necessarily has social effects [13].

Nor can the disorders from which man suffers be reduced to social sin [14]. One cannot postulate that all sin comes primarily from structures; 'structures whether they are good or bad, are the result of men's actions and so are more consequences than causes'. To seek radical revolution in social relations while neglecting personal perfection denies the meaning of the person and his transcendence, and undermines the distinction between good and evil. Charity is the principle of that perfection and charity is open to others in a spirit of service [15].

## V. The voice of the magisterium

The magisterium has frequently called attention to the need for solidarity with the poor [1] in documents such as *Mater et Magistra* [2]. The Second Vatican Council also confronted the question [3]. The Holy Father and CELAM have confirmed that the real truth about humanity is the basis for liberation [4]. The Synod of Bishops has also spoken on these matters [5] and the Pontifical Commission for Justice and Peace has been established [6]. Numerous episcopal conferences have also stressed the urgency of liberation [7] and at Medellín and Puebla, Paul VI and John Paul II dealt with the theme while emphasizing the distinctive nature of the Gospel [7–8].

## VI. A new interpretation of Christianity

An immense amount of selfless work has been done for the poor by dedicated people, clerical, religious and lay [1] but there is a danger that some of the cures sought for the social disease of poverty are just as damaging to man as that disease itself [2]. For the Christian the task of reducing poverty is part of the work of evangelization; the order cannot be reversed nor the two opposed [3], but some even suggest that the Gospel is a purely earthly message of economic and political salvation [4]. The option for the poor (and the young) of Medellín and Puebla [5] is diametrically opposed to such a vision [6].

It is also to be noted that the option for the young has almost been ignored [7]. There are in fact different theologies of liberation [8] and here we only deal with those that 'seriously depart from the faith of the Church' [9]. Concepts taken from Marxism and a rationalist biblical hermeneutic have no place in authentic liberation theology [10].

## VII. Marxist analysis

Impatience and a desire for results have made Marxist analysis attractive to some [1], it is said to be scientific and relevant to third-world needs [2]. Scientific knowledge of the situation is necessary for any social reform [3] but 'the term scientific exerts an almost mythical fascination, even though everything called scientific may not be scientific at all' [4]. The human and social sciences are far too complex [5] to fit into Marx's simple and univocal explanation in which ideology precedes analysis [6], an ideology which leads to the totalitarian State [7]. Marxism which remains true Marxism cannot be reconciled with Christianity. Those who use the phrase 'class struggle' cannot pretend that it means only 'severe social conflict'. Using such formulas 'while claiming to keep only certain elements of Marxist analysis and yet to reject this analysis as a whole' is confusing to those who hear and read the words of those who use them [8]. Atheism and the denial of the human person, his liberty and his rights 'are at the core of Marxist theory, and it therefore contradicts the Christian under-standing of the eternal destiny of man'. It also leads to 'a total subordination of the person to the collectivity, and thus the denial of the principles of a social and political life in keeping with human rights' [9]. Theologians must be careful about analytical methods borrowed from other disciplines. The ultimate criterion of theology, whose principles are provided by the light of faith, must be theology itself, not the social sciences [10].

There is, it is true, a certain plausibility about the application of Marxism to the situation in Latin America [11]. The lack of social conscience and disregard of human rights shown by oligarchies of the wealthy and their allies is blatant. In this context it is easy for criticism of the evil to be 'accompanied by a pathos which borrows its language from Marxism ... wrongly presented as though it were scientific' [12]. But it is not. Total openness to the reality to be described is the first requirement for any analysis. The nature of human science demands that a 'critical consciousness has to accompany any working hypotheses that are being adopted' but this 'is ignored by those who, under the guise of hypotheses recog-nized as such, have recourse to such an all-embracing conception of reality as the thought of Karl Marx' [13].

## VIII. The subversion of the meaning of truth and violence

The Marxist position cannot be reconciled with the Christian because it is deterministic, said to be 'scientific', true of necessity [1]. According to this view, analysis is inseparable from praxis [2]; consequently the analysis can only be correctly conducted by those involved in the revolutionary process [3]. The clear implication of this is that there is no truth except in partisan praxis [4] and that the class struggle is the fundamental fact and the source of this truth [5]. It is claimed that only the counter-violence of revolution will challenge the oppression of the poor by the rich [6]; in charity one must embrace the class war, and love of neighbour becomes an eschatalogical principle; it has no relevance in the here and now

[7]. The participation of opposing classes in the Eucharist is nonsense [8]. But in the Christian understanding the option for the poor includes the suffering of all social classes [9]. Theologies of liberation have brought to light prophetic teaching and so done the Church a service; but when they identify the poor with the proletariat of Marx, they pervert the Christian teaching [10]. The concept 'the Church of the people' can be another way of speaking of the Church as the people of God; it cannot be taken to mean the Church of one class [11–12]. Those who see it so, go on to challenge the whole of the hierarchical and sacramental system [13].

## IX. The theological application of this core

Some say that the Mass is a celebration of the people's struggle [1], for this struggle determines even ecclesiastical realities [2]. There is also consequently no distinction between profane and salvation history, and the kingdom of God and human liberation are identified, a position which 'is in contradiction to the faith of the Church as it has been reaffirmed by the Second Vatican Council' [3]. Some identify God and history [4] or reduce faith, hope and charity to fidelity to history, confidence in the future and option for the poor [5]. Every affirmation of faith or theology therefore depends on the class struggle [6], participation in which is a demand of charity itself [7]. Participation in the Eucharist by opposing social classes on this analysis makes no sense [8]. It is claimed that the poor, whatever the form of their poverty, are preferred by God [9]. Theologies of liberation which reason this way 'go on to a disastrous confusion between the poor of the Scriptures and the proletariat of Marx' [10]. The Church of the people means to some a class church with the people the object of faith [11–12]. The sacramental and hierarchical structures are seen as oppressive of the poor, and the people have the right to designate their own ministers 'in accordance with the need of their historic revolutionary mission' [13].

## X. A new interpretation of Scripture (hermeneutics)

Since for liberation theology of this kind hierarchy and magisterium represent oppression [1], it is difficult to enter into dialogue with its protagonists, for to them there is only the one true point of view, that of the revolutionary [2]. For them, orthopraxis, right practice according to the class theory, replaces orthodoxy or the right rule of faith. Sound theological method of course always takes the praxis of the Church into account 'but that is because the praxis comes from faith and is the lived expression of it', which is quite different from 'making praxis the supreme criterion for theological truth' [3].

The social doctrine of the Church is rejected by those who hold this point of view: 'it is said that it comes from the illusion of possible compromise, typical of the middle class which has no historic destiny' [4]. At the same time their beliefs lead to a political re-reading of the Scriptures; the exodus is primarily a liberation from political servitude. Likewise a political rereading of the Magnificat is proposed. The mistake is not in bringing to notice the political dimension of these readings, but in making it the exclusive one [5]. It leads to temporal messianism and the secularization of the kingdom of God [6]. While keeping the wording of the creeds, their meaning is perverted; so for example the radical message of Jesus, that he came to liberate us from sin which is the source of all evils, is denied [7]. The authoritative interpretation of the Church is dismissed as classist and the way left open to the rationalist, Jesus-of-history and Jesus-of-faith opposition [8]. The creeds are interpreted in a manner negative to the faith [9] such as that Jesus' experience was that of the poor in their struggle for earthly justice [10]. Faith in the incarnate word is replaced by Jesus the symbol of the oppressed [11]. Salvation is denied by this purely political interpretation [12]. It touches the whole Christian mystery [13]. The exodus prefigures not baptism but political liberation [14]. In the Church the relationship of hierarchy and people is one of domination [15]. The Eucharist is no longer a real sacrament of reconciliation but a celebration of the people in their struggle; the unity of the Church is denied [16].

## XI. Orientations

The defects of liberation theology do not mean that pastors and all Christians should not give work for justice high priority [1]. Quite the contrary: love for the poor is of the essence of the Church's mission [2] and work in this field goes ahead in communion with the bishop [3] and with theologians in collaboration with the magisterium [4]. Only in the context of evangelization can human progress and liberation be secured. The Church is for all classes [5]. The defence of human rights which the Church affirms is the authentic fight for justice [6], and that fight is to be non-violent, for violence debases human nature [7]. Poverty and the structures which conceal it are themselves forms of violence, but the source of the injustice is in the human heart; materialism inverts this order [8]. New structures will not of themselves produce new persons; the Holy Spirit alone renews man [9]. Revolutionary violence is not *ipso facto* a guarantee of better things [10]. The class struggle is an illusion; abandoning it means that the Gospel can become the inspiration for struggle for the poor [11] through the use of the Church's social teaching [12], and it also implies that those who work for the poor must put their experience at the disposal of the Church's pastoral and doctrinal reflection [13].

In this work 'the Church needs competent people from a scientific and technological viewpoint as well as in the human and political sciences', with the social teaching providing ethical guidelines [14]. Adequate catechetical work will help spread the knowledge [15] and pastors must see that theologies of liberation are placed within the context of salvation [16]. The transcendence and gratuity of liberation by Christ must not be forgotten, nor must the distinction between good and evil [17]. Nor must orthodoxy be a justification for complacency; 'spiritual conversion ... the love of God and neighbour, zeal for justice and peace' are among its requirements, 'effective witness in the service of one's neighbour ... the poor and the oppressed in particular' [18].

## Conclusion

The Congregation professes the faith expressed by Paul VI in his 'Profession of faith', that the kingdom of Christ is not of this world, though the love of Christ makes the Church ever concerned with the true temporal good of mankind. That however can never mean conforming itself to the things of this world.

## 2 *Libertatis Conscientia*: Instruction 'On Christian freedom and liberation', (March 22 1986)[3]

### (i) Background: the liberation theology of L. Boff

Nicaragua was not the only flash point of liberation theology in the middle 1980s; another was Brazil where the liberation theologian Fr Leonardo Boff OFM had a large following and whose book *Church, Charism and Power*, published first in 1981 and therefore ten years after Gutiérrez' seminal work, was under examination by the CDF.[4] The disagreement between the latter and Boff therefore came to a head in the period after the first critical Instruction (6

August 1984), just examined, and before the more positive one
issued in 1986. Boff's work is a much more radical critique of the
hierarchical Church and its teaching than was that of Gutiérrez,
and amounts to a total rejection of her self-understanding through
the centuries down to and through the Second Vatican Council. A
brief statement of the main themes of each Chapter reveals its
main drift.

The book has thirteen chapters. The first is entitled 'Models and
pastoral practices of the Church' and dismisses any notion of the
Church of pope, bishops and clergy, as the exclusive bearer of
man's salvation; this has been outdated by the Second Vatican
Council. It dismisses also the Church seen as mother and teacher;
that suited the colonial world in which the Church identified with
the *status quo*. Also rejected were the ideas of the Church as sacrament of salvation, accepting what was good in the world as
evidence of God's universal offer of salvation; that suited the
reformist and developmental mood of Vatican II and after. It is
only the fourth model, typified in the basic communities of the
third world, which is valid: a Church not only for the poor, but of
the poor.

Chapter 2, 'Theological tendencies and pastoral practices',
argues that the theology of captivity and liberation is the most
important today; other theologies, such as explaining the deposit
of faith, are secondary to this. This theology runs the risk that its
political implications may obscure the faith dimension, but this it
must not do. Chapter 3 suggests that the Church should take a
specific political option based on the preferential option for the
poor. The political party which best favours the poor is the one for
those who wish to walk with the Church. Chapter 4, 'Human rights
in the Church', asserts that from priesthood to papacy, the clergy
hold too much power, and so deny better-qualified men and
women, the laity generally, access to that power. Their hold over
the 'religious means of production' is comparable to that wielded
in civil society by those who control economic resources.[5]

Chapter 5, 'Power in the Church, can it be converted?', reasons
that, down to Vatican II, the hierarchy was totalitarian, brooking
no opposition, and that we now need a return to Gospel standards.
Chapter 6, 'Roman Catholicism, structures, health, pathologies',
suggests that the founding of the kingdom on the twelve apostles
was Christ's doing, but the institutional Church that evolved after
the resurrection was not according to his mind. The Church then
was in a sense truly Christ's and was equally truly not Christ's. The
New Testament possessed within it therefore, pluralities of theol-

ogy and churches, and dogmatic assertion cannot be valid for all times and circumstances. Catholicism also possesses pathological tendencies; rejection of Luther's reform leading to a 'total reactionary, violent and oppressive ideology'.[6]

Chapter 7, 'In favour of syncretism; the catholicity of Catholicism', depicts Christianity as a syncretism of Greek, Roman and Germanic cultures, and capable of a new syncretism to meet new needs. Chapter 8, 'Characteristics of the Church in class society', claims that the Church has legitimized the ruling capitalist class. The hierarchical Church parallels that class in its control of the religious means of production. At the same time the Church has a revolutionary potential because of the memories of the subversive Jesus Christ. It can break with capitalist society, and liberation theology and the base communities enable it to do this. Chapter 9, 'The base community, a brief sketch', presents these communities as essentially tuned to political action and as a new way of being Church through and by the poor.

Chapter 10, 'The underlying ecclesiologies of the basic ecclesiastical communities', sees those ecclesiologies as reducible to one, that of the people of God, of which the bishop is priest co-ordinator. Chapter 11, '*Ecclesia discens* and *ecclesia docens*' (The learning Church and the teaching Church), is of the opinion that Vatican II said that the whole Church is the teaching and learning Church, and that the bishops alone have no teaching prerogative. Chapter 12, 'An alternative view, the Church as the sacrament of the Holy Spirit', challenges the Church's traditional self-understanding. It is not founded on the incarnate word of God but on the faith of the Apostles informed by the Holy Spirit, and it is then always open to the new. The risen Christ knows no bounds of dogma, ritual, canon law or liturgy. Chapter 13, 'An alternative structure, charism as the organizing principle', tells us that the hierarchical model of the Church was accepted because it was adapted to the authoritarian political structures of the ancient and feudal worlds, but now one based on the CEB's was needed.[7] Collegiality involves the whole people of God, not only the bishops, whose function in the Church is as co-ordinators.

The *Notification* on the book was published on 20 March 1985 and specifies the more questionable views the book expresses. The remarks about the institutional Church not being founded by Christ, and the hierarchy as being the institutionalization of the feudalized Church, amount to a relativization of the truth about the latter, as does the assertion that its power is a simple function of service. The statement that the Second Vatican Council taught that the Church of Christ can subsist in other churches is shown, from the texts, to be the error it is. The book also relativizes dogma; the Church's dogmatic truths are truths for all time, though they can be further clarified and better understood as her theology develops. Nor are there contradictory teachings in the New Testament which would justify openness to all things. The deposit of faith perdures as it is clarified and as our understanding of it deepens. The parallel between the control of economic forces by the few in civil society, and that of the clergy's control of the spiritual forces in the Church is rejected. No one produces the sacraments in a manner equivalent to the production of wealth; they are gifts of God. There are imperfections in the Church and its members at all times, but the criticisms of the book tend not to the rebuilding in truth but to destruction. The hierarchy is not merely the co-ordinator of Church affairs; among its functions is that of judging whether movements within the Church are truly authentic or not.[8]

## (ii)  Summary of the text of the Instruction[9]

The English title of this document is 'Christian Freedom and Liberation' and it contains the assessment of the positive aspects of liberation theology which was promised in this document. It consists of an Introduction, five chapters and a conclusion. Chapter 1, 'The state of freedom in the world today', Chapter 2, 'The human vocation to freedom and the tragedy of sin', Chapter 3, 'Liberation and Christian freedom', Chapter 4, 'The liberating mission of the Church', and Chapter 5, 'The social doctrine of the Church for a Christian practice of liberation'.

### Introduction

The Church identifies with the modern world's desire to liberate man from all that oppresses him but knows that this desire sometimes assumes expressions 'which are not ... in conformity with the truth' and so *Libertatis Nuntius* remains apposite. This Instruction is the one promised by that document on the true Christian understanding of liberation; 'between the two documents there exists an organic relationship. They are to be read in the light of each other' [1].

Liberation is the heart of the Christian message. Here we will deal with it in its principal theoretical and practical aspects; local churches, in communion with each other and Rome, will work out applications to their particular situation. The ecumenical dimension of the theme is a valuable one. Freedom and liberation belongs to the patrimony of all the churches [2]. The truth that makes us free is centred in Jesus Christ, the way, the truth and the life. 'Redemption, which is at the heart of the mystery of faith ... is the root and the rule of freedom ... the foundation and measure of all liberating action' [3]. Man's moral conscience obliges him to be open to the fullness of truth; 'he must seek it out ... accept it when it presents itself to him'. Christ commanded the truth to be taught to all: the Holy Spirit, who guides the Church into all truth, is the 'root of courage, boldness and heroism' [4].

## Chapter 1. The state of freedom in the world today

*Achievements and dangers in the liberation process* 'By revealing to man his condition as a free person called into communion with God, the Gospel of Jesus Christ has evoked an awareness of the hitherto unsuspected depths of human freedom'. The Western quest for freedom and liberation, among the principal signs of the times for the modern world, has its first source in this heritage [5]. The Renaissance, Lutheranism, the Enlightenment and the French Revolution in modern times led to a belief in progress to the total freedom of man and human happiness [6] and, by penetrating the secrets of nature through science and technology, man has subjected it to his needs, and a life of dignity with freedom from poverty can reasonably be envisaged for mankind [7].

Political and social developments have done much to prevent the domination of man by man. The 'right of all to share in the benefits of culture has made significant progress' [8]. The modern liberation movement was intended to develop a new notion of man to help him gain a better self-understanding for personal growth and community formation [9]. Yet his ability to master nature, social and political life, or to master himself, have fallen far short of ambitions, while new forms of servitude threaten [10]. Abuse of technology threatens nature itself, puts at risk future generations [11]. Those who control modern technologies exercise immense power over others, and there are dangers of oppression latent in that power [12].

The Enlightenment view of social freedom was highly individualistic, favouring the unequal distribution of wealth, and during the industrialization process this had evil consequences, with the collectivism which was a reaction being a cure worse than the disease [13]. New totalitarianisms, genocide and a drug culture which destroys lives have flourished [14]. Mutual threats and weapons capable of destroying all human life challenge peace [15]. New relationships of inequality, resulting from the imbalances of rich and poor nations, are aggravated by arms importation [16]. The lack of economic and social advance to match political independence is a minus of recent years; on the other hand the growth of a sense of dignity and justice is a plus [17]. To some liberationists, however, man's freedom consists in rejecting the idea of God [18]. The tragedies of modern freedom are summed up in this sentiment. Yet in truth man, free of God, destroys his freedom: deprived of the measuring rod of truth he falls prey to the arbitrary, to terror, hatred, fear [19].

*Freedom in the experience of the kingdom of God*
The Church has always been aware of the ambiguity of freedom but, despite human errors in the course of the centuries, she insists that the revelation Christ entrusted to her is not in opposition to scientific freedom which has its own legitimate autonomy [20]. The Enlightenment's error was to think science, technology or economics alone secures freedom, whereas the knowledge that God loves us is the true liberating joy, and the poor especially know that. 'The first and most fundamental meaning of liberation ... is the salvific one; man is freed from the radical bondage of evil and sin'; true understanding and the proper use of freedom is rooted in love of God [21]. In their popular devotions the poor show this, and sense instinctively that this is the most radical of liberations [22]; in salvation humanity discovers true freedom [23] while where truth and love are missing, as they often are today, the process of liberation results in the death of freedom [24].

## Chapter 2. The human vocation to freedom and the tragedy of sin

*Preliminary approaches to freedom*
The spontaneous response to the question, What does being free mean? is that it means being free to do anything without restraint of authority [25]. But in fact

> freedom ... is the freedom to do good, and in this alone happiness is to be found ... Liberation for the sake of the knowledge of the truth that alone directs the will, is the necessary condition for a freedom worthy of the name.

Man needs others, needs to unite his will with theirs. Freedom only exists when truth and justice so links people [26].

*Freedom and liberation*
Freedom 'which is the interior mastery of one's own acts and self-determination ... entails relationship with the ethical order, choosing the good'. Man's freedom is not the absolute principle of his being and becoming, as 'historical praxis' would make it [27]. He was created in God's image, free and inclined towards the good so that he could choose friendship with his maker [28]. Hence man's capacity for self-realization is in no way suppressed by his dependence on God. It is from God that freedom comes: it 'takes its meaning from man's relationship to him' [29]. 'Authentic freedom is the service of justice ... the choice of ... evil [is] the slavery of sin' [30]. Freedom then always exists even when people are denied it. The downtrodden always have hope and so work to secure their freedom [31].

*Freedom and human society*
God created us as social beings. Social life, family, professional and political communities, help people grow as human beings [32]. Society must therefore give man his rights. The number and diversity of peoples in the Church, the body of Christ, reflects something of the richness of God's glory [33].

*Human freedom and dominion over nature*
Man needs the material world for his personal and social fulfilment, acting as a guardian of the things God has given him [34]. Man must be the master of his works, even though science and technology make them more complex [35], and scientific discoveries need moral control; they do not possess moral autonomy in themselves [36].

*Sin, the sources of division and oppression*
Called to freedom, and tempted to be like God, man refuses obedience [37]. Denying God, he is alienated from the truth of his own being [38]. He worships things instead of God and so perverts his relationship with them [39]; man makes himself his own centre, becoming enslaved to things [40]. In a single step the atheist 'rejects both the idea of God and the idea of sin'. The audacity of sin is the claim that it makes man adult and free [41]. 'Having become his own centre, sinful man tends to assert himself and to satisfy his desire for the infinite by the use of things.' Despising other people and using them, he helps to create 'the very structures of exploitation and slavery which he claims to condemn' [42].

## Chapter 3. Liberation and Christian freedom

The biblical message of freedom and hope enables the Christian community to work in love for justice, peace and freedom [43].

*Liberation in the Old Testament*
The exodus has both a religious and a political meaning. 'God sets his people free and gives them a covenant, a land and a law, but within a covenant and for a covenant.' The political aspect cannot be isolated from the religious plan of which it was part [44]. That plan included a law, the universal moral precepts of the decalogue and 'the religious and civil norms which were to govern the life of the people chosen by God'. Provision for 'the poor, the needy, the widow and the orphan' was made in it. It outlined a society 'centred upon worship of the Lord, based on justice and law inspired by love' [45].

The teaching of the prophets reminds Israel of, and condemns, the injustices done to the poor as being contrary to the covenant; Yahweh is their refuge and their defence [46]. The poor of Yahweh endure poverty, injustice and affliction but they hope for deliverance. Their communion with Yahweh is their most precious treasure 'and the one in which man finds his true freedom ... the most tragic misfortune is the loss of this communion' [47]. On the threshold of the New Testament the 'poor of Yahweh' are the people who live in hope of the liberation of Israel. Mary personifies this hope, above all in the Magnificat [48].

*The Christological significance of the Old Testament*
In Christ, exodus, covenant, law and prophets are fulfilled: the children of Abraham were invited to enter, together with all the nations, into the Church of Christ, to form the one People of God [49].

*Christian liberation*
Jesus Christ proclaimed the good news to the poor as the prophet had foretold; he was born of and lived with the poor [50] and his sacrifice on the cross procured for us liberation [51]. The heart of the Christian experience of freedom is in the justification received through faith and the Church's sacraments which free us from sin and place us in communion with God [52]. The freedom bought by Christ 'has freed us from disordered self-love, which is the source of contempt for our neighbour and human relationships based on domination'; but we still have to persevere not to fall back again [53].

The conflict within us of which St Paul speaks does not abolish this freedom but can affect its exercise. Yet Christ gained for us the grace to observe God's law perfectly. He also abolished the cultic regulations of the old law, and the juridical norms governing the social and political life of Israel were no longer binding.

This enabled the Christian communities to understand the laws and the authoritative acts of various peoples. Though respecting them in their time, in the light of the Gospel, many laws and structures seem to bear the mark of sin and prolong its oppressive influence on society' [54].

### The new commandment

The second of the two great commandments is to love thy neighbour as thyself [55] and the measure of this love is that we love one another as Christ has loved us (John 13:34–5). St Paul stresses the link between sharing in the body of Christ and sharing with neighbours in need (1 Cor. 2:7–34) [56].

Evangelical love, and the vocation of the children of God to which we are called, have as a consequence the direct and imperative requirement of respect for all human beings in their right to life and dignity. There is no gap between love of neighbour and desire for justice. To contrast the two is to distort both. Indeed the meaning of mercy completes the meaning of justice by preventing justice from shutting itself up within the circle of revenge.

Admitting the human failings of some of our fellow Christians, there have also been among them vast numbers who, from the time of the apostles onwards, have committed themselves to the liberation of their fellow men from every form of indignity and oppression. They are an example to us today [57].

### The Church, the people of God of the new covenant

The people of God of the New Testament is the Church of Christ looking to the new Jerusalem, to his coming again [58]. All those found worthy before Christ's tribunal for having, by the grace of God, made good use of the free will, are to receive the reward of happiness [59] but this hope strengthens rather than weakens commitment to the progress of the earthly city. There is a distinction between the two certainly; they do not belong to the same order, but there is no contradiction – rather, man's vocation to eternal life confirms him in his task of developing his temporal life. The expectation of the final coming includes perfect justice for the living and the dead which Christ will bring [60].

## Chapter 4. The liberating mission of Christ

Though the Church is determined to respond to man's yearning for freedom, ordering the political and economic life of society is not part of her mission. However, enlightening consciences is, and if her members remain true to the love of the Spirit, the source of solidarity, they will bring forth justice [61].

*For the integral salvation of the world*
The beatitudes express the spirit of the kingdom that is to come and free man from the illusion of a perfect world, so preventing the worship of worldly things which is the source of injustices [62]. By evangelization

> man is ... freed from the power of sin ... in this mission the Church teaches the way man must follow in this world in order to enter the kingdom of God; [it] ... extends to the whole of the moral order and notably to the justice which must regulate human relations.

Through her members she pursues the temporal good. She desires the good of man as a member of the earthly city also [63].

When she speaks of justice, therefore, the Church is not going beyond her mission, although she avoids over-involvement in temporal affairs at cost to her evangelical role [64]. 'It is by pursuing her own finality that she sheds light on earthly realities so that human beings may be healed of their miseries and raised in dignity.' She opposes oppression and forms of social life which exclude God, and also methods of fighting oppression which are contrary to the Gospel [65].

*The love of and preference for the poor*
Jesus Christ became poor for our sakes, teaching detachment, trust in God, sobriety, readiness to share. It was among the humble, the 'poor of Yahweh' who were thirsting for the justice of the kingdom that he found a response. But 'he also wished to be near those ... rich in the goods of this world ... publicans and sinners, for he had come to call them to conversion' [66]. The beatitude of poverty that he proclaimed 'can never signify that Christians are permitted to ignore the poor who lack what is necessary for human life in this world' as a result of human action or neglect [67]. Human misery 'material deprivation, unjust oppression, physical and psychological illnesses and finally death' is a sign of that human weakness that results from original sin and of the need for salvation; hence Christ

has compassion on it. The Church, despite the human weaknesses of so many of her members, has consequently always had a compassion for the poor, manifested in her numerous works of charity 'and through her social doctrine she has sought to promote structural changes ... to secure conditions of life worthy of the human person'. In loving the poor, she witnesses to man's dignity: 'man is worth more for what he is than for what he has ... this dignity cannot be destroyed' no matter how unjustly a man is treated. She shows solidarity with the rejected, especially those killed in the womb, the elderly, the abandoned.

> This special option for the poor, far from being a sign of particularism or sectarianism, manifests the universality of the Church's being and mission; this option excludes no one. This is the reason why [she cannot] make this preference a partisan choice and a source of conflict [68].

Basic communities in union with the local and the international Church, hierarchy and magisterium are welcomed [69] and theological reflection developed from a particular experience, highlighting aspects of the Scriptures, can be very positive if the theologian interprets it in the light of the Church's experience, particularly in the lives of the saints, and of her pastors in union with the successor of St Peter, discerning its authenticity [70].

## Chapter 5. The social doctrine of the Church for a Christian practice of liberation

'The salvific dimension of liberation cannot be reduced to the socio-ethical ... which is a consequence of it.' That liberation is implied in the new commandment of love and its practice [71].

### The nature of the social doctrine of the Church

> The Church's social teaching is born of the encounter of the Gospel message ... summarized in the supreme commandment of love ... with the problems emanating from the life of society. [It] ... has established itself as a doctrine by using the resources of human wisdom and the sciences. It concerns the ethical aspect of this life ... takes into account the technical aspects of problems but always in order to judge them from the moral point of view.

It 'develops in accordance with the changing circumstances of history'. Together with 'principles that are always valid ... it contains contingent judgements', 'it remains ... open to new questions', and it offers 'a set of principles for reflection, criteria for judgement and directives for action' [72].

Its fundamental principles are three. The first is that the human being, the person, made in God's image, is 'the active and responsible agent of social life'. The second is 'solidarity' which obliges a man 'to contribute to the common good of society at all levels' and the third the principle of subsidiarity which states that 'neither state nor any society must substitute itself for the initiative and responsibility of individuals and of intermediate communities at the level on which they can function'. Hence the Church is opposed to individualism and collectivism [73].

These principles are the basis of criteria for judgements on social situations, structures and systems: 'the institutions and practices ... national and international ... which orientate or organize economic, social and political life'. By these criteria they can be assessed and if necessary changed, but by the decisions of men, 'not [by] ... the alleged determinism of history'. For its part

> the social doctrine of the Church does not propose any particular system, but, in the light of other fundamental principles ... makes it possible ... to see to what extent systems conform or do not conform to the demands of human dignity [74].

The concentration primarily on sinful structures simply reflects modern materialism: sin is, however, primarily personal. That is not to deny the need to change unjust structures, but it underlines that sound structures do not necessarily secure the people's good; they must be administered honestly. 'The corruption which in certain countries affects the leaders and the State bureaucracies' proves this. Moral integrity is a necessary condition for the health of society. We must work 'simultaneously for the conversion of hearts and for the improvement of structures'. Intellectuals also have a responsibility to ensure that alien ideologies are not imposed contrary to a people's cultural tradition [75].

These principles and criteria provide incentives to action. 'The means of action must be in conformity with human dignity and facilitate ... freedom ... there can be no true liberation if from the very beginning the rights of freedom are not respected.' Systematic recourse to violence 'as the way to liberation has to be condemned ... one must condemn with equal vigour violence exercised by the powerful against the poor'. Neither is it possible to accept 'the culpable passivity of the public powers' in supposed democracies which lack 'constitutionally guaranteed individual and social rights' [76].

Encouragement of associations to fight for rights, e.g. trade unions, does not mean support for the class war, but for justice and solidarity; the Christian will always prefer dialogue. Liberation in the spirit of hatred is contrary to the Gospel [77]. Situations of grave injustice require the courage to make far-reaching reforms, but

> those who discredit the path of reform and favour the myth of revolution ... foster the illusion that the abolition of an evil situation [creates] a more humane society; they also encourage ... totalitarian regimes.

The fight must be for an order which conforms to justice; justice should mark each stage; there is a morality of means [78]. These things must be remembered when considering the teaching of the magisterium that there can be in the last resort a justification for the use of force to end an obvious and prolonged tyranny in which human rights are denied and the common good ignored. At no time and in no conflict are reprisals against the people generally, torture, terrorism and the deliberate provoking of violent demonstrations, the suppression of which gives excuse for slaughter, or smear campaigns aimed at destroying a person psychologically or morally, to be tolerated [79].

> It is not for the pastors of the Church to intervene directly in the political construction and organization of social life. This task forms part of the vocation of the laity acting on their own initiative with their fellow citizens.

In this they will be guided by their consciences; their options should not be such as to hinder collaboration among the Christian people. They also need to equip themselves with the essential technical and scientific skills as well as deepening both moral and spiritual formation and their understanding of the Church's social teaching which, though it offers principles and wise counsels, 'does not dispense from education in the political prudence needed for guiding and running human affairs' [80].

*Evangelical conditions for reform*
What is it that the commandment of love demands in order that the liberation of man from economic, social and political oppression may be achieved? It is a task of education for the civilization of work, for solidarity, for access to culture for all [81]. That Christ who was God became a manual worker, offers us the first principle of that liberation, the dignity of human work; as an expression of personal-

ity, work has a creative meaning [82]. Such work, done willingly and freely, issues in just working relationships with others, becomes the basis of a system of political community capable of favouring the integral development of every individual [83]. Such a culture affirms the priority of labour, whose rights are to be defended and duties are to be performed, and enables confrontation to be replaced by dialogue. Participation aimed at promoting the national and international common good will help political authorities to develop a true subsidiary role, especially in helping to ensure job creation [84].

The value of human work depends, not on the work done, but on the fact that a person does it; the subjective dimension in other words establishes its value, not the objective. And since all have a right to work, unemployment is a tragedy. Job creation is a task for private enterprise, with the State in a subsidiary role [85]. Wages cannot be considered a mere commodity but must provide the worker with access to a fully human standard of living: participation in the responsibilities of work is also needed [86]. Employers have an obligation to consolidate jobs or create new ones for the production of things that are really needed. Private property carries with it responsibilities to the common good. It is subordinated to the higher principle which states that goods are meant for all [87]. It is a primary demand of social justice that all have access to the goods needed for a human, personal and family life worthy of the same. The rural and agricultural workers are the majority of the poor and this justice is for them also [88].

*The promotion of solidarity*
A new solidarity must be created, solidarity of the poor among themselves, among the workers, institutions, nations, organizations [89]. This solidarity is a direct requirement of human and supernatural brotherhood. The serious socio-economic problems that occur today cannot be solved unless new forms of solidarity are created – the poor with the poor, the poor with the rich, among the workers and with the workers [89]. That goods are meant for all, and the principle of human and supernatural fellowship, are the two principles which express the responsibility of rich to poor nations and the need for solidarity [90]. International solidarity requires that new solutions be found, and the creation of a new mentality among our contemporaries [91].

*Cultural and educational tasks*
All have the right to the means necessary to develop their intellec-

tual capacities and moral virtues and so to relate better to other human beings. Education, initially the abolition of illiteracy, is the first task [92]. The State cannot use the pretext of public order or national security for the systematic restriction of cultural freedoms [93] and its role in education is subsidiary. Private schools deserve justice [94]. Authentic development is only possible if there is political freedom and participation by all of whatever sex, race, colour, social conditions, language or religion [95]. Christianity, present throughout the world, takes positive elements from every culture, intimately transforming them by integrating them with Christianity. Gospel and culture are inseparable [96].

**Conclusion**

The canticle of the Magnificat tells us that it is by faith, like Mary, that the people of God express in words and translate into life the mysterious plan of salvation with its liberating effects upon individual and society. Mary, as totally dependent on her son, and at his side, represents the most perfect image of freedom and of the liberation of humanity and the universe. This faith found in the poor leads to an acute perception of the mystery of the redeeming cross and to unshakeable trust in the Mother of the Son of God [97]. Accordingly it would be criminal to divert these energies into an illusion which would end in a new slavery. To surrender to the ideologies of violence is to abandon the hope, with its boldness and courage, which is extolled in the Virgin Mary's hymn to the God of mercy [98].

Liberation in its primary meaning is salvific. Its liberation is ethical, outlined by the social doctrine of the Church. The present document outlines some of the needed in-depth reforms, and the primary task is educational, it being a condition of success for all the others [99]. The task ahead is immense and might tempt to despair but that the Magnificat enfolds the Church and supports it in hope.

## 3. Letter of John Paul II to the Brazilian bishops on liberation theology, April 9 1986

*(i) Background*

In the 1980s the Brazilian Church continued to be convulsed by controversy over liberation theology. In his visit to Brazil in 1982, and then during their *ad limina* visits in 1985–6 when the 370 Brazilian bishops went to Rome in their regional groups, the Pope learned more about the situation. Finally there was a special meeting between the Pope and officials of the Roman curia on one side and the senior members of the Brazilian hierarchy and lay representatives from each of the regions on the other in 1986, after which, this letter was made public.

## (ii)  Summary of the text[10]

The controversy over liberation raises the question of the nature of the Church. That Church is above all a mystery, a response to the Father's saving plan, and 'an extension of the Incarnate Word's mission and the fruit of the creative action of the Holy Spirit'. It cannot therefore be defined in purely rational categories, socio-political or other. It is holy, though consisting of sinners; it is eschatological, that is, the first fruit of the kingdom but not its completion, unchanging in its fundamental being and mission but adaptable in outward features. The Church's mission is primarily religious, and its concern with social and political issues is to be understood accordingly. It is concerned with socio-political issues, but the proper exercise of this aspect of her mission requires discernment, and she is conditioned by certain basic requirements 'among them: a clear distinction between the function of the laity, committed by their specific vocation ... to temporal tasks, and the function of pastors, who train the laity'. It is not the Church's place to suggest technical solutions to social problems, but to illuminate the search for solutions with the light of faith. Further action in social and political matters must remain in unfailing harmony with the Church's constant teaching.

The Church in Brazil faces many fundamental problems, but it has great strengths based on its deep appreciation of spiritual realities and the quality of its people, clergy and laity, their dedicated work in the past and in the present day. Of those problems, the contrast between luxury and deprivation that exists in daily life is particularly challenging and cannot be ignored by the Church. The duties of the bishops are pastoral, teaching the truth, building community, helping all, especially those in most need of help, defence and protection.

As the bishops seek ways to respond to these challenges, the Holy See works with them: the instructions of the Congregation for the Doctrine of the Faith, *Libertatis Nuntius* and *Libertatis Conscientia*, addressed to the whole Church, are particularly relevant. 'We and you are convinced that the theology of liberation is not only opportune but necessary', constituting a new stage in the apostolic tradition of the Fathers and Doctors of the Church and 'the rich patrimony of the Church's social teaching expressed in documents from *Rerum Novarum* to *Laborem Exercens*'. The Brazilian church has an important role to play 'in perfect accord with the ... two previously mentioned instructions'. Christian liberation is primarily salvific, an aspect of salvation achieved by Jesus Christ 'and afterward socio-ethical or ethico-political'. To reduce the former to the latter is an error. On the other hand the bishops and the entire church in Brazil show themselves ready to undertake all that is derived from salvific liberation, what the Church has always tried to do by means of its saints, teachers and pastors and of the faithful engaged in temporary reality.

## 4 Summary analysis of the social teaching of the C.D.F.

### (i) Ethics and civil society

God did not create us as solitary, but as social beings. Social life then is not something which is exterior to us; it is only through that life that we grow and can develop. Inside its communities we learn to exercise responsible freedom, and a just social order assists us to develop as free persons, as an unjust one hinders us in this. Basic to our development is the recognition of our human rights [LC 32].

The supreme commandment of love results in the full recognition of the dignity of each individual, made as he is in the image of God in possessing intelligence and free will. From this dignity proceed natural rights and duties. Freedom is the essential prerogative of the human being, and persons are the active and responsible agents of all social life. The first principle of social living is that the dignity of man, intelligent and free, with freedom as his essential prerogative, is the end and purpose of all social organization. The second is that in his social living man is bound first of all to solidarity, to contribute to the common good of society at all its levels; it therefore rejects the individualism which ignores that good. The third, which is an extension of the first, is the principle of subsidiarity, that neither the State nor any society within it should substitute itself for the initiative of individuals or intermediate communities at the level at which they can function effectively, nor must they limit their freedom. It then rejects collectivism which needlessly tries to replace private initiative with public [LC 73]. Solidarity is a direct requirement of human and supernatural brotherhood. The serious socio-economic problems of today cannot be solved without it; solidarity of the poor among themselves, solidarity with the poor to which the rich are called, solidarity among the workers and with the workers. Institutions and social organizations at different levels as well as the State must share in this general movement [LC 89–91].

The modern desire for freedom, for liberation is one that is fully compatible with the biblical and theological understanding of freedom, though the latter is not freedom to do what one wishes but to do good, what is objectively right and true. Authentic freedom is in the service of justice [LC 25–26]. Such freedom in economic, social and political matters is then man's right. Encouragement of associations, e.g. trade unions, to fight for their rights, does not mean approval of class war as the structural dynamic of social life; in a struggle for justice and solidarity, the Christian will always prefer dialogue and joint action [LC 77]. On the question of social reform, reform of self, of individuals, cannot be separated from the reform of the structures, which are unjust precisely because of the injustice of individuals. Any structure will soon become oppressive if operated by individuals who are unjust, as we see in the operations of corrupt individuals in charge of political organizations. Both personal and structural reform are needed simultaneously where injustice exists. The moral integrity of persons and structures is needed for the health of any society [LC 75]. Reform on Marxist lines on the contrary introduces a cure worse than the disease. It is said to be scientific, but its atheism obliterates natural rights and introduces a disastrous identification of the poor with the proletariat of Marx [LN VII. 2, VII. 9, IX.9]. However, that some liberation theologians err in these matters does not excuse neglect of the needs of the poor by those who defend orthodoxy; on the contrary all those who follow the Gospel must see that justice towards the poor which moves us to help them in their need grows out of the love that we should have for them. It demands sacrifice, boldness and courage and all priests, religious and laity must respond to that need [LN XI. 1 to 5].

## (ii) Ethics and political society

In some parts of Latin America the seizure of the greater part of the national wealth by oligarchies who lack social conscience, and the activities of military dictators, careless of law, make a mockery of elementary human rights, and this, combined with the corruption of powerful officials and the savage practices of foreign capital interests, nurtures a passion for revolt among those who suffer from their injustices [LN VII.12]. Supposed democracies which lack constitutionally guaranteed personal and social rights, and show passivity in dealing with problems of injustice are also an abomination. So also is the use of violence by the powerful against the poor who seek justice [LC 76]. Where such injustices exist the task of reform must be faced courageously, but to abandon gradual reform in favour of the myth of revolution under the illusion that it will provide a more just society is an error: in fact it encourages totalitarian regimes. There does exist in the last resort the justification for armed struggle, when an obvious and prolonged tyranny gravely damages fundamental rights and the common good, but this should not be countenanced without the most rigorous examination of the situation, and, given the growing technology of violence, passive resistance is more conformable with morality and has the better prospects of success [LC 79].

## (iii) Ethics and economic society

The right to private property cannot be separated from the higher principle which states that goods are meant for all. So there is a moral obligation to make capital productive, and in making investments to think first of the common good. Access for everyone to the goods needed for a human, personal and family life worthy of the name is a primary demand of social justice, and it requires application in the rural and agricultural world as much as in the industrial; rural peoples in the third world make up the vast majority of the poor [LC 88].

Every person has a right to work, and the creation of jobs is a primary task facing individuals and private enterprise as well as the State. The State here has a subsidiary function but can be called in to intervene directly if need be [LC 85]. Wages must be such as will allow the worker and his family access to a truly human standard of life. Whatever his work, the worker must be able to express his personality through it, and there should be access to participation and a truly communitarian dimension to the undertaking [LC 86]. A work culture of this kind will acknowledge the worker as the principal subject and purpose of work, the priority of work over capital, and the fact that material goods are meant for all. It will be informed by a spirit of solidarity over not only rights but also duties, it will promote participation on a national and international level [LC 84].

# 27

# John Paul II's social encyclicals 1987–91

## 1 *Sollicitudo Rei Socialis* (1987)[1]

### (i) Background

This, the second strictly social encyclical of John Paul II issued on 30 December 1987, commemorates the tenth anniversary of Paul VI's *Populorum Progressio*, and deals with the same subject, the development of peoples, recalling the continuing significance of that document, looking again at its teaching in the light of events since and restating and developing the Church's attitude where needed. It is also notable, and caused controversy in some Catholic circles, because of its firm restatement of the validity of the concept of Catholic social doctrine as a developing corpus of knowledge which needs to be assimilated by all concerned with the Church's social apostolate.

As the documentation above indicates, a major part of John Paul II's concern with the Church's social apostolate and teaching since he assumed office, had been centred on the South American Church and liberation theology. The reason was pastoral, the Church there being deeply involved with the search for greater justice that her people in the region were seeking, but the ways to deal with it were not always easy to discern. These difficulties led to the sort of conflicts outlined. There was another area of major concern to the Church in terms of her social apostolate and teaching and that was in a very different context, that of Eastern Europe, and Poland in particular. The Pope had been much concerned with it before his election, and we shall be looking in more detail at the situation when we consider *Centesimus Annus*. But we will see

* The notes and references for Chapter 27 are to be found on p. 463ff

that *Sollicitudo Rei Socialis*, published in December 1987, a few months after the third of John Paul II's pilgrimages to his home-land after he became Pope, touched on problems that were coming to a head there and elsewhere in Eastern Europe, and would find their solution over the years 1989 to 1991. The struggle was about freedom, which included economic freedom, and the encyclical we are about to examine was emphatic about the issue of economic freedom properly understood, in the solution to the problems of economic injustice in the world.

## (ii) Summary of the text

There is an Introduction I [1–4], and five Sections: II. The origi-nality of *Populorum Progressio* [5–10], III. Survey of the contemporary world [11–26], IV. Authentic human development [27–34], V. A theological reading of modern problems [35–40], VI. Some particular guidelines [41–45], and a Conclusion [46–49].

## I. Introduction

The series of documents published by the popes since Leo XIII [1.1] constitutes 'an updated doctrinal corpus' built up under the guidance of the Holy Spirit as the Church seeks to help her people in their vocation as responsible builders of society [1.2]. *Populorum Progressio* of Paul VI (27 March 1967), the twentieth anniversary of which had been recently celebrated, is part of this corpus [2.1–2]. 'Continuity and renewal are proof of the peren-nial value of the teaching of the Church' [3.1–2]. The present document considers the course of later developments and looks to the future [4.1–4].

## II. The originality of *Populorum Progressio*

The encyclical captured the attention of the public when it was published [5.1]. It was an application of the teaching of the Council and the tradition on which it was built, but put in a much broader context. The Church's centuries-old traditional teaching, for example concerning 'the universal purpose of created things', was developed and applied to the economic inequality between nations. It further enlarged on the serious duty the developed countries had to help the undeveloped [6.1–7.2]. The term 'devel-opment' is taken from the social and economic sciences, which are, not in themselves the Church's concern. But ethical issues are, and Paul VI's encyclical looked at a socio-economic question from an ethical point of view [8.1–2].

The social question was now world wide and the social teaching of the Church responds to this situation. John XXIII and Vatican II had moved in this direction, but not so comprehensively nor with such precise application [8.3–9.2]. Paul VI drew out some of the moral implications and obligations of development far more clearly, and stressed that development is the new name for peace: war and military preparations are by definition its enemy [9.3–10.6].

### III. Survey of the contemporary world

The situation today (1987) is of course different from what it was twenty years ago [11.2]. The world is unfortunately not so optimistic about development as was that of the late 1960s [12.1–3]. It is not true to say that nothing has been achieved; much has been, yet on the whole the results have been disappointing. All the main indicators of development show that there is too great a difference between the two general groups of countries: abundance for the one, deprivation for the other; every quality of life indicator shows the disparity as to food, health, housing, literacy, education, life expectancy and so on, the gap between the two groups of nations growing wider instead of narrowing, cultural and value differences in many cases being most disturbing: they include illiteracy, limited access to higher education, lack of political participation in nation building, the existence of exploitation and oppression of all kinds [13.1–15.1].

The right of economic initiative, important for the person and the community, is often suppressed. Absence of it results in a levelling down instead of levelling up, in passivity, dependence, submission to the bureaucracy, similar to the traditional dependence of the worker-proletariat in capitalism. It has national counterparts, nations deprived of their rightful economic-political sovereignty. No social group, no party has the right to claim sole leadership, because this limits the rights of the citizens; it leads to denial of religious, of trade union and of economic freedom. True development in other words must include cultural development and freedom [15.2–6].

For the failures of the past twenty years there are many causes. One of them, and an important one, is the grave instances of omission on the part of developing nations themselves and especially those holding economic and political power. Another is the failure of the developed nations which have not always sufficiently felt the duty to help countries separated from the affluent world to which they themselves belong. Economic, financial and social mechanisms controlled by the developed world but which function almost automatically, penalize the underdeveloped [16.1–4].

As their designations, first, second, third and even fourth worlds, indicates, the world today is divided, but its interdependence remains real. Underdevelopment is in some respects a fact of life in the richer nations too; in other words it is both world wide and regressive. Marks of this regression in the developed world are its housing problems [17.1–4]. Another is unemployment and underemployment. Regarding the latter, the words of *Laborem Exercens* are recalled; such a phenomenon in the developed world shows that 'there is something wrong with the organization of work and employment, precisely at the most critical and socially most important points' [18.1–4]. Interdependence, and the need for justice in it, is apparent when international debt is in question. In fact, servicing the debts of the third world now leads to the crippling export of capital. A new approach is needed then to this question if justice is to be done [19.1–6].

The existence of the Eastern and Western blocs has had a considerable negative effect on development: while the tension is somewhat attenuated of late, it continues. Other countries get caught up in the ideological conflict the opposed blocs represent, and energies and resources are wasted in consequence. Politically it is a conflict of ideologies, of liberal capitalism versus Marxism, and these ideologies spark local armed conflicts, with the Cold War in the background [20.1–8]. The conflict is between two concepts of development, both being imperfect and in need of correction, namely the liberal capitalist and the Marxist, and the Church rejects both as being incapable of encouraging true human development.

Newly independent countries, seeking the support of one or other of these blocs, are drawn into their spheres of influence to the point of civil war – which diverts energies and resources away from development [21.1–3]. Caught in a neo-colonialist trap, they become appendages of this conflict instead of working for the full development of their peoples [22.1–5]. The leaders of both blocs fail humanity in imposing this pattern on it [23.1–5]. Meanwhile arms are available to all throughout the world and the misery of the masses affected by civil discord increases; companion to this evil is that of terrorism which seeks to create a climate of fear by its unpredictable nature. No cause which uses such methods can be countenanced, whatever elements of idealism inspire it: 'acts of terrorism are never justifiable' [24.1–4]. The demographic problem is also very much in people's minds. In the North of course it is one rather of an ageing population, in the South it is that of coping with population growth. In the latter case the pressure for restricting births is often from the developed world and the methods used often militate against human dignity and rights, becoming a form of racist eugenics [25.1–4].

However, there are positive signs in the development field also over the past decades. One is the growing awareness of human rights, among peoples and throughout the world. Along with it, the threat of conflict of every kind is encouraging an awareness of the need for international solidarity in the face of it. The idea that the happiness all are seeking cannot be obtained without renouncing personal selfishness is gaining ground. The respect for life is also apparent despite the pressure for abortion and euthanasia. People are becoming increasingly aware that peace and justice is one and indivisible: it is either for all or none. Concern for the environment is growing, as is the generous commitment of so many people in public life, in the sciences and in the professions, to the cause of peace and of improving the quality of life. The self-sufficiency in food, and the degree of industrialization that many of the third-world nations have achieved is in no small part due to them. There is above all a new moral concern, especially in regard to development and peace [26.1–12].

## IV. Authentic human development

Unfortunately progress in development is not automatic; the idea that it should be owes more to Enlightenment philosophy than to development theory [27.1–2]. The very idea of economic development itself is in crisis. Neither mere accumulation of goods, even for the majority, nor more modern technology, bring freedom in themselves.

> The experience of recent years shows that unless all the considerable body of resources and potential at man's disposal is guided by a moral understanding, and by an orientation toward the true good of the human race, it easily turns against man to oppress him.

There is also another lesson from recent experience. Along with unacceptable underdevelopment, there is an unacceptable over development 'which consists in an excessive availability of every kind of material good for the benefit of certain social groups' so that they become 'slaves of possessions and immediate gratification, with no other horizon than the multiplication or continual replacement of the things already owned, with others still better'. This consumerism discards a thing regardless of 'its value in itself, [or] of some other human being who is poorer'. The injustice is compounded in that the rich are comparatively few and the poor are many; 'it is the injustice of the poor distribution of goods and services ... intended for all'. The evil does not arise from possessions in themselves but 'in possessing without regard for the ordered hierarchy of the goods one has ... the subordination of goods and their availability to man's being and true vocation' [28.1–9].

Man needs created goods and the products of industry 'constantly enriched by scientific and technological progress', meeting his needs and broadening his horizons, but

> development cannot consist only in use, dominion over and indiscriminate possession of created things and the products of human industry, but rather in subordinating the possession, dominion, and use, to man's divine likeness and his vocation to immortality. This is the transcendent reality of the human being, a reality which is seen to be shared from the beginning by ... man and woman ... [and] is therefore fundamentally social [29.1–4].

Development in other words is not simply a lay or secular activity, but an essential part of man's vocation. He was created to 'have dominion' over created things and cultivate the earth, but subject to God's law, and when he disobeys it the exercise of his dominion becomes more difficult. Yet the descendants of Cain build a city, farm sheep, become musicians, work in metal, and throughout history man has developed himself and his world; modern development is part of this. Today's difficulties are examples of the difficulties of dominion that followed the Fall but they should not prevent us using the talents God has given us in development [30.1–8].

Given faith in Christ, 'the dream of unlimited progress appears radically transformed' because God the Father made us sharers in his glory. Some of the Fathers of the Church developed the meaning of history and human work in an optimistic way because man is redeemed by Christ and destined for the promised kingdom. So part of the teaching and most ancient practice of the

Church is her conviction that she is obliged by her vocation to relieve human need out of her abundance and even out of her necessities [31.1–8].[2]

The co-operation in the development of every person and every nation is the duty of us all throughout the world, cultural identity and openness to the transcendent being respected [32.1–3]. True development must be moral, it must respect the rights of the person, the State and international rights. Neglect of the rights of the person, of cultural and national community, does not satisfy the aims of development, and is in the end contemptible. The rights of young and old, of men and women, families, communities, the life of the political community, freedom of conscience, are involved. On the international level all countries should be treated with equal respect for their identity, history and culture. It must also be achieved within a framework of solidarity and freedom without sacrificing either, under whatever pretext. It must be based on the love of God and neighbour [33.7–8]. Development must respect also the natural world of which we have only a conditional, not an absolute dominion. Using all natural resources as if they were inexhaustible, or reckless development which puts the environment at risk, denies it this respect [34.1–6].

## V. A theological reading of modern problems

Since development has a moral character, obstacles to it likewise have such a character. The slowness of development since 1967 therefore has not only economic causes but also political. The political will for it has been weak [35.1–3]. Ideologies favour imperialisms rather than solidarity and interdependence. The 'structures of sin' do exist, the result of selfishness, shortsightedness, political and economic imprudence, moral failings which cannot be tackled without moral or ethical evaluations. These are positive if they are based on God and his law. There is a 'difference between socio-political analysis and formal reference to "sin" and the "structures of sin". The latter refers to the God who is rich in mercy, and his plan for mankind which requires from his people positive action in looking to the need of our neighbours [36.1–6].

Two attitudes in particular which are opposed to the will of God for man, and which contribute to sinful structures, are the all-consuming desire for profit and power at any price. They can and do exist together or separately: 'not only individuals fall victim to [them], nations and blocs can do so too'. In all cases it is a question of moral evil, the fruit of many sins that lead to the 'structures of sin' [37.1–3]. Deciding the path to be followed in overcoming these evils is difficult but not impossible; men and women of faith recognize that God's will is the only one true basis for ethical judgement. Those without explicit faith can perhaps see the need for something more than merely economic values, to change the spiritual attitudes which define relationships with self, neighbour, the human community, nature itself, for the full development of all. Christian theology speaks of the need for conversion, a turning to God, a recognition of sin committed, and an acceptance of its consequences for self and others, so that God can turn our hearts of stone into hearts of flesh. There are some signs that humanity is already on the road to conversion through the growing awareness of interdependence. This awareness can become in moral terms true 'solidarity ... not a vague compassion or a shallow distress' but a firm and persevering determination to commit oneself to the common good, of each and all, because all are responsible for all. What is hindering full development is that desire for profit and thirst for power already mentioned. It will be conquered by Gospel values, forgetting oneself in serving others rather than exploiting or oppressing them [38.1–6].

Solidarity in society is valid, when its members recognize one another as persons. 'Those who are more influential because they have a greater share of goods and common services should feel responsible for the weaker and be ready to help them. Those who are weaker for their part, in the same spirit of solidarity, should not adopt a purely passive attitude or one that is destructive of the social fabric, but while claiming their legitimate rights should do what they can for the good of all. The intermediate groups, in their turn, should not selfishly insist on their particular interests, but respect the interest of others. There are signs of growing solidarity in the world today especially of the poor among themselves. The Church stands by them, while she does not lose sight of the context of the common good. Internationally, interdependence must become solidarity based on the principle that goods were created for all so that the exploitation, oppression and annihilation of others, nation or person, is not countenanced. We are to see our neighbours as helpers, not things to be exploited, since all are made by God. '*Opus justitiae pax*' ('peace is the work of justice'), was the motto of Pius XII taken from the Bible: by extension of this, the same Scriptures tell us that '*opus solidaritatis, pax*' ('peace is the work of solidarity') [39].

Solidarity and faith are intimately linked. Like charity, solidarity seeks to go beyond itself because in one's neighbour is the image of God. Beyond human and natural needs there is a new model of unity for the human race, the reflection of the one God in three persons, in every human being. That is what we Christians mean by communion, and solidarity must help to build up this unity. The example of many saints, for example St Peter Claver and St Maximilian Kolbe, should be before us as models of this solidarity [40.1–4].

## VI. Some particular guidelines

The Church has no technical solutions to offer; 'she does not propose economic and political systems or programmes nor does she show preference for one social political system rather than another': she seeks only to defend human dignity and freedom to exercise her ministry. As an expert in humanity she has something to say on the moral aspect of development, because development cannot be considered merely as a technical matter. Drawing on her social teaching she applies her truth to the moral issues; her social doctrine is 'not a third way between liberal capitalism and Marxist collectivism, nor a possible alternative to other solutions ... it constitutes a category of its own'. Nor is it an ideology, but the result of

> an accurate formulation of the results of careful reflection on the complex realities of human existence in the light of faith, and the Church's tradition. Its main aim is to interpret these realities, determining their conformity with or divergence from the lines of the Gospel teaching on man and his vocation.

Its aim is thus to guide human behaviour; therefore it is theological and not ideological; it is part of moral theology. Teaching and spreading her social doctrine is part of the Church's evangelizing mission; it gives rise to a commitment to justice according to each one's individual role. Condemnation of evils is part of the Church's prophetic role, but 'proclamation is always more important than condemnation' [41.1–9].

Today certain of its propositions are particularly crucial. The option for the poor, that the goods of the world are for all and that accordingly all private property has a social mortgage on it, the defence of human rights and of religious freedom and economic initiative, are among them [42]. The reform of international trade and of the financial system to make them more just in their operations towards the underdeveloped countries, is needed [43.1–7]. However 'development above all demands a spirit of initiative on the part of the countries which need it'. The needs of each are different but more self-affirmation by citizens, the rule of law and promotion of human rights is necessary for all. Some countries need to increase food production, others to reform certain unjust structures and in particular corrupt political systems, replacing the latter by democratic and participatory ones [44.1–5]. In their turn all these measures require international co-operation in solidarity to make them fruitful [45.1–4].

## VII. Conclusion

People and nations aspire to be free; liberation theology responded to this deep need. The positive value and the deviations of this theology have recently been 'appropriately pointed out by the Church's magisterium'. Liberation and development 'require the exercise of solidarity especially with the poor; where love and truth are missing the liberation process results in the death of freedom (*Libertatis Conscientia* 24)' [46.1–6]. The Church has confidence in liberation because she has confidence in man himself, made in God's image and redeemed by Christ. This appeal is to all men to join in this task anew [47.1–9]. Though not identified with the kingdom, all temporal action in this direction is an anticipation of that kingdom. However limited and passing temporal things are, they are sanctified through Christ and the Eucharist [48.1–6]. To Mary we look for aid in our difficulties that she may intercede with her son for us, and all are invited to reflect on the prayer of the Mass for the Development of Peoples which asks God to give us a sense of our oneness in him so that in love we can ensure justice, peace and equality for all [49.1–5].

## 2 *Centesimus Annus* (1991)

### (i) Background; the collapse of real socialism

*Redemptor Hominis* gave us a powerful statement of John Paul II's teaching on man, and the human rights that are his. *Laborem Exercens* provided a statement of equal force on the nature of human work and the rights of labour, by hand and by brain, while *Sollicitudo Rei Socialis* updated John XXIII's, the Council's and Paul VI's teaching on the social problem world wide and gave us new insights into solutions. *Centesimus Annus* deals with aspects of all these questions in the context of a consideration of the ethics of economic systems and the light of the hundredth anniversary of *Rerum Novarum*, which famously happened to coincide with the collapse of those economic systems of real socialism which had once for millions held out the hopes of a better life, but ended only in cynicism and despair. That a man of his background, experience, talents and natural interests should have been called to the Papacy at this crucial juncture in the life of the Church and of society internationally has been of great significance and influence in the Church and in the affairs of nations. In nothing more does this appear than in his role in the events in Poland since his election, and his influence on the wider world in the light of the decline of Soviet power and the events that triggered it. The coincidence of the hundredth anniversary of the publication of Leo's great encyclical then gave him the opportunity of reflecting on the signs of the times over the last century, which he was uniquely equipped to do, as a person and in the discharge of his great office.

The collapse of real socialism[3] was one in which the Church, and the Church in Poland in particular, played an important role, though clearly it was only one of the many factors that led to the collapse; the system had been rotting from the inside from its beginning and the rot became terminal in the 1970s and 1980s; it is easy now to see with benefit of hindsight that it was only a matter of time before it would disintegrate. The question was, would it do so violently and in bloodshed on a massive scale, or would it do so reasonably quietly; that it did the latter owes much to John Paul II's influence as we shall see.

The teaching of the Church had realized the intrinsic impossibility of the Marxist dream from the beginning on both historical – sociological and theological grounds; the theory on which it was based disregarded the facts of human experience and completely misunderstood human nature; it also denied the reality of God and his plan for his world and his people. Yet until the analysis was confirmed dramatically by events, few accepted the Church's position. For a long time it was possible to believe it did work. In Russia where it took deepest root, the ruthlessness of Stalin and his policies in the 1930s, which continued and gathered strength in the conflict with Nazi Germany in the 1940s, resulted in rapid industrialization and then national survival. It was only as the 1950s progressed, and the Russian people began to realize how Stalin had perverted the idealism that was supposed to infuse the cause, and made it serve his megalomania, that it was made evident to all that the contradictions and impossibilities of the system were every bit as real and as cruel in their effects as calm thought and reflection in the light of human experience had known they would be.

The predictions of Leo XIII and Pius XI that exaltation of the collectivity over the person would destroy communism were proved to be correct. There was an increasing awareness among political and economic realists in the USSR that it was just not working. The growing lack of confidence in it, and that at the highest level, forced upon them the realization that it had to be reformed before it collapsed, if indeed it could be saved in time. Before them therefore yawned a chasm of uncertainty: could it survive the reforms necessary to make it work, in that those reforms would at the very least threaten profoundly the totalitarian basis of its operations, politically and militarily, and were likely to destroy them altogether? Once the old guard was gone, these questions would out, no matter what steps were taken to repress them.

Stalin died in 1953 and a triumvirate of Malenkov, Molotov and Beria ruled briefly, until the latter was executed for plotting against the others. In the aftermath of the power struggle that followed, Nikita Khrushchev, General Secretary of the Party in succession to Stalin, emerged as joint leader with Bulganin in 1955. There had to be change, but what change? Malenkov had sought to introduce consumer-oriented economic policies but they were not at the time acceptable; Khrushchev therefore compromised with the continuance of modified Stalinist economics combined with a conciliatory foreign policy. At the Twentieth Party Conference in 1956 he faced the problem of Stalin's legacy head on and denounced him as a tyrant whose persecution mania had resulted in mass arrest, torture and execution of thousands of party members, and in the next two years he introduced measures which were intended to stimulate production by giving greater responsibility and incentive to the local management. So confident was he of success that he openly announced his ambition of overtaking the economies of capitalist countries in so doing. Meanwhile he had ousted his rivals from power within the party in 1957, then ditched Bulganin in 1958, so that he exercised supreme authority.

His abilities, opportunities and luck did not match his ambitions; by 1962 his policies were failures and he gave way in 1964 to Leonid Brezhnev (1964–82) who chose to proceed by consensus and presided over 18 years of Stalinist stagnation which finally condemned the system; its decline accelerated so far and so fast in this period that nothing could redeem it. Yuri Andropov (1982–4) and Konstantin Chernenko (1984–5) attempted to tackle the problems but they were old and tired and they too failed; it was not until Gorbachev, a 51-year-old, took over in 1985 that a comprehensive attempt could be made to sort out the chaos. Gogol's *Inspector General* was a satire on the weaknesses of the Tsarist bureaucracy in the last century and

> ironically Soviet Communism reinforced some of the basest Tsarist traditions. Over the past seven decades, the system had degenerated into one that penalized initiative, efficiency, decency, and responsibility while rewarding opportunism, laziness, sloganeering and deviousness.[4]

Gorbachev set out to try to reverse these trends, his policies of restructuring (*perestroika*) the massive State organizations which inhibited efficiency and enterprise, and openness (*glasnost*) which made it possible openly to criticize those in authority at all levels, being the means he proposed. They turned out to be excellent for goading into opposition those who had benefited from the system, but they were quite hopelessly inadequate for reversing the trend of decline. The whole structure had to be replaced from the lowest to the highest levels. Greater participation by the people, which hopefully would revive the sense of personal moral responsibility which 70 years of culture of dependence on the State had almost destroyed, was the only hope; but one lesson that such participation had taught democratic societies was that it could only be built up on the infrastructure of a civil society, and above all a free economy. Yet it was precisely this that the Soviet State had almost entirely destroyed. Autonomous social organizations directing their own affairs in cultural, educational, academic, economic and professional fields did not exist in the USSR.

It remains to be seen whether the Russian people are going to make up for the terrible poverty of political culture that exists in their country, and in the long term lay the foundations for a cultural, political and economic freedom which is positive, open to change and development and yet firmly based and stable enough to absorb the shocks it is bound to experience as the effort is maintained, but major credit goes to Gorbachev for setting in train the events which led to the abandonment of the planned economy as the USSR had known it. He also refused to encourage any member of the Soviet bloc to use force, or try to use it to challenge peaceful protest against the Soviet system as discontent grew in the 1980s. He recognized the writing on the wall: the system as applied had failed, and he refused to inflict any more suffering on people who rejected it.

In East Germany in 1953 unrest had been met by violence and in 1961 it became the first modern State to try to fence in its people

from defection to, or corruption by, the West, in building the
Berlin wall. Riots and rebellion in Poland and Hungary in 1956,
and in Czechoslovakia in 1968, were crushed by the military. But
when in the 1980s, the first signs of what turned out to be the final
assault on the Soviet regimes appeared in Eastern Europe, especially in Poland, there was no encouragement from Moscow to
send in the tanks. There was a realism about Gorbachev's approach
which made him aware that it was useless, but there was something
else there too; Gorbachev exuded a genuine humanism; although
he had been steeped in the deceits and the cruelties of the old
regime, the experience had been unable to destroy his better
instincts. The danger was that as the Soviet monolith collapsed, as
he refused to defend it by repression, it might lead to widespread
armed revolution or counter-revolution and further tyranny.

Since force had established the Soviet system in Russia in 1917
against the social democratic majority wanting constitutional
change and evolutionary reform, force had been the communist
way everywhere; in some cases backed by popular support, active or
passive, in most cases not. In 1948–9 in China, it was revolution
which brought communism into control of the State with popular
support. In Cuba in 1959, it was the perversion of what was originally a social democratic revolution which put the communists in
power. Communism was co-opted to serve the revolution when
Castro found he needed a philosophy if he was to rule effectively.
Then throughout the 1960s and 1970s, bemused by Marxist
doctrine and the apparent success of the Soviet system in Russia,
China and in Cuba, South East Asia, Africa and South America
were afflicted with attempted socialist revolutions. Their main
effect on the one hand was to cause terrible suffering to the people
supposedly being liberated, and on the other to give aggressive
right-wing factions and regimes the excuse they needed to identify
every move for freedom, justified or not, as a communist plot to be
countered by any means available, and to use it as an excuse
further to oppress the people.

In the long run communism penalized the poor it was, theoretically at least, designed to help because its insistence on the State
ownership of productive goods, and the denial of economic
freedom meant that it could not harness the energies of man, who
wants above all to be free, to produce the kind of wealth that is
necessary if the poor were to be provided with access to the means
of a decent life. Denying him economic freedom meant denying
his political freedom too, and so a double slavery was fastened on
him. In countries where such social, political and economic

freedom exists, there are many unable to have access to a decent livelihood, it is true, but that is a defect of the political and social will to give justice to all; it is not a defect of freedom in itself. Be that as it may, the Russian people rightfully concluded that no tinkering with their system would improve it fundamentally, and they needed little persuasion to follow where Gorbachev led. With the home of the Revolution rejecting it, it could not be maintained in Eastern Europe.

Given the failure of the Soviet economy to meet the needs of the people, and the failure of confidence within the Party itself in the relevance of the dogma they had been led to believe would solve all problems, the whole vast enterprise was on the road to self-destruction without any outside help. It was a question of how and in what way the end would come, and here outside influences were important, not only for the Soviet system itself but for the world at large. For both, a reasonably peaceful transition to whatever followed the collapse of everything that had held State and society together was in their best interests. Even if such a transition passed off without too much destruction and violence, or with little or none, the problems were bound to be immense. Had it led to considerable violence or bloodshed initially there is no telling what widespread sufferings might have had to be endured, nor what the ultimate effects might have been; nuclear war might well have been one of them.

No State or society had ever tried to make such a fundamental adjustment in its aims and purposes so suddenly and violently, yet more or less peacefully, rejecting a founding ideal so absolutely, and doing so consciously while seeking an alternative, and trying to rebuild around it. Only desperation bred by the hopeless failure of the inherited system compelled the process. No evolution to an alternative would be other than painful nor could fail to avoid inflicting most of that pain on those who had the weakest defences against it, at least in the crucial first stages. Both the Industrial Revolution under liberal capitalism and the rapid growth of industry under the five-year plans in Russia taught as much. But in Britain the combined social strength of the forces against them had prevented the suffering registering any effective self-defence until the 1830s, some fifty years or so after industrialization began to gather pace. With a proletariat that had an effective basic education and thorough politicization under the Soviet regime, and in what was by the late 1980s an increasingly open society even in Russia, and which since then has become wide open, where the modern media of communication exist and which has the outward forms of democracy, not to say populism tending to extremes of right and left, there is still no telling where the experiment will take those engaged in it.

That the first stage of this revolution took place with a peacefulness that gave everyone, in the Soviet bloc and without it, at least a chance to catch their breath, was the secret of its success. That it was peaceful was in its turn due largely to its Polish origins and to the influence within that country of the Catholic Church. 'If I was forced to name a single date for the "beginning of the end" in [the] inner history of Eastern Europe,' writes Timothy Garton Ash who is one of the most knowledgeable Western commentators on these matters, 'it would be June 1979 ... the Pope's first great pilgrimage'. He accepts that the judgement may seem to be excessively Polocentric, but it is not so in the light of what that pilgrimage meant. Here for the first time we saw that

> massive, sustained and supremely peaceful and self-disciplined manifestation of social unity, the gentle crowd against the Party-State, which was both the hallmark and the essential domestic catalyst of change in 1989, in every country except Romania,

and even in Romania the violence did not emanate from the crowds. The Pope's visit was followed, just over a year later, by the birth of *Solidarity*, and without the Pope's visit it is doubtful that there would have been a *Solidarity*.[5] It was this organization, a variegated trade union, inexperienced, learning by doing, and with no native models to guide it, which had to work out, on the hoof and under pressure from all sides, not only how to do the unthinkable in challenging the communist State industrially in defence of workers' rights, but also to provide the umbrella within which an even more variegated cluster of opposition groups could rebuild civil society as a preliminary to exercising its right to elect a government and choose a form of State.

Garton Ash shows that Solidarity was the start of a new kind of politics in Eastern Europe, a politics of self-organization and negotiation of the transition to a new society. By the 1980s there had been nearly forty years of peace and stability, but the ordinary men and women in the eastern bloc had gained very little from it in economic terms and nothing at all in political terms. Successive attempts to challenge the regimes since the 1950s had all met with bloody repression, and in all this time all had been constrained to repeat the meaningless jargon about brotherhood and working together to produce the new socialist man and his new socialist paradise. An atmosphere of official lying produced a morally, intel-

lectually and spiritually devastated society, and this fatally weakened the structure of the State from the lowest to the highest.
Everyone had had a basic education under the socialist State, and
one that from the first had been highly politicized in the State's
favour; but now this basically literate and politicized people had
totally lost patience with the nonsense and dishonesty with which
they had been forced to live. Their sense of civic responsibility as
part of the system had been appealed to by the regime whenever
dissidents emerged, but that civic responsibility was now turned to
another purpose – self-defence against the regime of lies and
oppression.

The idea of civic society, a society older and with a greater moral
legitimacy than the State, was given practical expression by the
dissenters. Indeed it was only out of such a civic society that an
honest and morally legitimate State could emerge. It made possible a social structure in which people wanted to be frank with each
other because it was only on that basis they could work together
peacefully for common ends out of personal conviction, freely
using their own initiative. Citizenship came to be seen as a right
and a privilege, belonging to individual men and women who
became aware they possessed personal dignity and accepted
responsibility for their actions; citizens 'with rights, but also with
duties, freely associating in civil society'.[6]

John Paul II's presence in the country in 1979, and his moral
support afterwards gave the spontaneous formation of Solidarity
hope in its beginnings, and priceless assistance as it developed to
maturity. The gradual withdrawal from those who governed of the
moral right to lead and rule, and the transference of those rights
to this organization was the result of Solidarity's own self-disci-
plined search for a way through the moral wilderness of the official
order. It was seeking a better life, and self-discipline made it possible for the peaceful overthrow of the Socialist State to take place.
Inevitable as is seems now that Solidarity would succeed, that was
by no means certain at the time. The patience and self control
needed in waiting for the regime to self destruct by its incompetence required a self-discipline from the ordinary workers which
amounted to the heroic, given what they had been through and
the intensity of their anger at what still was. This is where the
recruitment of all the positive traditions of Poland, under the leadership of a Church, and above all a man such as John Paul II, was
the key to the peaceful process of the revolution.

The preaching of 32 sermons during 9 days, 2–10 June 1979,
during his first visit to his country as Pope, laid the foundations.

They did not preach politics or revolution: they preached the spiritual revolution in which conscience confronted 'the fear and acquiescence that kept society in the grip of "the power"'.[7] Peace, he told his people, can only come when basic human rights, including a nation's right to freedom, and its own culture, are assured. The Church, aware that the temporal dimension of life is realized in political, economic and cultural society, continually rediscovers its own mission by establishing a religious relationship with man in these sectors of life and society, consolidating him in his natural social bonds. Far from religion being the expression and cause of alienation, it was the evangelical and sacramental mission of the Church to defend human rights, to help humanity to live creatively, and to make men and women more devoted servants of one another, of their families and society. The only privilege the Church sought was that of freedom to preach her message.

The message was intensely christological. Christ cannot be excluded from human history; to attempt to do so is an offence against God and humanity, and the Pope had his listeners insisting, 'We want God, we want God in the family, in schools, in government orders'. Christ will never agree, he told them, 'that man is only a means of production'. The only danger is that man will resist the challenge of the honest truth as he knows it; he must resist the temptation to want only to fit into things, to float in conformity. He reminded them that the Christian faith and truth had been woven into the national cultures of the Slavic peoples and that religious freedom is the core and root of those cultural values. Respect for the rights of every member of a family or a nation go along with the rights of self-determination of nations and their own culture. Some 13 million Poles heard him in these nine days of June 1979. The seeds of Solidarity had been well and truly sown.

The call had been to break through the self-centredness and isolation, the atomization, of the culture of the lie; he had revived the Polish tradition of self-sacrifice and, much more difficult, he had shown that the tradition was to be reborn peacefully. He clarified that sense of civic society to which they had been groping. They had been sure who they were against; now they knew what they were for and who they were with. They could trust each other now; they were society and the country was theirs. But they had to be patient. So great was the emotion and the fervour that the situation could have ended in bloodshed and disorder, in disaster in other words, had his lead not been so calm and assured and utterly peaceful. As it was Poland turned not to violence but to Solidarity.

The organization was born in the two weeks of August 1979 at

Gdansk's Lenin Shipyard when a strike broke out in protest against price increases. With deadlock reached, and fear of violence and Russia intervention in the background, the bishops' conference disabused the regime of any notion that they would act as broker with the strikers; quoting the Vatican Council's assertion of the right of association in free trade unions, it backed the strikers' rights for such a union.[8] It was a breakthrough of immense importance; the communist State for the first time had to negotiate with a free trade union, one as yet without a clear legal status, and soon to be, for a time, made illegal with the declaration of martial law in 1981, but it was still trusted by the hierarchy as the agency through which freedom would come; above all it had opted for peaceful attainment of its aims, by the moral strength of its case and the moral strength of its members' discipline and self-control. They had demonstrated that revolution need not be violent if it was morally justified and morally pursued.

The foundation of Solidarity then was only a beginning. It had to prove itself. By early 1981 there were signs that it might not do that. There were wildcat and organized strikes in disorderly progress, and a bruising struggle over the formation of rural Solidarity. At this juncture, when all was fluctuating and in conflict, on 13 May John Paul II was shot in St Peter's Square and two weeks later, on 28 May, Cardinal Wyszynski died of cancer; the inspirer of Solidarity was out of the reckoning for a while and its staunchest support in the early difficult days was dead. Archbishop Glemp, who succeeded the Cardinal had not the experience, the stature nor the personal authority of his predecessor and he handled the situation less surely. The situation in Poland continued to deteriorate, General Jaruzelski took over as Communist Party leader on 18 October, and on 12 December a state of war, effectively martial law, was proclaimed; Solidarity was outlawed and remained so until 1988.

Martial law lasted until June 1983 and it was a time of gloom and hopelessness; when it was over there were tensions in the Church about how to respond to the situation of deadlock, Archbishop Glemp resisting any attempt to give the Church a more active role in opposition to the regime. But there was quiet progress too; the Solidarity leaders became aware that the reconstruction of civil society was a precondition of political and economic change, and its supporters began to take an even bigger part in the educational and cultural programmes which were being developed, while John Paul II's second visit to Poland in May 1983, just before the ending of martial law, stemmed the creeping despair and replaced it with hope. It also confirmed the union's position, since, in his dealings with Jaruzelski, John Paul rejected any Church alliance with the State in a form of corporatism. The proper channel for negotiations over resolving the problems was he insisted, Solidarity.

The depth of the antagonism of the regime was revealed in the kidnapping and death in October 1984 of Fr Popieluszcko, chaplain to the Warsaw workers, and this threatened to provoke a violent reaction, against which Lech Walesa pleaded passionately. In June 1987 came the Pope's third visit to his homeland, during which he preached on the theme of 'solidarity' in Gdansk and Gdynia, seeking to provide the movement with solid theological and philosophical foundations. In the April and May of 1988 there were strikes over pay at Nowa Huta and Gdansk, while demonstrations took place in other cities, and the end of Polish communism was in sight. After a last attempt to get the Church to negotiate with it in search of a settlement failed, the regime accepted the inevitable, and on 6 February 1989 Solidarity joined with others in round table talks. In the partially free elections of 4 June its candidates swept the board and on 24 August the first non-communist Prime Minister is an Iron-Curtain country took office in Poland.

The events in Poland were reflected in their different ways throughout the communist States of Eastern Europe in 1989 and 1990. Given the violent repression of its first attempts at freedom in 1956, Hungary's liberation was of great symbolic significance. The leader then had been Imre Nagy, who had been executed along with his closest associates after the defeat in that year. Their memory was kept fresh by the people, so much so that in 1988, as János Kádar, the Russian-backed leader who had replaced Nagy and had held power since, was dying, the Party decided to allow the posthumous rehabilitation of Nagy, in order to retain some credibility and support during the transition to a new regime. Accordingly on 16 June, he and those who died with him were duly honoured in a great celebration held in Budapest's Heroes' Square. Three days before the funeral, the authorities met with the various opposition groups in a manner that was roughly modelled on that between the Jaruzelski regime and the Polish round table.[9] There were confused negotiations and ambiguous agreements, combined with backstairs manoeuvrings between new and old political groupings over the next months before, on 25 March 1990, free elections paved the way for a free Hungary.

Events in Hungary were linked with those in Germany. As Hungary began moving to freedom in May 1989, so the trickle of East Germans escaping over the border increased, and by the end of October became a flood. The Church supported peaceful opposition which went on throughout the summer; Gorbachev's intervention meant the end of the Berlin wall, and he curtly warned the East German dictator that those who did not move with the times would be punished by events; it made no impression on Honecker who carried on as if nothing had changed. Meanwhile in Leipzig the same massive peaceful protests as had been seen in Poland began to rock the regime; by early 1990 the move for change, not only for the removal of the last vestiges of communism but the reunion of East and West Germany was irresistible, and so it came about.

Czechoslovakia's dash for freedom, at the end of a long battle with repression which was typified in the efforts of the Charter 77 group, began with the demonstration on 17 November 1989 in Prague to mark the fiftieth anniversary of the death of Jan Opletal, a student murdered by the Nazis. The occasion of this officially approved gathering by accident or design soon turned into a wholesale and growing demonstration against the current regime, and the riot police reacted violently. On the next two days a students' strike received wide support and larger and larger demonstrations over the next six or seven days kept the pressure on the government, while over the next weeks the various opposition groups came together to organize what became known as the Velvet Revolution; by 10 December the old regime had resigned and Václav Havel became President.

Finally in December 1990 Nicolae Ceauşescu, the Romanian dictator, like Honecker incapable of appreciating that his time was up, was overthrown and killed in a bloody coup. To all this the Russians turned a blind eye. Gorbachev had let it be known in the summer of 1989 that he would not intervene to prop up threatened regimes. Brezhnev's doctrine of 'limited sovereignty' which had justified the invasion of Czechoslovakia in 1958 was no more.[10]

There were then violent incidents on the road to freedom, but they were few and they were not the mark of the movement as a whole. That mark had been given to it by Solidarity. Poland, pioneering a new kind of politics of self-organization, negotiated the transition from communism to freedom. The failed economics of communism played its part in rousing the people, but it was their political hopes which bore them on, spurred by popular outrage at the attempt by the regimes to curb them. The overthrow of communism was achieved by the insistence of the people that they would no longer tolerate its mind-numbing daily lies and hypocrisies. The motto of 1989 was *magna est veritas et praevalebit*, as the Latin had it (the truth is great and it will prevail), and never was the truth of an adage more clearly demonstrated. It was the peaceful crowds, in their tens and hundreds of thousands, demanding freedom and the dismissal of all those who would prevent it, which conquered. What violence there was elsewhere was authoritarian police violence, and there was on the whole little of that.

The revolutions then were manifestations of the vitality of peaceful civil society. The demands were for the right of association, 'national, regional, local and professional, which would be voluntary, authentic, democratic, and first and last, not controlled or manipulated by the Party or the Party State'. People should be non-violent, polite, tolerant. Civil and civilian meant something again; the idea of citizenship had to be taken seriously.[11] The concepts of 'civic' and 'citizenship' survived the corruption of language that the Soviet system produced. In Poland it was Solidarity's 'Citizens' Parliamentary Club', the 'Civic Forum' in Czechoslovakia and the citizens' initiatives in East Germany, which were the focus of organization. People found they could defy the totalitarian State with its lies and pretences, and claim the dignity of being free, responsible individuals with the rights and duties which that dignity involved.

These events were occurring when the encyclical which celebrated the centenary of *Rerum Novarum* was in preparation. In the latter, Leo XIII had insisted that the basis of any concerted attempt to improve the conditions of labour had to be the maintenance of the right of the responsible private ownership of productive goods, tempered by just laws for the common good, and the right of association for labour to organize in its own defence. These principles were not new; they were embedded in the tradition, and while liberal capitalism had ignored those which concerned the rights of the workers and the community, its belief in the value of private enterprise, though exaggerated and taken out of its context, was born of that tradition also. The collapse of real socialism, and the increasing capacity of private enterprise economies to moderate their excesses in the light of the power of organized labour and the extension of the franchise, while at the same time showing their ability to supply the material needs of their people, proved the soundness of this analysis.

The reaction against the excesses and social irresponsibility of liberal capitalism had largely determined the political agenda in the capitalist democracies in the twentieth century. Roosevelt's New Deal in the 1930s still influenced American thinking in the post-1945 years, while in Europe the triumph of the Labour Party in the United Kingdom, and of the Social Democrats and Christian Democrats and their allies in Europe ensured that political, social and economic policies would take note of the needs of all the people. It was a time when left-wing politics were fashionable and socialism occupied the moral high ground. Now that had changed. The collapse of real socialism was accompanied by the resurgence of strongly ideological right-wing, market-favouring theorists and parties, and even the milder forms of left-wing politics were at a discount. All this challenged the Christian conscience and the social teaching of the Church had to take note of the changing situation. In his third social encyclical, John Paul II responded to this need.

## (ii)  Summary of Centesimus Annus[12]

There is an Introduction [1–3] and six Chapters: I. Characteristics of *Rerum Novarum* [4–11], II. Towards the new things of today [12–21], III. The year 1989 [22–29], IV. Private property and the universal purpose of material goods [30–43], V. The State and culture [44–52], and VI. Man is the way of the Church [53–62].

### Introduction

*Rerum Novarum* and subsequent documents constitute what has 'come to be called the Church's social doctrine, teaching, or even social magisterium' [2.1–2]. Its re-reading on the occasion of its centenary

> will not only confirm the permanent value of such a teaching, but will also manifest the true meaning of the Church's tradition ... built on what 'the Apostles passed down to the Church',

a tradition which contains things both old and new and which absorbs into itself the experience of the faithful. It will also reflect on recent events in the light of the needs of evangelization, without passing definitive judgements on them, since that is not within the magisterium's specific domain [3.1–5].

### I. Characteristics of *Rerum Novarum*

Towards the end of the last century, the final stages of the evolution of a new form of political and economic order were taking place. There had been radical changes in science, technology and ideology. In politics there was a new conception of society and State and of authority itself. In economics, science and its practical application had revolutionized production and property in the form of capital, and labour for wages determined by the need for profits, a mere commodity without consideration of human need, resulted in 'a society divided into two classes separated by a deep chasm'. Leo XIII intervened, drawing on his own previous encyclicals on political matters, the inspiration of his predecessors, together with the work of the Catholic social movement in the nineteenth century [4.1–5]. The conditions set man against man as if they were wolves, and Leo set out to restore peace, condemning the class struggle, while insisting peace could only be built on justice. In this situation he showed that the Church, as part of her evangelizing message, had a teaching to meet the needs of the time, dealing with a conflict situation without degrading the human dignity of those involved. The present world very much needs the proclamation of such a social doctrine. The new evangelization which it requires 'must include among its essential elements a proclamation of the Church's social doctrine' for there is no solution to the social question apart from the Gospel [5.1–6].

Leo's encyclical reaffirmed the dignity of work, work as personal and social. The right to property was also strenuously defended, though it was not an absolute right but conditioned by the universal destination of the world's goods. That it mainly spoke in terms of land ownership does not invalidate the necessity of affirming 'the right to possess the things necessary for one's personal development ... whatever concrete form that right may take' [6.1–3]. The right of association in trade unions was affirmed, a right which precedes the State and cannot be denied by it; the worker has also the right to conditions of work which respect human standards according to age and sex; labour agreements should protect these standards [7.1–3]. Wages should also be just and free; contract alone does not necessarily ensure that. Accordingly it is for the public authority to see that it does. These principles, laid down when liberal capitalism was sweeping forward unchecked, unfortunately need to be repeated today because such capitalism still exists [8.1–3]. The right of workers to Sunday rest should also be guaranteed; this is an aspect of that religious freedom which is so much the Church's current concern [9.1–2].

The duty of the State to defend the poor was also dealt with. Liberalism was not mentioned directly but its defects are clearly in mind here. The poor have no other defender and it is the State's duty in justice to fulfil its role in this, having special care to protect them. The lesson is apt today where poverty abounds still; it is a matter of justice then but it is also demanded by solidarity; Leo XIII used the term 'friendship' already found in Greek philosophy, Pius XI referred to 'social charity', Paul VI expanded the concept, speaking of a 'civilization of love' [10.1–3]. What we today call the 'preferential option for the poor' was always there, and Leo XIII saw that this gave the State certain obligations in the light of the common good, but he did not think State action could answer every social problem. The family and society are prior to the State and the role of the latter is to protect their rights. These and other themes are still relevant today. It is necessary

> to keep in mind that ... the guiding principle of Leo's encyclical, and all of the social doctrine of the Church, is a correct view of the human person ... the only creature God willed for itself.

On him God imprinted his own image; because of this he has rights which flow from his very dignity as a person, apart from those which correspond to work he performs [11.1–3].

## II. Towards the new things of today

The commemoration can hardly fail to take account of the events of 1989–90 which confirm Leo's insights and those of his successors. He saw the negative consequences of socialism before it was put into practice; aware of the terrible sufferings of the working class, he knew that the social ownership of the means of production would not solve the problems of their poverty [12.1–4]. The anthropology of socialism is wrong; it subordinates man to the social organism and deprives him of freedom. Christianity by contrast sees the social nature of man expressed in the family and other groups below State level, each with its own autonomy, subject to the common good. The error of atheism in this is closely allied with the rationalism of the Enlightenment which had a mechanistic view of human and social reality [13.1–4]. There is no denying that social conflict is a fact and Leo XIII 'did not intend to condemn every possible form [of the conflict] ... Christians must often take a position, honestly and decisively', and a struggle for social justice can be positive. But the socialist understanding of class struggle knows no moral restraint and puts force above the law; 'what is pursued is not the general good ... but a partisan interest which ... sets out to destroy whatever is in its way'. Inevitably this results in contempt for human beings. Marxist class struggle shares this latter characteristic with militarism and imperialism, and all three have their roots in atheism [14.1–2].

*Rerum Novarum* accepted that, while economic life is autonomous and independent of the State, the State must provide the right juridical framework for its functioning. Society and the State must protect the employee from exploitation and, according to the principle of subsidiarity, help to create the right conditions for economic freedom 'which will lead to abundant opportunities for employment and the sources of wealth [creation]' [15.1–6]. Such measures have been introduced by various States, often as a result of pressure by workers' movements. There is good reason for thinking that Leo's encyclical was not without its influence in all this. Unfortunately the need for reform was not fully accepted at the time [16.1–3].

The encyclical assumes the connection between freedom and truth also, and the failure to accept this was an even greater disaster because freedom then becomes merely self-love unrestrained by justice. Hence the destructive wars that ravaged Europe and the world between 1914 and 1945; only pent-up injustice explains them and the hatred they revealed. *Rerum Novarum* showed how violence and hatred could be overcome by justice [17.1–3]. A period of 'no general war' rather than real peace followed 1945, with its international arms race and sporadic violence. The scientific and technological effort that should have gone into solving the problems of poverty internationally were diverted into an ever more sophisticated arms race, and the major power blocs encouraged subversion throughout the third world, polarizing it for their own political purposes [18.1–3]. Some countries were moved to counter the communist threat by fostering democratic freedom, prosperity and social justice, free market mechanisms, social harmony, the right of association, steady economic growth, a better future for people and their families, and social security, combined with a measure of public control 'which upholds the common destination of material goods'. Others relied on the national security State, depriving their people of basic freedoms under the pretext of the necessity of preventing communist infiltration. Still others still resorted to simple materialism, the affluent or consumer society, excluding spiritual values, so making the same basic mistake as Marxism by reducing man to the role of a slave of things [19.1–4].

Meanwhile decolonization gave many new countries a freedom which turned out to be largely illusory because of the dependence on foreign powers or economic interests. In the new countries, social and political life often lacked cohesion and

> a class of competent professional people capable of running the State apparatus in an honest and just way, [and] qualified personnel for managing the economy in an efficient and responsible manner;

many therefore saw Marxist Leninism as the answer [20.1–2]. Finally, there has been a new awareness of human rights and the rights of nations, and a realization of the need to correct the imbalances between the various regions of the world. Yet the overall balance on aid and development is not all positive, while the United Nations Organization has not found it possible to find a way of settling international disputes by peaceful means [21.1–2].

## III. The year 1989

In the 1980s some democratic regimes replaced totalitarianisms in Latin America, Africa and Asia, but it was the events in Eastern and Central Europe in 1989 and 1990 which were the most significant. The Church contributed to the movement which brought them about, and now that the new democracies face the problems of establishing themselves, they deserve the continuing support of Christians and all men of goodwill [22.1–2].

Violations of the rights of workers were prominent in the causes of the discontents that got things moving, especially through Solidarity in Poland. There, experience taught people the truth of Catholic social teaching. Almost everywhere the protest that brought about the downfall of unjust regimes was peaceful; truth and justice were its only weapons. 'The non-violent commitment of ... people ... refusing to yield to the force of power ... succeeded time after time in finding effective ways of bearing witness to the truth' [23.1–3]. Economic inefficiency stemming from restricting economic freedom and private ownership aided the protesters, while atheism produced a cultural void which led to a search for the religious roots of their national cultures and the rediscovery of 'the person of Christ himself as the existentially adequate response to the desire of every human heart for goodness, truth and life' [24.1–2]. The events of 1989 are an example of the success of willingness to negotiate, and of the Gospel spirit, in the face of evil which was totally uninhibited by moral principle. The struggle against it called for sacrifice in some way unthinkable without trust in God and the cross of Christ; they prevented the cowardice that succumbs to evil, as well as the violence that is greater than the evil it seeks to combat.

Freedom is also unintelligible without Christian revelation. Man, created for good, has in him a tendency to evil that is the result of original sin. Those therefore who aim at a perfect social organization where evil is impossible put themselves in the place of God, because only in his kingdom does this perfection exist. It is a kingdom which is not of this world although it throws light on the proper ordering of the earthly kingdom, and grace penetrates that order to give it life. The Christian view, in the light of its understanding of human nature, is that self-interest should be harmonized fruitfully with the common good: the alternative is the imposition of a deadening bureaucracy which stifles all initiative [25.1–2].

The events of 1989 have world-wide significance. The crisis of Marxism revealed that the workers' movement was making demands 'for justice and the dignity of work, in conformity with the social doctrine of the Church'. In the recent past many believers sought 'an impossible compromise between Marxism and Christianity' but now a reaffirmation of 'the positive value of an authentic theology of integral human liberation' is being made. What happened in 1989 in Central and Eastern Europe, the search for its own path of development, is important also for the third world [26.1–5].

In Eastern Europe itself, the very enormity of the changes in train causes great problems. They need the support of the international community that they may adjust to the new need [27.1–3]. Assistance given to these new countries on the other hand should not restrict that given to the third world. The savings on military expenditure will provide the means; the poor must not be able to feel they are a burden [28.1–3]. Nor must developments be seen purely in economic terms, but must build up a human, a more decent life for all and foster the right values. Old authoritarianisms are not necessarily dead, and while in developed countries there is often a promotion of purely material values, the problem in the new countries can be new forms of fundamentalism which are denying others full religious freedom [29.1–4].

### IV. Private property and the universal purpose of material goods

*Rerum Novarum* reaffirmed the natural right to private property based on the autonomy and independence of the person. It also reaffirmed that the right is not absolute, being subordinated to the common purpose of created goods according to Christ's warning that all will be called to account for the use of their possessions; St Thomas's teaching remains relevant here and this tradition has been restated by the Second Vatican Council [30.1–3]. This common purpose of goods stems from God's gift of the earth to all. But the earth needs to be worked to yield its fruits to man, using the intelligence and freedom God gave him. 'In this way he makes part of the earth his very own ... the part he has acquired through work, this is the origin of individual property'. Nor must the individual stop others getting their own shares. 'Work and land therefore are the beginning of every human society' but they vary in the way they relate to each other. Today work, and work with and for others especially, is of greater importance as it becomes more productive [31.1–3].

Know-how, technology and skill, become the real source of wealth in the industrialized countries. 'The ability to foresee ... the needs of others and the combination of productive factors most adapted to satisfying those needs', an ability possessed by the person 'who produces something ... in order that others may use it after they have paid a just price ... through free bargaining' is increasingly such a source. Man's primary resource is man himself, working in conjunction with others in extended working communities; diligence, industriousness, courage, all are needed. Human freedom is the basis of all [32.1–3]. However, there are risks and problems connected with this process. Many today, perhaps the majority, do not have the means to take part in a productive system in which work is truly central. They have no likelihood of entering into the network of communication and knowledge which would make it possible for their qualities to be appreciated and utilized. So they crowd to the cities, especially in the third world. Attempts are even made to exterminate them by coercive forms of demographic control. Others face the conditions of ruthless capitalism which *Rerum Novarum* knew. These countries need fair access to international markets and the proper use of their human rather than their natural physical resources [33.1–5].

> It would appear that, on the level of individual nations and of international relations, the free market is the most efficient instrument for utilizing resources and effectively responding to needs but only for those needs which are solvent ... are endowed with purchasing power, whose resources are marketable ... capable of obtaining a satisfactory price.

Yet there are fundamental human needs 'which find no place on the market'. Those needs must be satisfied. People must be helped to develop their skills so they can enter the market: and even prior to the market there are things due to man as man, such as adequate wages, insurance for old age and unemployment, and protection for working conditions. In the third world situation the basic requirements of *Rerum Novarum* often still need to be met [34.1–2].

Here unions and other workers' organizations are particularly important in the struggle for justice; where the absolute predominance of capital remains, the aim should not be for real socialism which has failed, but for 'a society of free work, enterprise and participation', a market system which meets the needs of the whole society. 'The church acknowledges the legitimate role of profit ... this means that productive factors have been properly employed and ... human needs satisfied.' But profit making is not enough; profits can be earned while workers are 'humiliated and their dignity offended'. The purpose of business is 'not simply to make a profit ... other human and moral factors must be considered'. Nor is capitalism the only alternative model, given the collapse of real socialism, as said above. Barriers and monopolies which penalize underdeveloped countries also need to be dismantled; the problem of the foreign debt of the underdeveloped countries remains to be solved, if necessary by cancellation, as is happening to some extent [35.1–5].

Advanced economies have overcome the difficulties of supplying not only necessities but goods of sufficient quality and quantity to their people. They now face those of consumerism. An economic system 'does not possess criteria for correctly distinguishing new and higher forms of satisfying human needs' from those which 'hinder formation of a mature personality'. This has to come from sound education and the proper intervention of public authority. The widespread abuse of drugs, and the spread of pornography, are examples of artificial needs. It is not wrong to want to live better. What is wrong is to want more, solely to make enjoyment of material goods the end of life itself. 'Truth, beauty, goodness and communion with others' are the factors that should be predominant in determining lifestyles and all else. Where investment is concerned, for example, a moral choice is concerned; upon such choices depends the opportunity of the poor to use their labour [36.1–4].

Consumerism also leads to the irresponsible exploitation of the environment. Man was meant to co-operate with God the creator, in developing the world for his use: instead he sets himself up in the place of God and terrorizes it [37.1–2]. The human environment is also vandalized. It is right to worry about the natural habitat of animals, but there is too little regard for man's own moral habitat. Man is God's gift to man and he must respect the nature and moral structure of his being. Man receives from God his essential dignity, but he himself largely creates the environment which will mould his moral attitudes [38.1–2]. The family founded on marriage, the mutual gift of husband and wife, provides the environment in which children can develop their potentialities. But people are often discouraged from entering into stable relationships, the proper relationship for human reproduction. Children are 'things' one can have or not have according to taste. The family is the source of life, and yet society seems determined to destroy the sources of life, for example through abortion. Instead economic life has been absolutized, the possession of goods has become society's only value, ethical and religious considerations are ignored. Economic freedom is important, but it is only one aspect of freedom. When it becomes autonomous, man becomes a producer or consumer, rather than the subject who produces and consumes, and in consequence his very economic freedom oppresses him [39.1–5]. It is for the State to protect the common good such as the natural and human environment which the market does not protect, just as it once protected the workers against exploitation. The very importance and value of the market runs the risk of making it the subject of idolatry [40.1–2].

Marxism did not eliminate alienation; neither does Western consumerism whose work system diminishes its workers as human beings, using them simply as a means. But man needs to be recognized for his value as a person, made to transcend himself by giving himself to others and ultimately to God. A society which makes it difficult for him to make this gift of himself to others in solidarity is an alienated society. Western society is alienated; people use one another because they are concerned primarily with the possession and enjoyment of things; they are also manipulated by the means of mass communication [41.1–4]. After the fall of communism then, should capitalism be the model for the world? Yes,

if by capitalism is meant an economic system which recognizes the fundamental and positive role of business, the market, private property, and the resulting responsibility for the means of production ... free creativity in the economic sector ... although it would be better to speak of a 'business ... market ... or free economy.

The answer is No, however,

if by capitalism is meant a system in which the economic sector is not circumscribed within a strong juridical framework which

V · /·

places it at the service of human freedom ... and sees it as a
particular aspect of that freedom, the core of which is ethical
and religious.

Marginalization and exploitation still exist, especially in the third
world, as does alienation in the advanced nations. The collapse of
communism certainly removes an obstacle to facing these problems, but the danger is now of

a radical capitalist ideology which refuses even to consider them
in the conviction that any attempt to solve them is doomed to
failure and blindly entrusts their solution to the free development of market forces [42.1–3].

The Church presents no models; these only arise effectively out
of historical situations. Her social teaching 'recognizes the positive
value of the market and free enterprise' in the context of the
common good. It recognizes also

the legitimacy of workers' efforts to obtain full respect for their
dignity and gain broader areas of participation so that ... co-
operating with others and under the leadership of others ...
they can in a sense work for themselves.

The integral development of the person through work increases
productivity and efficiency, though it may weaken consolidated
power structures. A business is a society of persons, not only a
society of capital and there is still need for a broadly based workers'
movement.

In the light of today's new things we have to re-read the relationship between labour and capital. Man through his work uses
his freedom and intelligence to make the world serve him, working
also with and for others, fellow employees, suppliers, customers in
a growing solidarity. 'Ownership of the means of production in
industry or agriculture is just and legitimate if it serves useful
work.' The obligation to work implies the right to work, and
without this society is neither just nor can it be peaceful.
Ownership justifies itself in the creation of the opportunity to
work, and of human growth through it [43.1–4].

## V. The State and culture

Leo XIII saw the value of the legislative, executive and judiciary
distinction as one which protected political freedom. The totalitarian concept by contrast, in its Marxist Leninist form, gave the

State absolute power. Totalitarianism also denies there is a transcendent truth, in obedience to which man achieves his full identity, but without this 'there is no sure principle for guaranteeing just relations between people' [44.1–2]. Such a system consequently denied the Church her rights, as it denied the absolute moral values it taught; it absorbed also the nation, society and family [45.1–2].

The Church therefore values

> the democratic system inasmuch as it ensures the participation of citizens in making political choices, guarantees to the governed, the possibility of both electing and holding accountable those who govern them and of replacing them through peaceful means when appropriate.

Contrary to what is sometimes said, it is only in a democracy which accepts the reality of ultimate truth, that the democratic ideal is safe; otherwise ideas and convictions can be manipulated, and totalitarianism results. Christianity is not an ideology, does not claim to put 'socio-political realities in a rigid schema' but on the contrary accepts the diverse and imperfect patterns of history. But it insists on the transcendent dignity of the human person and its method is always to respect freedom which attains its full development in truth affirmed in dialogue [46.1–4].

The collapse of communism makes democracy attractive, and for that reason it needs to be stressed that human rights are essential to a sound democracy. Especially important are the right to life, even of the unborn, and the right to a full human development in the family, seeking the truth, and 'a share in the work that makes wise use of the earth's material resources' so that the family responsibilities can be met. In a sense, these rights are synthesized in religious freedom, and such rights are not necessarily respected even where democratic forms exist; some democracies seem at times 'to have lost the ability to make decisions aimed at the common good'. Electoral or financial power rather than justice or morality are the norm, and as a result of the absence of a coherent vision of the common good there is general disillusion among the people. That common good is more than the sum of particular interests; it is achieved through the integration of those interests in such a way that the dignity and rights of each person are correctly understood. The Church meanwhile respects the legitimate autonomy of the political order, expressing no preferences for particular institutions or constitutions; the dignity of the person is her concern [47.1–3].

Economic activity in a market economy presupposes individual freedom, private property, stable currency and efficient public services so that workers can enjoy the fruits of honest and efficient labour. The State has the duty to create conditions which will sustain business activity and job opportunities and remove obstacles to development. It can also intervene more positively to support weak systems on a temporary basis; the Welfare State's interventions to remedy poverty and deprivation must be in terms of subsidiary function, not of a Social Assistance State which creates self-serving bureaucracies and neglect of the real interests of those they are intended to serve. Some forms of need, that of refugees for example, are better served by those who are closest to them, acting as neighbours. They can only be really helped by 'those who offer them friendly support in addition to necessary care' [48.1–5].

Solidarity and charity, beginning with the support given by the family structure, is the need, and public policy should support this. Other intermediate societies between individual and State prevent life becoming impersonal. It can happen that the individual person is suffocated 'between two poles, State and marketplace'. But life does not have the market or the State for its purpose but truth, sought in dialogue with past and future generations [49.1–3]. It is from this search that a nation derives its character. Its heritage is always challenged by the young as they test its values in their own lives and distinguish true from false. Evangelization has a role in sustaining a culture in its progress towards truth [50.1–2]. The formation of a true culture requires the involvement of the whole man, and here the Church has a specific contribution to make. She teaches that God has placed the world in human hands so that man may grow through work, that the redemption has united all men, making them responsible for one another, especially in times of need; and today the need to find other ways of resolving disputes between nations other than through war is paramount [51.1–2]. Pope Benedict XV and his successors understood the need, and the Gulf War made it necessary to warn once more that war is no way to settle conflicts between nations. It must be remembered also that serious grievances are more often than not the root of war. Development is therefore the new name for peace; a world wide effort is needed to provide it for the less advanced nations [52.1–3].

## VI. Man is the way of the Church

With *Rerum Novarum* Leo XIII sought to help man to face the modern social question. The Church cannot abandon man, redeemed by Christ, and her social doctrine has developed with man as its main theme [53.1–2]. The human sciences and philosophy help him to understand himself better as a social being, but it is only from faith he understands his full identity. 'While drawing on all the contributions made by the sciences and philosophy, [the Church's] social teaching is aimed at helping man on the path of salvation.' It is because she has an evangelizing mission that she evolves this social doctrine with its implication for human rights [54.1–2].

Revelation gives her the meaning of man; it is in God's nature we know our own. Christian anthropology is part of her theology, and her social doctrine then belongs to her moral theology. Atheism, which deprives man of his spiritual dimension, and consumerism, which imprisons him in his own selfishness, both need a theological refutation. The Church's religious message enriches human dignity, although that message and the mission that brings it is today particularly difficult to preach. That is why she devotes herself with ever new energy to an evangelization which promotes the whole human being [55.1–3].

On the hundredth anniversary of the encyclical the Pope wishes to thank all those concerned with making the Church's social teaching better known, and in particular he would like it publicized in countries where real socialism has collapsed. The Western countries too may fail to make the necessary corrections in their own system and the third world nations face the problems of their underdevelopment. In the words of Leo XIII, everyone should put his hands to the work that falls to his share [56.1–3]. The social teaching of the Church motivates to action. Through the centuries Christians have responded to the needs of the poor, and today more than ever it is actions that count. So the preferential option for the poor, never discriminatory or exclusive towards other groups, not limited to those in material poverty only, impels us to help them in a world where there is so much poverty. In the West there are marginalized groups, while in the third world tragic crises need internationally co-ordinated measures [57.1–2]. Love for others is made concrete in the promotion of justice. But justice will never be attained 'unless the poor person who is asking for help in order to survive is not seen as an annoyance or a hindrance, but an opportunity for showing kindness and a chance for greater enrichment'. It is not a matter of giving from one's surplus but of changing life styles and models of production and consumption, so that whole peoples who are deprived can 'enter into the sphere of economic and human development'.

The increasing globalization of the economy argues for effective international agencies which are better able to oversee that economy than individual nations could, agencies which could give due weight to those in desperate need and lacking influence in the world market [58]. To meet the demands of justice the gift of God's grace is needed. Faith needs people to find solutions and makes suffering humanly bearable while sustaining human dignity. The Church's social teaching in particular has an interdisciplinary dimension touching the other sciences concerned with man; it opens them up to broader horizons, serving the individual persons acknowledged and loved in the fullness of his humanity. Its practical and experiential aspects are also important, manifested as they are in the lives of individuals involved in cultural and political life [59.1–4]. Leo XIII was convinced that the solution to the problems of industrial society required the co-operation of all, and this conviction is central to Catholic social teaching. Liberalism and Marxism at the time rejected such co-operation, but the world today is more aware of the importance of ethical and religious values in reform, and this openness and dialogue is required of all people of good will in building a society worthy of man [60.1–3].

One hundred years ago Leo XIII spoke out against 'the yoke little better than slavery itself' to which man was subjected, and since then the Church has continued to speak out in defence of man against economic exploitation and totalitarianism. Now, one hundred years later, the Church is faced with 'new things', new challenges once more [61.1–2]. The present encyclical has looked to the past but is directed to the future, the threshold of the new century, aware that in every age true and perennial newness of things comes from the infinite power of God. In conclusion John Paul thanks Almighty God who has granted his Church the light and the strength on her journey. In the third millennium she will be faithful in making man's way her own, knowing that she does not walk alone but with Christ her Lord and with Mary, on her pilgrimage of faith [62.1–4].

# 28

# John Paul II and CELAM IV

## 1 CELAM IV[1]

### (i) Background – the controversy over the anniversary of Columbus' landing

The first meeting of CELAM was held in Rio de Janeiro in Brazil in 1955; the second was at Medellín in Colombia in 1968 and the third at Puebla in 1979. With the five hundredth anniversary of the discovery of the continent due in 1992, it was fitting that this fourth meeting[1] should coincide with it. It was fitting also, though controversial, that it should take place in the Dominican Republic, which shares with the State of Haiti the island in the Caribbean on which Christopher Columbus first made landfall in the new world in 1492, and which was named Hispaniola by the Spaniards. The capital of the Dominican Republic, Santo Domingo, was the first settlement established on Hispaniola in 1496 and it therefore has the distinction of being the first city founded in the Americas by Europeans.

The coming of the Spaniards to the Americas is important in the secular history of the region. It is of course also important in the history of the Church in that the Spaniards and the Portuguese brought Christianity to the new world. But not everyone in Latin America was enthusiastic about celebrating this quincentenary;[2] there were many who considered the arrival of the Europeans a disaster first of all for the indigenous peoples, who were in places almost wiped out by disease and violence of one kind and another in the wake of settlement; secondly, disaster for the African slaves, imported to work on the plantations which followed on the settle-

* The notes and references for Chapter 28 are to be found on p. 464ff

ment. But these disasters were not the whole story. The Europeans brought a new and vital culture with them, one which, because of its vitality, was to mark and make the modern age.

It was a personal vitality based on the idea of the free and responsible person capable of independent action, however marred it became by the behaviour of unworthy Christians, secular liberalism, racialism and imperialism; an intellectual vitality, however marred it became by arrogance and contempt for other cultures; and an economic and technological vitality, however warped it was by the diversion of its energies into selfish exploitation of others and into war and violence. Other cultures have also had these defects, without having made so many advances as has Europe's in so many fields which have stimulated mankind to so many great achievements. The non-European world has adapted its philosophies, good and bad, the latter increasing the more the Europeans have distanced themselves from their Christian inheritance. Its political ideas and institutions, its scientific achievements, its mastery of exploration, physical, intellectual and technological, its military and naval skills have shaped the modern world. The English language is the international language of science, the social sciences, and communications. The parliamentary and representative government systems first developed in medieval Europe, adapted by the settlers in the United States and put at the service of republicanism, has become the democratic political system the world has taken to its own. The thrusting independence of the medieval and modern European entrepreneurs created the modern market economy. Disfigured as it was – and still is to some extent – by the liberal capitalist elements which dominated it from the seventeenth century, it has none the less been sufficiently mastered by society to see it purged of its most blatant evils, and today is the world's choice for economic prosperity.

European universities have been the pioneers of advanced education throughout the world, and European hospitals have been the models for those of the rest of the world in many important respects. Social responsibility for its poor, accepted by society from New Testament times and formalized in the medieval period, was obscured as liberal capitalism took over, but in reaction to the excesses of the Industrial Revolution secular society has given them something like their due. Above all Europe has given to the world an ideal of personal responsible freedom under the law – stemming from the idea of man made in Gods's image and likeness and given intelligence and free will. Although the rejection of this theological and philosophical framework has weakened that ideal, and in the

West threatens to destroy it, it remains a beacon for hope for all who do not have freedom and seek it. Europe then has ravaged the world with its wars of Empire and plundered its riches for its own economic purposes, but it has also brought benefits wherever its influence has reached. This is doubly true of Latin America.

The disasters that came upon the people of the region were the results of conditions and perceptions of reality that were accepted by the men of their time, which was crude, harsh and violent, and which we rightly deplore. But then ours is the century which produced the totalitarianism of Nazi Germany and Stalin's Russia, the holocaust, the Gulags, the atom bomb and a myriad of weapons, nuclear, chemical and others as lethal which have not as yet been put to the test; it has also produced absolute moral relativism which is undermining the cast of mind which fostered its most positive achievements of the past. By contrast, despite the negative aspects of the imperial tradition, the missioners took with them the best of the European achievements, its conversion to Christ and the sound spiritual and moral values that implied. Christ was preached to the people, and preached effectively despite all exaggerations and errors, as is witnessed by the deep faith and the holy lives of so many of its sons and daughters over the centuries and today. The Church and those of her members who were worthy of their calling, were, with all their faults, from first to last the best friends of the indigenous peoples and the slaves. Those who regard the secular achievements of civilization to be beneficial to mankind see also that the Europeans brought with them not only the best of the Judaeo-Christian tradition, spiritual, moral and temporal, but also those of Rome and Greece, which represent many of the greatest achievements of the human mind and spirit when enlightened by natural virtue and greatness alone, achievements which speak of the grace of God in pagan goodness and the power of that human mind and spirit which are gifts of God.

## (ii) The address of John Paul at Santo Domingo[3]

### I. Jesus Christ, yesterday, today and forever

Under the guidance of the Holy Spirit, and turning our eyes to Christ, we are gathered to give thanks to God for five hundred years of faith on this continent[1] ... and the founding of the Church here which fostered it [2]. With the coming of the gospel to America, the work of salvation expanded [3] ... and the Church from the first was a defender of the Indians, through men like Las Casas and prophetic work of the School of Vitoria at the University of Salamanca. The vitality of your Church today is a testimony to its people [4] ... now, in considering its new evangelization I wish to stress the need for a sound Christology, ecclesiology and anthropology in that process [5].

## II. New evangelization

This is not a new gospel; the riches of Christ are for all ages and cultures [6]. Reductive Christologies are to be rejected: culture is not the measure of the Gospel; rather, Christ is the measure of all culture and human endeavour [7]. The truth that will make us free does not accommodate pluralism to the point of relativism, or parallel magisteria of theologians, and pastors must be careful to avoid being led away by strange teachings. Theology is called to provide service to the new evangelization [8]. The new *Catechism of the Catholic Church* is to be the guide in catechetics, along with the Scriptures and the liturgy nourishing the lives of the faithful [9]. A new ardour, pastoral charity and steadfast fidelity to the Gospel expressed in ways accessible to your people should be its hallmark [10]. We know that faith is being assailed today by secularism and the weakening of spiritual and moral values without which it is impossible to build a truly human society [11]. The advance of sects is also a challenge; these must be countered by pastoral action centred on the whole person, a dynamic Church presence, based on sound piety and true solidarity [12].

## III. Human development

Stimulating human development must be the logical outcome of evangelization which shows solidarity with the poor, and respects the truth about God and the human being, God's rights and human rights [13]. The tackling of poverty requires an active, just and urgent solidarity internationally also, especially on the part of the wealthier nations [14]. Attitudes, behaviour and structures must be changed to bring about this solidarity; demographic problems must not be solved by immoral means [15]. The Church reaffirms the option for the poor, though it is not the exclusive gauge of our following of Christ. The best service we can offer them is evangelization which liberates from injustices and fosters integral development; the genuine praxis of liberation is to be inspired by the Church's social teaching [16]. Help must be given to indigenous groups, small farmers and Indians who suffer from poverty, and the Holy See has taken a small step by creating a foundation for the purpose. A greater unity and solidarity among your people is needed [17].

Neither is there genuine development without the support of marriage, the family and human life, the vital cell of society; in this context the needs of the street-children are apparent. Life is sacred from the time of conception and all that attacks and undermines it must be countered [18]. Only Christ can save man from the ideologies that threaten him; only the acceptance of the Holy Spirit as at Pentecost will bring forth a people capable of respecting human dignity.

> Latin America's greatest wealth is its people ... awakening their consciences through the Gospel contributes to the awakening of dormant energies that can be put forth in building a new civilization [19].

## IV. Christian culture

To proclaim Jesus Christ in all cultures is the Church's central concern, and the object of its mission [20]. Today's cultural crisis challenges Christian values in many ways, and only by the inculturation of the message of Christ can these aspects of culture be purified [21]. It is a crisis that challenges the moral dimension of culture altogether and the task of the new evangelization is to provide a Christian alternative [22]. Some cultural phenomena on the other hand, the interest in ecology for example, chime with the Christian concern for the proper use of the world for all [23]. The Church in Latin America has successfully been inculturated in the past, providing the people with their basic values; 'we need to face now the question of its renewed inculturation, under the patronage of Our Lady the Virgin of Tepeyac' [24].

## V. A new era – under the sign of hope

The path that the Latin American Church must follow in this time of hope is that of the unity of the bishops in the episcopal college with Peter at its head, and the unity of the communities at local level, with a clear ecclesial identity, finding that unity in the Eucharist presided over by the priest, and being in harmony with the Church's magisterium [25]. The vocations of evangelizers, priests and religious, deacons and members of secular institutes must be encouraged and they must be properly trained under the bishops' supervision [26]. The role of the laity here is indispensable, as new apostolic movements begin to emerge, reflecting the need for greater presence of the faith in secular society. The contribution of women is especially valuable and necessary, as is that of the young, and of the sick whose suffering has an evangelizing power [27]. All are called to help build a civilization of love [28]. Pastors of the flock must not forget that the primary form of evangelization is witness, that is, proclaiming the message of salvation through one's daily life [29]. Christ is in our midst, for we are gathered in his name and the communion of saints is watching over our labours [30]. What is spoken to you by the Lord will be fulfilled once again as, faithful to your baptism, you call upon the enormous graces that have been given to you [31].

### (iii) Message of CELAM IV to the peoples of Latin America and the Caribbean

### Introduction

This fourth Council seeks to provide an outline for a new impetus to evangelization that will put Christ into the hearts of all. The great majority of our people live in critical conditions and the bishops wish to help them overcome their problems, having primary responsibility for their own lives in Christ [1–11]. Christ on the road to Emmaus can be taken as a model for this new evangelization. Jesus walks with his people in their suffering and reaffirms the word of God to them. The Church's social teaching is an essential part of that word, and a renewed catechesis will sanctify all Christians and equip them to work for an integral development, with the poor as their main concern, the family occupying a privileged place, and the inculturation of the gospel the Church's aim [11–32]. The bishops' greetings go out to all who are working with them in their episcopal mission, observers of other Churches who are with them, and to all Latin Americans [32–42]. They wish to work for the greater homeland of the whole region, by encouraging reconciliation, solidarity and integration of their countries and deep communion with the Church which they commend to Our Lady of Guadalupe [43–48].

## I. Jesus Christ, Gospel of the Father

We celebrate Jesus Christ who died for our sins. He reveals God's self to us and draws especially near to those on the margins of society. Christ alone is our justice; he tears down the walls separating human beings. We confess our faith as Peter did and we acknowledge the situation in which sin has placed humanity; the collective evils that oppress the people of Latin America, the injustices, and the whole culture of death. In the Church, one, holy, catholic and apostolic, a pilgrim Church, and a missionary one, we proclaim that Christian truth which 'tends to heal, strengthen and advance human beings and establish a fraternal community' [1–13]. We believe that Christ will return to bring God's reign to its fullness, and we confirm the faith of our people by proclaiming Mary mother of God and the Church [14–15].

Five hundred years of evangelization, 'a valid, fruitful and admirable labour', has opened the way to Latin America knowing the truth about God and humanity, the Church becoming a tribunal which held accountable the irresponsibilities of many of the settlers [16–18]. The great evangelizers defended the rights and dignities of the indigenous peoples, who so cruelly suffered in the period of conquest and settlement, and of the African slaves on whom was inflicted what John Paul II has called an 'unknown holocaust'. We remember too the lives of holiness of so many of those who received the Gospel [19–21].

## II. Jesus Christ, evangelizer living in his Church

*Chapter 1: new evangelisation*
The starting point of this evangelization is that the riches of Christ are for every age and culture; it does not mean a new evangelization but it means activity and attitudes that can put the Gospel in active dialogue with modernity in a continent where divorce between faith and life results in injustice and social inequality. Christ bursts the barriers of secularism and returns man to his dignity as a child of God. The renewing power of this new evangelization will be found in faithfulness to God's word in the church community, its creative breath the Holy Spirit; it will be new in its ardour, its methods and its spirit [23–30].

The Church is called to holiness. Only holiness can guide true human development, a holy community formed by the word of God, which has a primary duty to preach the Gospel. We must proclaim Jesus Christ, died and risen again, according to the

Church's catechesis, with theologians aiding pastors in complete fidelity to the magisterium, serving all God's people who share in Christ's prophetic function [31–3]. The Church's liturgy also has an evangelizing power and must be prominent in the new evangelization. Popular religiosity, its values, criteria and behaviour, also has a role, as does the contemplative life [34–7]. Catechesis is crucial; despite the heroic efforts of so many, religious ignorance is too prevalent. Many are losing the sense of 'the day of the Lord'. Spirituality must be renewed, illuminating the light of faith. To the many who are looking to practices foreign to Christianity for an interior life, we should be able to offer the riches of the Church's teaching and experience. A liturgy faithful to the spirit of Vatican II can adapt the forms of native cultures within the norms laid down by the Church [38–53]. Local churches must be dynamic; they are organic communities and must be characterized by a diversity and complementarity of vocations and states of life, in the unity which springs from the Eucharist around the bishop, and in union with the whole episcopal college and Peter's successor [54–7].

The parish has an evangelizing mission also and must be renewed by the establishment within it of smaller communities with lay leaders. Basic communities as a living cell of a parish are a sign of its vitality, but must have a clear ecclesiological foundation, integrated into the Church [58–63]. The family is the domestic church, the primary evangelizing community and the first cell of society. Pastoral work for families is a basic priority [64]. There must be unity in the spirit with a variety of ministries and charisms, and the organization of the Church should reflect this; there is need too for a deeper spiritual life. These multiple needs reflect the importance of ongoing formation. The good shepherd also knows his sheep and they know him, and as servants of their communities they must be models for their flocks [65–75].

The permanent diaconate is important for the service of the Church, and its needs and its potential must be recognized. The promotion of priestly and religious vocations is crucial for evangelization and must be a priority, with selection and training being guided by the relevant Church documents [76–93]. The people of God being mainly made up of lay believers, their role is crucial in evangelization. Many do not feel they belong to the Church and consequently cannot take up this challenge. The experience of the Church as communion should lead to a shared responsibility for it, and such a Church must be fostered by, for example, forming lay councils in full communion with their pastors but sufficiently independent that they can facilitate dialogue, unity and a growth in spirituality [94–8]. The varied ministries, movements and associations of laity, and the contribution of the women of the Church especially, are all essential to the new evangelization [99–106].

The bishops are committed pastorally to the denunciation of all that demeans the dignity of women, and to the encouragement of all that underlies their importance in the Church community and society; they are committed too to the support of adolescents and youth, so many of whom are suffering from poverty, unemployment and other social evils; they reaffirm also the preferential option for the poor made at Puebla [107–20]. In proclaiming Christ's reign to all people they are mindful of the poverty that afflicts so many and they testify to the liberation of all in Christ, asking for forgiveness for their frailties. They also look to the non-Christian world, for the Church's mission is universal [121–5]. (The pastoral challenges and the necessary responses are then considered in detail [126–56]).

*Chapter 2. Human development*
The Church's commitment to human development is a key part of her social teaching, and development and liberation are closely linked [157–8]. The love and charitable care that Christ preached has been too often lacking [159–161]. Latin America has so far shown itself incapable of reforming the structures of injustice, and the advancement of women has suffered [162–3]. Human rights are too readily challenged by terrorism, oppression and murder, and by extreme poverty; children, women and the poor are especially afflicted. Damage to the environment requires to be reversed [164–73]. There is injustice in the way the land is distributed throughout the continent, and in the way it is managed. A just resolution of these problems is needed, involving changes in attitude, governmental policies and solidarity with those affected [174–8]. The world of work and the rights of workers are of concern also [179–8] as are those of migrants [186–9].

Politically the democratic system is to be valued as it gives the right of participation to all, but in some countries in Latin America democracy is deteriorating and efforts to underpin it are required, for example urging its importance and the need to get involved in such systems [190–3]. The new economic order, stressing the importance of the market system, has its virtues, but the sacrifice of everything to market needs results in the suffering of the poor; inflation and massive foreign debts are both evils, as are consumerism and its selfishness, and all these have been characteristics of the 1980s. The Church's pastoral activities must be directed to the preferential option for the poor and the values of hard work and sharing, combined with the search for better economic models, while denouncing the injustices at present suffered by so many [194–203]. No nation can live and achieve the desired results alone; solidarity is needed; particularly should the strong nations help the weak and, in Latin America, greater integration of peoples and nations is a basic need [204–9].

The importance of the family to development does not require urging; it protects, reveals and communicates love by encouraging personal development, being the sanctuary of life which is the basic human right; it is the primary cell of society and it is also the sanctuary of holiness, the domestic church [210–15]. It is challenged today in numerous ways and a priority in pastoral work must be to support it by teaching, example and practical help [216–27].

*Chapter 3. Christian culture*
When God became man in Jesus Christ the Word of God entered into human culture and all cultural values which relate to Christ foster the truly human. Authentic values such as this are necessary in order to incarnate the Gospel message in human culture, and when not only Gospel but basic human values are being challenged, the task of the new evangelization is formidable indeed [228–30]. Created in God's image, the standard of man's moral behaviour is Christ, and though many throughout Latin America remain faithful to their master, the attack on these standards is total and deceives many. Corruption is rife, justice is mocked, the weak are oppressed, human sexuality is debased, the dignity of man undermined; the cultural standard is taken as the minimum consensus of society at large. We must rebuild moral life in Christ, extol its virtues and defend its values by all means open to us, keeping in dialogue with those whose lives are not built on Christian ethics [231–42].

Latin America is the meeting place of many cultures, Indian, African, European, Mestizo, but all seek unity in their Catholic identity. The non-Europeans suffered from many injustices in colonial times at the hands of baptized Christians and this failing will always be before us, along with the outstanding examples of Christian living; the cultural traditions of peasants and people testify to Christianity's sound legacy [243–7]. We have asked our indigenous and African brethren forgiveness for our failings and we are pledged to inculturated evangelization, replacing mindsets imposed from outside with one of self-development, so that peoples can be artisans of their own destiny [248–51].

The good characteristics of modern culture are the centrality of the human being, personalization, and the social dimension, but there is also the illusion of absolute autonomy which excludes God; the result is an ethical vacuum which undermines social structures and causes injustice. Pastorally Christ should be presented as a model for human life, and there should be dialogue between faith, science and modern culture. Pastoral challenges lie in urbanization and its problems and the answer to them is to be found in the reshaping of the urban parish and the multiplication of small communities and ecclesiastical movements, including Christian basic communities; the evangelization of influential groups whose decisions affect the lives of others is also important [252–62].

Education is the assimilation of culture, and Christian culture is achieved through Gospel values being made evident in society; the Christian teacher is to be recognized as a representative of the Church in its evangelizing mission. We need to confront the new cultural values of our day with Christ who reveals the mystery of the human being. But in Latin America many do not get even a basic schooling. Given the technological orientation of much education, and of higher education particularly, the Christian educator must be in dialogue with it so that the human problems may be faced and solved on Christian lines. There are multiple other problems, which include, among others, those of the sects and of the relationship between State and Christian education; our pastoral response must take account of them all [263–78].

Social communications also pose challenges and problems. The communications industries reflect the influence of the dominant economic and social groups which can encourage hedonism and consumerism, and deprive cultures of their values and identities, and this at a time when the Church's presence in the media is limited. Support must therefore be given to all those defending their cultural identity, the Catholic media professionals particularly, while pastoral agents must be trained to use the media, and Catholic universities be encouraged to provide the expertise; information sciences must be adapted to evangelization with Catholic publishing houses responding to pastoral needs [279–86].

### III. Jesus Christ, light and hope of Latin America and the Caribbean

Jesus Christ, the same yesterday, today and forever, has made us new, and we commit ourselves to a new evangelization of our peoples, a comprehensive development of those peoples, and an inculturated evangelization. The first calls for a commitment from all, and the living out of that commitment in community. The clergy and religious are to encourage work for vocations, and ongoing education for all is to be based on sound catechesis, founded on the Word and the teaching authority of the Church, with the liturgy being carried out with joy through the participation of the people [287–95].

The second means that we make ours the cry of the poor, the preferential option of Medellín and Puebla, it being neither exclusive nor excluding. In that light we will seek a new economic, political and social order fostering justice and charity. We also say Yes to the family and action to defend life [296–7]. The third means evangelizing the urban areas where most of our people now live, and being close to the indigenous and the African American peoples. We likewise will increase our educational effort, and that in modern communications; in all this we place ourselves under the impulse of the Holy Spirit [298–301].

## 2  Summary analysis of the social teaching of John Paul II

### (i)  Ethics and civil society

Because he is made in God's image, and because through God becoming man the Son of God in a certain way united himself with every man, all social organization should respect man's dignity [RH 13]. Civil society and the people comprising it should be masters of their own destiny and their human rights secured [RH 17]. Man, the family and civil society, have rights that are prior to the State and they must be respected by it [CA 11] and since God has given man freedom he must use it properly, but many aspects of modern culture do not encourage him to do that.

Man was meant to co-operate with his creator in the development of the world for his use, but it is possible for him to thwart this purpose if he instead sets himself up in the place of God and terrorizes it, by for example vandalizing his human environment, his own moral habitat. Man receives his original dignity from God, but he must respect the nature and moral structure of his being; he largely creates his own moral environment; the family founded on marriage for example provides the best environment for the healthy development of children, the citizens of the future. But marriage can be downplayed and so unstable relationships result which do not provide that environment. Children can be seen as things one can have or not have according to taste. The family is the source of life, yet abortion is being encouraged. The possession of goods can become society's only value, ethical and religious considerations being ignored [CA 36].

Human initiative and the freedom to exercise it within a proper framework of law for the common good, is the essence of a healthy economy and society [CA 31–2]. The anthropology of socialism was therefore wrong; it subordinated man to the social organism and denied him freedom. The structure of society should be built on the family and other groups below State level, each with its own autonomy, but subject to the common good. The good of the individual cannot be realized without his free choice. Man is not to be subordinated to the social organism: he is the autonomous subject of moral decisions, and it is those decisions which build the social order. A man who is deprived of the possibility of owning property and the opportunity of using his own initiative in earning a living is reduced to dependency on the social machine and those who control it. His social nature is not completely fulfilled in the State but needs the various intermediate groups, the family, the social, political and economic organizations which he develops of his own initiative and which have their own autonomy, in the context of the common good [CA 13].

The perfect kingdom is not of this world, self-interest has to be reconciled therefore with the common good [CA 25]. Social conflict cannot be eliminated altogether, it is a fact of the human condition. The conditions of labour under liberal capitalism in the nineteenth century made workers' solidarity in defence of their rights necessary, and it is still right to defend those interests against unjust employers when necessary [LE 33]. But charity and justice must be the foundations of a healthy society. Of these, charity, love of God and of others for his sake is the more fundamental. Programmes which start from justice can continue to appeal to it when justice has been forgotten, and hatred and cruelty take over, the growing interest in justice while basic moral standards are declining is a disturbing development [DM 12]. The deeper power is love, which should shape human life in all its dimensions [DM 14].

Solidarity is the working out of love and justice in practice. Leo XIII used the term friendship, Pius referred to social charity, and Paul VI to the civilization of love [CA 10]. Solidarity exists when the members of society recognize one another as persons, whatever their social class or standing. Those who are more powerful or influential because of their greater wealth should feel responsible for the weaker and be ready to help them. Those who are less wealthy, should, while claiming their legitimate rights, do what they can for the good of all and refrain from passive or destructive attitudes. Intermediate groups in society should not selfishly put their own interests before the common good, but respect those of others. Solidarity should exist within nations and between nations; solidarity is the work of justice [SRS 38 and 39]. Political society, government, has a duty to help the weaker members of society, but this must be in accordance with the principle of subsidiarity which puts the onus on persons, individuals and intermediate societies to handle their own affairs; the State, however, has the duty to intervene when the common good requires it, helping the citizens to achieve independence in looking after their own affairs as soon as possible [CA 48]; a Social Assistance State is not acceptable.

## (ii) Ethics and political society

No group has the right to claim perpetual political leadership as did Marxist Leninism; such States absorb the individual, the family, civil society and nation, and by denying transcendent truth, in obedience to which man achieves his full dignity, deny the principle which guarantees justice [CA 44–5]. Democratic systems elect and hold accountable those who govern them, but authentic democracy is only possible in a State ruled by law and where there is a correct understanding of the human person. The claim that agnosticism, sceptical relativism and morality decided by majority opinion are the preconditions of effective democracy is false. Only when democracy accepts the reality of ultimate truth is it free from manipulation for the sake of power. History demonstrates that democracies which lack such values are prey to totalitarianism – to ideologies which seek to impose what they regard as good and true. Christian truth on the other hand is not an ideology; it recognizes that the conditions of human life differ in different historical circumstances and that socio-political realities cannot be fitted into a rigid schema. The transcendent dignity of man is a dignity which demands freedom, but freedom only attains full development in truth. Without that truth freedom loses its foundation, man is open to the violence of passion, and to manipulation by others [CA 46]. In the wake of the communist collapse the democratic ideal and human rights are in vogue, and for this reason those who are introducing these reforms must give democracy a solid foundation by the recognition of those rights, synthesized in the right to religious freedom understood as the right to live in the truth of one's faith and in conformity with one's transcendent dignity as a person.

Unfortunately these rights are not always fully recognized in democracies. Some seem to have lost all vision of the common good; the electoral or financial power of certain groups within them dominate. This creates apathy and disillusionment and it becomes impossible for particular interests to relate correctly to the common good, which can only be done when all interests are integrated on the basis of accepted values, ultimately stemming from a correct understanding of the rights of the person. The Church for its part accepts the legitimate autonomy of the political order and does not express preference for one form rather than another; her concern is with the dignity of man revealed in its fullness in the truth that God became man [CA 47].

The proper understanding of the role of the State in the economic order is necessary. The latter cannot be conducted in an institutional, juridical and political vacuum in a free society; it presupposes private property, stable currency and efficient public services, and the principal task of the State is to guarantee these things so that those who work and produce can enjoy the fruits of their labour, so as to be encouraged to work efficiently and honestly. Securing human rights in the economic sector is primarily the responsibility of individuals, groups and associations, but the State still has a role in stimulating business activities and creating conditions which will ensure job opportunities when this is necessary. Similarly it can intervene when monopolies are obstructive, and support weak sectors in order to get them under way, such activities to be as brief as possible and not to enlarge State intervention to the detriment of economic and civil liberties. Similarly, the Welfare State, introduced to provide conditions worthy of human dignity, should not become a 'social assistance' State; the principle of subsidiary function should be respected, otherwise human energies are undermined and enormous expenditures are incurred. Although public agencies may have to be called on to provide care, it is desirable that voluntary, fraternal support should meet the need [CA 48].

## (iii) Ethics and economic society

Economic activity is concerned with supplying man's material needs; at one time it was hard put to it to supply basic requirements but in many countries this is no longer the case. Problems of choice are then more crucial, and since economic mechanisms such as the market do not possess in themselves any moral criteria, education, culture and the public authorities must ensure such are there. Human needs are also spiritual and intellectual and material needs must be seen in this perspective. Consumerism, which exploits human weakness and ignorance, should be checked. It is not the wanting to live better which is wrong; what is wrong is the making of more material goods for their own sake the end of life when some do not have the basic needs [CA 36, SRS 28].

The Church has always insisted on the right to economic freedom and the possession of private property as essential to a healthy economy, one that will enable the earth to yield its riches abundantly and justly for all, though there are limits on ownership and use which are necessary in the light of the common purpose of material goods. God gave the earth to the whole human race for its sustenance, and all must find that sustenance. The earth does not yield its fruits without human effort. It is through his work, using his freedom and intelligence, that man makes it fruitful; it is through work that private property was initially obtained; by working, man made part of the earth his own. Work and land are there at the beginning of every society [CA 31].

The work by which man earns his daily bread is a uniquely human activity, and because it is a human activity subjective work, the work of the individual man, is more fundamental than objective work, the specific task to which he applies himself. All honest labour, however basic, is dignified in that a human being is doing it; the classical world regarded some human work as inherently dignified, most manual work as worthy only of the slave. Christ himself however was a manual worker, so this understanding of it was not accepted by the Church [LE 6]. The idea of the value of work and worker stemming from its human agency, not from any specific task, was however shattered by the materialistic economism of liberal capitalism during the Industrial Revolution. Labour was just merchandise, to be bought and sold like any other, irrespective of its human needs. The resulting injustices led to the workers showing solidarity through trade unionism, which is morally justifiable, and it has achieved much in bringing about improvements in working conditions and rewards. But the original liberal capitalism still exists to some degree in both industrialized and industrializing countries, and similar watchfulness is needed [LE 7].

The conflict between liberal capitalism and Marxism was born of the excesses of the former, the latter seeing the answer to those excesses in the class war leading to the collectivization of the means of production. Capital and labour are, in this schema, natural enemies, the one destined to destroy the other [LE 11]. But the priority of labour is a moral imperative; labour is the efficient cause of the process of production, whereas capital is only instrumental. Capital, in the sense of natural resources available to man, and the whole means that man uses in making them serve his purpose, finance, factories, plant, machines, tools, are of man's making also. Man, as the subject of work and independent of the work he does, man alone is a person [LE 12].

Since capital and labour spring from the same source, they cannot be opposed to one another in themselves. What brought about the opposition was liberal capitalism, the error of economism it contained, the idea that labour could be regarded simply as an economic factor. It was the result of a materialist philosophy, at the other end of the spectrum to Marx's. And that economism occurs today also [LE 13]. Property in the form of the means of production cannot be morally isolated in opposition to labour. The only legitimate title to its ownership, by private individuals or collectively, is that it should serve labour, providing useful work, so achieving the first purpose of productive goods, their universal purpose and common use. The social ownership of some productive goods can then be defensible, but they must serve labour too. Rigid capitalism, which sees private ownership as an untouchable dogma, is rejected. Capital is indeed being continually created by labour, not only manual but white collar and management. Schemes for joint ownership, sharing in management or profits, labour shareholding, are then of special significance. Abolition of private ownership on the other hand solves nothing if it means simply a change of management. Workers must in some way be part owners [LE 14].

The rights of the worker follow from this. Work is an obligation and a right; the creator commands it, man's humanity requires it and others need the products of work. One can distinguish between the indirect and direct employer although their functions naturally overlap to some extent. The former are those who considerably influence the economic factors and the activity which provides employment, and they must act responsibly and encourage productive labour and its proper treatment. The direct employer is one who primarily plans and manages the productive process; he too has a responsibility in maintaining employment opportunities [LE 17–18].

There is a right to adequate wages and this is a most fundamental requirement of justice. It is through them that the workers can gain access to the goods destined for all, and the means to support their families. Women should not be penalized if they work but treated justly on economic and other matters; women who wish to devote themselves entirely to their families should be not penalized either [LE 19]. The right to association in trade unions is a vital one. They are organizations for justice in what is in one way a class struggle, but in the final analysis employers and employed should be united by their work for the common good, not divided. There is a right to strike, but it must not be used for political purposes, and the authorities have the duty to keep essential services going [LE 20].

The purpose of economic activity is to provide man with what is necessary in material terms for the maintenance of life and its improvement, doing so in a way which respects his spiritual, moral, intellectual and cultural needs. In our time it is the possession of know-how which is becoming more important than other factors of production – the know-how first of those business men who possess the ability to foresee the needs of others and to organize the means of production to meet those needs at a price determined by bargaining in a free market. Theirs is a disciplined and creative role, one which requires initiative and entrepreneurial ability, demonstrating that man himself is man's principal resource. Diligence, prudence, industriousness, reliability and a capacity to develop satisfactory personal relationships are needed for the task, as is the creation of ever wider working communities transforming man's natural and human environments. This creativity has its basis in human freedom in the economic sphere; once land, and later capital in the sense of the instruments of production, were seen as the decisive factor, in wealth creation; now it is man and his knowledge, his organizing capacity and his ability to predict the needs of others. Man is mankind's most important resource [CA 31–2].

Production for sale in a free market is the most efficient way of utilizing resources for those who have purchasing power, or whose resources are marketable. Remembering that the purpose of economics is the provision of the material needs of man, there are some fundamental human needs that the market cannot meet because there is no profit to be had in supplying them. There are also needs which are prior to the market, human needs: adequate wages for example, insurance for sickness, unemployment and old age, decent working conditions, and access to the skills that are needed to be able to engage in working for the market. The poor whose needs are not provided for are faced by attempts to exterminate them by forced population control, or else they run the risk of being exposed to ruthless capitalism. Here workers' organizations are required to fight for justice. A market system which meets the needs of the whole of society is also necessary. Profit has a legitimate role in rewarding the efficient use of the factors of production and the satisfying of human needs, but it is not the sole measure of business performance. Humiliation and degradation of workers in its earning would be wrong. Nor is capitalism the only alternative model after the collapse of real socialism; a society of free work, of enterprise and participation, a market system meeting the needs of the whole of society, is another [CA 33–5].

Advanced societies, however, have not only been able to meet the needs of the majority of their citizens; they are now supplying the wants, the luxuries of a society which sees possessions as the only value which it should respect, making consumption an end in itself, irrespective of the needs of other who cannot obtain the necessities of life. Neither does the consumerist market differentiate between good and bad in human wants; the suppliers of pornography and drugs are responding to market demands, but it is an evil and corrupt market. Truth, goodness and beauty are possible criteria for determining lifestyles; were they acted on they would produce a better society [CA 36].

Consumerism leads to the irresponsible exploitation of the physical environment, and it is the State's duty to protect the environment from market excesses. It also leads to the destruction of man's moral environment, as material goods and more of them become society's only value. Stable marriage, the good of children, life itself is under threat. It is the State's duty to protect this human environment too. Economic freedom is important, but it is only one aspect of freedom, which is primarily ethical and religious; when it becomes autonomous man is defined as producer or consumer, not as person. The very importance of the market runs the risk of making it the subject of a new form of idolatry [CA 37–40]. Marxism did not eliminate alienation of the worker. Consumer capitalism does not do so either. Workers are still things, but man needs to be treated as a person. In the consumer society people use one another as things, preferring possessions to them; the media manipulate all [CA 41].

Is capitalism then to be the model for the world after the fall of communism? Yes, if by it we mean a free economy which allows creativity in the economic sector, and a predominance of private ownership of productive goods, but not excluding some public ownership. It also embraces the positive role of business, the market taking responsibility for the proper use of national resource; it must also show the proper respect for the rights of labour [CA 42, LE 16–23]. However, if by capitalism is meant a system in which the market does not operate in the context of good law and for the common good, and if it does not see its freedom as one aspect of a freedom which is primarily ethical and religious, then capitalism is not the model. In practice marginalisation and exploitation still exist, but radical capitalist ideology may produce the belief that these problems, in the former communist States and the third world, may be ignored, and that the free development of market forces will solve everything [CA 42].

The problem of the universal purpose of created goods is one that faces the international community and the international economy. All the main indicators of development, food, health, housing, literacy, education, life expectancy, show the gap between the rich and poor nations widening [SRS 15], and that there has been too little improvement since 1967. This has been partly due to the mistakes of the ruling classes in the underdeveloped countries, but it is also due to the failure of the developed nations to accept their duty towards their less affluent neighbours [SRS 16]. The interdependence of the two is seen most clearly in the problem of international debt; the servicing of debts incurred in the third world has resulted in a crippling export of capital [SRS 18]. Demographic problems result in pressure from the first world for restricting births by immoral means in what amounts to racialist eugenics [SRS 25].

Development itself has become controversial; neither the increase of goods, even for the majority, nor more modern technologies bring freedom in themselves, while the consumerism of the West, at a time when others in the third world are lacking necessities, is a scandal [SRS 28]. Yet co-operation in the development of every person in every nation in the world is the duty of all throughout the world; development which is moral, respecting the rights of the person, all persons, young and old, men and women, families and communities, respecting also the State and international rights. Natural resources must not be exploited recklessly or in a manner which puts the environment at risk [SRS 32–4].

Ideologies favour imperialisms rather than solidarity and independence, and the structures of sin do exist, the result of selfishness and other human failings which must be tackled by attacking their roots. Two in particular stand out: the overwhelming desire for profit, and for power at any price, which create structures of sin [SRS 35–7]. There is need for conversion so that interdependence can be seen in terms of solidarity – the firm and persevering determination to commit ourselves to the common good because we are all responsible for all; in this way we overcome that thirst for profit and power [SRS 38].

There must be an option for the poor, the realization that the goods of the world are for all and that accordingly all property has a social mortgage on it; human rights, religious freedom and economic initiative must be preserved and international trade and financial institutions reformed. A spirit of initiative is above all required in the underdeveloped countries themselves, acting in accordance with their own responsibilities, not expecting everything from the developed countries, using to the best of their abilities their own freedom, responding to their own needs as societies. The development of peoples is primarily a self-development, therefore they should favour wider culture and free access of information and literacy for their citizens. Nations should establish their own priorities [SRS 42–4].

The co-operation of the international community in all this is necessary, in a spirit of solidarity, the richer nations with poorer, and the poorer with one another. Solidarity also demands the readiness to accept sacrifices for the common good [SR 45]. There is no need for despair, or pessimism or inertia. We are all called, obliged, to face the challenges before us [SRS 47].

## 3 The social teaching of CELAM III and IV

### (i) Ethics and civil society

The ethical foundation of a healthy society is the personal dignity of everyone in it; it, calls for freedom, love of others and justice for all, to be 'our own person, act on our initiative'. The love of God, the root of that dignity makes possible loving communion with others and fraternal participation [Puebla 83–4]. In Latin America the majority of people live in difficult conditions, and the bishops wish to help them overcome their problems by helping them to have primary responsibility for their own lives [Santo Domingo 1–11].

The fundamental communitarian values which foster the common good are necessary for a sound social order. So, since the family is the basic unit of society, its values are to be protected and furthered [Santo Domingo 64, and 210–15]. They do not exist where there is social injustice, poor quality of life, inadequate rewards for work [Puebla 118–19]. Personal equality, essential rights for all, freedom, self-determination, justice secured through effective institutions that are adequate and operative, are needed. The rights of women are to be accepted and promoted [Santo Domingo 121–5] and the preferential option for the youth of the continent is reaffirmed. Christian culture provides the true human values that society needs for its basis [Santo Domingo 231–42]. Latin America is a region of many cultures and we support educational processes which respect that variety [Santo Domingo 248–51].

Liberation is needed, the liberation in Christ from personal and social sin [Puebla 103–4]. The preferential option for the poor that was asserted at Medellín is reasserted, though the option has been misunderstood by some [Puebla 118–19]. Neither determinism, psychologism, economism, Marxism or the National Security State respect the basic rights and dignity of the human being [Puebla 79–81]. Nor does Marxist class struggle or liberal capitalist economism secure justice, closed as they are to the transcendent values which secure the rights of man [Puebla 115–16].

## (ii) Ethics and political society

Political totalitarianism is too prevalent in Latin America and it is contrary to the good of peoples, as is Marxism and the National Security State; the latter claims to defend Christian values but does not; in particular it increases social inequalities [Puebla 107, 115]. Any violence used by the State in the form of torture, kidnapping and the persecution of dissidents is evil [Puebla 112]. The State in itself, however, in its proper role has a positive part to play in human development, and that its authority has sometimes been excessive should not obscure this [Puebla 114]. Politicians who are concerned to solve the social, political and economic problems of society have an essential role in securing communitarian values [Puebla 110]. The democratic system gives the people a right of participation; it is unfortunately under pressure in many countries, and efforts need to be made to underpin it, for example by urging people to get involved in it [Santo Domingo 190–3].

## (iii) Ethics and economic society

Worldly goods were intended to be shared by all, and in consequence the right of private property has a mortgage on it. The

right is one primarily of use and administration; it gives ownership and control, but these are not absolute or unlimited. Both
liberal capitalism and Marxism then have a wrong understanding
of the institution, and neither can be the basis of a healthy
economy. The idolization of goods and the reckless depletion of
resources that occur in many economies today are aberrations
[Puebla 106–7]. The new economic order, with its stress on the
free market, has its virtues, but pushing the claims of the market
to the point where the poor suffer is not one of them. Inflation,
and excessive and crippling foreign debt are evils. The preferential option for the poor and the virtues of hard work and sharing,
combined with the search for better economic models, are
needed in the face of the sufferings and deprivations of many
[Santo Domingo 194–210]. No nation can achieve solid results for
its people on its own; solidarity is needed, especially of the
stronger nations with the weaker.

# 29

# A summary of Christian social teaching

## 1 Ethics and civil society

*(i) Man, made in God's image, the purpose and end of every social organization*

God created man in his own image and likeness, male and female, as such he created them, and he sent his own Son to redeem them. What God has done for man therefore bestows on humanity a dignity which provides the only sure basis for human rights, and man and woman demonstrate that dignity when they respond to God's love and act according to his law [DR 37–40, RH 13–17, John Paul II at Puebla 1.9, LC 25–42].

The likeness to God which is in man lies in the possession of intelligence and free will which enable him to know and freely chose to do the good according to God's law. By nature man is social, born into the society which is the family, and needing civil, political and economic society in order to develop his full potential; and those societies are validated and have their purpose in fostering the dignity of man [PT 219], the only creature God has created and loved for his own sake.

Because he is a social being he cannot deny his responsibilities to these societies [PT 28–35]. To say that the social organization to which man belongs of his nature must make him their purpose and end does not mean advocating a selfish attitude to others and society, an atomistic individualism. On the contrary, man shows his true dignity as a son of God by loving others for God's sake and accepting his responsibilities towards them. [GS 24–32 and 43, CA 49–50]. They too are sons and daughters of God. Nor is man

* The notes and references for Chapter 29 are to be found on p. 464ff

absolutely autonomous, independent in the sense that, being given his freedom, he is free of the law of God. He can choose to disobey that law, but in so doing he enters into slavery, the slavery of sin. If, however, he lives according to it he will be truly free and will fulfil his human potential and find true happiness, at the same time helping others to achieve theirs. Selfish individualism cannot be reconciled with Christian belief.

The preservation of human dignity and a sound social order requires a framework of objective moral law and a sense of social responsibility under it, and Christian belief provides both [PT 1–10 and 36–8]. Man must be free, but freedom must be guided by an objective morality, based on divine revealed and natural law [John Paul II *Veritatis Splendor* 1994, 94–9, *Evangelium Vitae* 1995, 68–75], only under it will there be true freedom which secures human rights and dignity for all. It is this presupposition, that man is capable of choosing between good and evil and is responsible for his moral choices, that underpins all Christian morality, personal and social. There is no social teaching independent of the essentially personal nature of Christian ethics. Man must bring to society a sound personal morality, based on natural and divine revealed moral law, if a just society is to be built. Society in its turn can influence, does influence, personal morality, but in the Christian scheme of things, insofar as the accepted moral values contradict those of the Scriptures, then they must be resisted. Morality is what God wants; only if we follow in Christ's way can we be truly happy and build a just and loving society. Morality in the Western world was, theoretically at least, based on this understanding of things until what has come to be called the permissive society was ushered in during the 1960s after a long incubation by secular liberalism, and permissiveness has now almost entirely undermined this inheritance.

## (ii)  The family, the foundation of civil society and the State

The well-being of the individual person, of human society and of the Church depends on the well-being of marriage and family which have been established by God and are supported by his law. In marriage, which is founded in the irrevocable personal consent of the partners, they of their fruitful love give life and found the family which is the cornerstone of both State and Church [*Familiaris Consortio*, John Paul II 1981, 42–54]; where children cannot be born the love of the couple remains. Parents are to guide children to maturity and are primarily responsible for their education, especially their religious education. Children in their turn should love and trust their parents and stand by them if they are in need. That women have the same rights as men to a role in the professions, the world of work and public life should not be the reason for regarding the role of wife and mother within the family as of any less value than work outside the home [FC, 22–3].

Conjugal love enriches the partners; it remains steadfast in body and soul and is a stranger to adultery and divorce. It is within the family that children learn about the dignity of married love and, trained in chastity, they in their turn are prepared in due time to enter into marriage themselves. It is for the parents to decide on the number of children they shall have, taking into consideration the law of God, their own welfare, that of their children, and of society and the Church. Methods of regulating births should be in accord with God's law authentically interpreted by the Church [*Humanae Vitae* of Paul VI 1968, 8–16]. In the family the generations come together and learn to harmonize personal and social life. The Church has a special responsibility to support marriage and the family through its liturgical, educational and spiritual mission [GS 47–52, FC 65–86]. The public authorities also have their responsibility to provide the conditions in which stable strong families may grow and develop.

## (iii) Intermediate organizations

Self and society are given a sense of identity and purpose by the specific geographical region in which a community is situated. Duties to family, friends, parish, local organizations condition personal choice and help maintain the fabric of society. The family is the most basic social unit; in it are to be nurtured the virtues which make responsible citizens capable of acting on their own initiative in cooperation with others in building basic social structures, forming private associations. Markets develop and the economy is built up. Man also organizes for social and cultural purposes and religion and its practice helps him in this.

Civil society, with its private or intermediate associations, social, economic and cultural, is important in the Christian understanding of things [QA 84, 87, MM 65–7, PT 23–7, 31–5, GS 74, CA 13–14]. In it basic human rights and practices which stem from man's being made in God's image and likeness are established by the sound moral decisions of the citizens and the State and cannot deprive them of these. Civil society evolves into political society by its own inner logic. The capable individuals who build up the former do so in order that they and their fellow men may develop their potential as human beings and they are capable of doing this initially because of their desire to better themselves and their dependants, using their intelligence, free will and sense of responsibility to these ends. They see that they need the more formal organization, political society, for full development of their human potential; they need an authority capable of making laws for the common good and enforcing them [GS 74].

Without this political organization, civil society cannot perdure because there are needs of the common good which it cannot of itself fulfil. Conflicts of interest need to be settled and positive steps for the development of society need to be taken which the less formal civil organization cannot undertake. But political society should leave to civil society, the person, the family, the private associations and the local interests and their agencies, those functions which they can more efficiently discharge. So in local government a healthy political system requires active participation at every level and their authorities should be given as much initiative as they can handle subject to the overall common good.

Private associations are also essential to the working of the economy in a complex political society, a modern State. Basic to it is the institution of private property, and the different forms of economic organization that have evolved spontaneously – concerned with farming and fishing, mining, commerce, trade and industry, transport and communications, and other services. The profession which grow out of social needs, the practice of law and medicine, education, the scientific community, the engineers and other technologists each need their own orgnanizations to establish standards and foster common interests. So do the artists, the actors, writers, musicians the entertainers, the professional sportsmen and women. Those directly concerned with the productive, distributive and service sectors of industry, trade and commerce are organized in the individual workplace, the firm and the industry and require their own trade associations or trade unions for the same purposes. This complex of organizations provide essential infrastructures for social, political and economic society.

The organization of cultural life overlaps with local government in the provision of education for example, and with the professional groups or unions in the economic sphere. The academics, the artists, and those who work in the media, through publishing and newspapers, and those sections of the communications sector who work with them, also cater for the cultural aspects of life. The churches are crucial to the culture of a people, protecting and encouraging its fundamental values. The vast number of organizations which provide voluntary and charitable service to the community are central to it also – the youth organizations and the literary, dramatic and recreational groups, and those which work for the vast range of charities – all are necessary and supplement the work of the State in these areas.

The Church therefore puts great emphasis on the importance of a vital pattern of such intermediate organizations between the family and the State, because it is through them that the citizens and their free associations are enabled to exercise responsibility for their own lives and those of their dependants. The State, the national government capable of providing for the common good according to natural and divine revealed law, is essential to man in order that he may fulfil his human potential, but it is the rights of persons, families and private associations established in civil society which exist before the State, which that State exists to serve. Where the State totally fails its citizens, as it did in the former communist countries, it was the nations whose culture had been formed under Christian influences over the centuries which provided the antidote in a Godless system which was disintegrating. The people rediscovered their power as free citizens to form associations and reclaim their freedom and their self-respect to rebuild an alternative society and State.

### (iv) Community and society: solidarity

Because all men and women are made in the image and likeness of God and are called to serve him in love and to share the eternal happiness of heaven, we are brothers and sisters, sons and daughters of the one God. Wherever human beings are gathered together there is a community, a common origin and a common purpose between them, and this should be reflected in their relationships. Some communities have greater oneness or homogeneity of race or culture in all its aspects, and that gives them a greater tendency to realize their common humanity within themselves; this can be exaggerated and become the seed of racialism, which refuses to accept that all men and women possess the same personal dignity because they share the one human nature, no matter what accidental differences of birth, culture and socioeconomic background separate them; but such racialism is a

perversion of solidarity. Awareness of our common humanity is the
reality which should surpass all others; it is the basis of solidarity
[SP 35–43, GS 29–32, LC 73, 89–91, SRS 38–40] which should lead
the strong to care for the weak, those who have riches to share
them with the poor, and those who are poor to do their best by
their own efforts to overcome their poverty and other disadvantages so that they may better themselves and make a greater
contribution to the common weal aided by the community. The
secular creed of socialism has always grasped this communitarian
nature of man and stressed its implications in terms of brother
helping brother – yet the socialist movement has also produced
some of the greatest injustices of modern times by forgetting that
man, as made in God's image and redeemed by his Son, is the end
and purpose of every social organization, and not its slave.

Solidarity then is primarily the solidarity of all men in possessing
the same human nature and dignity; it is also the solidarity of
particular groups of citizens among themselves, national groups,
social and economic groups, all the intermediate organizations
that make political society possible. Such groups seek to ensure
that their legitimate interests are properly served and advanced. In
this they can conflict, actually or potentially, with other such interest groups, and it is the task of the political authority to harmonize
the various solidarities, if necessary curbing their excesses by force
of law. Despite this tendency of group solidarity to become anti-
social, that solidarity is in itself valuable because it is an exercise in
self-help and self-organization for acceptable ends which is part of
the pattern of a free society. If every right and every good thing
that could be abused were denied the right to exist, there would be
not be any social institutions at all because all are capable of being
misused, abused.

This solidarity should make Christians pre-eminent in helping
the development of every man. Conscientization is the ugly word
applied to the policy of some Christian activists in Latin America
who wanted to help the poor to help themselves. They were considered as innovators, and sometimes dangerous innovators, because
this made the poor more aware that they had been deprived of their
right to self-development which operates through the right of association to further their well-being. But the situation in which they
could be pressured into accepting such injustices was a denial of the
basic Christian ethic of civil society; not only must the rich show solidarity with the poor and vice versa, but the poor have the right and
the duty to do what they can to better themselves; conscientization
therefore is just the process of helping the poor to help themselves.

## (v) Justice in society

Justice[1] is the virtue which enables us to give to others what is theirs by right, that to which they have a moral right, and one that can be vindicated at law; the function of law being to secure justice. The way the legal system works does not always ensure that this is done; such defects are the result of human error and weakness. The truth that law should give justice is reinforced, not undermined, by this fact.

In society justice must be done at all levels. General justice primarily orders the individual towards the community, and for that reason is mainly the responsibility of the legislator; it is secondarily in the citizen, because the latter has the duty of obeying just law (ST IIa IIae, Q. 58, art. 6). General justice, properly understood and acted on produces justice in society, social justice, as the State which has the care of the common good, through humane legislation which enables the citizens and all the intermediate organizations to develop their potential. The citizens, and those intermediate organizations, also have a duty to contribute by their care for the needs of the community and to make their creative contribution to the common good. A major question is the proper distribution of property and the regulation of possessions, and it is the ruler's duty to ensure that access to the necessities of life is available to all, because this is necessary for virtue, and the absence of justice in economic matters is a cause of social disorder (ST Ia IIae, Q.105, art 2 ad 3, Aquinas *de Reg. Princ.* Bk. 1. 15, Aristotle *Polit.* ii 4) In return the citizen has to make his contribution to the common good by being prepared to work for what he needs.

Besides the general, there is a particular justice in two respects. Firstly there is commutative justice, justice primarily in economic exchange, which concerns justice between individuals and covers the keeping of contracts and agreements between them. What is justly promised or contracted must be justly fulfilled by the partners. This justice is arithmetical, therefore exact equivalence according to contract is demanded by it (ST IIa IIae, Q.61, art. 1, art. 2). Secondly, there is distributive justice, and this concerns the State's distribution among the citizens of the honours and goods it has in its gift (ST Ia, Q.21, art. 1, IIa IIae, Q. 61, art. 1 and 2). Under general or social justice all are entitled to access to the necessities of life, and it is the duty of the State to see this is the case, the citizen in return being prepared to work for his needs. Distributive justice is not about the necessities of life, but about the honours and goods which are in the State's gift, and these are distributed proportionately. All citizens are to be given access to the means of a decent livelihood in return for readiness to work; some are to receive the goods of the State and its honours, not according to the principle of exact equality between individuals, but in accordance with their greater service to society. Those whose contribution to the common good is greater, should have a greater share of the honours of the State.

Justice at all levels is then a mark of a sound and healthy society, but justice alone cannot knit society together; it needs to be supplemented by love, by charity (ST IIa IIae, Q. 29, art. 3), respecting others as persons, members of the same human family, an awareness that all are children of one common Father. Charity, love of others for God's sake, is the cradle of justice; without it the latter can be harsh and unfeeling; true love for our brothers and sisters in Christ, solidarity with them whatever their colour, creed, or social class is the only force which will bind society together. If that is the underlying attitude in society, and informs its leaders and its structures, then justice will be firm but tempered with mercy. Where unjust structures exist in society then the Christian must work for change, but this change will not be achieved unless, at the same time as seeking the necessary peaceful change, the hearts and minds of those who perpetrate injustices are changed also [LC 74–5, SRS 35–8], or else the evil will appear in another form even if a particular unjust structure is eliminated.

### (vi) Human rights and responsibilities

Justice is about rights and the securing of them by law. The question of human rights in general overlaps with that of justice, but is at once much broader than the reach of justice, and it is therefore not always practicable to seek legal redress for human rights; for example, there is in general a human right of access to higher education in order that those capable of benefiting from it may fulfil their potential, but whether and to what extent it is available depends largely upon the state of development of a particular society. It would be futile therefore to try to claim a legal right to that education if the State had not the means, for no fault of its own, to provide it. The failure of a right to exist in practice tells us something therefore of the defects of a particular social order. Other rights are of course absolute and not conditional, the most fundamental being the right to life and the basic means to sustain it.

These rights are founded in man's being made in the image and likeness of God and redeemed by his Son. They therefore existed before the State was founded and cannot be taken from him by that State [DR 27–31, MBS 29–31]. They embrace [PT 11–27, SRS 32–3, CA 47–6] the right to life – the most fundamental of all rights, now challenged by abortion and euthanasia. The right to the means to sustain and develop it, to adequate food, clothing, shelter, medical care, rest, social services, the right to be cared for in ill health, after accidents at work, and during periods of unsought unemployment. There is a right to be respected, to a good name, to freedom to seek the truth, to freedom of speech and publication (within the limits of the common good), to choose a profession and to be informed about public events and to share in the benefits of culture, to general and technical/professional training and advanced studies according to talent and the country's state of development. The right to worship God according to conscience and to profess religion privately and in public, according to the freedom the apostles and martyrs claimed, most truly safeguards the dignity of the human person.

There is a right to choose to marry or not to marry, and the right to choose priesthood or religious life. The family, founded on true marriage, one and indivisible, is the primary cell of society and must be protected by it. The support and education of children is the right primarily of parents. There is a right to work and to personal initiative in it, under conditions which respect human dignity and development, of adults and juveniles, male and female. There is a right to economic freedom and rewards from it, according to responsibilities in its process. The right to private ownership of productive goods is included in this; it permits an assertion of personality, exercise of responsibility, and prosperity for the State. It brings with it social obligations.

There is the right of groups to meet together, form private associations with their fellows and to give them the purposes and organizations adequate to suit their aims; such intermediate organizations are essential for freedom with responsibility. People also have a right to freedom of movement and residence in their home country, and of emigration where there are just reasons for it, because all are members not only of a particular State but of the whole human family. There is a right to take an active part in public life and make a contribution to it for the common good; man is the end and purpose of the State, not an inert element within it. Each has also the right to legal protection of rights, effective, unbiased and just. These rights are then for all, men and women, of whatever race, colour or creed [PT 44, 86, PP 62, OA 16]. Racialism is particularly repugnant because it strikes at the very root of the dignity of the human being, a dignity that stems from the common Fatherhood of God and redemption by God made man. The rights of women to full participation in all aspects of cultural, professional and public life has been increasingly recognized in recent years [PT 41, GS 9, 29, OA 13].

These rights therefore stem from man's nature as made in the image of God and entitled to freedom so that he may freely respond to God's love; they bring with them and are inseparable from the responsibilities that go with the dignity of possessing reason and free will. To claim our rights while neglecting our responsibilities is to build with one hand and destroy with the other [PT 28–34]. It is because she understands the high dignity of man that the Church insists these rights and responsibilities are for all. They are fruitful for the person, civil society and the State, but without the understanding of men and women as children of God human rights become meaningless. Those who deny these rights can only be challenged on the grounds of absolute and unchanging moral standards. Those within society who try to corrupt it by introducing concepts of rights which are perverse and challenge human dignity can likewise only be challenged by those who have a firm and well-founded belief in moral absolutes. Only such standards provide a sound basis for freedom and human dignity [MBS 29–31, SP 47–70, PT 36–8, CA 46–7].

### (vii)  Social class and social conflict

The Christian vision of society is not egalitarian [RN 16–19]. That there should be different social classes, and differences of fortune and prosperity between them, was accepted by the inspired writers of the Old and New Testaments. God's dealing with his chosen people, building them up to a great nation in all aspects of social, political and economic life, did not reveal an egalitarian plan. All men and women are equal before God in their human dignity, it is true, because that stems from their being his sons and daughters, redeemed by Christ our brother; none then may be denied their human rights, and, if they will work for it, all must have access to a fair share in the wealth of the world that God has given to all so that all might enjoy a good life from it. Within this framework worldly fortunes may differ, justice and charity in the gaining and the use of their wealth being binding on those that fortune favours more markedly. Provided everyone who is ready to work, and is capable of working, has access to the means of earning a living, then differences of fortune are compatible with the teaching of the Scriptures and the apostolic tradition, but not every pattern of wealth distribution has to be accepted as a fact of life, and reforms in these matters may be not only legitimate but necessary for the greater social good. All should be encouraged to become property owners, and should have the opportunity to become so through their own efforts [RN 47, MM 112–15, GS 71].

The question of the significance of class differences and their effect on society were brought to the fore by Marx and Engels in their writings on the industrial revolution and its aftermath. Marx reasoned that the injustices inflicted on the proletariat by the bourgeoisie, the capitalists, were not only intolerable, but of their nature were going to bring about the self-destruction of capitalism; socialism, above all the social ownership of the means of production, was the way of the future. Its advent, they said, was scientifically predictable. In facing these predictions, the Church did not deny there was a considerable degree of class conflict in modern industrial society, and that the working classes and their employers faced one another in a form of industrial and social war which had to be ended. Unlike the Marxist, however, she believed in gradual social reform, achieved by recognizing that all men were brothers in Christ and should act accordingly, by the proper intervention of the State to improve the lot of the proletariat and protect it from those who were effectively enslaving it, and by the action of employers and employees in industry, working out fair wage contracts and properly human conditions of work. The wage earners had a right of association in free trade unions aimed at improving their condition in body, soul and property. The State was to limit its intervention to cases where it was necessary for it to act in order that the common good should be fostered. Any attempt by the workers to use violence in their cause was wrong, as was any attempt to deny the right of association in free trade unions and the peaceful working for improvement of the lot of the wage earners. As to the class war – it was specifically repudiated; labour needs capital and capital needs labour; they should work together rather than spending their energies in futile conflict [RN 16, 48, QA 65, 81–7, MM 75–7, 91–2, LE 8, 20].

The decision then was not for the *status quo* of liberal capitalism and its evils. The injustices of the Industrial Revolution [LE 29–37], against which socialism was a reaction, were repudiated as contrary to the dignity of man. Where liberal capitalism exists today it is to be condemned [CA 8, 33–4]. But the extreme socialist remedy for these evils, namely, class warfare and the social ownership of the means of production, were rejected also [LE 11, 14, CA 13–14]. With justice and charity governing their relationship, labour and capital could both make their contribution to a more just social order. At the time this judgement was made in the late nineteenth century, it seemed that such an answer had avoided the issues. It was only after the collapse of real Socialism that it became plain that the analysis had been sound and prophetic.

### (viii)  Community and society: subsidiarity

That the citizen then has rights which the State cannot take from him, and that man is the end and purpose of every social organization, are fundamental principles of the Christian ethic of civil and political society. Nurtured in the family, which is the foundation of both civil and political society, citizens must receive from their parents the essential moral education which enables them to accept their responsibilities as citizens, free but using freedom for good and not for ill, and because of this ability becoming valuable members of political as well as civil society. The natural and the divine revealed moral law are the sources of sound morality, and it is in the State's interest to see that this morality is fostered in educational and cultural institutions.

The Christian social ethic therefore is oriented to producing citizens who relish their freedom under the natural and divine laws; the latter prevents freedom giving way to licence, and because of this it encourages independent-minded people capable of running their own affairs without excessive reliance on others. This strong sense of independence is not anti-social or anti-communitarian: on the contrary, the Christian is his brother's keeper; all men and women are God's children and have the same rights stemming from that dignity. Solidarity with others is a theory and a practice which is nurtured by the Christian understanding of man as a social being, joined with all men in oneness in Jesus Christ.

Yet while accepting his social responsibilities of solidarity with all, he retains his personal identity and the need to follow that vocation to self-development which God has given to all men and women according to their talents and their opportunities. So the Christian is more rather than less able to use his own initiative in social, cultural, economic and political life, and in this should not be shackled or thwarted by the unnecessary interventions of other social organizations in his affairs. Since, however, he is a social being, and joins with others in society for mutual support, there may come a time when as a person, or as a member of a social organization or organizations, he needs the help of other social authorities, the State locally or nationally in particular, in achieving his aims. When he does need this help, the principle of subsidiarity [QA 79–80, MM 53, 117, 152, LC 73] comes into play, the word being a derivative from the Latin *subsidium*, which means assistance, help. Subsidiarity then does not see person, civil society and political society as in conflict; on the contrary, they are mutually supportive. The person in the context of family life comes first, but person and family need society beyond the family, so that they may achieve ends with others corporately which they would be unable to achieve alone. However, since there is a danger that socialization, the proliferation of social organizations, can get out of control and threaten the individual initiative which is essential for a healthy society, the principle of subsidiarity must be clearly kept in mind. There are cases when intervention of the higher organization or authority is needful in order that the person on the smaller organization may fulfil his, or its purposes. But any such intervention should be temporary and aimed at making the person or the smaller organization independent again.

## 2 Ethics and political society – the State

### (i) *The origin, purpose and nature of the authority of political society and the State*

Civil society, families and private organizations, or 'intermediate organizations', i.e. those that come between the person and the State, by definition exist before the State, and civil society is then the more fundamental social organization [QA 76–80, MM 59, 65, GS 25, 74–5]. Because of this priority of person, family and civil society, the citizens bring with them into that society rights of which they cannot be deprived. Yet properly understood there is no natural animosity between the two societies. Political society, that is, a society which can make law and enforce it in a way which private societies cannot, is necessary in order that persons, families and private organizations might fully achieve their ends; it grows out of the need to ensure that the common good, the good of each and the good of all, is achieved because right reason and experience confirm that without such a political organization civil society cannot function effectively [QAM 6, DI 4–5]. The State has a positive function; the liberal idea of its purely negative role is rejected, its true task is to develop both public and individual well-being, and in this it has a special duty to care for the poor [RN 33–46, QA 25–8, PT 46–66]. Where there is mass poverty the State must do all in its power to relieve it. Positive action by the State is also needed to maintain economic prosperity once it is achieved; it must be based on the encouragement of private initiative and the principle of subsidiarity. The State should not absorb the individual or the family, but allow them full freedom consistent with the common good and the needs of others [RN 35]. The rights of persons, families and private associations inevitably overlap or conflict at some point, at many points, and the limits of each must be determined by just law. So if strikes threaten the peace, or employers impose on workers unjust wages and conditions which lead to their spiritual, moral and physical degradation, the State could legislate insofar as the common good requires [RN 36].

Because such political authority is needful for a fully ordered life of man in society, it is necessary to society and as such its authority comes ultimately from God [ID 8–16, QAM 6, PT 46–50, GS 74]. Without the backing of the law of God, political authority lacks the sanction to bind the citizens to obedience in conscience: it needs to have this backing if it is to discharge its responsibilities successfully. That there should be a political society therefore is implicit in the spontaneous evolution of civil society, because civil society needs a directing agency within it so that all the members of that society can achieve their legitimate aims without depriving others of theirs.

## (ii) Forms of State

Man, created by God as a social being, forms States to further his social needs. The Church is not identified with any particular form of State, and peoples are free to choose their own form of government; political pluralism is positively accepted; the identification of freedom with licence she will always condemn [ID 36–7, 48, DI 4–7, SC 78–9]. The key legislation which secures basic human rights and social justice must then be able to bind its people to obedience in conscience, in spirit as well as law, if it is to do this.

Positive prescription is not enough; man needs more enduring standards, from natural and divine law, if his choices on these issues are to be properly guided. But that the power of all legitimate political authority and the State is God-ordained, does not imply that those who exercise political authority get it directly from God. No one has a divine right to rule; and the people may choose the form of State and their rulers [QAM 6, DI 4–7]. The form of State chosen may be a traditional or monarchical form, aristocracy, plutocracy or democracy, or a combination of more than one of these; it may be chosen passively, that is, by peaceful acquiescence in an existing order, or actively, through the casting of votes, but it must have the approval of those over whom it is exercised; it cannot be imposed. Legitimate political authority must be respected because its power to act for the common good is derived from God through the people.

When we consider in practice that man's dignity requires that he take an active part in government, that all States must protect human rights and clearly set out what are the respective rights and duties of the public authorities and the citizens, it is clear that a democratic form of government is the best way of providing that this pattern is established (Pius XII Radio Message December 1944, 74–5, [CA 46]). But for democracy to be of true service to man it must serve the truth as revealed in natural and divine revealed law, or else it is open to manipulation, tends to totalitarianism, and loses sight of the common good, with its rulers serving only the electoral or financial purposes of those who elected them rather than justice or morality, so that the people become disillusioned [CA 47].


## (iii)  The common good and party politics

The moral foundations of the State therefore rest on its function in guiding society, its individual members, its families, and the other intermediate organizations, social, cultural, political and economic, towards the true common good, that is into a situation where all are helped to achieve their individual aims in such a way that they do not deny others, individuals or organizations, their respective rights, and all make their contribution to the general welfare in pursuing their aims in accordance with just law [SP 55–9, PT 53–7].

Partisan politics, in which various interest groups join together in advancing a shared set of beliefs about political life and ask their fellow citizens to elect them on their programme, have been found by active and stable democracies to be the best way of ensuring that changes of government are managed peacefully through proper democratic channels. It is not the task of the Christian social ethic to determine particular political forms; these are for secular society to decide, provided the ends and the means they use are compatible with natural and divine law. Party politics, like representative government, grew out of perceived need and no other theory or practice seems adequate to meet that need. The question then is, are party politics and the pursuit of the common good mutually exclusive? Briefly, the answer is in principle no, provided that the existence of an overall common good is accepted, and with it a basic solidarity with all in society – including political opponents – and that parties work within this framework, each insisting on its understanding of how that good is to be achieved, but accepting the right of other parties to disagree with them and abiding by the decision of the electorate on who is to govern [GS 75]. In other words the magisterium has accepted that such a system is reconcilable with right reason for the operation of the secular order [GS 75, OA 46–50]. The plural- ist State assumes such parties, and the pluralist State was accepted by Leo XIII [ID 37] though the question of Christian democracy clouded the issue for a while; Leo, however, accepted the value of the Centre Party in Germany, and Benedict XV the PPI in Italy after the first world war; the existence of parties in democratic society gradually proved their worth and the Second Vatican Council recognized them explicitly. The legitimacy of different points of view about the organization of worldly affairs is recog- nized, and the associations or parties which people form to advance them. Each will consider its own policies the best way of achieving the common good, but must never make the mistake of thinking that it is superior to that good. Christians are to take their political options within the limits allowable by the Church's social teaching, but they must not expect to claim the Church's name or authority in support of their own legitimate opinions when other good men may legitimately differ from them. Nor can Christian partisan politicians commit the Church to the support of a particular party option [GS 43, 76]. Should it happen that one party was favouring an option on a particular matter which was compatible with Christian social teaching, and an opposed party was not, it would then be for the hierarchy to judge the degree to which the party with the right option should be explic- itly supported by the Church. The experience of alliances formed with political parties ostensibly in favour of Christian policies have not been encouraging; it suggests that such parties are much more interested in using such alliances for party than for specifically Christian purposes, and the Church's mission has accordingly suffered in the long term.

## (iv) The law, morality, justice and human rights

We have seen that respect for human rights, the rights of man, is the best rule of thumb for judging whether in a particular society the common good is being achieved, and we have also considered the questions of general, distributive and commutative justice. These ideas and their interaction stem from a particular understanding of Christian morality and its relation to those rights and to law. Society must be rooted in freedom, guided by justice and animated by a love which enables men to feel the needs of others as their own. It must be based on freedom, each having and assuming moral responsibility for his own actions; human society in this perspective is primarily a spiritual reality, through participation in which men can share their knowledge of truth, claim rights and fulfil duties, sharing their enjoyment of the wholesome pleasures of this world. Such order can only come to be through belief in a universal, absolute and immutable good, stemming in its turn from belief in the one, true, personal and transcendent God [PT 35-8].

Belief in the divine eternal law, the divine revealed law, and the natural law is the only basis on which a healthy political society can be built. To allow moral law to be left to the whim of man's subjective opinions instead of anchoring it in the will of God and his commandments is to destroy it. Natural law is written in the hearts of men, and it can be understood by sound reason when it is not obscured by sinfulness. Every positive law can be judged by this law; nothing can be useful if it is not morally good; man has rights that he holds from God and these must be protected by the State [MBS 29-31, EV 68-74].

Totalitarianism of the left and of the right denies transcendent truth and consequently has no respect for persons and their rights; they are expected to be totally at the service of race or State. Only in the light of their transcendent destiny is there firm protection for people and their rights. Without ultimate truth founded in God the citizens of democratic States are subject to manipulation, as are those in the totalitarian. The Church by contrast is not trapped by the rigid schema of worldly ideologies, but can respond to human need without reservation, insisting only on the dignity of man made in God's image and likeness, the human person, who can know the moral truth and follow its dictates freely. Some democracies, however, have rejected the belief that society must have a sound, objective moral basis with rights and duties for its citizens established in just laws and protected by effective sanctions. That basis cannot exist unless the value system on which it can be established exists, and this must be fostered, in freedom, by the public authorities. They cannot avoid their responsibilities in this matter. Societies and political systems which are not so based produce politicians who are interested only in electoral and financial power and the selfish interests of their partisans [CA 46–7, EV 70–1].

## (v) Justified war

Once Christianity had been accepted by the Roman Empire, and Christian statesmen and military leaders faced their responsibilities to defend the State, it was inevitable that moralists would be involved in trying to help them determine the circumstances when, regrettably, force might have to be used, and the manner in which it should be used once hostilities had started. It was then not a matter of determining in the abstract whether it was just or not, but of trying to prevent abuses of the right of self-defence once it became impossible to preserve the public good without resort to arms. There was therefore always a certain hesitancy about positively commending death-dealing violence; it was always to be seen as a regrettable necessity; there was then always a paradox here. In an imperfect world there were circumstances in which it was necessary that military virtues could be, and should be respected, praised and encouraged for young men called on to fight, yet there was always regret that it should be so.

The modern social teaching has not dealt with the matter, though the tradition has recognized and defended the concept, and the Second Vatican Council reminded us that, since there is no international authority with the competence and power to ensure the peaceful settlement of disputes, which is the ideal, then the right of lawful self-defence remains [GS 79]. With the publication of the *Catechism of the Catholic Church*, however, the theory has been briefly restated. The aggressor must have done lasting, grave and certain damage to a State or to the international community; all other means of ending it must be shown to be impractical or ineffective; there must be a reasonable prospect of success, and the use of force must hold out the reasonable hope that it will not produce greater evils than those which it is hoped to eliminate; it is for those who have the responsibility for the common good to evaluate these conditions of moral legitimacy in the light of the power of modern weapons and their capacity for unimaginable destruction, especially of non-combatant civilian populations, which the Council also declared was totally immoral [GS 80]. Once war is started, non-combatants, the wounded and prisoners must be treated humanely, and actions contrary to international law are forbidden; blind obedience does not excuse those who carry them out [CCC 2307–14].

### (vi) Political dissent and Christian ethics

The acceptance of party politics means that respect for legitimate political authority, when it is exercising that authority in accordance with natural and divine law, does not rule out the right of dissent for the Christian. Party politics is a form of such dissent in a democracy; the concept of 'loyal opposition' allows a democrat to differ with the particular government, or some of its policies, while accepting its right to make laws which, despite his disagreement, he will obey while it is the rightful government; such dissent, peacefully made, is one way of keeping government under constant scrutiny lest it overreach its authority, while respecting its right to rule until replaced by due democratic process.

   Not all legitimate differences of opinion can find effective outlet through party politics and the formal procedures of democracy, and most democratic States allow peaceful demonstrations by private associations on specific issues – subject to protesters meeting the reasonable needs of public order. This is not always easy to preserve when passions are running high, as for example on racialism, trade union rights or abortion. In cases where the police are prepared to use what seems to be disproportionate force to control protesters on the one hand, and on the other, some protesters are clearly going beyond peaceful protest, it may be prudent for protesters not to invoke their full right to protest for a while, or for the law to be applied minimally by the authorities – for the sake of the public and private good. Exposing oneself to serious injury, or being imprisoned, however unjustly, for a just cause, affects not only the injured or the imprisoned, but also spouses, children and colleagues, and those risking such things should remember this; it could also lead to serious public disorder from which all would suffer; quieter and less conflictual means of asserting the right of protest should be found. Pursuing the full force of the law, even where they are entitled to do so, may inflict such disproportionate suffering on individuals, and on public well-being, that the authorities may be well advised to ease off in its application in specific cases, while maintaining the principle.

The case of conscientious objection by individuals on the grounds that the shedding of blood is wrong, even in a necessary war of self-defence, is also acceptable in most modern States. However, the objector, while being able to claim right of conscience in this matter, can be expected to help the community by performing some peaceful service to the community war effort, such as assisting the medical services or working in another useful capacity specified by the State. Nor can the Church's acceptance of the moral legitimacy of conscientious objection in war be opposed to the equal right of a citizen to decide that service of his country in a just war is a good and honourable way also [GS 79].

A particular difficulty for many during the Cold War years was the morality of building, and intending to use in a possible future war, the weapons of mass destruction which modern technology had spawned. Primarily this meant the nuclear weapons which the splitting of the atom had made possible, but it included also the many new biological and chemical devices which had never been used in war but promised to add new dimensions of horror to any future conflict [GS 80]. The matter came to a head when some sections of the American Church had become determined that means should be found for a total outlawing of these weapons – so that construction of them for intended military use, and any co-operation in their deployment for that purpose, should be declared intrinsically immoral.[2]

If this had been the case the Church would have had to warn her people that it was their moral duty to disobey the orders of the State in this matter, whether they were military personnel or civilians, a course of action which would have involved the Church in open conflict with the secular order on a disputed matter of the application of moral principle in a dangerously hypothetical case; this was a contest she could not enter and, if she did, she could not win. The degree to which the believer in the God of the Scriptures and in the Church's tradition based on that belief can compromise with evil in a fallen world has always been difficult to decide; but the attempt to prevent a possible disaster in the secular order by putting at risk the Church's freedom to go on with her work of preaching the Gospel would have meant the complete repudiation of her Master's example and instructions; his kingdom was not, and is not, of this world, its beginning in it not withstanding.

Beyond these cases of dissent from political authority by peaceful and legal means, there also exists, in principle, a moral right to use violence to try to overthrow a government if it rules for the private good of the ruler or of any one group instead of for the common good. The conditions for considering this step in theory are very exacting. It is never the Church's role to initiate such action, and she must be careful not to influence the laymen on whom the responsibility for it would rest, to take such action. It must be the last resort when all other means have failed; the rebels must in some way represent the opinion of the majority of the citizens that this violence is necessary, and they must be morally sure that greater good will come from the proposed course of action than from tolerating the evil ruler and hoping that things may improve. The whole stress of the teaching Church is that peace must be the way, but if this fails and the situation cannot be tolerated because of grave and persistent denial of human rights, then as a last resort rebellion may be justified [PP 30–1, LC 79]. That is to be determined by the laity in response to the promptings of their informed consciences; at all times, the hierarchical Church's option must be for peace.

## (vii)  Church and State

The Church is not bound to any political community or system but, being a sign of the transcendence of the person, is independent of them all. Church and State are autonomous organizations, each of which has its own specific purpose, and neither may hinder the other in discharge of its responsibilities; the State exists for the sake of the secular order and its purpose is to secure the common good of society, the good of each and of all, and must make dispositions accordingly. The Church has no direct role in the social, political or economic order [GS 76, LC 80]; each has its own legitimate autonomy under the natural law, and it is only on the moral issues involved in these areas that the Church has any authority; what sort of State and form of Government there should be is for the people to decide, with the statesmen, politicians and political scientists working out the practical implications of the people's choice. This does not mean that Church and State are in any fundamental way in opposition to one another; on the contrary, since they both deal with the same human beings, it is desirable that they co-operate as much as possible in their missions, always keeping in mind that the two missions differ.

The Church is concerned with spiritual and moral truth and the preaching of the kingdom of God which is not of this world, but, far from this dividing the two, this concern increases the importance of the secular order. Christians have a duty to participate in politics according to their talents and the needs of the community; the minimum requirement is to cast a vote in elections, deciding on the best of the knowledge available which candidate or party is more likely to serve the common good. Party politics are a means of serving the common good, and Christians must respect other Christians whose choice of party or political philosophy is different from theirs. No sectional group or party may claim that theirs is the only Christian way, and to use, or seek to use, the Church's name, teaching or action as a vindication of partisan political views is not acceptable [GS 43–4, OA 24–8, 45–51]. There may be circumstances in which one party is strongly in favour of policies, for example on the family, which are more in line with Catholic teaching. In this case it would seem that the Church could recommend her people to vote for the party in question. Experience, however, has shown that any such identification with one party is counterproductive, as it eventually involves the Church in the secular conflicts of partisan politics. It is better to proceed by recommending policies, irrespective of which party is saying what, and leaving the people to make up their own minds.

The question of the Church 'interfering' in politics is one that causes confusion. The way it is proposed assumes that if the Church does take a stance with political implications then it is always wrong for her to do so, but the Church's concern with man's eternal destiny leads her to different conclusions. The whole of human life and morality is regarded by her as under her care, and this means that some political issues, those concerning human rights and the good of souls, are part of it. Since she sees the person as the purpose and end of all social organizations, such organizations which deny or undermine human rights are open to criticism, and since man's first obligation is to know, love and serve God, any interference with religious freedom is also open to criticism. What she must avoid, and her clergy must avoid, is an identification with partisan politics, a particular political, social or economic group (Address of John Paul II to priests and male religious at Guadalupe 27 January 1979, Bishops' Statement 'Evangelization in Latin America' at Puebla.)[3] Her aim must be to encourage active involvement in politics and public service for citizens of all political persuasions, and to give spiritual and moral guidance to them in pursuing their legitimate though frequently conflicting ends. She must avoid supporting any particular group; where the majority of Catholics are of one political persuasion rather than another, this may cause problems, but the opinions of the minority of dissenters must be respected.

## (viii) Solidarity and subsidiarity

The one proviso on the question of the necessity of giving all and any organizations the right to carry on their activities, is that they respect an underlying solidarity which prevents healthy political debate from being corrupted by incompatible ideologies of left or right; these are not interested in democratic freedoms, but only in the furthering of their own brand of political intolerance which ultimately leads to totalitarianism [CA 44–6]. There must in other words be a respect for opponents. That I disagree entirely with what a man says should not move me to want to deny him the right to say it; on the contrary, I should defend his right to free speech. A true democrat has to be prepared to say that all true democrats have the same right to rule as does his party, so that when the country does ask another party to take over in government he is prepared to give them his loyalty in the ordinary discharge of their responsibilities, whether he agrees with their policies or not that, if he disagrees with them, his loyalty will take the form of a loyal opposition when convention allows, involves no contradiction. Far from undermining democracy, it will ensure its continued vitality.

Providing the basis on which this solidarity can be firmly founded is beyond the brief of any particular political party. Dealing as it does with answers to the ultimate questions concerning man, and not with party differences, it must be derived from the cultural values, philosophical and theological, which underpin society. Christianity provides such values in its teaching concerning the dignity of man, and the rights and responsibilities he possesses in the light of that dignity. A particular party may share those values; it can hardly provide them. A society which has abandoned the standards which previous generations accepted when that society emerged, and has not found and cannot find an alternative on which to base a morally sound consensus, cannot be in anything but the profoundest decline and such, unfortunately, is the case with Western post-Christian society today.

Solidarity requires a theological, a moral philosophical or meta-physical basis, therefore, if it is to be effective. Subsidiarity, however, the moral principle which ensures maximum freedom of initiative for the person, the family and private association, is also a matter of practical politics which should form part of any political party's basic thinking.

In civil society, which is prior to political society, the citizen possesses rights which political society cannot take from him – basically the right to life and to self-development in freedom. At the same time, in entering into political society in order that through social-political association he may fulfil himself, he must expect to give up some part of some of his pre-political freedoms so that he may be helped by the community to achieve what he could not achieve without that community. Civil society, with its values and potential, is not of its nature in conflict with political society; the latter grows out of the former and in it the values possessed in civil society are supplemented so that they may be more easily and completely fulfilled. In particular there may be difficulties in adjusting the rights under the one with the responsibilities that come from the other, but given the essential coherence of the two societies such adjustments can be made.

The Christian social ethic being based on the dignity of the person who is the purpose and end of all social organization, that social organization must always be at the service of the person in the context of the family and of the spontaneously developing social groups which form intermediate society; at the same time political society and the State are necessary for the fulfilment of the ends of persons, of families and private social organizations [GS 74]. It comes to be because they realize they need such a political organization to achieve their ends. All this is summed up in the idea of subsidiarity, a concept which tells us that the larger organization and ultimately the State can, in circumstances alone give to individuals, families, organizations the help that they need to achieve their aims. Implicit in Judaeo-Christian social teaching from the first, it was spelled out explicitly by Pius XI; the aim of all social activity should be to help the smaller groups, not to destroy them; it is wrong to withdraw from the individual and to give to the group things he can do himself, and wrong also to take from the smaller group and give to the larger, tasks that they can do for themselves [QA 79–80]. The political authority, local and national, should only intervene in the affairs of those groups as a last resort and temporarily, to enable them to be independent again.

The State has a role in the control of a country's economic life, but it is a secondary one. It has the right to own productive goods where the common good requires it [QA 114, GS 71]; it has the right and the duty of influencing the economy to ensure a high level of employment and of overseeing it as a whole for the common good; in all this, however its function is secondary, guiding and supplementing so that private initiative serves the community better, but not replacing that initiative [LE 17, PT 60–6, CA 48]. There is a particular problem in the State's role in social welfare. That it has such a valid role is clear; at one time in Europe, and wherever the Europeans colonialized, it was the Church which was responsible for social welfare, but from the fourteenth century it became clear that voluntary organization was no longer enough to meet the need; the State had an essential role here as well as the private organizations. When the modern social magisterium began to develop from the late nineteenth century, it emphasized that provision by the State to meet the needs of the poor – by which was meant the working class in general – was imperative, while the ideal of each wage earner being able to provide for the essential needs of his family remained. The State's action was necessary but should be complementary to what the individual, or what the first-line social organization could do.

There was concern among social Catholics in the 1950s that State welfare was becoming excessive and threatening the capacity for individual responsibility that was the benchmark of the Christian social ethic. John XXIII responded to this concern specifically in *Mater et Magistra* [59–67] and while he did not attack the principle of State welfare where it was clearly necessary, he did note that care should be taken lest it bred dependence. The purpose of all welfare should be to enable the person concerned to become independent once more. This acceptance of the need for State welfare systems remains; it is a demand of justice in any society that the right to life and proper maintenance of it, for those unfortunate enough to be unable to provide the means to do so for themselves, should exist. The dangers of a State welfare mentality are becoming more apparent in some societies and this undermines human dignity and produces a Social Assistance State [CA 48].

### (ix) International relations

The relations of States and heads of States are, like those of individuals, the subject of reciprocal rights and duties based on truth, justice and freedom according to the natural law and the needs of humanity [PT 80]. There are great differences between States in terms of population and resources, stages of development and of power, but this does not mean that the larger and stronger powers have the right to dominate the smaller; justice should be the norm in all things [PT 88–9]. No State may defend its rights at the expense of the rights of others, and conflicts between them should be settled by negotiation, not by force of arms. The complexity of modern life and the ease of communications between States underline that the good of each State and of the international community of States, depends on co-operation each with each; as with individuals, so the co-operation of States enables them to achieve collectively what they cannot individually.

Given this complexity and their growth, the older methods of organizing and regulating international relations through diplomacy and treaties, are no longer enough. Some international authority is needed with the power, organization and means adequate to achieving the international common good; it must be built up by agreement, on the principle of subsidiarity, and so with the full co-operation and support of individual States [PT 130–41]. The United Nations Organization has done much to these ends and the hope is that it may gradually be able to fulfil the expectations resting in it more fully. The problems of conflict between the nations must be handled by negotiations where this is possible; where there is a justified resort to arms it must be conducted humanely. The indiscriminate bombing of civilians and civilian targets for terror purpose is of its nature to be condemned, as is any State resort to terror and torture of any kind and on any scale [GS 79, 80, LC 78–9]. Arms races between nations, especially the larger ones, absorb energies and resources which are needed for more constructive purposes, and this scandal must be ended.

## 3 Ethics and economic society

### (i) The origin and purpose of the economy

The purpose of economic society is to supply man's material needs in such a way that his spiritual, intellectual, moral and cultural life is strengthened and supported. Though concerned firstly with the material things, therefore, the manner in which this is done should be in harmony with his non-material needs [GS 64]. The economic system must be based on private enterprise and be innovative, improving the economic agencies through which it works and which engine progress, meeting human needs through the market in accordance with its own methods and laws but also according to the moral law [RN 13, QA 41 and 136, PP 25, CA 31–2]. Economic freedom must be seen as a particular aspect of a freedom which is at its core ethical and religious [CA 42]. Satisfying material needs and wants, by using means which degrade or dehumanize human beings, can never be a legitimate end of economic activity. What constitutes a legitimate material end or means varies according to cultural factors and the stage of development of a people, but what is good for a truly human existence must be the norm in all cultures and circumstances. Excessive dependency on goods of any kind; consumerism, which means they become an end in themselves; having, for the sake of having instead of having for reasonable use generously interpreted, demeans human nature. Needs and wants must also be satisfied in a manner which is socially responsible; to want to satisfy my own requirements while ignoring the legitimate needs of others, for example by paying those who supply me less than is just, is disordered. The production of superfluous goods to meet neither need nor reasonable wants, but simply to enable possession for the sake of possessing, raises the question of the maldistribution of resources. The capital invested in that production should be used, earning a reasonable market-determined profit, for the production of basic goods which others need and of which they are deprived. The earth's resources are for all, and it should not be beyond the wit of mankind, whose creativity in economic and technical matters grows by leaps and bounds, to find ways of directing market forces into these more constructive channels [QA 135, CA 34, 36, SRS 27–30].

## (ii) Labour

If the end of the economy is to satisfy human needs, then the essential means to that end is labour. God gave the earth to all for their sustenance, but the earth does not yield its fruits and products on the scale which satisfy his needs without human effort; it is through his work, his use of his intelligence and freedom in developing the world, that man does this. Initially man had no private capital, no property; he had only the land God had given him and his capacity for applying his energies to it in order to make it yield its riches; all private capital, all property then originated in labour, and this is why labour ethically always has priority over capital [LE 4, 10, 12].

Work has a spiritual as well as an economic significance. It is man, made in God's image, who shares by his work in the creative activity of his maker, who is depicted as working in the creation of his world. That work has been given a new dignity by the example of God the Son made man, the carpenter of Nazareth. Manual work was the occupation in which he spent most of his adult life on earth, and manual workers and their families were his social milieu; by this the lives of all who work for a living, particularly manual workers, have been incalculably ennobled. Work is natural to man and in it he finds fulfilment, as the lives of artists and skilled workers especially can show forth. There is a punitive side to man's work also. Much of it is inseparable from a toil that is often hard and unrewarding, part of the punishment for the sin of our race. Uniting ourselves with Christ in our work is one answer to this, more so if we unite ourselves to him in his passion and death suffered for our sakes [LE 25-7].

Work is a uniquely human activity, the subjective activity of the person; it issues in a particular product or activity, something made or done, an objective something, but subjective work is more important than the type of work done, or product produced. The worker is more important than the work. All honest labour, however basic, is dignified by the fact that it is a human being doing it. That Christ was a manual worker overcame the contempt in which the classical world in general held the ordinary work of mankind [LE 6, 26].

The materialistic economism which was the result of liberal capitalism of the Industrial Revolution did not accept this understanding of work, but saw labour only as an inanimate commodity, a factor of production, to be bought and sold like any other, irrespective of the needs of the human subject who worked. The workers reacted in solidarity through trade unionism, a manifestation of that right of association of which man cannot be deprived by the State, and unionism has achieved much in bringing about improvements in working conditions. But the original liberal capitalism still exists to some extent in both industrialized and industrializing countries and watchfulness is still needed. Marxism sees the answer to the excesses of liberal capitalism as resting in class war leading to the destruction of its enemy. But capital and labour are not natural enemies, since all capital is a product of labour; labour is the efficient cause of production, capital the instrumental only. Man uses capital, in the sense of all natural resources, and makes them serve him, finance, factories, plant, tool and machine; these also are of man's making [LE 11–12].

It was the materialistic economism of liberal capitalism which opposed labour and capital, regarding the former as simply an economic factor, whereas in truth the only legitimate title to ownership of capital rests in that it serve labour, so achieving the first purpose of productive goods, their universal purpose and common use [LE 13]. This is true also of socially owned productive goods: they too must serve labour. Rigid capitalism, which regards the labour/capital divide as a dogma beyond questioning, is therefore not acceptable. Workers must become part owners in some way and schemes of joint ownership, worker shareholding or sharing in management or profits are significant in this context. Replacement of private by public ownership on the other hand of itself solves nothing unless the workers are in some way part owners [LE 14]. The worker's rights follow from these considerations. Work is an obligation as well as a right; God commands it, man's humanity needs it, and society is dependent on its products. It has therefore a personal and a social aspect.

Employers can be classified as indirect or direct. The former are those whose actions and decisions affect the level of employment and its conditions; these powers are to be used responsibly in favour of work and the proper treatment of workers. The latter are those who directly own and manage firms and companies; they too must sustain employment and respect workers' rights [LE 17]. The right to work is the most fundamental of those rights [LE 18]; also fundamental is the right to a wage which will enable workers to gain access to the goods destined for all and to support themselves and their families adequately. Women with families should not be compelled to work outside the home, and should they make this choice they must be treated justly [LE 19]. The right of association in free trade unions is essential, but their ethos must be primarily that of co-operation, though not of class struggle. There is a right to strike, though not for political purposes, and the authorities have the responsibility to keep the public services going where they are affected by strikes [LE 20]. The dignity of the agricultural worker is also to be fostered. Frequently they are unjustly treated by landowners in the third world, and they are at times also denied advancement in the industrialized nations [LE 21]. The disabled worker likewise needs catering for; much has been done in this respect but much still remains to be done so that such workers are not cut off from the world of work but can make their contribution to society [LE 22]. The emigrant worker too is entitled to justice. Those who wish to leave their homeland to better their lot are entitled to do so, but there are usually difficulties for them and for the new lands they enter, and all means must be taken to ensure that such difficulties are overcome – with due respect for the rights of all who are involved [LE 23].

The community of work embraces all those who make a contribution to providing it and executing it. It includes those whose knowledge and business skills create wealth and put it at the service of the economy; such wealth is becoming more important to the production process than are the natural resources used in that production. The decisive factor in the economic process is thus demonstrated most remarkably to be man himself. The businessman's insight which enables him to foresee a need and the ability which enables him to organize the factors of production so that the need can be met, is central to the modern wealth-creating process. So too is the scientific and technical knowledge and skill that enables man to exploit the resources of nature in increasingly sophisticated and profitable ways. All this is disciplined, highly creative and socially valuable work at the centre of a process which requires the co-operation of many other skills and talents, mental and manual, in the vast community of human workers. Such communities transform man's natural and human environment. They demand of those in them industriousness, diligence, prudent risk-taking, reliability and fidelity in working relationships, and courage in making often difficult decisions. They are built on economic freedom and they increasingly demonstrate that human energy and talent are the most important elements in the economic process [CA 30–2].

## (iii) Property

Need then is the first and fundamental fact of economic life, and in seeking to satisfy needs, man is linked with the external world and nature, and expresses his essential freedom in relationship to that world. But that freedom is not clearly set out in this relationship itself. It is the fact of property, and its implications in terms of the spiritual personality, which does that. Animals appropriate to themselves property, but they do so in a way which is entirely

temporary and instinctual, for purposes of self-protection or propagation of the species. Man alone of the animals, having reason,
has the right to possess things not only temporarily but in stable
and permanent possession [RN 5]. He can possess not only the
fruits of the earth but the earth itself. He does this initially through
work, which establishes a conditional *dominium*; only man can
create between himself and nature a more intimate relationship
than mere consumption. Property can also be obtained by gift,
purchase or inheritance by legal title, but all such property is the
fruit of someone's labour.

Work is of its nature internal to this property relationship and
property is bound up with human liberty. It secures both man's
temporal and transcendent ends, the freedom of man, made in
God's image and given conditional *dominium* over his creation. It
expresses corporeal man's involvement in nature but as a reasoning
being. Property is therefore always primarily a defence of work and
human personal liberty, not of the acquired rights of ownership.
Private ownership of the means of production is justified in so far as
it serves useful work. A society in which the right to work is systemat-
ically denied cannot be ethically justified, nor can it attain social
peace [LE 73, 82–7].

The right to property is a natural right [RN 4–14, QA 44–52, MM
104–21, CA 30–1], and property in productive goods, property
used for profit and wealth creation, in addition to consumer
goods, durable and fungible, because we are by nature able to use
best for ourselves and for others the world which God has given us,
if we possess part of it for ourselves. God gave the world to
mankind in order that all might get from it the means to live
according to their human dignity, but how that world could be
made to do this was left for society to work out, it not being
intended for the whole of mankind to use the whole of the world's
wealth in common. That would have made man subject to the
collectivity, and therefore deprived of liberty in his economic life
from the beginning. In logistic terms it was also impossible,
whereas from the beginning it was possible for men or groups of
men in a local region to take possession of the land, the most basic
form of property, and make it productive for themselves and for
others. It was a natural right, not indeed by explicit initial gift, but
implicit in that gift, developing from it and therefore in that sense
natural; it was a logical conclusion from and an addition to it.

Man has a natural right to property in productive goods, but
the original purpose of created goods, to serve the needs of all,
remains [GS 69, CA 30–1]. Because man has a natural right to

private property, as many as possible should own it; political society is then compelled to see property as widely distributed as possible. It is always possible to question how that property is distributed and the magisterium has consistently said, and says today, that its distribution is too narrow, and more should have access to it [MM 112–18, GS 71]. Further, the right to use private property is not absolute; it must be used for the common good, and this is not left to the private decision of the owners, but is the legitimate concern of the State, in this the State does not undermine the institution but protects it. The State can also own productive goods and work them, although such ownership should not predominate (QA 114, GS 71). The initiative of the private owner is necessary if production is to respond to the complex economic needs of humanity.

Private enterprise must remain the basis of the economy, but the State has the right and the duty to see that private property meets its social obligations both as regards ownership and use. Where the common good requires it can take certain firms or sectors into public ownership after paying compensation; nor is any particular distribution of goods so sacrosanct [QA 49, MM 112, 116, GS 71] that it cannot be readjusted if need be, saving the principle of the social value and necessity of private ownership as the dominant form.

In God's plan then, the institution of private property is an essential part of the social order, a presupposition of private initiative, a stimulus to work; and the owner of property must see himself as a steward of the possessions God has given him, for which he will have to render an account. Those who control financial resources have a moral duty to save and invest. The goods God has given us should neither be left idle and unused, nor serve the enrichment of the few, but should satisfy the needs of all, so demonstrating both the personal and social function of the property [GS 69–70].

The personal ownership and the social dimension of such ownership must be kept in balance; both are essential to a proper understanding of private property in productive goods, and neither must be exaggerated at the expense of the other. Overemphasis on the personal aspect produced liberal capitalism and its injustices. This in turn bred the excesses of Marxist socialism and its even greater injustices. The social teaching of the Church avoids both dangers, not by splitting the differences between them, but by emphasizing there are positive values in both, while warning against the abuses of both.

## (iv) Capital

Capital and capitalism, which have been demonized by Marxism, are in themselves neutral in their moral import, and we must summarize what we have said earlier about the development of these phenomena before we can also summarize the development of the Church's modern teaching on them. The word 'capital' refers primarily to savings – all resources not used up in meeting consumption needs; it is what is saved when all necessary expenses have been met. If people are very poor, producing at best little more than enough to cover the needs of basic subsistence, they will have nothing left over to take to market, hence little or no surplus or capital, in cash or in kind. If they are more fortunate they will have something to take to market; they can save more, buy better tools and develop better methods of producing their goods so that they will be more competitive in the market and so become more prosperous still. They have become capitalists.

Investment, applying capital to improve productive efficiency, is the path to economic development, and man understands this is necessary to meet the material needs of society. In this sense, capital is a natural and beneficial development in itself, all things else being equal – which unfortunately they were not as capitalism began to dominate economic life. Capitalists and capitalism are as old as mankind, but with the revival of trade, commerce and industry in the medieval West from the eleventh century a more systematic capitalistic development occurred as the long-distance trades and the great industries, woollen cloth manufacture especially, responded to the growth of the market for their goods. They began to produce and sell on a scale which required more investment, more capital, than the craftsmen who served only small local markets, could muster, and which required commercial and business organizational talents that few possessed. They became increasingly powerful, and in the succeeding centuries down to the eighteenth, what they had begun continued and expanded until by the time of the Enlightenment the social and economic systems was increasingly dominated by them; the capitalism which had been concentrated in certain trades and areas became increasingly general in Europe. Reflecting on the lessons it was teaching the world, writers like Adam Smith developed the science of economics, and the principles of *laissez faire* capitalism which it endorsed.

Since human experience showed capitalism was necessary if the economy was to meet the increasing needs of a growing population, it is in its nature socially beneficial when it acts in socially responsible ways. Capital and capitalism, as represented by liberal capitalists, notoriously did not do this, and they merited the criticism of the socialists and other social critics, and of the Church, for these abuses; what capitalism did not merit was to be judged solely on its excesses. The abuse of a thing does not indicate that the thing is evil in itself. Every good institution that man has developed to serve his honest purposes has been abused because of the corruption that is in him. The answer is to curb the evil so that the institution works for the common good. This the social teaching of the Church has tried to do. Leo XIII in *Rerum Novarum* sought to purge a good thing of its excesses. Pius XI in *Quadragesimo Anno* made the point precisely. The system is not to be condemned in itself; it is not of its own nature vicious, but it violates right order when it scorns the human dignity of the workers, the social character of economic activity, social justice itself and the common good [QA 101] and it needs adjusting according to the norms of right order.

Britain, the home of the liberal capitalism of the Industrial Revolution, and the scene of its worst excesses, was by the 1830s ready to see the law used to provide a corrective. The growth of the labour movement later added its pressure in this direction with some effect. But this in practice left intact the basic theory and instinct of liberal capitalism, that the law of the market is a God-given moral force, embodying a natural law in which man interferes with peril to national economic well-being; legislation to curb excesses was accepted because society insisted on it, but the readiness today to speak as if the market was always a moral force for good indicates that liberal capitalism is alive and well, and it leads to so many modern capitalists neglecting their social responsibilities. This makes it impossible for the magisterium to accept that what has come to be called 'democratic capitalism' is always as socially benign as some claim it to be. It still bears the marks of its philosophical origins. Its liberal ideology, of which Paul VI noted the modern rebirth, has its roots in philosophical liberalism, the child of the Enlightenment [OA 35]. The market is not in itself a moral force; it is a social mechanism, created by the social needs of man; it will meet morally good and morally bad demands equally if the price is right. Hence democratic states have been compelled to legislate to control its abuses. Its freedom must be a moral freedom, not an immoral one. Legislation however may not be used to reduce the responsible freedom in which it can work for the common good; it must facilitate that freedom – as it will do if it curbs the evil tendencies to which it is prone and encourages its virtues.

Both liberal capitalism and Marxist socialism have been rejected
by the Church, not in the search for a soggy 'middle way' but
because both had ignored the first way, the right way which she has
always taught, namely, that the moral good of private ownership of
productive goods depends on its personal and social aspects being
rightly balanced. Private ownership of capital is essential for
economic freedom – the basis of a thriving economy responding to
the needs of the people. The economic error of Marxism was to
deny this, but capital has in it of its nature, from divine revealed
and natural law, social obligations which, if they are ignored, make
it the enemy of human dignity. The Church's way is not a third way,
because she and her teaching on economic freedom preceded
liberal capitalism and Marxist socialism. Hers is the first way, and
the only way, for private ownership of productive goods to serve
the true common good.

## (v) Exchange, the market, price and profit

Liberal capitalism was judged by the magisterium to have been
defective in its understanding of the right of ownership of productive goods, and of the workings of exchange, market, price and
profit, because it failed to accept that all these must work within
the framework of objective moral law, embodied in just law by the
State which has care of the common good. But since these institutions, working in accord with sound moral principles and good law,
are essential if the economy is to provide properly for the material
and cultural needs of the people, the system could not be
condemned outright; the magisterium therefore had confidence
that men of good will could correct the evils of liberal capitalism.

The sources of wealth would run dry if the communist alternative of the social ownership of all the means of production were to
be adopted, because the incentives to economic creativity would be
removed from the system; no one would have any interest in exerting the talents which are necessary if the wealth that will provide
for the needs of the poor is to be produced [RN 15]. The system
itself was not vicious, only its excesses, its contempt for the human
dignity of the worker, the social character of economic life, social
justice and the common good [QA 101]. Many Catholics refused to
accept the Church's moral guidance in this [QA 124], although
there is no doubt of the moral evil of many aspects of liberal capitalism. Those who organize production and increase the nation's
wealth, however, are not denied the right to prosper proportion-

ately from their efforts for the community [QA 136], although the general picture of how the system was working was sombre in the 1930s.

Excessive competition had given free rein to the ruthless who heeded conscience least, and resulted in too much economic power being in the hands of the few, particularly the few who controlled investment, money and credit, and could exercise too much control over production. The struggle for control was first for economic domination, then for power over the State, and finally led to clashes between States and a detestable imperialism in international affairs. Profit was gained by any means and defended by any means; the search was for easy returns in an uncontrolled market with least labour; there was speculation for selfish gain without regard for its impact on manufacturing industry, the abuse of limited liability and the betrayal of trust by those concerned; the exploitation of base passions for purpose of gain. With these injustices perpetrated by the leaders of business, it is no wonder many workers were led astray, the more so since they were conscious that they were treated as mere tools by such men [QA 132–5].

The market economy, nevertheless, shorn of its liberal economic excesses, is in itself essential for human life. Man is a social animal, and the social relationship which is economic exchange is the foundation of economic activity, through which the material and cultural needs of society are met. Free traffic in goods by exchange or gift is a fundamental human right and need. It serves to establish and maintain economic equilibrium in society. It is the agency by which the priority of human needs is established through fair competition, that is, competition in a market in which none of the parties concerned can exploit or be exploited by others. If competition is not within the bounds of justice it becomes a battle for the greatest possible financial gain at whatever the cost to others; social justice and charity must regulate all economic activities including those of exchange.

Exchange of goods is part of society's natural structure, and the whole pattern of exchanges constitute, 'the market', the central institution of that economy as goods move to the place where demand and supply dictate. The market as a whole then is a unity, whether it is territorial (local, regional, national) or organized by branches (retail supplies for the consumer or commodities for the wholesalers, e.g. cotton, copper, coffee, timber, etc.). The market is a powerful society-forming force in directing the economy towards its end of meeting the material and cultural requirements of the people. Through demand it conveys the order of the consumer to the producer, and tells him what goods he will be able to sell at what prices. The market best serves economic progress, mobilizing economic forces in the manner best calculated to meet the economic and cultural needs of society, facilitating improvement in standards of living in the full sense. If the sellers secure a surplus, a profit, in their operations in a truly competitive and morally ordered market, this means that they have made the best possible use of the resources available to them and that profit is a just reward for their service to society [CA 35].

The exchange value of goods in the market therefore, expressed in monetary terms, is their price. It results from the interplay of supply and demand, and provided none of the parties involved is in a position to exploit the weaknesses of the other, or to rig the market in their own interests, that interplay provides a just price. Demand in the market therefore means demand backed by purchasing power. Accordingly it does not indicate the sum of human needs and wants in economic society, but only those which can be satisfied by the supply of goods and services at equal exchange value. Effective such demand therefore only represents part of total need. Those who lack purchasing power cannot take their needs to market, no matter how basic those needs are. Social policy or social charity must then make up their lack, and if whole classes of the community cannot provide for the necessities of life out of their earnings, or if their living standards are disproportionately low, this means that there are defects in the system and it is socially divisive to a dangerous degree. All members of society should be able to find work and income, and this means a level of employment which will enable this to happen. Better distribution of income and better distribution of property are also necessary if divisive defects are to be overcome.

The market, working in accord with the moral law, is then the most efficient instrument for utilizing economic resources and responding to human need for those who have money, but throughout the world the majority, perhaps, do not have the opportunity to earn through meaningful and profitable work the purchasing power which gives them access to the market place [CA 33–4]. They must be helped to develop their skills so that they can enter it; there are also needs which are prior to it – adequate wages, social security and protection for wages and conditions; while profit has a legitimate and necessary role to play it must not be earned at the price of denying workers their human dignity [CA 35].

Nor does the market of itself distinguish the moral quality of needs that are presented to it. A civilized society must recognize that a socially healthy market economy depends on the moral quality of such needs, which in its turn means that the consumer has to be able to opt for the moral good in his or her choices, and to be supported in this by the public authority, otherwise consumerism and wrong moral choices destroy the moral climate of society [CA 36]. The family especially suffers as people are discouraged from permanence in relationships, children are seen as 'things' one has or has not according to taste, and abortion is accepted. This happens if market-oriented economic life is absolutized, and the possession of goods becomes society's only value [CA 37–9, *Veritatis Splendor* [VS] 100]. It is for the State to protect the common good, the natural and human environment which the market does not protect; the very importance of the market leads to the danger of it becoming the subject of idolatry [CA 37, 40].

There are specific dangers of some aspects of business practice in the market economy of which Christians should be aware [VS 101, CCC 2409–14]. They include business fraud, the paying of unjust wages, forcing up prices by trading on the ignorance or hardship of another, the misappropriation and private use of corporate property, work badly done, tax fraud, forgery of cheques and invoices, excessive expenses, waste, the theft or retention of goods. Prices can be manipulated to gain unfair advantage over others, and corrupt business practices warp the market. Contracts are not always honoured. Profit cannot be made the exclusive norm of business performance, nor can the disordered love of money.

Is capitalism then a suitable economic model for the world after the fall of communism? Yes, if by it is meant an economy in which the fundamental and positive role of business, private property, free creativity in the economic sector are central, though it would be preferable to call this a market or free economy. A capitalism on the other hand which lacks a strong juridical framework, which places it at the service of a freedom which is at core, ethical and religious, is however not acceptable [CA 41–2]. Nor is a morally unobjectionable form of capitalism the only alternative to communism. A society of free work, enterprise and participation, a market system which meets the needs of the whole of society, should be possible [CA 35].

One market has the power ultimately to control all the others, and that is the financial market. Financial resources are, like all forms of private ownership, to be used in a socially responsible form. The animus against usury, which so exercised the minds of

earlier generations of the Church's canonists and moral theologians, was based on the determination to try to make those who
lent money do so in a socially responsible manner. Investment, in
which risk was taken and the hope of a profit commensurate with
skill, risk and effort was hoped for, should be encouraged and safeguarded. At the same time the inflated profits of the usurer
lending to desperate men at a price which could be fixed by the
greed and cruelty of the former was curbed; the price of money was
thus kept down, which, other things being equal, is socially beneficial, while the poor seeking consumption loans had some
protection. Usury, in the sense of loan sharks battening on the
poor, and of excessive interest rates taken by the less scrupulous
kind of investor or businessman, still exists and is in the Church's
estimation still gravely sinful.

However, because of the way money markets, speculative dealings
and stock markets work, it is almost impossible for any social control
to be exercised over some of their dealings, and forms of monopoly
and ways of making profits whose speculative nature panders to the
gambler's instinct rather than to rational analysis and hard-earned
knowledge of markets are given free rein. Speculation on the movement of prices and the market is so wide open and volatile that only
a few are able to keep up with it, and they can exploit their position
as they please. The machinations which accompany major takeovers
on the stock market are so obscurely understood that, when wrong-
doing is suspected and the law seeks to prosecute those concerned,
it defies platoons of lawyers and experts to disentangle who did what
and when, and the case collapses.

Major insurance companies are shown to have been operating in
an unacceptable manner with companies training sales forces to
unload dishonest and deceptive insurance policies on those who
trusted them for their supposed expertise. Then when legislation
is passed to make them disgorge, they make the procedure for
claimants so complex that the legislation is in effect almost nulli-
fied. Similarly large firms, and large public authorities, frequently
delay payment to smaller firms who have done work for them, on
the purely cynical calculation that there is little the latter can do to
force them to pay up.

In the financial markets, knowledge and information, and the
technology that enables them to be handled, is power. Here secu-
rities, bank deposits and a complex system of credit and debt is the
property that matters. Those who have the requisite information
and positions of power, through the technologies they control, can
operate most efficiently while fostering the opportunities for spec-

ulators to operate and manipulate prices. The difficulty for the outsider, or anyone with the obligation to find out what is going on, so that if necessary any anti-social activity can be monitored, is that those insiders who wish to exploit the situation without regard for the common good can always outsmart them, because of their fuller grasp of the situation and their knowledge of how to deal with awkward questions. Modern moralists have their work cut out in dealing with all these issues.

### (vi)  The firm or enterprise: management and labour

Private enterprise, private ownership of productive goods, exchange in a free market where there is true and fair competition, prices set by such a market, and profit earned by those who foresee its needs and meet them most efficiently, these are the foundations of an economy best capable of meeting the material and cultural needs of a nation, though a degree of social ownership is acceptable where the common good indicates that some key sectors should be owned and controlled by it [QA 114, LE 14]; the State has the responsibility for helping to provide the conditions in which the economy can flourish, and it must oversee its working so that the common good can be achieved.

The individual firm, enterprise or corporation in the various sectors of the economy, is its basic unit. The human implications of the division of labour under the liberal capitalist system of the eighteenth and nineteenth centuries were such as to raise the whole question of whether endemic long-term conflict between capital and labour could be eliminated; could such capitalist enterprises be shorn of the class conflict overtones which bedevilled them in the first instance? *Rerum Novarum*'s judgement was that they could; the evils that were evident in liberal capitalist industry in the nineteenth century – and are evident today when conditions favour them – were not to be seen as intrinsic to private ownership of productive goods and a market economy in themselves. They were the result of the liberal philosophy with which these things had become identified, a philosophy which assumed that it was not necessary for any social control to be exercised over the capitalist to ensure he met his social responsibilities. By the action of the Church, the State and the parties themselves, however, society could see that such control was exercised. That capital and labour need each other and are capable of co-operating in the productive process was its conviction, given its understanding of man and human society. At the same time it saw the trade unions as a morally legitimate and socially beneficial development for the protection of the workers against capitalist exploitation. They are still necessary in that role; exploitation of labour by capital still exists, especially in the third world; therefore the unions have a proper function to perform. Insofar as, like all other sectional social and economic interests, they can act against the common good, the unions must also be subject to just law. They are agents of solidarity, but not of class egoism; the right to strike, for example, is limited by the needs of the common good, and requires that public services be maintained, but where there are genuine injustices which have lead to strike action, the way to deal with it is to remove those injustices [RN 39, 49–57, LE 20].

All capital has its origin in labour of some kind [RN 19, LE 12]. Though each has a right to defend its own interests, they can and must do this within a generally co-operative context. They have more in common than divides them, conflict which can occur between groups should be the exception not the rule. The question of making sure that modern industry meets the needs of the common good poses considerable problems. The firm must become a true society in which all meet as personal equals [MM 91–2, LE 20] but it is also a society in which the wage relationship is a contract between two parties, and it must above all be a just one. The employer must not cheat the worker, and a free agreement must be a fair agreement that does not exploit the worker's weakness [RN 17, 34]. In return the worker must carry out his agreements honestly and well, protect his master's property and never resort to violence [RN 20, and 42–5]. What is a just wage is difficult to determine in the abstract; only specific cases can render an intelligible answer. The general framework within which that answer can be given is, however, clear. The wage must be sufficient for the support of the worker and those dependent on him or her, it must not be such that granting it to all the workers would challenge the economic viability of the enterprise, and it must take into account the needs of the economy as a whole [QA 63–75, LE 19]. Clearly these norms depend mainly on society's, and above all the State's, ability to see that they are embodied in the ordinary process of wage negotiations. This can be done by helping to provide the conditions in which the enterprise can flourish, the bargaining procedures are clearly worked out and all concerned in them believe in honest negotiations within this framework.

The wage contract is not then unjust in itself [QA 64]; it is the basis of the relationship between employer and employee, but that relationship must also exist in a broader context of co-operation within what is also a community of work [CA 43]. The wage contract should be modified so that the employees can share in some way in ownership, management or profits [QA 65, MM 91–2, LE 14]. A form of free work, enterprise and participation, while working in the market economy, is an alternative to capitalism after the failure of socialism [CA 35]. The worker must in a true sense be working for himself [LE 15].

### (vii)  The command economy

The capitalist, or market economy, is one in which the pull of market forces is the main influence in shaping that economy as individuals and organizations make clear what goods they want, and are ready to pay for. The result is that the pattern of economic life and its structures, industrial, financial and commercial, is determined by consumer choice; the 'consumer is king', as it has been said. To meet the demand for these desirable goods, businessmen are ready to invest in the plant, the raw materials and the rest which is necessary for their production, because they calculate that the demand will continue and with it their profits, while the industries making products which people no longer want will decline, because there is no longer profit to be had in maintaining them. Economic activity in the market economy then, and in particular the investment decisions which promise further growth, is determined by the needs of organizations and individuals.

The market economy as it developed under liberal capitalism, produced the Marxist socialist reaction and in due time the emergence in Soviet Russian of a major modern industrial economy which allowed little or no private enterprise. The problem of mature liberal capitalism in the 1920s and 1930s led many in the West to assume that the system was played out, and the future, they thought lay with the command, or centrally planned, economy[4] in which investment decisions, and every other economic decision, was made in response not to what they saw as private greed but to social need. The trouble was that between the fine rhetoric of Marxist – Leninism and the realities of economic life there was no nexus. Marx and Engels had delivered a judgement on the capitalist economy, but had not left any convincing account of how a non-capitalist economy would operate, and the alternative that emerged under Stalin, and remained substantially intact until the collapse of real socialism, notoriously failed its people.

On theological grounds the Church could not support Marxist socialism, and her social ethic told her that theoretically it was unworkable sociologically, politically and economically, as indeed it turned out to be. That did not mean that where she had to live with Marxist socialism, as she did in Eastern Europe for example, the Church could not do so. But the whole of her teaching and life contradicted its values and in time they undermined it. Her social teaching defended basic human rights, including the right of association in free trade unions, which the system denied because the state planners and managers would not tolerate their activity. In time it was this particular Achilles' heel of the Marxist socialist planned economy that the Christians sons of Poland exploited, and in so doing began the process which hastened the crumbling of the communist monolith already doomed because of its contradictions.

## (viii) The market economy and the State

If the command economy is incompatible with the Christian social ethic, that ethic gives the State a real role in guiding the economy: because the market is a social institution, the body which has care of society's common good, namely the State, has a right and a duty to oversee it to that end [QA 49, 88, 133, MM 51–8, GS 64, 65, PT 51–3, CA 15, 40, 42, 48]. It has then a much more positive task to perform than that of merely 'holding the ring' as liberal capitalism envisaged. It has to make sure that the law and institutions, the general character and administration of the country and its people work for the common good, seeking to encourage public well-being and private prosperity, in the light of the principle of subsidiarity. That principle does not make persons and private organizations the enemy of the State, but is concerned that where necessary the latter should intervene to help secure the well-being of the former.

The economy cannot be conducted in an institutional, juridical and political vacuum in a free society. The market is a social institution, created by social forces and serving them. It must therefore be subject to social supervision. The market responds to need backed by purchasing power, but many have human needs which they cannot pay for, and it is for society to ensure that they are met by ensuring that all have access to the job market and can earn to pay for these needs [CA 34]. Economic freedom requires a stable currency and efficient public services, and the task of the State is to secure these, so that those who work and produce can enjoy the fruits of their labour and so be encouraged to work efficiently and honestly [CA 48]. The State has a role in stimulating business activity by sound economic policies and by encouraging the growth of job opportunities [MM 51–3, LE 17–18]. Similarly it can intervene when monopolies are obstructive and support weaker sectors when they need it to make them stronger, its activities here to be as limited as possible and not to enlarge State intervention on a permanent basis [MM 54–8, CA 48]. The crucial thing is to give both political society and economic society their legitimate freedoms and, not to allow the one to swallow the other. The dangers of the State taking over the running of the economy completely were illustrated in real socialism, and that will remain the danger wherever real socialism remains or reappears. The danger that particular economic interests will dominate the State was seen in liberal capitalism, and this still happens where liberal capitalism becomes the dominant force in society.

National States therefore have the duty to supervise the functioning of national economies, subject to the principle of subsidiarity; that is, they must facilitate the freedoms of persons, families and intermediate organizations, not stifle or replace them. This does not, however, mean that the State has only a negative and restrictive role, but that it is to be a supportive one only, helping those given assistance to become more effective in helping themselves and so no longer be in need of the State's intervention.

## (ix) The international economy

The international economy, like the national, must work for the common good, and it is necessary that some form of overall effective international organization must be established, on the principle of subsidiarity, to do this, facilitating the capacities of nations to help themselves, by developing sound, self-sustaining economies [GS 84–6, PP 43–61, SRS 27–31]. The need for this central authority is both political and economic. States have to deal with one another on both matters and the two are interrelated, with economic issues becoming of particular importance as the world grows smaller, and modern communications making the injustice of the widening gap between the economic fortunes of nations become more evident. The enlightened self-interest of the wealthier nations should make them aware of the need to span this gap.

It is, however, the underdeveloped States themselves which are primarily responsible for their own development [GS 86, PP 54, 77, SRS 16, 44, CA 20]. It is particularly incumbent on them to see that

political structures are sound and operate justly, because otherwise
they lack the first requirements for effectively handling any assistance given – namely, good laws, sound social and economic
institutions, and infrastructures capable of supporting the task of
development. This does not reduce the moral responsibility of
richer, stronger nations to assist them, but it makes it more likely
that any help given them will be effective and not just be chan-
nelled into futile schemes or the pockets of unscrupulous
politicians or officials.

The moral obligations of the more developed nations to help the
less fortunate, results from that universal purpose of created things
which lies behind any possession and use of the natural riches of the
world, and their development by a nation for its own purpose [GS
85, PP 22–3 and 43–53, SRS 5–10]. The total of the resources and
the talents God has given us for the use of the human race are for all
of the race, not for part only of it. A nation has the right to exploit its
riches first for its own use and enjoyment, but it equally clearly has
the duty to do this while helping others who have been less well-
endowed. The ways in which this help can be given are two – aid and
trade. Aid is the transfer of resources. It can be in finance – grants or
gifts or loans – or it can be in kind: either for example as the emergency transfer of food, medicines or other commodities in times of
sudden crises, or by transferring technical knowledge which will
help the nations concerned to avoid such crises in future. Such
transfers can be made by technicians and academics going to the
countries concerned to train local labour or experts, or by their
nationals studying at universities or other educational institutions
in the developed countries. It can also be made by allowing foreign
companies to operate in underdeveloped countries where they will
trade for profit while bringing training facilities for local labour and
transferring funds for development of their operations to such
countries. In all this there is the danger of neo-colonialism, but,
given sound government and adequate watchfulness in the developing regions, this can be avoided by specifying quite clearly what
forms of activity are welcome there by the commercial and national
interests of would-be co-operators from the developed countries
[MM 161–77, GS 83–9, PP 43–61].

## (x) Population and resources: the environment

The concern over the population and resources equation first
became acute in the 1950s, though Malthusians had been insisting

all along that the crisis was upon us. John XXIII first faced the issue, noting the warnings that the growth of population over the next few decades would outstrip man's capacity to provide food for it and that disaster would follow. The only answer was to take steps severely to reduce the world's population growth. But, he said, these arguments are based on unreliable and controversial data and are of uncertain validity. The resources of nature are, collectively inexhaustible, and man by his intelligence has the means to make them available for his needs; the answer to the problems of the population/food supplies ratio is therefore a renewed scientific and technical effort on man's part to deepen and extend his dominion over nature.

The very real problems of the poorer nations are more often the result of defective social and economic organization and of lack of social solidarity than any other factor. The answer lies in international co-operation and the exchange of knowledge, capital and manpower [MM 186–92]. Government population policies must be such as respect the law of God, especially the right of parents to decide the size of their family, using only moral means in such policies and programmes based upon them [GS 87, PP 37, SRS 25].

John XXIII's analysis of problems and their lines of solution in 1961 were well supported by the scientific knowledge of those many experts, demographers, economists and agronomists, who found the Malthusian thesis faulty. And his analysis was proved right. We have not been plagued since the 1960s by world-wide famine. Famine there has been in places, but on nothing like the scale predicted, and it has mostly been the result of the failure of corrupt political and economic systems to respond to the needs of the people or the disasters caused by needless wars, by drought or other natural calamity. Internationally and overall, food supplies outstripped population growth as economic, social and other pressures led to the search for new answers to the age-old problem of supply shortages, and as it had been in the past, necessity and the natural development of knowledge and expertise was the mother of invention; new crops, new strains of seeds, new fertilizers and techniques developed.

The problems of poverty, hunger and deprivation were not and have not been finally solved. These evils remain in the immensely rich world God has given us. What experience has shown us is that it is political and economic will that is lacking in their solution, not the resources of nature; the same is true regarding supplies of other resources besides food – raw materials and fuel for example, and the question of a proper regard for the environment [OA 21,

SRS 34, CA 37]. These are not insoluble either, but all need to be tackled energetically by the co-operation of nations and the application of the skills and ingenuity God has put at our disposal through our intelligence and technology.

# Notes and References

## 16 Leo XIII (1878–1903)

1. R. Aubert, *The Church in a Secularized Society* (London, 1978), chs. 1 and 6; Philip Hughes, *A Short History of the Catholic Church* (London, 1970), chs. 9 to 12; Derek Holmes, *The Triumph of the Holy See* (London, 1978).
2. There were excesses in this matter. Some ultramontanists overstated their case and have been rightly criticized. Their opponents were guilty of excess too, and generally the latter disregarded the development of doctrine in this area. H. Jedin and J. Dolan (eds.) *Handbook of Church History*, Vol. 8 *The Church in an Age of Liberalism*, pp. 312ff.
3. John Molony, *The Worker Question* (Dublin, 1991), p. 14.
4. Jedin and Dolan, *Handbook*, Vol. 9 *The Church in an Industrial Age*, pp. 3ff.; Aubert, *Secularized Society* pp. 7ff.; H. Daniel Rops, *A Fight For God* (London, 1966), pp. 40ff. and ch. 3.
5. E.T. Gargan, *Leo XIII and the Modern World* (New York, 1961), p. 18.
6. Molony, *Worker Question*, p. 13.
7. Molony, *Worker Question*, p. 13.
8. *Acta Sanctae Sedis* 10. 585–92 Claudia Carlen, *The Papal Encyclicals 1878–1903* (Ann Arbor, 1991) pp. 5ff.
9. *ASS* 11: 372–9 Carlen, *Encyclicals 1878–1903*, pp. 11ff.
10. On the conditions in which rebellion might in principle be morally justified, see Vol. 1 of this work pp 185f and 253f.
11. *ASS* 14: 3–14 Carlen, *Encyclicals 1878–1903*, pp. 51ff.
12. Leo XIII's political ethics were analysed in articles by J. C. Murray in *The American Ecclesiastical Review* CCXXIV (1951) 'The problem of "the religion of the state"' 329–32 and *Theological Studies* XIV (1953) 'Leo XIII on Church and State' 1–30, 145–214, 551–67..
13. Footnote 2 to the text of the encyclical refers to the *philosophes* of the French Enlightenment.
14. Footnote 13, referring to James 4:12. Also quoted in footnotes in these paragraphs are, Romans 13:1–4 and 1 Peter 2:13–15. St Augustine *De Civ. Dei* Bk 21 and John Chrysostom *In Epist. ad Rom. Homil.* 13.1.

15.  Text *AAS* 18: 161–80 Carlen, *Encyclicals 1878–1903*, pp 107ff.

16.  Footnote 26, Tertullian *Apol.* 27.

17.  *AAS* 22: 385–404 Carlen, *Encyclicals 1878–1903*, pp. 211ff.

18.  Gargan, *Leo XIII*, p. 30.

19.  AAS, 24: 519–29 Carlen, *Encyclicals 1878–1903*, pp. 277ff.

20.  Gargan, *Leo XIII*, p. 69.

21.  George's single tax would yield 100 per cent from unimproved land values and according to him would make all other taxes redundant, remove the State from most areas of public life and resolve the labour management conflict. In Father Edward McGlynn, pastor of an important New York parish, it had a strong supporter and this caused the Church some problems as the debate waxed hotter, with the usual misunderstandings on both sides; it was a time when some in the fledgling Church in America were finding the restraints of the Roman dimension a little taxing. In the end, though neither Cardinals Manning nor Gibbons thought him a serious threat, McGlynn was excommunicated on 3 July 1888 and George's book was placed on the Index on 6 February 1889. Molony pp. 50ff.

22.  Moloney, *The Worker Question*, p. 48.

23.  Moloney, *The Worker Question*, p. 130.

24.  A. Freemantle, *The Papal Encyclicals in their Historical Contexts* (London, 1963), pp. 21ff.

25.  Charles Curran, for example, makes much of what he sees as 'The changing anthropological bases of Catholic social ethics' (C. Curran and R. A. McCormick (eds.), *Readings in Moral Theology* No. 5 (New York, 1986), pp. 188ff. He first bowdlerizes Leo XIII's teaching on political ethics, alleging it was invalidated by its elitist slant (the inaccuracy of this judgement can be seen from the summary of it given above), but then allows that 'he always upheld the basic rights of individual human beings which might be abused by totalitarian democracy' and 'similarly that the human being is prior to the state and has natural rights which do not depend on the state' (pp. 192f.). These and the other unchanging principles, which are the core of the teaching, can be applied to new situations, and since those situations differ so markedly, the manner of their application brings out new aspects of the moral theory on which they are based. Each pope also brings his personal insights, experience and knowledge to bear and will be either be too much, or too little, in sympathy with the men of his time, or affected by this or that school of thought on detail or approach or prescription, but he will always work within the same moral framework and his insights will be guided by them. The differences of emphasis of each fill out our understanding of the principles and the policies and situations to which they are relevant. This is the point; it is precisely because this core is drawn from the apostolic tradition that, though popes and their world views and advisers change, as do the situations to which it is applied, the social teaching is always valid, relevant and developing.

26. On the question of the authority of the teaching in general see J.-Yves Calvez and J. Perrin, *The Church and Social Justice* (London, 1961), pp. 7ff, 36ff and 54ff.

27. The 'magisterium', the Church's teaching authority, is vested in the Pope and the College of Bishops acting with him. The Church *'under the guidance of the Church's living magisterium* unfailingly adheres to [the] faith' so the truth can be known without error [*Catechism of the Catholic Church* (London 1994) sections 888–890: my italics]. The ordinary magisterium exists in the constant teaching of the Church on revealed doctrinal and moral truth. The extraordinary magisterium is exercised when the Pope in consultation with the Bishops decides that some truth which has always been held by part of the Church is now to be made binding on all, or when in a General Council Pope and Bishops infallibly clarify or develop the constant teaching by specific acts. Infallibility is invoked so that it is clear that although it may be unfamiliar to some it is now part of the accepted teaching. The difference between the ordinary and extraordinary magisterium then is not in the quality of the teaching. The difference is in the act or acts by which they are put forth [*Catechism* 890–892]. The extradinary magisterium is only exercised when occasion demands it; most of the Church's teaching does not require to be declared infallible. For example the ten commandments have never been so defined but they are binding on all from the scriptures and the constant teaching. R. Latourelle and R. Fisichella *Dictionary of Fundamental Theology* [London 1994] article on 'magisterium' and J. Kwitny *Man of the Century* New York 1997 p 556.

28. *AAS* 23 691–70 Carlen *Encyclicals 1878–1903*, pp. 241ff.; Jedin and Dolan, *Handbook*, Vol. IX, pp. 224ff.; R. L. Camp, *The Papal Ideology of Social Reform* (Leiden, 1969), pp. 77ff.; Calvez and Perrin, *Church and Social Justice*, pp. 76ff.; Donal Dorr, *Option for the Poor: One Hundred Years of Papal Social Teaching* (Dublin, 1992), pp. 13ff.; *The New Dictionary of Catholic Social Thought* (Collegeville, 1994), article on *Rerum Novarum.*

29. Molony, *Worker Question*, pp. 46ff., 66ff. The genesis of the text was unearthed by the (later) Cardinal Domenic Tardini when he was Under-Secretary of State; among the papers of Mgr Volpini who was the principal translator of Leo's letters into Latin, he discovered several drafts, corrections and some page proofs of the encyclical. Tardini's work was continued and published by Mgr Giovanni Antonazzi (ed.), *L'enciclica Rerum Novarum; testo autentico e redazioni preparatorie dai documenti originali* (Rome, 1957).

30. It has been claimed that Leo XIII's teaching here was derived from John Locke. But Locke had no place for the common use of private property which had been central to the teaching of the Fathers and of St Thomas and was to that of Leo. Also, as L. Strauss in his *Natural Right and its History* (Chicago, 1953), pp. 202ff., points out, the

owners of property Locke had in mind when defending the institution were the large landowners, whereas the Catholic tradition, and Leo XIII in particular, insist on the widest possible distribution of property. See M. Habiger OSB, *Papal Teaching on Private Property* (London, 1990), pp. 345f.

31. This is an application of the principle of subsidiarity; that the higher organization should not involve itself in the affairs of the smaller unless it is to help the latter achieve its purposes.

32. Footnote 10, Luke 6:24–5, 'alas for you who are rich, you are having your consolations now ...'

33. Footnote 11, Aquinas, *Summa* IIa IIae, Q. 66, art. 2, 'Whether it is lawful for a man to possess a thing as his own'.

34. Footnote 12, Aquinas, *Summa* IIa IIae, Q. 32, art. 6, 'Whether one ought to give alms out of what one needs'.

35. Footnote 17, St Gregory, *Hom. in Evang.* 7 n. 9.

36. This is the principle of solidarity, love of others as children of the same God which reinforces the natural attraction between individuals and groups, while preventing that attraction becoming anti-social through injustice to others. Solidarity is ordained to the common good which also gives the particular groups in society a just framework within which to work.

37. Footnote 25, *Apol.* 2. 39.

38. Footnote 27, Aquinas, *Summa*, IIa IIae, Q. 61, art. 1, 'Whether two species of justice are suitably assigned: commutative and distributive', ad 2.

39. The reference to distributive justice here is a little puzzling. Distributive justice concerns the distribution of the State's goods according to the degree of service to it (see Vol I of this work pp209f.). It is legal justice properly understood which requires that all citizens have access to the means of a decent livelihood which it is the sense of the paragraph that the State should secure . The next footnote makes this clear.

40. Footnote 28, St Thomas Aquinas, *On the Governance of Rulers*, 1. 15.

41. The principle of subsidiarity again; it assumes the right of the higher organization to intervene for the common good's sake.

42. Again the principle of subsidiarity, the State intervening in order to facilitate the obtaining of justice when necessary.

43. Footnote 36, St Thomas Aquinas *Contra impugnantes Dei*, Pt 2, ch. 8.

44. Carlen, *Encyclicals 1878–1903*, pp. 479ff.

45. Jedin and Dolan, *Handbook*, Vol. ch. 14; Aubert, *Secularized Society*, pp. 151ff.; Paul Misner, *Social Catholicism in Europe* (London, 1991), pp. 87ff., 213ff., and chs. 11, 12, 13.

46. Aubert, *Secularized Society*, pp. 153ff.; Misner, *Social Catholicism*, pp. 222; E. H. Kossman, *The Low Countries* (Oxford, 1978), pp. 480ff.

# 17   Pius X (1903–14) and Benedict XV (1914–22)

1.   R. Aubert, *The Church in a Secularized Society* (London, 1978), pp. 15ff; H. Jedin and J. Dolan (eds.) *Handbook of Church History*, Vol. 9, *The Church in an Industrial Age* pp. 381ff.; H. Daniel Rops, *A Fight For God* (London, 1966), pp. 51ff.

2.   Jedin and Dolan, *Handbook*, Vol. 9, chs. 26–33; Daniel Rops, *Fight*, pp. 51ff and chs. 5–6.

3.   Jedin and Dolan, *Handbook*, Vol. 9, p. 387.

4.   Paul Misner, *Social Catholicism in Europe* (London, 1991), pp. 253ff., 278ff., 300ff. and 306ff; R. L. Camp, *The Papal Ideology of Social Reform* (Leiden, 1969), pp. 13ff., 32f., 57 ff., 87ff., 116ff.; Donal Dorr, *Option for the Poor: One Hundred Years of Papal Social Teaching* (Dublin, 1992), pp. 61ff.

5.   *Acta Sanctae Sedis*, 36: 127–39 Claudia Carlen, *The Papal Encyclicals (1903–1939)* (Ann Arbor, 1991), pp. 5ff.

6.   CTS *The Pope and the People* (London, 1929), pp. 182ff.

7.   ASS, 37: 741–67 Carlen, *Encyclicals 1903–1939*, pp. 37ff.

8.   First Consistorial Address, 9 November 1903, quoted in Jedin and Dolan, *Handbook*, Vol. 9, p. 388.

9.   Camp, *Papal Ideology*, p. 121.

10.  Jedin and Dolan, *Handbook*, Vol. 9, p. 486.

11.  It was in this context that ODC was dissolved in 1904, its diocesan committees continuing under the control of the bishops. Aubert, *Secularized Society*, pp. 139ff and 159ff.

12.  Misner, *Social Catholicism*, p. 254. He renamed it the Catholic Social Economic Union. There was also an Electoral Union and a People's Union for the purpose of training an active laity. He called this the *Unione Cattolica Popolare* (Popular Catholic Union) in imitation of the German *Volksverein*.

13.  Jedin and Dolan, *Handbook*, Vol. 9, pp. 475f.

14.  *Acta Apostolicae Sedis* 4 (1912) 657–62 Carlen, *Encyclicals 1903–1939*, pp. 136ff.

15.  Jedin and Dolan, *Handbook*, Vol. 9, pp. 503f.

16.  Aubert, *Secularized Society*, pp. 163f.; Misner, *Social Catholicism*, ch. 14.

17.  Jedin and Dolan, *Handbook*, Vol. 10, pp. 21ff. and 35ff., Aubert, *Secularized Society*, p. 536.

18.  E. Hobsbawm, *Age of Extremes* (London, 1994), pp. 25ff.; P. Calvocoressi *Total War* (London, 1989); Marc Ferro, *The Great War* (London, 1973); Gabriel Kolko, *Century of War* (London, 1994).

19.  R. Eatwell, *Fascism: A History* (London, 1995), pp. 39ff.

20.  Camp, *Papal Ideology*, pp. 15ff., 35ff., etc.; Dorr, *Option*, pp. 63ff.

21.  *AAS* 6 (1914) 565–81 Carlen, *Encyclicals 1903–1939*, pp. 143ff.

22.  Daniel Rops, *Fight for God*, pp. 241ff., Jedin and Dolan, *Handbook*, Vol. 10, pp. 38f.

23.  Daniel Rops, *Fight for God*, pp. 246f.

24.  Jedin and Dolan, *Handbook*, Vol. 10, pp. 39ff.

25. Jedin and Dolan, *Handbook*, Vol. 10, pp. 42ff.; Daniel Rops, *Fight for God*, pp. 242ff.
26. Eric Eyck, *A History of the Weimar Republic* (Oxford, 1992), p. 20.
27. Daniel Rops, *Fight for God*, p. 249.
28. Carlen, *Encyclicals 1903–1939*, pp. 171ff.
29. See ch. 18, pp. 000.
30. Camp, *Papal Ideology*, p. 92.
31. M. P. Fogarty, *Christian Democracy in Western Europe 1802–1953* (London, 1957), pp. 323ff.
32. Camp, *Papal Ideology*, p. 16.

## 18  Pius XI (1922–39)

1. H. Jedin and J. Dolan (eds.), *Handbook of Church History*, Vol. 10, pp. 23ff.; R. Aubert, *The Church in a Secularized Society* (London, 1978), pp. 545ff.; H. Daniel Rops, *A Fight For God* (London, 1996), pp. 69ff.
2. E. Hobsbawm, *Age of Extremes* (London, 1994), chs. 1–4; Paul Johnson, *A History of the Modern World: from 1917 to the 1980s* (London, 1983), chs. 1–10.
3. The word is taken from the Latin *fasces*, the bundles of rods enclosing an axe which was the symbol of the Roman State. The creed was a mixture of right-wing extremism and semi-socialist populism, embracing racism, militarism, statolatry, and excessive nationalism. Yet it had enough intellectual coherence to appeal to many able and intelligent people. R. Eatwell, *Fascism: A History* (London, 1995), pp. xviiff.
4. Jedin and Dolan, *Handbook*, Vol. 10, p. 47ff; Daniel Rops, *Fight for God*, pp. 305ff.; A. C. Jemulo, *Church and State in Italy 1850–1950* (Oxford, 1960), ch. 6; R. Binchy, *Church and State in Fascist Italy* (Oxford, 1941).
5. E. Wiskemann, *Europe of the Dictators* (London, 1966), p. 28.
6. D. Mack Smith, *Italy: A Modern History* (Michigan, 1959), p. 326.
7. Mack Smith, *Italy*, pp. 367ff.
8. It was never complete nor effective, except in 'disciplining labour without controlling management'. E. F. Tannenbaum, *The Fascist Experiment* (London, 1972), p. 91.
9. Jemulo, *Church and State in Italy*, pp. 205ff.
10. Jemulo, *Church and State in Italy*, p. 225.
11. R. Webster, *The Cross and the Fasces* (Stanford, 1960), p 79. In compensation, the long-term effect of his support of Catholic Action was to nurture the seeds of Christian democracy, which otherwise 'would have been crushed by Fascism' (p. 111).
12. Charles Delzell, *Mussolini's Enemies* (London, 1961), p. 102.
13. Aubert, *Secularized Society*, p. 552. They had been worked out in some two hundred meetings of from three to four hours duration, after

each of which the Pope had been thoroughly briefed by his negotiators. Daniel Rops, *Fight for God*, pp. 264ff.

14. Jedin and Dolan, *Handbook*, Vol. 10, pp. 52ff.
15. Daniel Rops, *Fight for God*, pp. 307ff.
16. Claudia Carlen, *The Papal Encyclicals 1903–1939*, Ann Arbor, 1991) pp. 255ff.
17. His vision was then of a new Christendom, independent of the forms of the old but informing the new with its spirit. Jedin and Dolan, *Handbook*, Vol 10, p. 25; Aubert, *Secularized Society*, p. 548.
18. *AAS* 23 (1931) 285–312 Carlen *Enyclicals 1903–1939*, pp. 445ff.; P. Hebblethwaite, *Paul VI: The First Modern Pope* (London, 1993), pp. 110ff.
19. Binchy, *Church and State*, p: 527ff.; Delzell, *Mussolini's Enemies*, pp. 100ff.; Webster, *Cross and Fasces*, pp. 110ff.
20. Binchy, *Church and State*, pp. 614ff.; Webster, *Cross and Fasces*, p. 114; D. Mack Smith, *Mussolini* (New York, 1982), p. 222.
21. P. Lapide, *The Last Three Popes and the Jews* (London, 1967), p. 115.
22. R. Cameron, *A Concise Economic History of the World* (Oxford, 1993), ch. 14; W. Ashworth, *The International Economy since 1850* (London, 1965); G. Rees, *The Great Slump 1929–33* (London, 1970); A. G. Kenwood and A. L. Loughton, *The Growth of the International Economy 1820–1990* (London, 1992). Hobsbawm, *Age of Extremes*, pp. 92ff. and Johnson, *History*, pp. 246f. graphically remind us how traumatic the experience was for the Western nations affected.
23. J. K. Galbraith, *The Great Crash* (Harmondsworth, 1961), p. 98.
24. Wiskemann, *Dictators*, p. 90.
25. K. Pinson, *Modern Germany* (London, 1958), p. 452.
26. R. B. Nye and J. E. Morpurgo, *A History of the United States* (Harmondsworth, 1965), Vol. 2, *The Growth of the U.S.A.*, p. 660.
27. Andrew Boyle, *The Climate of Treason* (London, 1979).
28. S. E. Morison, *Oxford History of the American People* (Oxford, 1965), pp. 970ff.
29. *AAS* 23 (1931) 177–228 Carlen, *Encyclicals 1903–1939*, pp. 415ff.; O. Nell-Breuning, *The Reorganization of the Social Economy* (New York, 1939); M. Novak, *The Catholic Ethic and the Spirit of Democratic Capitalism* (New York, 1993), pp. 62ff.; *NDCST* 'Quadragesimo Anno'; R. L. Camp, *The Papal Ideology of Social Reform* (Leiden, 1969), pp. 36ff., 65ff., 95ff., Dorr, *Option*, pp. 75ff.
30. Footnote 31 refers to *Rerum Novarum*, para 36. However, the proper use of property is ruled by justice according to the needs of the common good, as the next paragraph [49] shows. See Vol 1 of this work pp. 208f.
31. Footnote 37, Aquinas, *Summa Theologiae*, IIa IIae, Q. 134.
32. This concept of social justice has been cause for much comment and Novak (*Catholic Ethic*, pp. 63ff), for example, makes much of it, but it is overdone. Legal or general justice, as we have seen, is primarily the responsibility of the State and among other things it

obliges the ruler to see that the goods needful for a virtuous life are available to all. See M. Habiger OSB, *Papal Teaching on Private Property* (London, 1990), pp. 106ff. In fact 'social justice is to be equated with legal justice properly understood'. J. Hoffner, *Fundamentals of Christian Sociology* (Cork, 1964), p. 51. St Thomas 'postulates that the person responsible for the common good ... "architectonically" visualizes in his intellect the order which is to be realized'. Legal justice is born of the creative and ethical political mind; this social, or commonweal justice is not limited to the State legislator but it should be in local government, professional and occupational organizations and intermediate societies generally, to produce the 'justice in society', which along with social charity, binds it together.

33.    The main element in the reconstruction of the social order here advocated is the proposal for a corporate order [see para. 83]; the text would suggest that the destruction of intermediate organizations, such as the guild system at the time of the French Revolution encouraged rampant individualism on the one hand and excessive State power on the other. Corporatism, it is suggested, will put an end to this. Meanwhile, the next paragraph [79] goes on to set out the principle of subsidiarity which will secure them from that excessive State interference. What is not clear is what form the excessive State interference here feared took in the 1930s.

34.    This then is the principle of subsidiarity, as it has come to be called. The word is derived from the Latin word *subsidium* which means 'help'. It states that it is better for individuals and private organizations to do what they can for themselves; the role of the larger organizations, the State above all, is to help them attain their ends rather than to stifle them.

35.    The labour troubles that were experienced intermittently in the period from 1919 to the early 1930s justified this analogy. The labour unrest that helped give Mussolini his chance, the unrest among the miners in particular which led to the 1926 General Strike in Britain, the street fighting between the Nazis and the communists during the early thirties, and the march of the unemployed on Washington, were all part of the pattern and had their long-term consequences for society.

36.    This is a specific recommendation in the practical order, suggesting what kind of industrial organization is needed, and as such would seem to have constituted a 'matter of technique' which the encyclical had specifically said was beyond its mandate [QA 41]. It would seem that its most insistent advocate, Von Vogelsang, was not interested in the Church's social teaching so much as in forcing this idea on it, while being prepared to ignore other aspects of that teaching. See A. Diamant, *Austrian Catholics and the First Republic* (Princeton, NJ, 1960), p. 170. The circumstances of the time called for profound reform but there was confusion about precisely what form it should

take. The answer turned out to be maintaining a high level of employment and providing better social legislation to give everyone a stake in the system. Providing this sort of security was one aspect of what corporatism was aiming at. The end was the right one, the means were not. On the influences at work on the drafting of the encyclical and which clearly caused the confusion of these paragraphs see Habiger, *Papal Teaching*, pp. 92ff. and O. Nell-Breuning SJ, 'The drafting of *Quadragesimo Anno*' in C. Curran and R. A. McCormick (eds.), *Readings in Moral Theology* No. 5 (New York, 1986).

37.    Here a note of realism returns. The recommendation of corporatism in the encyclical was a step too far; the tone of the document generally was that of the more cautious solidarist school. What the document was saying about industrial organization in practical terms was that the ethic of industrial relations should be co-operative rather than adversarial, though employers and employees should be able to deliberate separately on things that concerned their interests, if they wished. There had been spontaneous developments which encouraged such organizations. See R. Charles, *The Development of Industrial Relations in Britain 1911–1939* (London, 1972). It is notable more recently that the techniques of labour management relations the Japanese have introduced into the Western world, while not without their problems, are based on a non-adversarial approach which accounts for so much of their industrial efficiency.

38.    This sentiment is the key to understanding the complexities of these paragraphs. The growing realization that something was seriously wrong with a social and economic system which cared so little for the welfare of the ordinary people when circumstances beyond their control robbed them of a decent livelihood was what led to Roosevelt's New Deal in the 1930s, and the concern for maintaining employment levels and adequate social security systems that characterized the democracies from 1945 to the 1970s.

39.    This is a reference to Mussolini's reorganization of Italian industry and many have taken mention of it here as a recommendation of that system. But it was not. QA did not envisage a State corporatist system; it was to be established by free agreement of the parties and makes specific the right to negotiate outside the syndical structure. Mussolini's was a system created by the State and for the State, and outside it there was no effective independent trade union movement. The reaction of the Fascists to QA showed that, far from the Pope recommending their system, he rejected it.

40.    In fact it was right-wing regimes with their own agenda which cottoned on to the idea – in Argentina and Brazil, for example, and in Portugal. In Austria, the extreme right-wing Social Catholic Party sought to establish a corporatist regime against a highly unstable social and political background. E. Baker, *Austria 1918–1972*

(London, 1972); A. Diamant, *Austrian Catholics and the First Republic* (Princeton, 1960). Pius XI seems to have regarded the latter as hopeful at first (Nell-Bruening, 'The drafting'). Had he been more fully appraised of the nature of Austrian social, political and economic problems at the time he would not have done so. It was the last place where any such experiment should have been tried – if indeed it had been a sound or practical proposition – which it was not.

41. The message of these passages is clear enough. If class war and the attack on private property as such are mitigated, then these aims of socialism are acceptable; some forms of property give too much power to private interests and must be under State control. One does not have to call oneself a socialist to recommend these things; they are all in accord with the Christian tradition. True socialism, that is, advocacy of the class war, rejection of private property, and of God as the source of social authority, are incompatible with Christian belief and no Christian can be a socialist in this sense.

42. A. J. P. Taylor, *The Course of German History* (London, 1953), p. 219; Pinson, *Modern Germany*, pp. 343ff.; C. Craig, *Germany 1866–1945* (Oxford, 1973), pp. 398ff.; Golo Mann, *The History of Germany since 1789* (Harmondsworth, 1990), pp. 564ff.

43. Pinson, *Modern Germany*, p. 395.

44. Cameron (*Concise Economic History*, pp. 350ff.) tends to the view that the terms were so punitive as to be self-defeating. Craig (*Germany 1866–1945*, pp. 425ff.) is less convinced of that, while Taylor (*German History*, pp. 219ff.) is certain that the Germans had little to complain of.

45. W. Ashworth, *The International Economy since 1850* (London, 1965), p. 223.

46. A. Bullock, *Hitler: A Study in Tyranny* (Harmondsworth, 1967); W. Shirer, *The Rise and Fall of the Third Reich* (London, 1991).

47. Craig, *Germany 1866–1945*, pp. 539ff.

48. Wiskemann, *Dictators*, p. 88.

49. Pinson, *Modern Germany*, pp. 473ff.

50. Who started the fire is a matter of dispute but Pinson (*Modern Germany*, p. 505) identifies it as a Nazi plot; it seems likely it was an SA/SS operation under the direction of Heydrich. Craig, *Germany 1866–1945*, p. 572.

51. Pinson, *Modern Germany*, p. 505.

52. Pinson, *Modern Germany*, p. 506; Jedin and Dolan, *Handbook*, Vol. 10, pp. 539ff.; Daniel Rops, *Fight for God*, pp. 315; Shirer, *Rise and Fall*, pp. 189 and 199.

53. Shirer, *Rise and Fall*, pp. 214ff. The official number of the victims was 77; unofficial ones have ranged from 400 to 1000.

54. British MPs were given a first-hand account of the system by Gerhart Seger, a Social Democrat and member of the Reichstag. He had been imprisoned in one of the first concentration camps,

Oranienburg, in 1933, escaped and made his way to Czechoslovakia where he published an account of his experiences under the title *A Nation Terrorized* (1934), which sold nearly 250,000 copies in Europe and later appeared in an American edition. When the Nazis retaliated by putting Seger's wife and child in a concentration camp, Lady Astor arranged for him to give a lecture at the House of Commons, at the same time telling the German Ambassador that if Seger's family was not released the matter would be raised in the House; they were, and later escaped from Germany also. 'After this episode, no British MP could claim to be unaware of what was happening in Germany.' Duff Hart-Davis, *Hitler's Olympics* (London, 1988), p. 16.

55. Michael Power, *Religion in the Reich* (London, 1939), p. 6, on the implications of the 24th point from the Nazi programme. Alfred Rosenberg's *Myths of the Twentieth Century* was explicit on the matter; the Church had to be eliminated (Power, p. 21). See R. Eatwell, *Fascism: A History* (London, 1995), p. 119.

56. Power, *Religion*, p. 15.

57. Power, *Religion*, p. 37.

58. P. Lapide, *The Last Three Popes and the Jews* (London, 1967), p. 99.

59. Lapide, *Last Three Popes*, p. 98.

60. Aubert, *Secularized Society*, p. 555.

61. Daniel Rops, *Fight for God*, p. 320.

62. Taylor, *German History*, p. 249.

63. Pinson, *Modern Germany*, p. 512.

64. Aubert, *Secularized Society*, p. 556.

65. Lapide, *Last Three Popes*, pp. 109ff; Aubert, *Secularized Society*, p. 557; E. E. Y. Hales, *The Catholic Church in the Modern World* (New York, 1960), p. 275.

66. *AAS* 29 (1937) 145–67, 168–88 Carlen, *Encyclicals 1903–1939*, pp. 526ff.

67. A pastoral letter warning the people that their Catholic schools were under threat was confiscated by the Gestapo in 1934. Then, against a background of Nazi propaganda about the incompatibility of Catholicism and German patriotism and the disloyalty of parents who sent their children to Catholic schools, a series of plebiscites were held on the future of the latter. Sixty-five per cent of parents in Bavaria supported them still in 1935, but constant pressure and increasingly shrill propaganda took its toll. It was clear there was to be little future in the educational system for children, especially boys, from Church schools; in 1936 35 per cent of parents opted for them still; by 1937 it was only 4 per cent. The Nazis could then pretend that the end of confessional schools was the parents' choice when it was no such thing. Power (*Religion*, pp. 50ff), a journalist who had been in Germany in this period, saw the whole process as it unfolded.

68. This is an ecclesiology which the Second Vatican Council has modi-

fied, but in the context of the time it helped the Church in strengthening the resolve of her people to resist totalitarianism. Hitler undermined Christian determination to stand for the truth of Christ by claiming that a German national church, subject to him, could preserve the truth of Christ. It could not; he wanted it to act as a Trojan horse in the Christian community for his own evil purposes.

69. T. Prittie, *Germans against Hitler* (London, 1964), p. 77.
70. Lapide, *Last Three Popes*, p. 110.
71. Daniel Rops, *Fight*, p. 323.
72. Richard Pipes, *Russia under the Old Regime* (Harmondsworth, 1977).
73. B. Wolfe, *Three Who Made a Revolution* (Harmondsworth, 1964), p. 53.
74. David Shub, *Lenin* (Harmondsworth, 1976), p. 37.
75. L. Shapiro, *The Communist Party of the Soviet Union* (London, 1966), p. 38f.
76. Shub, *Lenin*, p. 210.
77. Shub, *Lenin*, pp. 320f.
78. Shub, *Lenin*, p. 411.
79. Shub, *Lenin*, p. 432.
80. A. Nove, *Economic History of the USSR* (Harmondsworth, 1976), p. 146.
81. R. Conquest, *The Great Terror* (London, 1992), p. 20.
82. R. Conquest, *Harvest of Sorrow* (London, 1988), p. 258.
83. Conquest, *Harvest*, p. 260.
84. Shapiro, *Communist Party*, p. 333.
85. Shapiro, *Communist Party*, p. 461.
86. Shapiro, *Communist Party*, pp. 462f.
87. Conquest, *Great Terror*, p. 283.
88. Isaac Deutscher, *Stalin* (Harmondsworth, 1966), p. 370.
89. Deutscher, *Stalin*, p. 356.
90. Deutscher, *Stalin*, p. 370.
91. R. Conquest *Great Terror*, p. 486.
92. Daniel Rops, *Fight*,. p. 326.
93. Jedin and Dolan, *Handbook*, Vol. 10, p. 60.
94. Jedin and Dolan, *Handbook*, Vol. 10, p. 742.
95. Jedin and Dolan, *Handbook*, Vol. 10, p. 743.
96. Jedin and Dolan, *Handbook*, Vol. 10, p. 743.
97. Raymond Carr, *Spain: A Modern History* (Oxford, 1982), p. 400.
98. Carr, *Spain*, p. 484; Jedin and Dolan, *Handbook* Vol. 9, p. 125.
99. William C. Atkinson, *A History of Spain and Portugal* (Harmondsworth, 1960), p. 323.
100. Carr, *Spain*, pp. 517 and 523; Atkinson, *Spain and Portugal*, p. 324.
101. Carr, *Spain*, pp. 516, 523; Atkinson, *Spain and Portugal*, p. 324.
102. Atkinson, *Spain and Portugal*, p. 327.
103. Carr, *Spain*, pp. 607ff.
104. Atkinson, *Spain and Portugal*, p. 327.
105. Carr, *Spain*, p. 635.

106. Deutscher, *Stalin*, pp. 411ff.
107. Atkinson, *Spain and Portugal*, p. 330.
108. Jedin and Dolan, *Handbook*, Vol. 9, p. 124.
109. Carr, *Spain*, p. 456.
110. Carr, *Spain*, p. 469.
111. Carr, *Spain*, p. 656, 678. Twelve bishops, 4,184 priests and 2,648 male and female religious were to be killed before the war was over. Jedin and Dolan, *Handbook*, Vol. 10, p. 607.
112. Jedin and Dolan, *Handbook*, Vol. 10, p. 606.
113. Carr, *Spain*, p. 678.
114. *AAS* 29 (1937) 65–106 Carlen, *Encyclicals 1903–39*, pp. 537ff.
115. The Stoics were aware of the dignity of man, but they were only one voice among the philosophers of antiquity in a society which most decidedly did not accept that dignity. From the first, the Church in helping to rebuild society during Roman times made practical charity, the treating of all, especially the poor and the sick with respect and kindness, for the first time a rudimentary social virtue. This was because it saw them especially as the special representatives of Christ. It was the rooting of human dignity and brotherhood in Christ which gave the Christian vision its universalism.

# 19 Pius XII (1939–58)

1. H. Jedin and J. Dolan (eds.) *Handbook of Church History*, Vol. 10 *The Church in the Modern Age*, pp. 29ff.; R. Aubert, *The Church in a Secularized Society* (London, 1978), pp. 558ff.
2. D. Caute, *The Fellow Travellers* (London, 1973), pp. 5f.
3. Caute, *Fellow Travellers*, p. 7.
4. John Keegan, *The Second World War* (Harmondsworth, 1990), ch. 2.
5. For purposes of analysis the social teaching of the two periods of Pius XII's pontificate are divided because of their very different backgrounds. On the social teaching as a whole see R. L. Camp, *The Papal Ideology of Social Reform* (Leiden, 1969), pp. 40ff., 101ff., 128ff., 149ff.; J.-Yves Calvez and J. Perrin, *The Church and Social Justice* (London, 1961), pp. 85ff., 91ff.; Donal Dorr, *Option for the Poor: One Hundred Years of Papal Social Teaching* (Dublin, 1992), pp. 96ff.
6. *AAS* 39 (1939) 413–53 Claudia Carlen, *The Papal Encyclicals 1939–1959* (Ann Arbor, 1991), pp. 5ff.
7. Guido Gonella, *The Papacy and World Peace* (London, 1945), pp. xvf.
8. Gonella, *World Peace*, pp. xvif.
9. Gonella, *World Peace*, pp. 200ff.
10. Gonella, *World Peace*, pp. 205ff.
11. F. S. Northedge and M. J. Grieve, *100 years of International Relations* (London, 1965); W. H. McNeill, *America, Britain and Russia: Their Cooperation and Conflict 1941–45* (London, 1953).

12. Michael Chinigo, *The Teachings of Pope Pius XII* London 1953.
13. A. J. P. Taylor, *English History 1914–1945* (Oxford, 1965), p. 528.
14. Jedin and Dolan, *Handbook*, Vol. 10, p. 244.
15. Radio Message to the World, 24 December 1944, Gonella, *World Peace*, pp. 318.
16. Address on the 50th Anniversary of *Rerum Novarum*, M. Habiger OSB, *Papal Teaching on Private Property* (London, 1990), p. 178.
17. Address of 2 September 1944, Camp, *Papal Ideology*, p. 103.
18. Address of 7 May 1949, Camp, *Papal Ideology*, p. 103.
19. Address of 1 September 1944, Camp, *Papal Ideology*, p. 104.
20. Speech of 13 June 1943, Camp, *Papal Ideology*, p. 106.
21. Speech of 12 March 1945, Camp, *Papal Ideology*, p. 131.
22. Address to UNIAPAC 27.4.41, Chinigo, p. 335.
23. 13 January 1943, Chinigo p. 330.
24. Address to UNIAPAC 27.4.41, Chinigo, p. 335.
25. P. Lapide, *The Last Three Popes and the Jews* (London, 1967); G. Lewey, *The Catholic Church and Nazi Germany* (New York, 1964); J. S. Conway, *The Nazi Persecution of the Churches* (London, 1968); G. Zahn *German Catholics and Hitler's Wars* (New York, 1969); T. Prittie, *Germans against Hitler* (London, 1964); F. R. Nicosia and L. D. Stokes (eds.), *Germans Against Nazism* (Oxford, 1990). Some testimonies are more worthy of credence than others and that by Lapide must have a particular authority. The author was Jewish and was more than a little critical of the Church's historical record in her treatment of his people, but while he points out what Pius XII and the Church did not do in these years, he records the many good things both did and which their critics ignore.
26. Aubert, *Secularized Society*, p. 563.
27. Lapide, *Last Three Popes*, pp. 230ff.
28. Lapide, *Last Three Popes* pp. 244ff, 264.
29. Lapide, *Last Three Popes* p. 250ff.
30. Lapide, *Last Three Popes* pp. 132ff, 256ff.
31. Lapide, *Last Three Popes* pp. 138ff.
32. Lapide, *Last Three Popes* pp. 162ff, 170ff.
33. Lapide, *Last Three Popes* p. 183 and Norman Davis *God's Playground: a History of Poland*. 2 Vols [Oxford 1981] Vol 1 pp. 78ff, 190ff, and Vol 2 pp. 240ff, 407ff and 463.
34. Lapide, *Last Three Popes* pp. 188ff, 197ff, 202ff.
35. Lapide, *Last Three Popes* pp. 214, 223, 227, 269.
36. W. Shirer, *The Rise and Fall of the Third Reich* (London, 1991), pp. 5f.
37. *The Past is Myself* (London, 1990). The author, who is Anglo-Irish, had married a German lawyer in 1933 and spent the war years in Germany. Her day-to-day account tells how this well-to-do professional-class, well connected and anti-Nazi family in Hamburg, at the centre of a group of such families totally opposed to the regime, were all but powerless against the all pervasive power of the totalitarian state. Michael Baigent and Richard Leigh *Secret Germany: Stauffenberg*

*and the Mystical Crusade against Hitler* (London, 1994) deal with a military family which did get involved with a plot against Hitler; the book also brings out that in a totalitarian gangster state fighting for its life, the normal structures of civil society, necessary for plotters to communicate and bring their plans to effect, almost entirely disappeared.

38.  Hitler later admitted that he could not have survived the disaster which would have resulted had he been opposed. But he cynically, and rightly, judged that neither France nor Britain would risk confrontation. Shirer, *Rise and Fall*, pp. 290, 293.

39.  Conway, *Nazi Persecution*, p. 301. The regime accepted that it had to handle the situation carefully while hostilities were in progress because the Church still had strong support among the people and national unity would be undermined by an open attack on her. However, Hitler made clear that once the war was won necessary steps would be taken to break her and all the other churches. The way they were treated in Poland (Conway, pp. 311ff.) shows what he meant by this.

40.  D. Dietrich 'Catholic Resistance to Biological Eugenics in the Third Reich', in Nicosia and Stokes (eds.), *Germans Against Nazism*, p. 147.

41.  Nicosia and Stokes (eds.), *Germans Against Nazism*, p. 152.

42.  Nicosia and Stokes (eds.), *Germans Against Nazism*, p. 147.

43.  Nicosia and Stokes (eds.), *Germans Against Nazism*, p. 150.

44.  Nicosia and Stokes (eds) *Germans Against Nazism* p. 145.

45.  Lapide, *Last Three Popes* p. 239.

46.  Lapide, *Last Three Popes* pp. 229, and 215ff.

47.  See above p 122.

48.  Nicosia and Stokes (eds) *Germans against Nazism* p. 151.

49.  Lapide, *Last Three Popes* p. 267

50.  Fr Rupert Meyer SJ was beatified by John Paul II in 1986 and Mgr Bernhard Lichtenburg and Fr Karl Leisner in 1996. A major biography of Mgr Lichtenburg was published in Germany in 1996.

51.  Conway, *Nazi Persecution*, p. 299.

52.  Johnson, *History*, ch. 13; E. Hobsbawm, *Age of Extremes* (London, 1994), ch. 8; Peter Calvocoressi, *World Politics Since 1945* (London, 1989), pp. 225ff.

53.  W. H. McNeill, *America, Britain and Russia. Their Cooperation and Conflict 1941–45* (London, 1953), p. 760.

54.  Johnson, *History*, p. 440; Bayard Price, *The Marshall Plan and its Meaning* (Cornell, 1955).

55.  Johnson, *History*, pp. 442ff; Calvocoressi, *World Politics*, pp. 15ff.

56.  'Europe's Christian Democrats' *The Economist*, 17 March 1990. M. P. Fogarty, *Christian Democracy in Western Europe 1920–1953* (London, 1957); G. Baum and J. Coleman, *The Church and Christian Democracy* (London, 1987).

57.  Johnson, *History*, pp. 577ff.

58.  J. Frederick Dewhurst et al., *Europe's Needs and Resources* (New York,

1956). Germany's was the most remarkable performance, the economic miracle of them all. Jeremy Leaman, *The Political Economy of West Germany 1945–1985* (London, 1988).

59. Camp, *Papal Ideology*, pp. 101f.; Hobsbawm, *Age of Extremes*, ch. 9.
60. Johnson, *History*, ch. 14; Hobsbawm, *Age of Extremes*, ch. 7; Calvocoressi, *World Politics*, chs. 5 and 12–20.
61. Camp, *Papal Ideology*, pp. 71ff.
62. Camp, *Papal Ideology*, p. 74.
63.. Allocution of 20 Feb. 1946. Camp, *Papal Ideology*, p. 42.
64. Christmas messages 1949 and 1951. Camp, *Papal Ideology*, p. 42.
65. Christmas message 1949. Camp, *Papal Ideology*, p. 43.
66. Discourses of 26 April 1950 and 18 June 1950, Radio Message of 24 Dec. 1952 and Address of 22 June 1956. Camp, *Papal Ideology*, p. 105.
67. Address of 7 May 1949. Camp, *Papal Ideology*, p. 103.
68. Camp, *Papal Ideology*, pp. 128f.
69. Christmas message of 1952. Camp, *Papal Ideology*, p. 131.
70. *Osservatore Romano* 4 July 1950. Camp, *Papal Ideology*, p. 133.
71. Camp, *Papal Ideology*, pp. 129f.; Jedin and Dolan, *Handbook*, Vol X, pp. 596f.
72. Camp, *Papal Ideology*, p. 150.
73. Address of 1 June 1941 on the fiftieth anniversary of *Rerum Novarum*. Camp, *Papal Ideology*, p. 50.
74. Letter of 14 July 1954. Camp, *Papal Ideology*, p. 151.
75. Carlen, *Encyclicals 1939–1959*, pp. 189ff.
76. Carlen, *Encyclicals 1939–1959*, pp. 321ff.
77. Calvez and Perrin, *Church and Social Justice*, p. 100.
78. Discourse of 13 June 1943. Camp, *Papal Ideology*, p. 72.
79. *Osservatore Romano* 2 Sept. 1944; Camp, *Papal Ideology*, p. 103. Address of 7 May 1949. Camp, *Papal Ideology*, p. 103.
80. Radio Message of 1 Sept. 1944. Camp, *Papal Ideology*, p. 104.
81. Address to Italian Catholic workers, 11 March 1945. Camp, *Papal Ideology*, p. 130.
82. Chinigo, 329ff. Radio Message Dec 24. 1940.
83. Chinigo, 335f Radio Message 24 December 1943. Radio Message 1 Sept 1944. Camp, *Papal Ideology*, p. 152.
84. Letter of 14 July 1954. Camp, *Papal Ideology*, p. 151.

## 20 John XXIII (1958–63)

1. H. Jedin and J. Dolan (eds.), *Handbook of Church History*, Vol. 10, *The Church in the Modern Age* pp. 96ff.; Aubert, *Secularized Society* pp. 569ff.; Peter Hebblethwaite, *John XXIII* (London, 1984).
2. E. Hobsbawm, *Age of Extremes* (London, 1994), p. 256.
3. Hobsbawm, *Age of Extremes*, pp. 258ff., 267ff., 273ff.; W. Laqueur, *Europe in Our Time* (London, 1992), pp. 231ff.

4.  The practice of speaking of the first world (the industrialized West), the second (the less industrialized nations of the communist bloc in Eastern Europe and the USSR), and the third (most of the rest of the world which was agricultural or produced raw materials), grew up in the 1950s. The overall picture is of course more complex. Many of the oil-rich States for example were in the 'underdeveloped' regions, and other individual States in those regions varied widely in their economic fortunes; Argentina, at least until the 1960s, had a European standard of living, Bolivia was at the other extreme. In Africa, the Republic of South Africa was wealthy by any standards though it was the whites who mainly benefited from this. In Asia, Taiwan, Singapore, South Korea and Hong Kong were soon to show remarkable growth rates. *World Development Report* (Oxford, 1992), p. 218.

5.  Andrew Schonfield's *Attack on World Poverty* (London, 1961) was one of the first general studies of the subject that caught public attention. He shows that from between 1955 and 1960, the amount of financial aid given by governments to the underdeveloped countries increased by 50 per cent. The major reason for this was political, with America and the USSR directing aid to nations important to them in the Cold War conflict.

6.  *The Population Bomb* (New York, 1968), pp. xi and 39.

7.  *Economist* 3 Sept. 1994, p. 22.

8.  *Economist* 20 Jan. 1990, p. 23.

9.  *World Development Report* (Oxford, 1980), p. 67.

10. *Human Development Report* (Oxford, 1990), p. 2.

11. *Economist* 3 Sept. 1994, p. 21.

12. FAO *Journal*, July/August 1971.

13. *Population Growth and Land Use* (London, 1977), p. 153.

14. *US News and World Report* 12 Sept. 1994.

15. OECD report *Facing the Future* (Paris, 1979), Part 1; Julian Simon, *The Ultimate Resource* (Oxford, 1981), Part 1.

16. Simon, *Ultimate Resource*, pp. 27, 21f.

17. B. L. Hodges, *Environmental Pollution* (New York, 1977), p. 442.

18. Prof. J. Park of Yale University, *Sunday Times* 21 July 1996; his findings were reported in *Geophysical Research Letters*.

19. *A Moment on the Earth* (Harmondsworth, 1996), Stephen Schmidheiny and Frederico Zorraquin, *Financing Change* (MIT, 1996); Stephen Budiansky, *Nature's Keepers* (London, 1996) and William Cronon (ed.), *Uncommon Ground* (London, 1996).

20. *Human Development Report 1990*, p. 27.

21. R. Charles with D. Maclaren, *The Social Teaching of Vatican II* (San Francisco, 1982), pp. 344ff.

22. Charles with Maclaren, *Social Teaching*, pp. 355ff.

23. *The Washington Monthly*, Sept. 1988; *US News and World Report*, 5 Oct. 1987 and *Commentary*, April 1986, pp. 30ff quoted in the *Population Research Institute Review*, Jan./Feb. 1991, p. 2.

24. *Time*, 5 Dec. 1988, pp. 43ff and *US News and World Report*, 6 Feb. 1989, pp. 34f.

25. John Mellor and John Gavian, 'Famine, Causes, Prevention and Relief' in *Science*, 235 (30 Jan. 1987), p. 541, quoted in *Population Research Institute Review* Jan./Feb. 1991, p. 2.

26. John Kearney, 'The Sahel, tragedy of underdevelopment', *America*, 24 Aug. 1974, pp. 67ff.

27. Wolfgang Lutz (ed.), *The Future Population of the World* (London, 1996), pp. 225ff, 248, 197ff, 233ff.

28. Claudia Carlen, *The Papal Encyclicals 1958–1981* (Ann Arbor, 1991), pp. 59ff; J.-Y. Calvez, *The Social Thought of John XXIII* (Chicago, 1964); *NDCST* 'Mater et Magistra'; Hebblethwaite, *John XXIII*, pp. 361ff. R. L. Camp, *The Papal Ideology of Social Reform* (Leiden, 1969), pp. 44ff., 108ff., 136ff., 153ff.; Donal Dorr, *Option for the Poor: One Hundred Years of Papal Society Teaching* (Dublin, 1992) pp. 113ff.

29. Footnote 7, Aquinas, *De Reg. Princip* 1, 15.

30. The word *Sozializzazione* was used in the Italian translation and the English translation 'socialization' seemed appropriate; from this it could be concluded that it was some form of socialism which was being recommended, although from the context it was clearly a social, and not a political phenomenon that was being considered. The equivalent word *socializatio*, however, was not used in the Latin, the authoritative version of the encyclical; nor did John XXIII use the word when introducing it on 14 May 1961. He spoke of 'the continuing multiplication of forms of association covering different aspects of life'. See J. Kirwan's note in *The Social Thought of John XXIII* (Oxford, 1964), p. 90.

31. The ideal would be that the market forces themselves were so balanced that they rendered to the workers adequate wages according to their needs and reasonable expectations; this requires that workers should have sufficient bargaining power to deliberate with their employers as equals and, in return, they should use that power responsibly. Experience tells us that neither of these conditions will come to be automatically. There is no option in a free society but to let market forces assert themselves, but such forces never work in a vacuum; society, nationally and internationally, helps establish the framework which contain them. Only the public authority can see that the framework exists. The statement of the case tells us just how far the capitalist system in democratic countries is from working in that way – because of the defects of the employers, the unions and the public authority. Only when the latter seeks the true common good will the problems be on the way to solution.

32. The relationship between employer and employee in economic terms is determined by commutative justice, but the harsh liberal interpretation of that relationship completely neglected the fact that those who work together to the same end, employer and employee, involved in producing goods and services for the market, are governed by the prior obligations of all human relationships,

solidarity in particular. Wage contracts which depersonalize or seek to make labour a mere commodity, deny this solidarity. In this sense, the firm as a society or community is a valid and indeed a governing concept. Calvez *John XXIII*, pp. 40ff.

33. Footnote 32, Pius XII, Broadcast 1 Sept 1944.

34. Footnote 36, *Rerum Novarum*, para. 22, St Gregory *Evang. Hom.* IX, n. 7.

35. This reflects the ethos of peasant farming. Most modern agriculture in the developed world is highly capital intensive. Where it is not, and it is not in many parts of the third world, the ethical insight of the encyclical is still valid.

36. P. Calvocoressi, *World Politics since 1945* (London, 1990), pp. 90ff.; J. D. and I. Derbyshire, *World Political Systems* (London, 1991), pp. 192ff. *Year Book of the United Nations* (annual).

37. Derbyshire, *Political Systems*, pp. 200ff.

38. Calvocoressi, *World Politics*, pp. 26ff and 503ff; Michael Beschloss, *The Crisis Years: Kennedy and Krushchev* (New York, 1991).

39. Calvocoressi, *World Politics*, pp. 28ff.

40. *AAS*, 55 (1963) 257–304 Carlen, *Encyclicals 1958–1981*, pp. 107ff; Hebblethwaite, *John XIII*, pp. 484ff.; Donal Dorr, *Option for the Poor: One Hundred Years of Papal Social Teaching* (Dublin, 1992), pp. 113ff., 127ff.; *NDCST* 'Pacem in Terris.'

41. Footnote 27 Aquinas, *Summa Theologiae* Ia IIae, Q. 19, art. 4, cf. art 9.

42. Footnote 29 *In Epist. ad Rom.* c.13, vv.1–2, *Homil* 23. PG 60.615.

43. Footnote 35 *Aquinas, Summa* Ia IIae, Q. 83, art. 3 ad 2.

44. That the principle of subsidiarity should operate here is to be expected. The intervention of the larger organization should only be made when it is necessary to enable the smaller to achieve its ends; the main responsibility for the development of a nation, as of individuals, is with the nation itself. Experts on economic development differ on what the best forms of aiding nations in this matter are. The social encyclicals have naturally tended to take the received wisdom of the majority on the matter; individuals like Peter Bauer in his book *Reality and Rhetoric; Studies in the Economics of Development* (London, 1984) have criticized the Popes for doing this and labelled their efforts as 'essays in ecclesiastical envy'. But he seems unaware that central to the Church's teaching on this matter is that, as John quoting Pius XII says, the burden for a nation's development rests primarily on itself. Making them clients of rich nations is not the end of the exercise. Enabling them to develop themselves is. If these nations can achieve development by their own efforts, or with much less help from outside, then critics like Bauer should show us how in a fully argued case and preach their message as do the misguided majority they criticize. The examples Bauer gives and the power with which he argues his case show that one could be attempted. Meanwhile the Church has to try to give guidance in the face of the sufferings of common

humanity; she has to come down from the ivory tower and try to help her people to assist in reducing those sufferings. If those who say the experts the Church relies on are wrong to fail to provide a proper statement of the right, it would seem that they are less concerned about the urgency of the matter.

45.     Many within the Church from the 1960s began to interpret this to mean that since we can, on practical matters, work with others whose value system differs from our own, there was no difference between value systems. But there is, as the Encyclical makes plain. The Christian value system is outlined in para. 160 and the hierarchy has the right and duty to defend it when necessary.


# 21     The Background to the social teaching of the Church 1962–78

1.      W. Laqueur, *Europe Since Hitler* (London, 1982), p. 314.
2.      Julian Becker, *Hitler's Children* (London, 1979).
3.      A. Marwick, *British Society Since 1945* (Harmondsworth, 1982), p. 86.
4.      M. A. Jones, *The Limits of Liberty: American History 1607–1992* (Oxford, 1995), pp. 548ff., 553ff.
5.      Crane Brinton, *A History of Western Morals* (London, 1959), p. 169. See Henry Sidgwick's classic *Outlines of the History of Ethics* (London, 1967), ch. 3.
6.      John L. Hallowell, *The Decline of Liberalism as an Ideology* (London, 1946), p. 4.
7.      Hallowell, *Decline of Libralism*, pp. 7ff.
8.      Hallowell, *Decline of Liberalism*, pp. 11ff.
9.      Norman Dennis *Rising Crime and the Dismembered Family* (London, 1993), pp. 2f. E. Hobsbawm *Age of Extremes* (London, 1994) ch. 11 'The Cultural Revolution' traces the decline of traditional morality, especially family and sexual, in the affluent countries.
10.     R. Charles with D. Maclaren, *The Social Teaching of Vatican II* (San Francisco, 1982), pp. 167ff.
11.     Steve Humphries and Pamela Gordon, *A Man's World* (London, 1996); Joanna Bourke, *Dismembering the Male* (London, 1996); George Mosse, *The Image of Man* (Oxford, 1996); David Popenoe, *Life Without Father* (London, 1996); Edward Humes, *No Matter How Loud I Shout* (London, 1996). Office for National Statistics: General Household Survey (1997).
12.     For example by J. D. Unwin, *Sex and Culture* (Oxford, 1934) and Abram Kardiner *Sex and Morality* (London, 1955).
13.     Dennis, *Rising Crime*, p. 5. *The Economist* 31.1.98.
14.     Norman Dennis and George Erdos, *Families Without Fatherhood* (London, 1993), who describe themselves as 'a firm Jew and a lax Anglican' refer to this as 'the type of pre–1960s family' and 'impar-

tially call it the "Catholic" family in whatever sections of society, "sacred" elements are still found'. (p. 57).

15. Dennis, *Rising Crime*, p. 64.

16. M. B. Norton et al., *America: a People and a Nation* (Boston, 1944), chs. 32–4; Benjamin Muse, *The American Negro Revolution* (Indiana University, 1970); W. H. Chafe *Unfinished Business: American Society since World War Two* (Oxford, 1988).

17. W. Laqueur, *Europe in Our Time* (London, 1992), p. 441.

18. The philosopher Herbert Marcuse was born in Berlin in 1898 and educated Berlin and Freiberg, leaving Germany for the USA shortly after Hitler came to power in 1933. Professor of Philosophy at the University of California from 1965, he became a cult figure in the next decade with his theory that modern bureaucratic societies are oppressive and manipulative and must be treated like other oppressive and manipulative States. A. MacIntyre, *Marcuse* (London, 1970).

19. R. Aubert, *The Church in a Secularized Society* (London, 1978), ch. 15; Jedin and Dolan, *Handbook*, Vol. 10, ch. 24; Edwin Williamson, *Penguin History of Latin America* (London, 1992), pp. 359ff.; J. Lloyd Mecham, *Church and State in Latin America* (Chapel Hill, 1966); Edward L. Cleary, *Crisis and Change: the Church in Latin America* (New York, 1985); Trevor Beeson and Jenny Pearce, *A Vision of Hope* (London, 1984).

20. Trade unions existed but were generally weak, though in Chile and Argentina for example they came to play a crucial role politically: H. Spalding, *Organized Labour in Latin America* (New York, 1977); Latin America Bureau, *Unity is Strength: Trade Unions in Latin America* (London, 1980). In Peru, Guillermo Billinghurst, a self-made millionaire manufacturer, President in 1912, introduced an eight-hour day for some groups, and legalized strikes and collective bargaining. But his mobilization of workers in support of his programme roused conservative opposition and he was removed from office by an army coup. B. Keen and M. Wasserman, *A Short History of Latin America* (Boston, 1984), p. 386.

21. Aubert, *Secularized Society*, p. 347. Williamson, *History of Latin America*, pp. 360ff.

22. Aubert, *Secularized Society*, pp. 348ff. Argentina was a case in point. The right-wing Catholic nationalists helped bring down a Radical Party government in 1930 and General Uriburu tried to establish a corporative State to counter the levelling tendencies of individualistic liberal democracy. He failed, and the country turned to Peron in the 1940s to liberate the masses from liberalism, socialism and communism. Argentinian society and politics however could not stand the strain of such experiments; the problems of adjustment to the political and economic realities of the twentieth century destabilized Argentina economically and politically from the 1940s.

23. Jacob Arbenz, the Revolutionary Action Party (PAR) candidate, was elected President of Guatemala in 1950. The PAR was a 'spiritually

Socialist' Party with communists as members, but it was not a communist party, it was reformist, and in 1950 communists split off from it, dissatisfied with its progress. Arbenz introduced land reform, which some feared was communist inspired, and Che Guevara was among those who advocated arming the peasants to protect their gains. That the President's wife was a communist made it easier to believe that PAR planned to run a communist state; communists were active in the country and had easy access to him and were generally influential; Guatemala also was, in international relations, gradually aligned with the Eastern Bloc and it was the arrival of Czech arms to Guatemala in the spring of 1952 which convinced the new Eisenhower Presidency that the USA had the right to intervene. They arranged for two anti-communist exiles to return, armed them for an invasion which took place on 16 June, and Arbenz was deposed. R. Woodward, *Central America* (Oxford, 1985), pp. 235ff. How far the communists were in a position to bring about a coup and take over the government of Guatemala is not clear, but certainly the American intervention set back the cause of democratic movement in the country indefinitely.

24.   Aubert, *Secularized Society*, p. 364. Cleary, *Crisis and Change*, pp. 75ff.
25.   Williamson, *History of Latin America*, p. 281.
26.   W. Woodruff, *Impact of Western Man* (London, 1966), p. 53. A. G. Frank concluded in his *Capitalism and Underdevelopment in Latin America: Historical Studies of Chile and Brazil* (New York, 1967), that only socialist revolution could solve their problems. This was reflected in J. D. Cockroft, A. G. Frank and D. L. Johnson, *Dependence and Underdevelopment: Latin America's Political Economy* (New York, 1972). Dependency analysis is concerned with the development of peripheral capitalism and the interplay between internal and external economic structures; it became increasingly centred on this question of whether capitalism is capable of developing the productive forces of third-world societies, with Frank and others concluding it could not. See John Eatwell (ed.), *New Palgrave's Dictionary of Economics* (London, 1967), 'Dependency theory'.
27.   Williamson, *History of Latin America*, p. 320.
28.   Williamson, *History of Latin America*, pp. 339ff.

## 22   The Second Vatican Council

1.   Xavier Rynne, *The Fourth Session* (London, 1965). H. Vorgrimler (ed.), *Commentary on the Documents of Vatican II* (London, 1969), Vol. 4, pp. 49ff, on the background to the document on religious freedom and Vol. 5, pp. 1ff., on that to the document on the Church in the modern world.
2.   *Constitutiones    Decreta    Declarationes    Sacrosanctum    Oecumenicum*

*Concilium,* Vatican II Secretaria Generalis Concili Vatican II (1966) pp. 681–883 A. Flannery (ed.), *Vatican II, the Conciliar and Post-Conciliar Documents* (Tenbury Wells, 1975); R. Charles with D. Maclaren, *The Social Teaching of Vatican II* (San Francisco, 1982); Donal Dorr, *Option for the Poor: One Hundred Years of Papal Social Teaching* (Dublin, 1992), pp. 150ff.; *NDCST* 'Gaudium et Spes', 'Dignitatis Humanae'.

3.   Footnote 117. After referring to *Casti Connubii* and other Church documents, which repeated the Church's traditional teaching on the rejection of any form of contraception, the footnote goes on

> ... certain questions requiring further and more careful investigation have been given over to a commission for the study of population, the family, and births, in order that the Holy Father may pass judgement when its task is completed. With the teaching of the magisterium standing as it is, the Council has no intention of proposing concrete solutions at this moment.

The disputes within the Church on the matter of the contraceptive pill were at this time very lively, and hopes were raised that it would be approved for general contraceptive use, and not merely to regulate periods. Since the drafters of the document accepted that the matter would eventually be for the Pope to decide, these were premature; those who had hoped for a change had misread the situation. See Vorgrimler, *Commentary,* Vol. 5, pp. 397ff.

4.   Footnote 10 to the text refers to Basil, Lactantius, Augustine, Gregory the Great, Bonaventure, Albert the Great and John XXIII.

5.   The question of what is binding in conscience on Catholics concerning the hypothetical use of nuclear weapons and on deterrence came to a head when it looked as though the United States bishops' letter on the matter would declare deterrence and all war immoral in the nuclear age because of the scale and nature of the destruction it would threaten or bring about. Rome became involved in the discussions before the letter was issued and as a result the bishops noted that 'in concert with the evaluation provided by Pope John Paul II, we have arrived at a strictly conditional moral acceptance of deterrence'. *The Challenge of Peace: God's Promise and our Response: the US Bishops' Pastoral Letter on Peace and War in the Nuclear Age* (London, 1983), p. v. Though with the demise of real socialism in Russia and Eastern Europe, the terrible threat that hung over all when the Cold War was at its height had passed, the danger of the use of these weapons is by no means ended. That even if they were used on a limited tactical scale initially, this would escalate to their use strategically and therefore wholesale, is beyond reasonable doubt but cannot be stated categorically. If however it was made binding on the conscience of Catholics to repudiate any participation in preparations for a deterrence policy, and a possible tactical use of nuclear and chemical weapons, this would mean that no member of the

Church, in the military or in civil life, could co-operate in any way directly in such a policy. The State might then, and with justice, decide that the Church was hindering its legitimate freedom to carry out its duty in defending the nation against aggressors. In other words the Church would have embarked on a collision course on a political matter, one on which the State could not allow her to win, and even if she did, it would be only after a prolonged and bitter dispute which would politicize her the more. Whatever was right, opening up this possibility was wrong. In many ways this problem parallels the one the Church faced on slavery. To have challenged that system, though there were good grounds for doing so, would have had political implications of the same kind and politicized the Church to the point of self-destruction. There are limits to what the Church can and should do in pursuit of a sound social ethic when men and nations are determined to pursue a course whose moral legitimacy is doubtful but which could, at a pinch, be theoretically justified. To become involved in the politics of opposition on such matters is not the Church's role.

6.    Flannery, *Vatican II*, pp. 799ff.
7.    Leo XIII called attention to his teaching in *Immortale Dei* [36].


## 23   Pope Paul VI and the Council of the Latin American bishops (CELAM II)

1.    Jedin and Dolan, *Handbook*, Vol. 10, *The Church in the Modern Age* pp. 115ff and 159ff., Peter Hebblethwaite, *Paul VI: The First Modern Pope* (London, 1993).
2.    *Acta Apostolicae Sedis* 59 (1967) 257–99 Claudia Carlen *The Papal Encyclicals 1958–1981* (Ann Arbor, 1991), pp. 183ff.; Hebblethwaite, *Paul VI*, pp. 483ff. Donal Dorr, *Option for the Poor: One Hundred Years of Papal Social Teaching* (Dublin, 1992), ch. 8; *NDCST*, Populorum Progressio; Barbara Ward, 'Looking back on *Populorum Progressio*' in C. E. Curran and R. A. McCormick, *Official Catholic Social Teaching* (New York, 1986).
3.    *The Church in the Present Day Transformation of Latin America in the Light of the Council II, Conclusions* (Second Council of the Latin American Bishops, NCCB (Washington DC, 1979); *NDCST* Medellín.
4.    See footnote 27 above.
5.    Cleary, *Crisis and Change*, pp. 68 and 77ff.
6.    The Congregation for the Doctrine of the Faith issued 'Ten Observations on the Theology of Gustavo Gutiérrez' in March 1978. Text in A. T. Hennelly, *Liberation Theology: A Documentary History* (New York, 1990), pp. 348ff.
7.    G. Gutiérrez, *A Theology of Liberation* (London, 1973), p. 6. The statement, thus baldly presented, reveals the illusions of the new theory. Charity, the love of God and of neighbour for his sake, the central

core of the Christian ethic, personal and social, was, we are to believe, absent from Christian witness in previous generations. Liberation theology discovered it once again.

8.  Given the role of the Church in developing social charity and justice from Apostolic times, and Christianizing and civilizing the barbarian tribes after Roman power disappeared in the West, and then helping the new civilization which emerged after 1050, a contrary view might be possible.

9.  Gutiérrez, *Theology of Liberation*, p. 13.

10. Gutiérrez, *Theology of Liberation*, p. 9.

11. Gutiérrez, *Theology of Liberation*, pp. 29–30. This analysis, with its naïve belief in Marxism, ignores what the Catholic tradition had always been critical of in Marx on sound philosophical, theological and sociological grounds and which was so spectacularly confirmed by the collapse of real socialism in 1989.

12. Gutiérrez, *Theology of Liberation*, p. 49.

13. Gutiérrez, *Theology of Liberation*, pp. 82–91. The appeal to Che Guevara's theories after the fiasco in Bolivia which showed that he and his mentor Castro were completely out of touch with the real situation in the country, is curious. The peasants of Bolivia had been given possession of the land by the National Revolutionary Movement of 1952 and positively allied with the Bolivian army, mainly manned by peasants anyway, in opposition to Guevara's guerillas. He himself was captured and executed by the military on 9 October 1967. D. James, *The Complete Bolivian Diaries of Che Guevara* (New York, 1979), pp. 59ff.; H. S. Klein, *Bolivia* (Oxford, 1982), pp. 248ff. Klein describes briefly the lot of the Bolivian peasant until the 1950s, graphically depicting the oppression to which they had been subjected (pp. 228ff.). He suggests that Guevara was primarily interested not in Bolivian revolution but in establishing a base for wider insurrection. James shows that this was not so; Bolivian revolution was his first goal. See also Leo Sauvage, *Che Guevara: the Failure of a Revolutionary* (Englewood Cliffs, 1973), pp. 154ff.

14. Gutiérrez, *Theology of Liberation*, p. 112. In fact, Allende's romantic revolution in Chile was doomed at the outset; he never had a majority in either the Senate or the Congress, while his policies produced social disorder on such a scale that what responsible middle-class support he had, and needed, was alienated and his overthrow was inevitable. That the Americans wanted that overthrow and plotted to achieve it is true; but it was Allende's own incompetence and contradictory policies that brought him down. Edwin Williamson, *Penguin History of Latin America* (London, 1992), pp. 498ff. A socialist constitutional revolution was never on. John Drury (ed.), *Christians for Socialism* (New York, 1975), traces the background to this movement in Chile.

15. Gutiérrez, *Theology of Liberation*, pp. 136ff.

16. Gutiérrez, *Theology of Liberation*, p. 255.

17. Gutiérrez, *Theology of Liberation*, p. 265.
18. B. Davies and M. Walsh (eds.), *Proclaiming Justice and Peace* (Mystic, CT, 1991), pp. 245ff; annoyingly, the document is referred to throughout as *Octagesima Anno*.
19. This was regarded by some as a significant recantation by the Pope. In truth Paul VI was saying nothing new. The social teaching of the Church was never intended to be a party political programme, detailing what technical answers States should give to the problems before them. She has neither the mandate for that nor does she possess the requisite knowledge of situations and possible alternatives that the experts and those they advise possess in proposing and executing them. Her concern is with the moral implications of such policies and advising her people on that aspect of them. Some took these observations to indicate that the very complexity of modern life had destroyed the Church's, and in particular the Pope's, confidence in her capacity to give that advice, despite the fact that this paragraph actually says that the corpus of the Church's social teaching is there for the guidance her people needed, and in paragraph 7 goes on to say that he intends to draw their attention to specific points from it. The misunderstanding did not result from anything Paul VI said; it resulted from individuals misreading his words.
20. *AAS* 68 (1976) 5–76 Davies and Walsh, *Justice and Peace*, pp. 284ff., Hebblethwaite, *Paul VI*, p. 651; Dorr *Option*, pp. 240ff.

## 24 John Paul II and CELAM III

1. Tad Szulc, *Pope John Paul II; The Biography* (London, 1995); George Weigel, *The Final Revolution* (Oxford, 1992); G. Hunstun Williams, *The Mind of John Paul II; Origins of His Thought* (New York, 1981). Jonathan Witney *Man of the Century* (New York 1997).
2. André Frossard, *Be Not Afraid* (New York, 1984), p. 15, quoted by Weigel, *Final Revolution*, p. 80.
3. M. Craig, *A Man from a Far Country* (London, 1982), pp. 81 and 107f.; Weigel, *Final Revolution*, p. 92.
4. Weigel, *Final Revolution*, p. 128.
5. H. Wiarda and H. G. Kline, *Latin American Politics and Development* (Boston, 1979), ch. 18; James Dunkerly, *Power in the Isthmus* (London, 1988), chs. 6 and 7.
6. Joseph Mulligan, *The Nicaraguan Church and the Revolution* (New York, 1987), p. 26.
7. John Paul II, *Puebla, Pilgrimage of Faith* (Boston, 1979), pp. 71–2.
8. *Opening Address at the Puebla Conference*, 28 January 1979; *Puebla: Third General Conference of the Latin American Bishops: Conclusions* (London, 1980) p. 1. The bracketed figures in the text refer to the

page numbers of the book, not to the paragraphs of the address.

9.    National Security States were right-wing military regimes which, under the pretence of defending Western civilized values, were prepared to deny human rights in countering those they saw as its enemies.

## 25   John Paul II's social encyclicals 1979–81

1.    *Acta Apostolicae Sedis* 71(1979) 257–324 Carlen, Claudia *The Papal Encyclicals 1958–1981* (Ann Arbor, 1991), pp. 245ff; J. H. Miller, *The Encyclicals of John Paul II* (Huntingdon, Ind., 1996), pp. 31ff., 46ff.; *NDCST* 'Redemptor Hominis'; Donal Dorr, *Option for the Poor: One Hundred Years of Papal Social Teaching* (Dublin, 1992), pp. 270ff.
2.    *AAS* 72 (1980) 1177–1232 Carlen, *Encyclicals 1958–1981*, pp. 275ff.; Miller, *Encyclicals of John Paul II*, pp. 97ff., 110ff.
3.    *AAS* 73 (1981) 577–647 Carlen, *Papal Encyclicals 1958–1981*, pp. 299ff.; Miller, *Encyclicals of John Paul II*, pp. 151ff. and 167ff *NDCST* 'Laborem Exercens'; Dorr, *Option*, ch. 1.
4.    Footnote 25, Aquinas, *Summa Theologiae*, IIa IIae, Q. 62, art. 2.

## 26   Congregation for the Doctrine of the Faith 1984–86

1.    Text in A. T. Hennelly, *Liberation Theology: A Documentary History*, (Maryknoll, NY, 1990), pp. 393ff.
2.    Hennelly, *Liberation Theology*, pp. 329ff., 335ff., 338ff.
3.    Text in Hennelly, *Liberation Theology*, pp. 461ff.
4.    The Archdiocese of Rio de Janeiro's Doctrinal Commission had criticized it and it was Boff's sending to the SCDF his defence of what he had written which led to the latter examining the book. They decided it was in error and the author was invited to discuss the matter further. This was done but the Congregation was not satisfied with the outcome and it issued the *Notification Sent to Fr Leonardo Boff Regarding Errors in His Book 'Church, Charism and Power'* 11 March 1985. Hennelly, *Liberation Theology*, pp. 431ff.
5.    Boff, *Church, Charism and Power* (London, 1981), p. 43.
6.    Boff, *Church, Charism and Power*, p. 86.
7.    Boff, *Church, Charism and Power*, p. 156.
8.    Hennelly, *Liberation Theology*, pp. 431ff.
9.    Hennelly, *Liberation Theology*, pp. 461ff.
10.   Text in Hennelly, *Liberation Theology*, pp. 498ff.

## 27   John Paul II's social encyclicals 1987–91

1.    *Acta Apostolicae Sedis* 80 (1980) 513–590, Miller, J.M. *The Encyclicals of John Paul II* (Huntingdon. Ind., 1996), pp. 411ff and 426ff; *NDCST*

'Sollicitudo Rei Socialis'; Donal Dorr, *Option for the Poor: One Hundred Years of Papal Social Teaching* (Dublin, 1992), pp. 323ff.

2.   Footnote 59 to the text quotes St John Chrysostom *In Evang. St. Matt. Hom.* 50.3–4, etc.

3.   M. Kort, *The Soviet Colossus: the Rise and Fall of the USSR* (London, 1993); Robert. G. Kaiser, *Why Gorbachev Happened: His Triumphs, His Failure and His Fall* (New York, 1992); H. Smith, *The New Russians* (New York, 1990).

4.   D. Doder and L. Branson, *Gorbachev: Heretic in the Kremlin* (London, 1991), p. 201.

5.   T. Garton Ash, *We The People: The Revolution of '89* (London, 1990), pp. 133f.

6.   Garton Ash, *We The People*, p. 148.

7.   George Weigel, *The Final Revolution* (Oxford, 1992), p. 131.

8.   Weigel, *Final Revolution*, p. 138.

9.   Garton Ash, *We The People*, p. 56.

10.   Doder and Branson, *Gorbachev*, p. 387.

11.   Garton Ash, *We The People*, p. 147.

12.   *AAS* 83 (1991) 793–867 Miller, *Encyclicals of John Paul II*, pp. 571ff. and 588ff. M. Novak, *The Catholic Ethic and the Spirit of Capitalism* (New York, 1993); R. J. Neuhaus, *Doing Well and Doing Good* (New York, 1992); Dorr, *Option*, pp. 340ff.; *NDCST*, 'Centesimus Annus'.

## 28   John Paul II and CELAM IV

1.   *Santo Domingo: Conclusions*, Fourth General Conference of the Latin American Bishops 'New Evangelization, Human Development, Christian Culture', (CIIR, London, 1993).

2.   Arthur Schlesinger, 'Was America a Mistake?', *Atlantic Monthly*, September 1992; Arthur McGovern, 'A 500th Anniversary: the Church in Latin America', *America*, 16 May 1992.

3.   *Conclusions* of CELAM IV (London, 1993), pp. 3ff. The numbers in brackets indicate the paragraphs of the text.

## 29   A Summary of Christian social teaching

1.   The concept of justice is not dealt with comprehensively by the social magisterium in any one place, though specific problems concerning the virtue are the stuff of its teaching. The concepts of general (or legal/social) justice and of particular (distributive and commutative) justice are referred to and the teaching of St Thomas, the Church's *Doctor Communis*, is accepted as normative. I therefore here summarize his teaching as being synonymous with that of the magisterium on this matter.

2.   See note 5 p 222 Chapter 22.

3.  *Puebla: a Pilgrimage of Faith* (Boston, 1979), pp. 67ff.; *Puebla: Evangelization at Present and in the Future of Latin America: Conclusions* (London, 1980), p. 110.
4.  R. Charles with D. McLaren, *The Social Teaching of Vatican II* (San Francisco, 1982), pp. 273ff., 290ff., 296ff.

# Index

# Index of Modern Authors